# KNOWING THE SOCIAL WORLD

# KNOWING THE SOCIAL WORLD

edited by
**Tim May** and **Malcolm Williams**

**Open University Press**
Buckingham · Philadelphia

Open University Press
Celtic Court
22 Ballmoor
Buckingham
MK18 1XW

email: enquiries@openup.co.uk
world wide web: http://www.openup.co.uk

and
325 Chestnut Street
Philadelphia, PA19106, USA

First Published 1998 



A catalogue record of this book is available from the British Library

ISBN 0 335 19768 X (hb) 0 335 19767 1 (pb)

*Library of Congress Cataloging-in-Publication Data*
Knowing the social world/edited by Tim May and Malcolm Williams.
p. cm.
Includes bibliographical references and index.
ISBN 0-335-19768-X (hardcover). – ISBN 0-335-19767-1 (pbk.)
1. Sociology–Philosophy. 2. Sociology–Methodology. 3. Social sciences–Philosophy. 4. Social sciences–Methodology. I. May, Tim, 1957– . II. Williams, Malcolm, 1953–
HM26.K58 1998
301′.01–dc21 98–13161
CIP



Typeset by Type Study, Scarborough
Printed in Great Britain by Biddles Ltd, Guildford and King's Lynn

# Contents

# Acknowledgements

We embarked on this project about three years ago while discussing the issues which arose from our joint authorship of a book on the relations between philosophy and social research. During this time we have a number of hostelries and breweries, as well as the email system, to thank for how the final proposal took shape. In the end it was the cooperation and contributions of the authors in this volume to whom we are grateful for agreeing to be part of this project.

We would like to thank those whose interest directly motivated us to produce this work, as well as those with whom we share our lives. They are Dee, Liz, Calum, John, Cian and Laura, as well as Justin Vaughan, Gaynor Clements and the marketing and production teams at Open University Press.

Finally, the editors and Margaret Archer would like to thank Les Presses de l'Université de Montréal for permission to reproduce an English translation of her article 'Théorie sociale et analyse de la société' which appeared in *Sociologie et Sociétés* 30(1).

# Contributors

**Margaret Archer** studied sociology to doctoral level at the London School of Economics before moving to the École Pratique des Hautes Études, Paris. She became Professor of Sociology at the University of Warwick in 1979. Her previous ten books include *Social Origins of Educational Systems* (1979), *Culture and Agency* (1988) and *Realist Theory: The Morphogenic Approach* (1995). The latter two are part of a trilogy which will be completed by *Human Being*. She is a former editor of *Current Sociology* and past President of the International Sociological Association and was the first woman to be elected to this position. In 1997 she became a founding trustee of the Centre for Critical Realism.

**Alan Bryman** is Professor of Social Research in the Department of Social Sciences, Loughborough University. His main research interests lie in social research methodology, leadership theory and research, organization studies and theme parks. He is author or co-author of numerous books including *Quantity and Quality in Social Research* (1988), *Charisma and Leadership in Organisations* (1992), *Disney and his Worlds* (1995), *Quantitative Data Analysis with SPSS for Windows: A Guide for Social Scientists* (1997) and *Mediating Social Science* (1998). He is series editor of the Open University Press 'Understanding Social Research' series.

**Rom Harré** graduated in mathematics and physics and then in philosophy and anthropology. He did postgraduate work at Oxford under J.L. Austin. His published work includes studies in the philosophy of both natural and human sciences, such as *Varieties of Realism* (1986) and the trilogy *Social Being* (1979), *Personal Being* (1983) and *Physical Being* (1991). His current research interests have concerned the ways that language enters into all aspects of human life, including the sense of self – reported in *Pronouns and People* (1990, with P. Muhlhausler) – and the emotions. His most recent book in this area is *The Discursive Mind* (1994, with Grant Gillett). Other recent research has included theoretical studies of the computational model of mind. He is currently Professor of Psychology at Georgetown University, Washington, DC.

**Derek Layder** received his doctorate from the London School of Economics in 1976. From 1974 to 1992 he was Lecturer in Sociology, from 1992 to 1997 Reader in Sociology and now Professor of Sociology, at the University of Leicester. He is author of numerous articles, mainly on social theory, research strategy and methods. He is also author of the following books: *Structure, Interaction and Social Theory* (1981), *The Realist Image in Social Science* (1990), *New Strategies in Social Research: An Introduction and Guide* (1993), *Understanding Social Theory* (1994), *Methods, Sex and Madness* (1994, with Julia O'Connell Davidson) and *Modern Social Theory: Key Debates and New Directions* (1997).

**Tim May** is a Lecturer in Sociology and Social Policy at the University of Durham. He gained his PhD (1990) from the University of Plymouth where he then taught until moving to Durham in 1995. His published works include: *Probation: Politics, Policy and Practice* (1991), *Situating Social Theory* (1996), *Introduction to the Philosophy of Social Research* (1996, with Malcolm Williams), *Social Research: Issues, Methods and Process* (2nd edition 1997) and as co-editor, *Working with Offenders* (1996) and *Interpreting the Field: Accounts of Ethnography* (1993). He is currently working on an edited collection on qualitative research, editing a new book series entitled 'Issues in Society' (Open University Press), writing a book on reflexivity, social science and social life, and via a research grant continuing his research interests on the themes of management, power and organizational change.

**Mary Maynard** is a Professor in the Department of Social Policy and Social Work at the University of York, where she was previously Director of the Centre for Women's Studies. She has long-standing interests in social theory and research methodology, especially from feminist perspectives. She is currently engaged on a project relating to older women and widowhood and is completing a book on feminist research. Previous publications have included *Women, Violence and Social Control* (1987, edited with Jalna Hanmer), *Women's Studies in the 1990s: Doing Things Differently?* (1993, edited with Joanna de Groot), *Researching Women's Lives from a Feminist Perspective* (1994, edited with June Purvis) and *The Dynamics of 'Race' and Gender: Some Feminist Interventions* (1994, edited with Haleh Afshar).

**William Outhwaite** studied at Oxford and Sussex. He is now Professor of Sociology in the School of European Studies at Sussex, where he has taught since 1973. His research interests include the philosophy of social science (especially realism), social theory (especially critical theory and contemporary European social theory), political sociology and the sociology of knowledge. He is the author of *Understanding Social Life: The Method Called*

*Verstehen* (1975; 2nd edition 1986), *Concept Formation in Social Science* (1983), *New Philosophies of Social Science: Realism, Hermeneutics and Critical Theory* (1987) and *Jürgen Habermas: A Critical Introduction* (1994). He edited *The Habermas Reader* (1996, with Tom Bottomore), *The Blackwell Dictionary of Twentieth-Century Social Thought* (1993), and (with Luke Martell) *The Sociology of Politics* (due to be published in 1998). He has been a deputy editor of *Sociology*, editor of *Current Sociology*, chair of the International Sociological Association's Publications Committee, and is now an associate editor of the *European Journal of Social Theory*.

**David-Hillel Ruben** is Professor of Philosophy at the London School of Economics. He received his PhD from Harvard University and has previously taught at the universities of Edinburgh, Glasgow and Essex and City University, London. He is the author of numerous articles and sub-editor for *Philosophy of the Social Sciences* and the *Routledge Encyclopaedia of Philosophy* (1998). He is the author of *Marxism and Materialism* (1979), *The Metaphysics of the Social World* (1985) and *Explaining Explanation* (1990) and editor of *Explanation* (1993).

**John Scott** is Professor of Sociology at the University of Essex and Adjunct Professor at the University of Bergen. He was previously Professor and Head of Department at the University of Leicester. His recent publications include *Sociological Theory* (1995), *Stratification and Power* (1996) and *Corporate Business and Capitalist Classes* (1997).

**Malcolm Williams** has been an academic since 1990 and has worked at City University, London, and since 1992, the University of Plymouth. His empirical research interests are in rural–urban population change and housing need and he has published several articles in these areas. He is also interested in problems of methodology, the philosophical foundations of research and the relationship of science to social science. He is the co-author of *Introduction to Philosophy of Social Research* (1996, with Tim May). He is currently working on a book on science and social science.

# Introduction: knowing the social world

**Tim May** and **Malcolm Williams**

The aim of this book is to provide a forum for philosophers, social theorists and methodologists to discuss the issues which inform, either directly or indirectly, the practice of social research. In so doing, it seeks to enable a dialogue between disciplines which often tend to talk across, rather than directly to, one another. For us as editors, this results in an unfortunate and unproductive polarization between those who reflect on the nature and possibilities of the social sciences and those who, more particularly, produce theories as part of those disciplines, as well as social researchers themselves.

The theme of the book is encapsulated in its title: *Knowing the Social World*. The title is deliberately broad and the contributions comprise a range of perspectives. Nevertheless, implicit in the title are two assumptions. First, that attempts to know the social world are worthwhile and second, that, to one extent or another, the social world is knowable. From these further issues require illumination: for example, what is the nature of the 'social'; in what ways can we 'know' it and what is the status of the knowledge which is then produced? These are matters which preoccupy ontology, epistemology and methodology. In addition, the often assumed means through which researchers illuminate such questions is the realm of social theory. Therefore, in addition to these issues, we must ask to what extent and in what ways does social theory relate to and assist in empirical illumination? This, in turn, requires an examination of how social theory incorporates and relates to matters of ontology, epistemology and methodology.

To explore these issues the book is divided into ten chapters which, broadly speaking, cover the areas of philosophy of the social sciences, social and sociological theory and methodology. However, as will be clear from the contributions themselves, not only is there an absence of simple lines of demarcation between each of these topics, but also the interests and experiences of authors in this collection range right across the spectrum of issues that we have sought to cover. As such, their writings reflect these preoccupations.

In terms of the content of the chapters, Malcolm Williams's and William Outhwaite's chapters both serve to provide the book with a general basis upon which to evaluate the themes and issues raised in subsequent contributions. In Malcolm Williams's chapter, we find a journey from philosophical considerations through those of methodology to the desire to have some impact on the understanding and policy issues which surround a social, economic and political issue: homelessness. Then, in William Outhwaite's chapter the theme is the social–natural divide. This relationship has witnessed the social sciences, in different intellectual and cultural contexts, running from the hermeneutic turn, via the Vienna Circle and Popper's critical rationalism and his debates with Adorno, through to the linguistic turn, social constructionism, Habermas's coherence theory, Rom Harré's and Roy Bhaskar's varieties of realism, right up to poststructuralism and postmodernism, with their critiques of the mind–body duality. Quite where the social sciences now stand is a frequent source of bemusement. From this point of view, part of the aims of these first two chapters is one of conceptual clarification via a discussion of the history and analysis of the status of understanding and explanation in the social sciences.

Rom Harré's chapter links directly into discussions concerning the ontological status of the social. At a sociotheoretical level, his discussion has parallels with Randall Collins and Aron Cicourel's 'aggregation hypothesis' (see Knorr-Cetina and Cicourel 1981). Broadly speaking, this suggests that if we can talk of macro social phenomena, then it is in relation to their being composed of aggregations and repetitions of micro-episodes. As Rom Harré then argues, in relation to the status of social explanations, reduction theory holds the social sciences to account at the level of micro-episodes. Methodologically, therefore, we arrive at the idea that we can know the social world discursively via an analysis of the symbolic systems through which life worlds are constructed and acted upon. However, we cannot 'know' macro phenomena in the same way. Allusion to such an entity as 'class', therefore, is rhetorical, not empirical.

David-Hillel Ruben's chapter draws upon the themes already raised in the first three chapters. In particular, he assists in clarifying the following question: in what sense can the social sciences lay claim to their status in view of the arguments which continually reoccur in relation to the 'transparency thesis'? Broadly speaking, this states that as the 'social' is the creation of knowing agents, then the workings of society and the dynamics of social relations must be transparent to them. If that thesis is rejected, then upon what basis are we able, in epistemological and ontological terms, to warrant the findings of social sciences? The illumination of these issues takes place in this chapter through a focus on what the social 'is' and what 'properties' may be ascribed to it. In so doing, it enables a further basis for discussions in subsequent chapters.

Following on from issues raised in the previous two chapters, the ontological status of action and structure and how this informs the construction of social theory is the subject of Margaret Archer's contribution. Taking the relations between structure and agency, she draws a distinction between three types of theorizing. First, downwards conflation in which structures appear as determinant and agency is accorded little or no autonomy in social relations. Second, upwards conflation which subscribes to a methodological individualism that admits of no other social properties than the actions and attitudes of people. Third, central conflation, which seeks to bring action and structure together, not as dualisms, but a duality. The best known example of this form of theorizing is Anthony Giddens's theory of structuration. Finding each of these unsatisfactory in terms of their ontological assumptions and their translation into methodological injunctions she argues, following the work of Roy Bhaskar, for an 'analytic dualism' that provides for a more adequate explanation of the relations between action and structure.

Derek Layder continues with this theme in his chapter. Arguing that unimodal ontologies are inadequate as bases to explain social relations, he moves towards an understanding of ontological differentiation and epistemological pluralism in order to examine structure and agency as separate elements informing social relations. In so doing, he holds to an argument concerned with 'domains of social reality' that accords autonomy to agency, alongside the ability to adequately analyse structure and how these relate to one another. Social reality is thus seen as stratified and multifaceted.

John Scott then raises another central issue in knowing the social world: that between particularism and generalization. In relation to social theory and methodology, a clear tendency towards relativism is now evident and is particularly aided by the 'postmodern turn'. However, we are also entering a period of reconstruction after the postmodernist critique. In terms of these debates and maintaining our thematic overview and addressing some core issues, John Scott argues that Karl Mannheim's ideas on relationalism provide a valuable perspective in thinking through the relativism–objectivity divide. Finding the Cartesian 'view from nowhere' as an insufficient basis for claims to objectivity requires an understanding of situated knowledge which is difficult, if not impossible, to transcend. A recognition of this, however, as John makes clear, does not mean an open embrace to relativism.

Mary Maynard's contribution is concerned with questions of epistemology, ontology, theory and research practice in feminist inspired thinking. In this sense it links in with all prior chapters; in particular, John Scott's discussion of the work of Nancy Hartsock on feminist standpoint epistemology. In terms of understanding situated knowledge, this chapter brings together elements of positioning and belonging via a gendered identity and what this means to know the social world from the point of view of a feminist social science. In so doing, this chapter makes clear the important and valuable contribution that feminisms have made to knowing the social world. In addition, Mary Maynard examines the issue as to whether there is something distinctive that can be called a feminist 'method' of knowing the social world. Her conclusion for feminist research practice is a call for a return to middle range theory.

Alan Bryman then brings us to the question of the relationship between the themes throughout the book and their translation into what are often seen as technical decisions as to the efficacy and applicability of different methods of social investigation. What is novel about his approach to the issues of quantitative and qualitative research is how each employs rhetorics of persuasion in the reporting of their results. While not suggesting that rhetorical allusion is all we have, in opening this up as a possible way of reading the differences between these research strategies, he clearly adds to an understanding of how it is that researchers claim to know the social world via what is a relatively neglected dimension of social scientific practice.

Tim May then looks back over the issues raised in each of the contributions and what their consequences are for knowing the social world. This takes place through drawing out their implications for an understanding of reflexivity, along two dimensions, not only in social scientific practice, but also in social life in general. Tim May argues that debates around reflexivity have a clear tendency to reproduce an inward looking practice. This, by default, moves the focus away from a number of key issues: for example, the need to understand the epistemology of reception, as well as production, of social scientific knowledge and how and under what circumstances reflexivity itself is heightened in the relations between knowledge, action and social circumstances.

The need to understand social relations and social life has never been so great as the modes of ordering societies become ever more complex and abstract and yet inform our everyday lives in ways that are often beyond our immediate comprehension. Therefore, it is our hope that through the medium of an edited collection, with contributions by scholars who are at the forefront of their respective disciplines, this book will contribute towards what will be more constructive encounters and dialogues between philosophy, social theory, methodology and methods in the spirit of seeking to know the social world.

# 1 | The social world as knowable

**Malcolm Williams**

To say we 'know' the social world implies different usages of the verb dependent on whether one is a philosopher, social theorist or methodologist. Yet in whichever sense one uses the phrase there is an implication of a correspondence between the thoughts of the knower and the world. Things become much more complex when we ask what it is we know about the social world and what might be a reliable route to that knowledge. Had the editors of this volume been of more pessimistic temperament it might have been titled 'Problems in Knowing the Social World', for there are many – philosophical, methodological and technical. But these problems should not blind us to the apparent success of social science, particularly in the form of empirical social research. Unless one is very sceptical, or very pessimistic, it is evident that researchers are able to produce explanations and understandings of the social world that possess both operational validity and practical utility. One could of course insist that the millions spent by government, academia, campaigning organizations and others are simply an investment in an ideological justificatory strategy (or strategies). It is possible that this is the case, but even if it is it remains that we have found out an awful lot about the world as an unintended consequence. Indeed historically, social research has played an important role in providing empirical evidence from which measures to tackle poverty, poor health and discrimination were based (Bulmer 1978). To say we 'know the social world' is, at the level of practical application at least, self-evidently true.

In this opening chapter I want to focus on two key questions that arise from the assertion of knowledge of the social world through social research. The choice of questions will be selective and the focus 'soft', and although I will attempt to sketch out a broad solution to the problems I illustrate, I am just as concerned to show how questions of how we can know the social world require an interplay between philosophy, social theory and method. In one sense the chapter represents a journey from the practical questions of the method of social research and how this can be a tool in the betterment of social life, to the abstract problems of philosophy and back again. Because this journey mirrors my own experience I will begin with some autobiography. Before entering academia I spent several years active in local politics and the trade union movement. My first interests as an undergraduate on a social science degree were empirical and practical. How could social science give valid and accurate results that would allow effective intervention to resolve social problems? The ethos of my undergraduate department was however Marxism and neo-Marxism and I soon realized that the presumption of effective intervention presupposed a particular ideological framework. Doubt crept in and this doubt was compounded by methodological questions about what counted as validity and accuracy anyway. By my final year the green shoots of ideological and methodological doubt had become a tangled undergrowth of philosophical problems. In an attempt to cut through some of the undergrowth I went off to study philosophy at a different university. The new literature I discovered was a carefully crafted and rigorous attempt to resolve the philosophical problems that underlay those of methodology, but what struck me as rather odd was the complete absence of reference to or (apparent) interest in recent empirical problems. Did investigative social science really end with Durkheim's *Suicide* (1897) or Weber's *Protestant Ethic* (1902)? Yet despite the apparent desire to refer only to the pasteurized examples of historical sociology there was so much work with important methodological value that was unheard of, or bowdlerized in the contemporary methodological literature. What became very apparent was that methodological and ideological stances adopted by researchers had very deep and often unacknowledged roots. This observation is not meant to imply the opposite, that every study of poverty or crime should indulge in philosophical navel gazing, but rather to lament the lack of effective debate between philosophers, social theorists and methodologists.

A glance at almost any methods textbook will quickly show that empirical social science follows two very different methodological routes, those of quantitative and qualitative research. These methodological approaches are not wholly a technical matter of difference but instead result from two different, even rival, philosophical and social theoretical traditions of interpretivism and naturalism. Many empirical and theoretical problems and questions flow from the adoption not just of one or other methodological approach, but from the assumption (usually implicit) of philosophical or methodological positions. Some maintain that it is perfectly possible for a particular methodological approach not to have philosophical implications (Bryman 1984; 1988), while others regard the technical advances in quantitative and qualitative methods to be complementary (Abell 1990). I do not deny that each of these views has merit, but through the use of examples from each methodological approach I will try to show that to understand the problems of method and to realise its potential, requires a symbiosis between the philosophical-theoretical and the methodological.

## Interpretivism

Depending on the context, what I shall here refer to as interpretivism is variously described as 'hermeneutics', 'ethnography', 'field research' or 'qualitative methods'. No one term adequately describes what is a huge range of theoretical views and technical approaches. In using the term 'interpretivism' I mean all of those approaches to research that prioritize the interpretation of the actions and meanings of agents, over measurement, explanation and prediction.

Though some of the exponents of 'interpretivism' claim their approach for science (for example Schutz 1965; Taylor 1994), this variant of 'science' is exotic with most denying that interpretivism can or should be a 'science' and more strongly, usually deny that investigations of the social world can utilize the methodological devices of science. Of course there are many intermediate positions and increasingly multimethod approaches utilize the strategies of interpretation and measurement (Bryman 1988: ch. 6), but these approaches often bypass the questions raised by each of their constituents, perhaps assuming the virtue of one will cancel the evil of the other out.

Interpretivism is usually treated as a counter to 'scientific' approaches, more properly called 'naturalist' approaches to research. Historically it is regarded as a humanist response to the scientific hegemony of the late nineteenth and early twentieth centuries (Manicas 1987: 121–6), but its origins have a longer methodological pedigree in classical hermeneutics and adopted as an investigative method in social analysis by Dilthey, Ast and Schleiermacher (Føllesdal 1994: 233). The methodological work of Norman Denzin is illustrative of the assertions and arguments advanced by interpretivists. This said, I do not suggest that Denzin's work is necessarily typical of interpretivism, nor do I use this example as an ideal type; instead I use his work to bring into focus some of the methodological issues arising from philosophical assumptions.

Denzin terms his approach 'interpretive interactionism', which he describes as 'an interpretive phenomenological symbolic interactionism' (Denzin 1983: 129). The theoretical underpinnings are therefore eclectic and give rise to methodological prescriptions deriving from each tradition. Interpretation is a strategy employed by phenomenologists and symbolic interactionists, so the 'interpretive' part of the description is rather superfluous, but serves to underline its centrality to his methodology.

Consider the following:

> Interpretive interactionism is founded on the study, expression and interpretation of human experience.
>
> Interpretivists participate in the life world so as to understand better and express its emergent properties and features.

> The interpretivist rejects generalisation as a goal and never aims to draw randomly selected samples of human experience.
>
> (Denzin 1983: 132–3)

Though Denzin's interpretivism in its attempted synthesis with structuralism has unusual characteristics, the above quotes well illustrate the central tenets of the approach. Implicit in the above is a 'folk psychology' that depends essentially on the intersubjective understanding of the meaning of actions and utterances. Because agents are participants in the 'lifeworld', then this participation is said to effect such an understanding. In the case of Denzin generalization is rejected because of 'an inherent indeterminateness in the lifeworld' (1983: 133). This concept of lifeworld indeterminacy is taken from phenomenology and can be found in Merleau-Ponty and Schutz (Merleau-Ponty 1967; Schutz 1967). Broadly speaking individual consciousnesses are free to attach different meanings to the same action or circumstances and conversely different actions can arise out of similarly expressed meanings. The attribution of causality to human actions is not considered legitimate, because meanings arise from 'mind' which is not observable or measurable. This position leads to a number of consequences. Some of these are recognized, but methodologically ignored, while some are largely unrecognized.

### *Generalization is not possible*

Janet Ward-Schofield (1993) notes the apparent lack of discussion of generalization in qualitative research and indeed uses the same quote (above) from Denzin to suggest the denial of generalization. Nevertheless in empirical research the conclusion that the intentional nature of individual consciousness produces far too much variability for generalizations to be made from one interaction to another has never really embarrassed interpretivists, whose attitude is somewhat akin to that of the Victorian middle classes toward sex: they do it, they know it goes on, but they never admit to either. Almost every classic interpretivist study, while acknowledging the subjectivity of the researcher and the uniqueness of the repertoire of interactions studied, nevertheless wishes to persuade us that there is something to be learned from that situation that has a wider currency.

Denzin is absolutely right. If there really is so much variability then any similarity between individual expressed meanings or actions would be coincidental. Research findings should be interpreted as unique events and any similarity with other sets of events should be seen as a coincidence. However this would seem to render most research a pointless exercise in the reconstruction and interpretation of a unique set of events. On the other hand if the researcher makes *moderatum* generalizations of the kind 'if *X* occurs in situation *S*, it is likely that in a situation resembling *S*, *X* may well occur in the future' (Williams and May 1996: 79) then she is asserting at least the existence of some similarities (however weak) between situations. This assertion seems far more plausible than its denial for if it is the case (as phenomenologists would assert) that we can employ a repertoire of typifications in the lifeworld then these are forms of everyday *moderatum* generalizations and precisely the means by which the researcher can know the world of the researched.

Implicitly the search is for difference and typicality in any research. More specifically is it the case that findings are typical of the wider group, or that they are different in important ways to those found in the wider group. A typical example is Sue Fisher's (1993) ethnographic work on children's gambling with fruit machines. The research utilized the method of participant observation of how children and young people use fruit machines in an 'arcade'. Fisher's research is richly descriptive of the cultural strategies and individual skills of the young people. From her data she constructs a sociological typology of 'Arcade Kings and their Apprentices', 'Machine Beaters', 'Escape Artists', 'Action Seeker' and 'Social Gamblers'. The construction of typologies, even though, as Fisher points out, these can be fluid, suggests categorization of the form of *p* and not *p* and one, moreover, which is presumably intended to have analytic value beyond the particular research. The typologies must be considered typical!

Denzin claims (1983: 133) that interpretivists never aim to select random samples of 'human experience', but unless one is making folk psychological assumptions about the extent of typifications or experience there is no guarantee that the findings are not just quirks. The interpretivist is on the horns of a dilemma. Assert that generalization is impossible because of the variability between agents and the research can suggest nothing beyond itself. If on the other hand it is accepted that we can make *moderatum* generalizations what is the basis upon which we can claim these hold?

### *There can be no explanations*

The denial of generalization implies the denial of explanation. Explanations are 'why' questions. Social researchers are interested in 'why' questions at two levels. The first is how agents themselves answer 'why' questions. The second is why do agents themselves believe *X*, or do *Y*? The first relates to agents' own explanations of their behaviour, the second to the researcher's explanation of the agents' behaviour. The word explanation, however, does not figure that often in interpretivists' descriptions of what they do. 'Why' questions imply a causal description of agents' actions or views. Instead emphasis is on understanding (*verstehen*), whereby through empathic understanding we can come to know the meaning an agent had for what she did, or said what she said. The difficulty is that ten different people performing the same action could give ten different reasons for doing so, conversely ten different actions could be motivated by the same reason. Therefore even if we can allow that an individual doing *X* and giving reason *Y* has adequately explained their actions (the first level), we cannot legitimately move to the second level and say that certain persons do *X* when they believe *Y*, because they just as easily could have done something else when holding those beliefs. This is often 'explained' at a metalevel by reference to a range of frequently mutually exclusive theories: the cultural specificity of rationality; reference to inner mental states etc. Methodologically however, the rejection of the possibility of wider or 'social' explanation is related to generalization in so far as if it is the case we cannot explain reasons or actions in a group of individuals it is because such characteristics in an individual cannot be inferred to the group. If there can be no generalizations there can be no explanations and if there can be no explanations beyond the individual then there can be no generalizations. Once again we can turn to Denzin for a clear statement of how this comes to pass in interpretivist research.

> The 'why' question [of science] is replaced by the 'how' question. That is, how is the social experience, or a sequence of social interaction organised, perceived and constructed by differentially wide awake, self reflexive, social constrained, free individuals.
>
> (Denzin 1983: 132)

Denzin's views here are very close to those of ethnomethodology; however, as with generalization, the denial of the possibility of 'second level' explanations is more honoured in the breach. Indeed Denzin's importation of structuralism and all of the *a priori* description and explanation that it implies of society, or parts thereof, surely contradict the former claim to answer only 'how' questions? As with generalization the avoidance of 'why' questions is either impossible or leads to sterile accounts. Actually the choice of a research topic, location, or set of agents is an implicit answer to an earlier 'why' question. The asking of 'how' questions about (for example) how power is distributed in a certain group suggests that at some point the question of why power was an interesting topic and why its distribution in that group was also interesting must have been asked, which in turn suggests some sort of elementary and speculative explanatory framework that is being tested by the research.

The denial of generalization and explanation, if taken seriously, would lead to denial that theories of the social world can be formulated, yet alone tested. Ethnomethodology, to pay it its due, does indeed insist that 'social' explanation is not possible (Heritage 1984). However, as we have seen through the Fisher example (and here I would assert this *is* a typical piece of interpretative research) explanations are offered and generalization is implicit. The rejection of either would make social research impossible or pointless. If however it is accepted that generalization and explanation are possible then there is an acceptance that enough characteristics are held in common between individuals for this to be possible.

The moral of the foregoing might be that if one wishes to produce practically useful research findings using interpretivist strategies it would not be wise to take the kind of philosophical strictures Denzin makes too seriously. Indeed Bryman (1988: 173–4) maintains that empirical research is relatively independent of such epistemological strictures. The problem is that these things are often foundational and part of the intellectual justificatory strategy that researchers employ in defence of the validity of their findings. If these are shaky, contradictory or even absent the practical authority of the research is undermined. It would be as if engineers, upon completing a bridge, were asked about the principle upon which they relied to prevent the bridge from collapsing, simply shrugged their shoulders and said 'Well it's standing isn't it? Does it matter?' Let me illustrate how this might be problematic in social research through a brief hypothetical example. It is widely agreed that certain research problems can be tackled only through interpretive methods. Studies of football hooliganism might employ survey method to ask how people felt about the experience of hooliganism, but to get at the meaning of hooliganism for its participants require more unobtrusive methods (Shipman 1988: 64). That this and other studies of (for example) cults, right wing political organizations and youth gangs, *can* be accomplished is testimony to the effectiveness of interpretive methods. But those who wish to know about football hooliganism do not wish to know simply about why some supporters of a particular team are hooligans, but something about hooliganism in general. What is it about the findings from a study of supporters of a particular team that make it generalizable to supporters of other teams? The technical problem of how to research such matters leads to the interpretivist strategy of (say) participant observation and in adopting this strategy we inherit a philosophical problem, namely whether hooligan behaviour is as varied as there are numbers of hooligans, whether hooligan behaviour is intersubjectively constructed, but locally specific, or whether the hooligan has universal characteristics!

## Survey research

It is upon the assumption that characteristics are held in common that survey research is based. That it is indeed possible to generalize from a sample to a population and to explain why particular groups do, or believe certain things, or to explain individual actions and beliefs in terms of pre-existing influences or determinants. While interpretivism mostly rules out the possibility of causal explanation, survey research relies upon such a possibility (though what is meant by 'causal' may differ), but does not however usually rule out a study of meaning (Marsh 1982: 98).

Survey research is a form of naturalistic inquiry and asserts that human beings are part of nature and that the social world is continuous with the physical world. It is said to follow from this, that with appropriate adaptation the same methodological approach can be used to study the social and the physical world. However the adoption of a naturalistic position with regard to inquiries in the social world, as with interpretivism, entails several philosophical difficulties. Here I will consider some aspects of just one problem, that of 'social reality' and how we can measure it.

### *Empiricism and its discontents*

Confirmation through sense data became the unquestioned hallmark of science until the mid-twentieth century and its predictive and technological success were important in its adoption as the model for the early social sciences (Williams and May 1996: 14). This doctrine of empiricism rules as illegitimate ontological assumptions that cannot be verified by sense data. However empiricism in its rawest form would commit us to the belief that the world presents itself to us in an unmediated form without the benefit of any prior conceptual schema. Empiricism does not rule out theories, but theories still take a back seat in relation to sense data. Theories may propose, but science through experimental method disposes. This however, leaves empiricism in a tricky position *vis-à-vis* the status of theories and observations. Are observations themselves innocent of prior theories? That they are not is now, post-Kuhn and post-Popper, something of a received wisdom. But if we accept that our observations are 'theory laden', this merely postpones the problem. If theory *T1* is to be tested through observations O and it is accepted that O is structured (perhaps through a particular research design, choice of sample etc.) by theoretical assumptions (let us call these *T2*), then *T1* is subject to test by *T2*, rather than some theory neutral algorithm of observation (expressed through language). In survey research attempts to overcome the problem of potentially self validating theories and instruments take a number of forms such as the alternating use of positive and negative statements in Lickert scales, etc. (de Vaus 1991). However the operationalization of theories into measurements implies a deeper philosophical problem and one with technical consequences. The problem can be simply stated: do our theories postulate reality and do our measurements measure that reality?

Empiricism postpones 'reality' by insisting we can measure only what is manifest. Indeed the character of the world depends on our description of it (Passmore 1988: 89), because there is no *a priori* real world against which we can compare it. Questions of 'reality' therefore become either irrelevant or metaphysical speculation. If theories are to be scientific they must propose the existence of phenomena that can be observed. Of course we can propose the existence of anything we like, from unicorns to UFOs (unidentified flying objects), but science relies for its authority on what Russell called 'hard data' (Ayer 1956: 84). The prediction and description of observables is a goal of science. Carl Sagan (1996) amusingly illustrates the significance of sense data to plausible explanation with the following. You assert to me that a fire-breathing dragon lives in your garage and I ask to see the dragon. Upon looking in the garage all I see are old paint tins, a ladder, etc., but no dragon. Ah you say, but the dragon is invisible. I suggest spreading flour on the floor to catch her footprints. You reply that the dragon floats on air. I suggest an infrared sensor to detect the invisible fire, but you respond that the fire is heatless, and so on (Sagan 1996: 160). We need the hard data.

Yet the reliance on sense data to represent reality has relativistic consequences, as the physicist Poincaré noted early in the twentieth century (Kolakowski 1972: 158–9), in that intersubjective agreement about the characteristics, or existence, of those data may well be local with several rival explanations or theories equally logically sound. This has a particular resonance in investigations of the social world, as we will see. Now either we can embrace this relativism, as in the case of Goodman (1977) for example, shifting the emphasis in science from the discovery of the world to elegance and simplicity of concepts, or we can adopt some form of what I would term 'standardization', thus retaining the focus on the objects of discovery as non-relative. The standardization can take a number of forms such as conventionalism (the view that Poincaré adopted that the choice of theory is simply a convention), (cf. Tudor 1982), but in survey research a common empiricist strategy is that of operationalism, whereby the measurement itself is used to define the characteristics of what is measured (Blalock and Blalock 1971: 8).

Naive operationalism is commoner than one might suppose in survey research. Definitions of ethnicity, social class, homelessness and so on, all depend on operational definitions that result not from an attempt at an authentic translation of the phenomenon into measurable definitions, but rather definitions that result from what can be measured. Take homelessness, for example. Bramley (1988) has produced what is acknowledged as one of the most comprehensive definitions of homelessness. However while some of what Bramley defines as 'homelessness' is both measurable and recognizable to those who experience it, many of Bramley's states of homelessness are subjective. For this reason the social sciences are more likely to adopt (or suffer from, depending on your view) operationalism. In investigations of the physical world, while it is possible to produce different operational definitions of phenomena (such as temperature) at least that definition will be universally operationalizable. Homelessness is not and will depend on (among other things) the local cultural norms pertaining to the concept of 'home' (Jencks 1994). Attempts to measure overall homelessness, or to quantify aspects of it, usually adopt definitions that arise from what it is (and is possible to) measure. As Blalock put it in relation to IQ testing: 'If one is asked what is meant by the concept "intelligence", he [*sic*] should be told that intelligence is what IQ tests measure' (Blalock and Blalock 1971: 8). Such definitions have been much criticized as being tautologies, as indeed they are. The problem, however, for the homelessness researcher, is that such definitions do not adequately capture the experience of homelessness – experiences which, if not quantifiable, can be shown to exist through the use of interpretive strategies.

Though some social scientists (for example Lundberg 1961 or Blalock and Blalock 1971) have embraced operationalism, it is perhaps more often, methodologically, an unintended consequence of *operationalization*. Is operationalism then simply bad research or is it an inevitable consequence of attempts to quantify the social world? What I have termed naive operationalism simply fits descriptions to what has and can be measured and is perhaps typified by Lundberg's work. A more sophisticated version, as originally advocated by Eddington and Bridgeman in physics (Bridgeman 1959), postulates specific definitions within a network of formalized axioms. The implication for commonsense definitions, such as homelessness, is that they would be broken down into a number of separate, measurable and related definitions. The obvious problem, as Pawson (1989) notes, is that this would lead to a proliferation of definitions and 'We would end up with a proliferation of concepts . . . that would be hypothetically endless as each modification of measurement apparatus came along'(1989: 230).

For example counting homeless people is hampered by the lack of existence of an adequate sampling frame (Williams 1996). If, however, as a result of an official campaign of voter registration, most homeless people (whether living rough, in squats or in hostels) appeared on electoral rolls, our definition would not then be constrained by who we could measure. In principle all homeless people could be counted using a standard sample frame. Should we earlier have produced operationalist definitions based on different measurement approaches they would be then redundant, leading to the ludicrous conclusion that homelessness had changed as a result of our ability to better measure it! The 'proliferation' criticism holds for both investigations of the physical and social worlds, but the more open (and often subjective) character of the social world renders operationalism more obviously a problematic strategy.

Operationalism is not synonymous with empiricism, but what I wish to illustrate is what happens when the notion of an objective reality is replaced with observables. Realism, in social science, though still committed to naturalism and often employing the same, or similar methods, begins from different ontological assumptions, namely that an objective reality exists. While a lot of quantitative research is naively operationalist, paradoxically a lot is also naively realist, in so far as the 'reality' of the social world is taken

for granted (Bunge 1996: 327). This means that a lot of research manages to be both operationalist and realist at the same time, asserting both the necessity of practical definition and the reality of the concepts so defined! However other forms of realism are less naive and while asserting the existence of a not always visible reality, nevertheless offer prescriptions of how that

reality might become known. One of the best known expressions of this is found in Bhaskar's 'transitive' and 'intransitive' objects of science (Bhaskar 1989: 18–21). For Bhaskar our theories and derived hypotheses are the transitive objects of science which aim to represent the intransitive objects of reality. This strategy, Bhaskar recommends, should be achieved through the measurements of effects. From this hypothetical entities can be postulated, which if they exist, would explain the effects. How would, or does, this approach work in social science?

Attempts to translate a realist programme into empirical social science are rarer than one would expect. A notable exception is that of Pawson who uses a number of examples – especially those of class – to argue that it is possible to be empirical without being empiricist (Pawson 1989: 126). In most survey research class is a key variable, but one that is notoriously difficult to operationalize. Pawson takes the bull by the horns, as it were. He examines three 'generative models' used to establish class categories (those of Wright, Boudin and Goldthorpe) and concludes that

> these case studies show remarkable similarities in terms of their explanatory and measurement strategies. None of them relies on common sense categorisation in establishing the measurement properties of key explanatory variables. . . . All of them meet the requirement of defining class positions prior to and independently of any operational criterion. . . . All of the theories receive support from empirical data and that evidence exonerates not only the substantive theorics but also the measurement and classificatory units that go to make up the theories.
>
> (Pawson 1989: 186–7)

The obvious objection here is that they each propose different 'generative models' of class (equivalent to Bhaskar's hypothetical entities), so how could each be an equally good approximation of reality? As Pawson notes:

> For Wright class is the context of production which identifies the economic resources and coercive powers open to members of particular class positions. For Boudon class is an emergent property resulting from the cultural assets and patterns of decision making by different groups. For Goldthorpe both class resources and perceptions combine to generate a developing system of hurdles and boundaries which identify the key class position.
>
> (Pawson 1989: 186)

Hall (1996: 194) takes up this point and suggests that similarities resulting from attempts to measure class may be explained by two possibilities. Either there is

> one fundamental generative and real process, which must be disentangled from externalities and described

or

> there may be manifold mechanisms, processes, events, recipes of action, and other phenomena that are tapped by alternative measurements of stratification.
>
> (Hall 1996: 194)

What we term 'class' may not be fully described by any one theory, but this does not mean that different theories are mutually exclusive, but may instead describe different social experiences. To hope for *a* theory of 'class' is perhaps analogous to hoping for *a* theory of movement. Hall ends up as pessimistic of a realist programme such as Pawson's arguing that the complexity of the socio-historical phenomena (of class) undermines a realist agenda for three reasons: the emergent complexity of the 'real' processes would prevent a complete or accurate description; the complexity of the phenomena overwhelms our ability to investigate it; historical change in the phenomena is faster than our technical ability to identify its properties.

The first of these objections is perhaps the most telling, but of course would equally apply to non-linear systems in the physical world. However the social world is not just complex in the same sense as, say, liquid turbulence, but arises from the reflective character of human minds. The contingency of human behaviour arises not just from the complexity that characterizes open systems, but from individual subjectivity. In saying this I am not denying that the social world can enable or constrain individuals, but rather that any specification of reality must allow that its constituents have a reflective character. An attempt to access 'social reality' will depend upon whether reality is to count as that which is experienced by individuals or whether we seek reality in common antecedents of these subjective experiences. The first of these, though realist in a minimal sense, is for all intents and purposes pragmatism and exemplified in the work of W. I. Thomas (Thomas and Znaniecki 1958). The second, though precisely the programme advocated by Bhaskar, brings us full circle back to the problem of the operationalization of variables. The first, applied (say) to homelessness would ask 'what is the experienced reality of homelessness, for the homeless'?. The difficulty here would be that a comparison of cases would require an *a priori* definition of homelessness, the alternative of self definition not only would preclude comparison, but also would not be at all certain that what individuals experienced was anything like the same phenomena. The second requires us to formulate hypotheses to explain observed effects (such as sleeping rough or in squats) which we have termed homelessness. In doing this we are assuming that it is likely that experienced reality (for the homeless) is underwritten by processes and mechanisms which are not transparent to the homeless. While the processes and mechanisms proposed could not (and perhaps should not) fulfill Schutz's postulate of adequacy for those experiencing homelessness, but in order to be corroborated the hypotheses

must propose objects that can be made visible and intelligible to someone, otherwise realism becomes jam tomorrow! Moreover for corroboration to be achieved the postulated mechanisms and processes must be shown to have been the cause of that which is experienced by the homeless. Yet the kinds of explanations we will seek and may find will depend in the first place on what kind of living conditions we wish to subsume under the theoretical term 'homelessness'. The 'causes', or generative mechanisms, that give rise to homelessness will depend on what counts as homelessness to begin with. By adopting a realist strategy of trying to identify the generative mechanisms we may have avoided operationalism, but have we ended up with a form of conventionalism? That is more than one theory of 'homelessness' allows us to explain the observed effects. To avoid the conventionalist charge the realist must make reference to layers of reality, as yet unobserved, that will (to use Bhaskar's terminology) constitute the 'intransitive' objects. While it is always the intention to find ontological agreement between these and the transitive objects of our hypotheses the intransitive objects begin to look like a dragon in the garage.

## Conclusion

In the foregoing I have considered two important philosophical problems facing research, or to put it another way two important problems of researching the social world facing philosophy, namely in interpretivism, how can research lay claim to explanatory utility that goes beyond the here and now and in survey research how do we achieve a correspondence between social 'reality' and the measures employed?

As the late Cathy Marsh once remarked, these are lawyer's problems and we should not forget that the work of the detective goes on in social research almost as if the problems did not exist. Indeed Alan Bryman (1984; 1988) has long held the view, developed in this volume, that there is a separation between the technical and the epistemological, with the latter taking the form of 'rhetorics of persuasion'. I would not deny that *de facto* this is indeed the case. However to continue my own analogy, when I travel over a bridge I do not want to know how it stays up, but I do want to feel secure in the knowledge that someone does. Building bridges is an interplay between scientific laws and engineering principles. In the same way I believe that the enterprise of social research should be an interplay between philosophy, social theory and technique. The difference between bridge construction and social research is that in the former the scientist can tell the engineer why the bridge stays up. In social research philosophical problems often take the form of telling researchers why their 'bridge' cannot stay up! Let me return to the two problems and try to offer some observations that might contribute to a solution(s).

That generalization can and does take place in interpretivism is manifest from the reliability of its results. Clearly agents within 'cultures' hold stocks of typifications that allow them to move from place to place and depend on the consistency of certain features. It seems perfectly reasonable that a gaming arcade in Devon, will in key physical and interaction characteristics, resemble one in Durham. Perhaps more importantly an observer of the former would immediately note any key differences and these would be interesting. In the following quote Guba and Lincoln (1982) consider the possibilities of interpretivist generalization:

> The aim of inquiry is to develop an idiographic body of knowledge. This knowledge is best encapsulated in a series of 'working hypotheses' that describe the individual case. Generalizations are impossible since phenomena are neither time- nor context-free (although transferability of these hypotheses may be possible from situation to situation, depending on the degree of contemporal and contextual similarity).
>
> (cited in Ward-Schofield 1993: 206)

I have no problem agreeing with the first and last sentence. The building of idiographic knowledge that can form (testable) hypotheses seems reasonable, but why in the same breath deny generalization? The denial, I believe, conflates the generalization of the total situation, with statistical generalization and *moderatum* generalization. No social researcher is in the business of generalizing the characteristics of total situations. In open systems such generalizations are almost certainly impossible. The survey researcher is interested in the second and while the isolation of specific variables for further survey work is not impossible, the interpretivist makes and cannot help but make *moderatum* generalizations about identifiable aspects of the research situation. That this particular bridge stays up seems to be the result of cultural consistency and precisely the domain of the social theorist, who in turn can produce testable theories as to why there might be cultural consistency.

The second problem can be seen as a question of what is social reality? The empiricist view is that this is not a useful question to ask because all we can ever know is that which we apprehend through the senses, while the realist insists that there is more to social life than we apprehend. History is on the side of the realist, while method, or more specifically its constraints, appear to be on the side of the empiricist. Our understanding of the social world is both deeper and different from one hundred years ago; moreover we can easily demonstrate that those things that crucially influence the life course of an individual are not always apparent to that individual. We get social life wrong and we know we don't know all of it. In this respect the realist argument is simple and compelling.

Against this the empiricist could demand how can we avoid conventionalism, when our theories are intersubjective constructs about a subjectively experienced world? At the level of method how can we avoid some form of operationalism, at least that our variables extend to what it is logically possible to measure, even if not technically possible? Yet among naturalist social scientists, realism seems to be like goodness: we all favour it, but how do we turn it into a methodological strategy?

First, the ontological question of 'social reality' is far from settled even among realists. While Bhaskar and his followers propose a view of social reality which, though acknowledging the greater variability and instability of social systems, nevertheless propose a model of society not unlike that of the physical world. Rom Harré takes a view, represented in Chapter 3 in this volume, that to know social reality we must know local 'grammars' – a view not dissimilar to that advanced by Winch and since by the ethnomethodologists. It is certainly true that our experience of reality is local and intersubjective, but that we also know from experience that reality transcends the local both as cultural consistency and as manifestations of structures that extend beyond us. For example I know that my cultural reality is very local in some respects, but wider in others. Some dialect expressions are local to my own town, but other colloquialisms would be understood in San Francisco or Sydney. This is the reality I experience. However I also know that it is possible that a decision of government may lead indirectly to my losing my job, or having my house compulsorily purchased. I do not know the details of these structures, but I know they exist and can potentially have effects that become part of my experience.

To return to the problem of homelessness research, we know that the reality of being homeless is what is experienced, but we also know that the reasons for that state are not always transparent to those experiencing homelessness. However what is important here is that the structural factors contributing to homelessness manifest themselves at some point to someone as first order experience, though again they may not know the nature of structure, or its effects, beyond them. Yet the homeless will be aware of the existence of such structures and will have folk psychological theories as to their nature. As will those who occupy other parts of the structure responsible for the situation of the homeless. All parts of the social structure are known to someone, somewhere at some time. A key role for the researcher is to make transparent as much of the structure as possible and indeed exposing the misapprehensions of those who occupy parts of the structure.

It might be objected that this assertion of experience as the definition of reality is a denial of realism in favour of empiricism. I don't think it is. First, it *is* a denial that *social* reality can consist of anything other than social constructions. However, those social constructions take on a reality to those who experience their effects. The job of social research is to know the effects and to provide explanations of the processes and structures that lead to those effects. It would seem that we are dealing with two different kinds of entities: first the effects, the reality as meaningfully experienced, and second, the abstract processes and structures. If it is the case that these processes and structures live somewhere in someone's experience (in the case of homelessness, housing officers, politicians and others) then a task of research is to turn these abstract entities into reality as meaningfully experienced. In other words it is fine to propose that the experiences of agents are produced by abstract processes and structures, but these must be translated into empirically testable propositions about experience.

At the level of method this implies pluralism. Interpretivism can make clear the meaningful experiences of agents and specifically why they believe the world is the way it is. If these experiences can be *moderatum* generalizations then they can form the basis of theories about process or structure. Conversely researchers' theories about process and structure can be exposed to the meaning criteria of those whose experiences the researcher wishes to explain. Through the use of interpretivist method the researcher produces representations that are created and tested by the meanings of the researched. But of course this is not enough, for the *moderatum* generalizations remain working hypotheses, but these hypotheses should be operationalizable into survey questions. The cultural consistency that led to the moderatum generalizations are some kind of guarantee that the operationalization represents the reality of those it is intended. Furthermore though the operationalization of specific variables into measurements must be meaningful to respondents it is not the case that the respondent will, or needs to, understand the overall analysis implications for explaining her experience.

Finally I have only touched on the problem of conventionalism, but again I believe this is less problematic methodologically than might be first supposed. It is possible that our theories are conventions in social research where the boundaries of what they purport to explain are culturally limited. In the physical sciences this is more problematic because if falsification or corroboration are a matter of cultural convention then they can hardly explain physical characteristics that exist independently of our ideas about them. In the social world things exist *only* by virtue of people's ideas about them,[1] therefore the researcher is testing theories (themselves social constructions) against the socially constructed reality of the researched.

Two things emerge from the foregoing: first, though occupying a great deal of the philosophical literature about the social world, the problems are those of the lawyer and on analysis turn out to be less troublesome than first thought. Generalization (and explanation) is not only possible in interpretivism, but indeed unavoidable. The problem seems to be one of importing a very rigid definition of generalization from survey research (worse still the 'straw person' of total generalization of all characteristics). The possibility of generalization seems to lie in intersubjectively shared meanings, what I have termed cultural consistency. Intersubjectively shared meanings seem also to be the experiences which comprise social reality. In survey research our representations (and thus our theories) must either come from these, or be subject to test by them in a reflexive process and this is the closest we can get to representing social reality, avoiding operationalism and conventionalism.

Second, these problems cannot be understood as problems of the nature of social reality, or as purely technical problems. By treating them simply as the first we run the risk of either philosophical or theoretical sectarianism (into, for example naturalism, interpretivism, empiricism or realism), or we end up producing elegant objections to what is manifestly the case. By treating them as technical problems not only do we fail to explain why something works, or doesn't work, but more dangerously we are likely to sanction a common sense and naive empiricism.

## Note

1 I speak of the social world as socially constructed. It does not follow from this that the physical world is thus. Indeed I would wish to deny this. Much of the physical world is socially produced (though not that much), but once produced has properties very different to those of the social world. Social structures, though 'real' to those they effect, require constant reproduction to continue to exist. Social structures have only social properties; physical structures may have social meaning, but, by definition, always have physical properties. A motor car is socially produced and has social meaning. This meaning is socially constructed, but the physical reality of the car is not. This proposition can be corroborated by stepping in front of a moving one!

# 2 | Naturalisms and anti-naturalisms

**William Outhwaite**

If we assume that there is a domain which can be usefully discriminated from the (rest of the) material world under the description 'social' or 'cultural', the question immediately arises whether such study should be seen as roughly similar to the study of 'nature' or fundamentally different. The position generally known as naturalism denies that there is any such fundamental difference; the position which affirms a radical difference between the natural and the social sciences has often been called methodological dualism and I shall refer to it here as anti-naturalism.

Most versions of anti-naturalism rely on one or other, or some combination of the following claims:

1 The social world is intrinsically different from the (rest of the) material world; thus our knowledge of it will be fundamentally different.
2 Our 'cognitive interest' in the study of the social world is radically different from our interest in the rest of the world, and thus our knowledge of it is radically different.

Although the first of these claims has an ontological flavour, and the second an epistemological or methodological one, in practice they tend to interpenetrate and reinforce one another.

## Historical

The first move in this debate substantially predates the emergence of the 'social sciences' as we know them. Giambattista Vico (1688–1744), in his *Scienza Nuova* of 1725 and 1744, formulated the basic principle that our knowledge of what we ourselves have made (individually or collectively) is different from what we have not made. Thus the world of human society and culture is in some sense 'our' product; the rest of the universe is attributed to a residual maker known as God. 'We' know the human cultural world because 'we' have made it; only God, whose omniscience of course includes perfect memory, can know the rest of the world in this way.

This distinction is taken up in a rather more speculative form in Hegel's differentiation between reason (*Vernunft*) and the understanding (*Verstand*), though the maker here is the world-spirit coming to recognize its own productions (including, ultimately, the world itself) and its learning processes as rational, in contrast to the essentially contingent states and relations found in nature and described by the mathematical and natural sciences. Something more like Vico's idea returns again in the second half of the nineteenth century, when Hegel's concept of objective mind is extracted from its surrounding developmental 'grand narrative' and treated more as a descriptive category, which is then used as the basis for a critique of the original (Comtean) version of positivism. (As the philosopher of history J.G. Droysen wrote in 1852, in terms which became familiar again just over a century later, 'Crass positivism unfortunately is finding great support': quoted in Spieler 1970: 20).

To put matters very briefly, Droysen and his contemporary Wilhelm Dilthey (1833–1911) developed an anti-naturalist programme based on the distinctiveness of human psychic expressions – the first of the two claims described above. In a more methodological vein, two other neo-Kantian thinkers, Wilhelm Windelband and Heinrich Rickert, focuses more on the second claim. The study of culture, they argued, is essentially interested in individual processes and in relating them to shared human values, whereas the natural sciences are concerned with general laws concerning objects which are essentially remote from questions of value. In other words, we are interested in the French Revolution not just as a member of a class of revolutions exhibiting certain common features (this would be, for Rickert, a natural-scientific mode of approaching it), but as a unique event embodying, and perhaps violating, certain crucial human values.

This opposition between positivism and methodological dualism comes to structure the emergent human or social sciences, as the term culture increasingly gives way to society or, for those suspicious of the objectivistic overtones of the latter term, 'sociation' (*Vergesellschaftung* in German). There is a fairly strong direct line of influence from Rickert to Max Weber, and also through Georg Simmel, who discusses our knowledge of the social world in particular in his *Die Probleme der Geschichtsphilosophie* (*Problems of the Philosophy of History*) (1892) and in his *Soziologie* (1900), notably in a classic 'excursus' on the question 'How is society possible?' – an essay which can now be seen as the founding text of social constructionist theory.

For Weber, as he put it in an early essay, 'the course of human action and human expressions of every sort are open to an interpretation in terms of meaning (*sinnvolle Deutung*) which in the case of other objects would have an analogy only at the level of metaphysics' (Weber 1975: 217–18 ). He therefore later defines sociology, in the first sentence of his *Economy and*

*Society*, as a science which aims at an interpretative understanding of action in order thereby to understand its course and its effects. Whether by this Weber means that explanatory understanding is itself a form of causal explanation, or merely complementary to it, the crucial point for him is that explanations of social phenomena must be both 'causally adequate' and 'meaningfully adequate'.

Our need for a causal interpretation (*unser kausales Bedürfnis*) demands that where an 'interpretation' (*Deutung*) is in principle possible, it be carried out; i.e. for the interpretation of human behaviour it is not sufficient for it to be related to a merely empirically observable regularity (*Regel des Geschehens*), however strict that law may be (Weber 1975: 128).

It is clear, I think, that for Weber our access to knowledge of the social world is importantly different from our knowledge of nature. It is not, however, in his view any less objective. He heroically attempts to hold together Rickert's principle that our perspectives on cultural phenomena, and our knowledge of them, are shaped by values (and for Weber, unlike Rickert, values are a matter of ultimately ungroundable existential choices), with the idea that the social sciences can attain a bedrock of solid and 'value-free' knowledge which would have to be accepted, as he sometimes curiously puts it, 'even by a Chinese'. But for all that one can distinguish between explicit value-judgements and the establishment of a relation between social phenomena and a potentially infinite set of possible value-standpoints – a position which one finds restated in Karl Mannheim's *Ideology and Utopia* of 1929 (Mannheim 1991) – the suspicion remains that in the end Weber is telling us how to steer a straight course in an ultimately arbitrary direction. *Faute de mieux*, of course, this is quite a good strategy to adopt if you are lost in a wood or at sea but, together with Weber's concept of the ideal-type, whose explanatory adequacy is again a matter of ungroundable judgement, it puts an uncomfortably heavy burden on the sensitivity and finesse of the individual researcher.

For this and other reasons, Weber's synthesis was pulled apart in both directions in the decades following his death in 1920. First, there was now a more stridently naturalistic and indeed reductionist variant of positivism: the logical empiricism of the Vienna Circle, in whose 'unified science' (*Einheitswissenschaft*) the statements of all sciences should be ultimately reducible to material-object language or to statements in physics, and *verstehen* was of no more importance, in Otto Neurath's vigorous formulation, than a good cup of coffee which sustains the social scientist. From this perspective, as Hempel and Oppenheim (1936) argued, the concept of ideal type was a mere preliminary to the serious business of constructing empirical indicators for theoretical concepts, and explanations in the social sciences and history could be shoehorned into a covering-law model (cf. Outhwaite 1987b). This formed what has been called the 'standard view' in Anglo-American philosophy of social science in the middle decades of the century.

From the other direction, Alfred Schutz initiated the tradition of social phenomenology with a book published in Vienna in 1932 with the title *Der sinnhafte Aufbau der sozialen Welt* (*The Meaningful Constitution of the Social World*), a title chosen for the sake of the contrast with the empiricist philosopher Rudolf Carnap's *Der Logische Aufbau der Welt* (1928). Schutz felt, unlike Hempel and Oppenheim (1936), that the problem with Weber's ideal types was not that they were insufficiently scientific, but precisely the opposite: Weber was too quick to impose them on the phenomena he described, paying insufficient attention to their grounding in acts of typification performed by ordinary members of society. In other words, the social scientist is constructing second order typifications based on those already carried out in the lifeworld. This theme was taken up by the phenomenologist Aron Gurwitsch in the United States, where Schutz had also settled, and by Peter Berger and Thomas Luckmann (1961), who finally put the term 'social construction' on the map, offering in the guise of a sociology of knowledge a paradigm more directly adapted to use in social research. By the time Schütz's book was republished (in Germany in 1970 and in the United States in 1967), the way had been prepared by Schutz's own later work (his *Collected Papers* appeared in 1962–6) and by the influential work of Berger and Luckmann.

Social phenomenology also of course had affinities with the well established minority North American tradition of symbolic interactionism, which also experienced a certain resurgence in the 1960s with, for example, the republication of the work of G.H. Mead (1962; 1964) and that of Herbert Blumer (1969), and also the publication of various studies by Erving Goffman (1959; 1961; 1963). But where the interactionists tended not to spend time on formal critiques of empiricism, Harold Garfinkel's (1967) ethnomethodology was more aggressive. A former student of the structural functionalist Talcott Parsons, Garfinkel was led by his study of the deliberations of a trial jury to emphasize, like Schutz, the importance of practical reasoning in everyday situations. He showed, in a kind of implicit homage to the Weberian principle mentioned earlier, that our drive to interpret leads us to impute a meaning even to random processes in the social world, as in one of his experiments in which an interviewer playing the role of a counsellor replied to the clients' questions by a random 'yes' or 'no', leading them into more and more contorted interpretive efforts. The production of meaning is at the same time the production of social order – Parsons's major concern. Unlike his former teacher, however, Garfinkel insisted that social actors are not simply bearers of their social roles ('cultural dopes'), but active subjects obliged to practise social analysis in order to function in everyday society.

Social phenomenology found a somewhat unexpected ally in a convergent move within analytic philosophy. On the margins of the Vienna Circle, Ludwig Wittgenstein had drawn the main intellectual inspiration for his brilliant *Tractatus Logico-Philosophicus* (1921) from Frege, Russell and

Whitehead. Coming to abandon the simple conception of a picturing relation (*abbildende Beziehung*) between propositions and the world, Wittgenstein was drawn into a more sensitive and holistic analysis of the practicalities of 'language games' based on implicit rules and themselves embedded in what he enigmatically called 'forms of life'. Where Frege had insisted that it is propositions rather than individual words which have meaning, Wittgenstein went further to direct our attention to the *use* of words and expressions in more complex ensembles of what came to be called 'speech acts' and other forms of human practice. In 1958, an important book by the Wittgensteinian, philosopher Peter Winch, *The Idea of a Social Science and its Relation to Philosophy*, drew the consequences for social theory, again using Max Weber as one of the foils for his argument. For Winch (1958), knowing a society means learning the way it is conceptualized by its members. He thus revived the central principle of nineteenth-century German historicism, according to which every age must be understood in its own terms. Winch explicitly cited Lessing in his frontispiece: 'the same moral actions do not always have the same names, and it is unjust to give any action a different name from that which it used to bear in its own time and amongst its own people' (Winch 1958: frontispiece).

Winch went even further. He directly identified himself with the German idealist tradition by insisting that social relations are 'like' logical relations between propositions (Winch 1958: 126). He also identified himself more concretely, in this book and in a later article, 'Understanding a Primitive Society', with an ethnographic fieldwork approach (Winch 1964).

Hermeneutic theory also took a new turn with the philosophical hermeneutics of Hans-Georg Gadamer, whose *Wahrheit und Methode* (published in 1960 and translated into English in 1975) insists, in opposition to historicist hermeneutics, on the *practical* dimension of interpretation, conceived in the Heideggerian sense of an encounter (*Begegnung*) between the 'horizon' of the interpreter and that of the text itself.

Gadamer's radicalization of hermeneutics was taken up in Jürgen Habermas's version of 'critical theory', which can be seen, along with certain realist positions and Anthony Giddens's structuration theory, as one of three particularly influential attempts in the final third of the twentieth century to reconcile, as Max Weber had done, the rival claims of explanation and understanding. At the outset of his career, Habermas participated in the famous 'positivism dispute' (*Positivismusstreit*) which began at the German Sociological Association conference in 1961 and ran on for some years. The initial exchange between Theodor Adorno and Karl Popper was continued by their respective supporters (Adorno 1969). Habermas, with the same narrative skill with which he traced the history of positivism and its critics in *Erkenntnis und Interesse* (*Knowledge and Human Interests*) (1968), shaped the three thinkers discussed above, Schutz, Winch and Gadamer, into an argument which he presents in *Zur*

*Logik der Sozialwissenschaften* (*On the Logic of the Social Sciences*) (1967). The positivist thesis of unified science falls in Habermas's view, because of the intimate relationship between the social sciences and history, and the fact that they are based on 'a situation-specific understanding of meaning that can be explicated only hermeneutically' (Habermas 1967: 43). As he put it some ten years later:

> the problem of 'understanding' (*Verstehen*) in the human and social sciences only achieved its great methodological importance because access to a symbolically prestructured reality cannot be gained by observation alone, and because the understanding (*Verständnis*) of a participant cannot be so easily subjected to methodological control as the perception of an observer.
>
> (Habermas 1982: 549)

Habermas therefore reviews the three principal modern approaches to *verstehende* sociology: phenomenological (Schütz), linguistic (Winch) and hermeneutic (Gadamer). Each of these approaches goes beyond or transcends the previous one(s). In

> the phenomenological approach [which] leads to an investigation of the constitution of everyday life-practice . . . language has not yet been understood as the web to whose threads the subject hang and through which they develop into subjects in the first place.
>
> (Habermas 1967: 117)

Similarly, Winch's linguistic approach which 'concentrates on language games that at the same time transcendentally determine forms of life' neglects the Gadamerian requirement to mediate between alternative frameworks. 'Winch seems to be contemplating a linguistic version of Dilthey. From his free floating position the linguistic analyst can slip into the grammar of any language game without himself being bound by the dogmatism of his own language game, which would be obligatory for linguistic analysis as such' (Habermas 1967: 136). Finally, the hermeneutic approach opens up the issue of the practical fate and historical effectivity (*Wirkungsgeschichte*) of traditions, and thus points beyond hermeneutics to a sociological account of the power relations which shape and distort human communication. Habermas, along with his close collaborator Karl-Otto Apel, argued for a complementarity between an empirical-analytic approach oriented to the explanation, prediction and control of objectified processes and a hermeneutic approach concerned with the extension of understanding, in an emancipatory model of critical social science, instantiated by psychoanalysis and the Marxist critique of ideology, which aims at the removal of causal blocks on understanding. Although Habermas has since come to abandon this model in its details, the basic idea remains in his more recent theories of reconstructive science and communicative action. Critical theory, it is worth noting here, is anti-naturalist by inclination, but in an increasingly muted way.

In Oxford, at much the same time, the late 1960s and early 1970s, Rom Harré and Roy Bhaskar were developing their realist metatheory of science, drawing in particular on the work of Mary Hesse. Both Harré and Bhaskar, like Habermas, were substantially motivated by the desire to undermine positivistic theories and approaches in the social sciences. Harré and Secord (1972) developed a philosophy for social psychology based on the work of Wittgenstein and the analytic philosophy of language practised at Oxford by J.L. Austin. Ordinary language, they argued, is better suited to the description of the mental processes of social actors than apparently more scientific artificial terminology, and they drew attention to models of research practice of this kind in the work of Goffman, Garfinkel and others.

Harré and Bhaskar were in any case interested in giving a more adequate account of science as a whole. For Bhaskar, accounts of the possibility of science had traditionally focused on facts about *us*: our experiences for empiricism, our cognitive structuring capacities (rationalism) or both (Kantianism). A more adequate account, he suggested, would have also to reflect on what had to be the case *in the world* for science to be possible – namely that the world be composed of relatively enduring structures and mechanisms, some of which could be isolated in scientific experimentation, given the entirely contingent emergence upon the earth of *Homo sapiens* and *Homo scientificus*. Thus a transcendental argument from the nature of science as an intelligible activity sustained the idea of a structured universe. The epistemic fallacy, for Bhaskar, consisted in the swerve from direct questions about the nature of reality, most of them properly the concern of the sciences, to anthropocentric questions about the possibility of our knowledge of reality, leading inevitably, once you grow out of the search for protocol sentences, to the dead ends of scepticism and conventionalism.

An important aspect of the realist programme developed by Harré, Bhaskar and others was a conception of explanation as involving not an essentially semantic reduction of causal *statements* to covering-laws plus initial conditions but, in what Harré later called a 'referential realism', a reference to the causal powers of entities, structures and mechanisms. The constant conjunctions of events which, for empiricists following Hume, were all that we could know about causal relations, were in fact neither sufficient, given the problem of induction, nor necessary for the justification of causal statements. Such law-statements should properly be understood as statements about tendencies which might or might not be outweighed by countervailing tendencies. Two causal tendencies may neutralize one another, as do the centrifugal force of the earth's rotation and its gravitational attraction, with the convenient consequence that human beings and other animals are safely anchored to the earth's surface.

This and other features of realism meant that, as Russell Keat noted in a classic article in 1971, the whole issue of naturalism could be rethought (Keat 1971). Human beings could be seen as having causal powers and liabilities, just like other entities; the fact that their relations rarely sustained any universal generalizations of an interesting kind, but rather sets of tendencies regular enough to be worth exploring. The fact that many of the entities accorded causal force in social scientific explanations were necessarily unobservable was not, as it was for empiricism, a problem of principle. Finally, in a move which I shall return to later, it would seem natural to include among the causes of human action the agents' reasons for acting. The realist critique of traditional epistemology found an echo in social theory, notably in the work of Anthony Giddens, who had become similarly impatient with the residues of positivist social science as well as the more radical contentions of social constructionism. As Giddens put it in *The Constitution of Society* (1984):

> Rather than becoming preoccupied with epistemological disputes and with the question of whether or not anything like 'epistemology' in its time-honoured sense can be formulated at all, those working in social theory, I suggest, should be concerned first and foremost with reworking conceptions of human being and human doing, social reproduction and social transformation.
>
> (Giddens 1984: xx)

Giddens's concept of the 'duality of structure' was designed to replace the traditional dichotomy between theories of social structure and social change, to do justice to the interplay of structure and agency in the social world and the fact that social structures enable as well as constrain our actions. Structuration theory aims to transcend the micro–macro divide, offering analyses both of intimate interpersonal processes and of longer run historical trends such as the rise and fall of the major world empires. What Bhaskar called the transformational model of social activity converges substantially with Giddens's approach. Realism does not however entail naturalism. Rom Harré, in particular, remains resolutely anti-naturalist in his social theory and sceptical of any claims made about social structures other than those immediately observable in behaviour or discourse.

So far I have been skirting around the issues of understanding and explanation or of reasons versus causes, and it may be helpful to return to these questions in rather more detail. As with naturalism and anti-naturalism in general, the issue is once again between those who see the understanding of action, including the understanding of people's reasons for acting, as a radically distinct activity from causal explanation, and those who see a more or less adequate understanding of an action as explanatory of that action, reasons for acting forming part of a complex causal nexus. Martin Hollis (1977) may be right to stress that 'rational action is its own explanation', but we still need to know what causes us to act sometimes rationally and sometimes irrationally, or to choose between equally rational alternatives such as red and black at roulette.

In realist terms, for example (though again realism does not in my view prejudge the issue), it seems natural to analyse the process of someone trying to give up smoking as a complex interplay between physical addiction and habituation on the one hand, and rational considerations of health on the other, with social pressures coming down on either side, depending on whether the agents involved are one's fellow addicts or an increasingly hostile non-smoking *umwelt*. And it is clear that, for better or worse, our explanatory narratives tend to bridge, if not make nonsense of, any simple differentiation between causes and reasons. Take for instance the following banal narrative:

> Around midday I began to feel hungry, realized it was lunch time, remembered that I would not be dining until late and that the queues for food would be shorter earlier rather than later in the lunch time period, thought resentfully that the University owed me a lunch break and optimistically that I would be more alert after a break, so I went to lunch.

Narratives of this kind effortlessly combine physical and social causes and individual reasons and intentionality in a way which defies any clear cut attempt to separate them.

## Theory

In the rest of this chapter I shall address some of these issues rather more systematically, building on the historical background outlined in the first section. My main message will be that it is useful to distinguish issues of principle from more pragmatic choices between alternative theoretical research programmes. The fundamental issue is perhaps best described as the differential slope of the typical learning curve in the natural and the social sciences or the different degree of built-in obsolescence of theories in these domains. Aristotle's insights into the natural world are now, *pace* Feyerabend, of rather little direct use to us nowadays, whereas we can still learn a good deal from his theories of society and politics, just as we can from, say, Machiavelli. And although a movement which has been influential in Germany, the 'protophysics' developed by Paul Lorenzen and other members of the 'Erlangen School' stresses the continuity between the natural sciences and everyday operations in the world – for example measurement; it remains the case that we have very little commonsense understanding of all but the most basic physical and chemical processes compared to our rather well developed pretheoretical knowledge of the social world. The age of the earth, continental drift, the relations between mass and energy or between quarks and atoms are not things we can have any meaningful knowledge of without getting into the relevant areas of science, whereas even a small child has quite a sophisticated conception of social relations and processes. Thus the constitution of society as an object of study, its conceptual *découpage*, as Lucien Goldmann used to put it, is in large part, though not, I think, *pace* social constructionism, entirely, a matter of reflecting on the real processes by which human beings, through their definitions of social situations and other, more material acts, reproduce the social world.

The good news is that this gives social theory a head start over most natural science; the bad news is that it means that the social sciences, in Anthony Giddens's phrase, do not possess the 'immense revelatory power' of the natural sciences. I was involved for a time in the Sociology section of the British Association for the Advancement of Science, and it was embarrassing to have nothing to offer the annual meetings of the association to compare with the discovery of a new elementary particle or some breakthrough in genetics. It wasn't just that these were bad years for the social sciences. The point is that their 'discoveries', such as they are, will inevitably tend rather to be refinements, illustrations, refutations or confirmations of existing beliefs, and will often be rapidly assimilated, in however garbled a form, into everyday 'knowledge', as Anthony Giddens has pointed out and Anne Mesny (1997) has shown in more detail.

We need also to look at the other end of the learning curve and to confront the fact that social scientific knowledge is very often less precise, less secure, more disputed and less cumulative than knowledge in the natural sciences. This contrast should not be overstated. A considerable body of work in the history and sociology of natural scientific knowledge has shown how flimsy has been the rational basis of many scientific paradigms, how strong the influence of habit, dogma, authoritarian pedagogy and patronage and so on. But for all this, it remains the case that the natural sciences can very often achieve a greater degree of certainty, both ontological and explanatory, than the social sciences.

A second issue which I mentioned earlier in relation to Rickert and Max Weber concerns the evaluative presuppositions and consequences of the social sciences: their actual or potential relation to practice. It is clear that even if one avoids making explicit value judgements, it is hard to imagine giving any reasonably sophisticated account of the social world without making at least characterizing, as distinct from appraising value judgements (Searle 1969). To say that people were murdered in an act of genocide is not just to append a value judgement to the statement that they were killed; it is to give a fuller and more adequate account of what happened. Moreover, as Bhaskar has argued, it is not just that a social scientific account of some social process is, like any other scientific account, implicitly or explicitly critical of others which conflict with it; we are often led more or less inexorably from an explanatory critique of a false belief to a critique of the social conditions which gave rise to the false belief. Thus Marx's contribution to political economy is designed also to be a critique of political economy and a critique of the capitalist society which generated it and makes it appear less false than it actually is. All this suggests that there is an evaluative dimension built into much social science which is absent from most work in the natural sciences.

This relates to a further issue: the 'insider' quality of much social scientific knowledge: the possibility of imaginatively 're-experiencing' the mental processes imputed to social actors in the explanation. Thus whereas it is absurd for me to ask what it would be like for me to be a bat (Nagel 1979), it is not at all absurd for me to ask myself how I would feel and behave if I were an ascetic Protestant entrepreneur in Early Modern Europe; indeed the plausibility of Max Weber's (1992 [1902]) interpretation of the role of the 'Protestant ethic' requires that we see his account of a set of largely unconscious practical inferences as at least a meaningful and possible one.

All this however leaves open a substantial area of pragmatic choice in our knowledge of the social world, marked by the rival insults of crass empiricism and idle speculation which haunt intellectual debate in the social sciences. Here, I think, we need to be genuinely pragmatic, recognizing that there are advantages and disadvantages to alternative approaches and to varying combinations of them. A useful rule for scientific, including social scientific metatheory is that it should not rule out by fiat important elements of the ongoing practice of the sciences concerned.

One way of making all this a little more concrete is to focus on the concept of reflexivity. A reflexive orientation has been variously identified as intrinsic to modernity, intrinsic to (or at least only fully exemplified in) postmodernity, and as marking a difference within modernity between its original forms and those characterized as 'high', 'advanced' or 'late'. In the latter formulation, most clearly expressed by Giddens, the distinction is between the relatively unreflective and confident modernism of what Groethuysen called '*les bourgeois conquérants*' and a more recent development in which an awareness of the institutional and cultural conditions of our action becomes itself a central precondition for action. As Giddens (1991: 14) puts it, 'Anyone who contemplates marriage today . . . knows a great deal about "what is going on" in the social arena of marriage and divorce'.

The notion of reflexive modernity is I think a useful one in marking a qualitative shift in ways of thinking and acting since the mid-1960s in many parts of the world. What Habermas calls a communicative orientation, which both relies on and reinforces a reflective orientation to social life, is now more strongly entrenched in modern societies and has in part displaced more authoritarian patterns of speech and action. This is a message which has perhaps not been fully internalized by postmodernists in the social sciences. There is however a measure of agreement that we now inhabit a world of the kind described, for example, by Ulrich Beck (1986) and

Anthony Giddens (1990) with the notion that modernity has become reflexive (see also Beck *et al.* 1994). This is a world in which individuals are increasingly thrown onto their own resources to define their own social relations – what Habermas (1990: 88) calls 'risky self-steering by means of a highly abstract ego-identity'.

Tim May (1998) has usefully distinguished between what he calls endogenous and referential reflexivity. Endogenous reflexivity concerns the process described in the previous paragraph;

> the ways in which the actions of members of a given community contribute to the constitution of social reality itself. . . . Referential reflexivity, on the other hand, refers to the consequences which arise from a meeting between the reflexivity exhibited by actors within the social world and that exhibited by the researcher as part of a social scientific community.
>
> (May 1998: 8)

In the first mode, it may seem enough to meticulously record and present the accounting practices of the members of society under investigation, under the quasi-transcendental presupposition that members of society are not cultural dopes. Alternatively, of course, the researcher may come to the conclusion that people are after all to a considerable extent cultural dopes, and that their reflexivity is correspondingly limited. Here the social scientist abruptly switches roles from a neutral or celebratory recording angel to a severe judge of the confused and incoherent behaviour and testimony of the subjects.

Only with a turn back to the theoretical and practical stakes of the constitution of social reality in the discourse of the social sciences does the dimension of referential reflexivity come to the surface. When Sartre criticized Lévi-Strauss for studying people as if they were ants there is the sense of both a theoretical and a practical error – in the everyday and the moral sense of the word practical. At the limit, social scientists may be brought to such anxiety about the enormity of what they do – the pretensions apparently inseparable from the role of the social scientist – that they are driven, like Oedipus, to self-blinding or self-castration.

The 'question about reflexivity', then, is essentially a question about how far to go. Where, in other words, can or should one stop on the slippery slope from a post-empiricist awareness of theory dependence, textuality, epistemic constitution or whatever to a paralysing scepticism which swallows its own question marks? Postmodernism in its deconstructionist variant tends to assume that everything follows from the first bite of the apple taken from the tree of *Entzauberung*, after which the only question is how long the process takes to set in. It follows, as in strong versions of social constructionism, that we should be sceptical about all forms of knowledge; there is no particular problem about knowing the *social* world – rather about knowing in general.

This raises a broader issue about the terms in which these questions should be posed. Postmodern, deconstructionist or antifoundationalist thinkers tend to assume that if we cannot have apodictically certain foundations of knowledge then more or less anything goes; strong foundationalists, usually these days in some sort of Kantian clothing, make the same claim as a horrific hypothesis; those who take some sort of intermediate position are open to attack from both sides, until it seems that there is no hiding place between dogmatism and sceptical pragmatism.

More optimistically, however, one can seek reassurance in something like a convergence between several of the positions described above. As I have argued elsewhere, the *prima facie* opposition between philosophical realism and critical theory is in the end one of emphasis rather than principle, and the convergences around the themes of hermeneutic understanding and emancipation are more striking than the differences. Theorists like Giddens and Bourdieu who are less concerned with metatheoretical issues will again find much to agree with in such a synthesis. The real opposition in contemporary social theory is between a somewhat ecumenical centre and the empiricists, functionalists, system theorists, rational choice theorists and perhaps poststructuralists outside. In the individual social sciences, of course, the picture is a rather different one, with 'theory' as a whole often being somewhat marginalized.

It may be helpful to focus, in conclusion, on the activity of theorizing itself. Both critical theory's critique of methodological reductionism, i.e. the positivistic reduction of epistemology to methodology, and the realist critique of the epistemic fallacy, i.e. the reduction of ontology to epistemology, are combined with a critique of traditional conceptions of epistemology and metaphysics in favour of a conception which sees human cognitive activities as embedded in other aspects of human practice. (Very few humans, after all, are capable *only* of cognition.) Despite differences of orientation and emphasis, which I am personally inclined to minimize, all these conceptions open up and I think encourage a certain conception of theoretical activity in science. 'Theory', on this account, is not limited by empiricist strictures on unobservables, counterfactual conditionals and so forth – a conception which resulted in the tug of love between formalized theory and the empirical which tore logical positivism apart. Nor, however, is it cut loose in a conventionalist free-for-all in which, in Pascal's phrase, 'nothing is freer than definitions' (cited in Tönnies 1964). A rationalism of the kind defended by Martin Hollis (1977) and realism converge in upholding a conception of real definition, in which definitions may be truth-functional statements, corrigible in the further development of the sciences, about the natures of (natural and social) things. Theory, as one can see from Giddens's remark which I quoted earlier, can be understood in what Habermas would call a reconstructive sense: systematizing our intuitions with respect to natural and social processes and sensitizing us to causal and meaningful connections.

This conception of social theory has sometimes been criticized as conservative (cf. Fuller 1992; 1998). It would be more appropriate however to see it as required by the very project of social science, based as this is on the very substantial pre-understanding of social relations which we can hardly deny we have. Our conception of theory, in other words, is now again a much more traditional one, in which it is seen as an organizing framework of sensitizing concepts rather than as something susceptible of formalization or of what Adorno used to call 'drastic' verification. Concomitantly, the acceptance or rejection of theories is seen as more a matter of judgement and argument about explanatory and interpretative adequacy.

What may be called the autonomy of theorizing is of course only a relative autonomy; theory without empirical content or at least illustration is empty. And having tried to keep metaphysics and methodology in their place we should clearly be cautious about letting theory take up too much space. There is I think a clear danger of piety about 'theory' – what one might call 'theory as the Holy Ghost' (cf. Outhwaite 1993). We should beware of the implicit conjugation: 'I theorize; you (just) do research; he/she is a crass empiricist who just collects facts . . .'. Indications of the aura of sanctity surrounding 'theory' are perhaps that it tends to appear in the first place in journal and catalogue rubrics and that it tends also to be something of a male preserve.

This is, if you like, 'theory' in the singular – a problematic concept, just like 'society' in the abstract singular. And although I would actually defend the singular use of 'society' and of 'social theory', it may often be safer to speak of theorizing, rather as Weber systematically avoided the term society (*Gesellschaft*) in favour of the process term *Vergesellschaftung*. 'Theories' in the plural suggests a further set of anxieties, which, to continue the patriarchal imagery, one might call 'theory as God the Father'. Here, the attachment to a particular theory-family is seen as an essential part of a claim to legitimacy, with associated issues of boundary drawing, loyalty, subordination to the discipline of testability, professorial domination and other aspects of traditionalism. The more professionalized the discipline, the greater the danger perhaps that the boundaries between theories will be used, along with methodological sophistication, as an ordering device at the expense of creative work with and across theories and indeed across disciplines (Weingart 1997).

Despite, and in part because of these anxieties, I think that we need a very broad term such as social theory to refer to work which does not fall squarely within the boundaries of sociology or the other social sciences, or of philosophy or any other single academic discipline. It would clearly be imperialistic to hijack not just the Marxist tradition, but also such thinkers as Sartre or Foucault into the camp of *sociological* theory. At the same time, any systematic account of contemporary sociology which did not address the contributions of such thinkers as these would be seriously incomplete. A number of sociologists, as well as people whose intellectual roots are in philosophy or cultural studies, have therefore tended to describe their work using a broad term such as social theory. Whatever their various motives for this choice, the more important point to make is that the rise of social theory reflects the fact that both our conceptions of sociology (and, to varying degrees, the other social sciences) and our ideas about the nature of scientific theory as a whole have changed in important ways over the course of the twentieth century. The distinctions between theory and reality, theory and metatheory, explanation and description, or philosophy and social theory have all rightly been problematized and made more flexible. In particular, the lines between theory and metatheory become blurred, for good reason, when, for example, a critique of a particular functionalist theory spills over into the question whether teleological explanations are possible at all in the absence of a reference to some kind of acting subject.

The question of our knowledge of the social world is a paradigm case of such a question which inevitably lies on the borders of theory and metatheory. My recommendation is to adopt a relatively open metatheoretical position of the kind I have been outlining, and to turn to the nitty-gritty question of the status of the various descriptive and theoretical accounts which we have so far been able to give of the social world. The diversity of such accounts, in particular, may be seen less as a problem than a resource for our reflections.

# 3 | When the knower is also the known

**Rom Harré**

The title of this collection, *Knowing the Social World*, reverberates with misleading implications, and that is what makes it an interesting phrase. There is another world, the material world, and it too seems to be an object of knowledge. Human beings are present in that world too, but not as knowers. They are present as molecular clusters, and, of course, as active interventionists. They are a species among other species. While modes of knowing are social phenomena, they are not material phenomena, though they may have profound impacts upon the material world. How complex a tapestry we discern here. In this chapter I want to trace out some of the consequences of applying two well known philosophical distinctions to the complex patterns of cognitive and practical relationships between people and their *umwelt* (which includes other people) hinted at above.

The distinctions to be deployed are

1 that between knowing by acquaintance and knowing by description, between phenomenology and discourse, if you like. It is often explicated by reference to the distinction in Romance languages between, for example, the Spanish *conocer* ('*Conozco José*' as '*I am acquainted with José*') and *saber* ('*Sabes como se llama el gerente*?'as 'Do you know what the manager is called?', that is, 'Are you able to tell me?') This distinction was important to Russell as a way of privileging sensations as the foundations of knowledge, taking knowledge by acquaintance to have priority as a way of knowing.

2 that between knowing how, the basis of trained or habituated skills, and knowing that, knowledge expressed propositionally. This distinction was important to Ryle (1949) as a way of debunking the intellectualist tradition in psychology, in that some concepts such as 'cleverly', 'competently' and so on could as properly be used of football playing as of explicit propositional reasoning.

Neither distinction is sharp. Both have something of the other in them. In what follows I shall try to interrelate these traditional distinctions in modes of knowing to the changing conceptions of the nature of 'the social' and to differing ideas of its modes of production and the conditions that make them possible.

## What is it all about?

### *Entities and discourses*

Knowing is a complex relational concept. There is the one who knows, the knowledge he or she possesses and that about which the knower has knowledge. At first sight it looks as if there are three entities in play, and in the context of this discussion they might be 'persons', 'representations' and 'societies'. The last item might be quickly decomposed into institutions, structures and practices. But then we realize that forming representations of social matters is itself a social practice. This insight is bothersome since it throws into doubt the easy assimilation of the form that the three-term knowing relation takes in, say, astronomy, as the best exemplar of knowing about something. There is the astronomer, his or her photograph, say taken by Hubble, and the galaxy represented in the picture. All three are material things, clearly distinct as entities, standing in well-defined relations to one another. Astronomers have to be able to interpret photographs, and Hubble has to be able to be causally touched by radiation from the distant galaxy. These relations are tricky to analyse, but, at least at first sight, the problems look tractable. Transferring this problem to social matters is not without its drawbacks. Galaxies are not assemblages of astronomers, but social institutions are assemblages of people, and some are assemblages of sociologists. The knower is a part of the known. Clearly, also, the relevant knowledge ought to be practical (knowing how) as much as overtly representational (knowing that). En route to a radical account of all this, I want to pause to offer a reminder of how the discursive conventions of our ways of talking and writing create the ontological illusions that beset our efforts to make sense of 'the social world'.

In the London *Times,* among hundreds of similar remarks, we find the following:

> The BBC has a strong commitment to reflect the UK's regional and cultural diversity in its television programmes. Our success in achieving this has been acknowledged by the Royal Television Society in its annual Programme Awards.
>
> (*The Times*, 3 June 1997: 12)

What have we here by way of entities? We can begin to answer the question by taking a quick look at the grammar of the paragraph. First of all there are some nouns with definite articles which give us a clue to the upfront ontology in use in this remark. 'The BBC' and 'the UK' are given entity like status. Less directly, but no less clearly, the ontology includes 'regions', 'cultures', 'programmes', 'awards', a 'Society' and 'years'. But now let us ask in a deliberately naive way 'What went on?' Well –

> Some people got together and had a conversation about certain broadcast conversations, and then they invited, by writing or ringing up, or even maybe by email, a lot of other people to assemble and then there were some more conversations and some of the people who had been invited were given bits of paper with writing on them, and more conversation then went on, culminating in the writing quoted above and similar inscriptions. Some of the people who received these pieces of paper laughed, and said nice things to each other. Others grumbled.

The strong impression that one derives from the first, 'official version', of entities other than people in relation to one another, has disappeared. In the second version nothing but speakers and what they say and do has been mentioned. There are just people talking and writing to each other. But not any old talking and writing will do to create the phenomenon described in the original quoted version. In order for the discourse to have been about the BBC, the Royal Television Society, programmes, regions and even years, certain discursive conventions would have to have been adhered to, including ways of counting nights and days. It looks as if we are closer to an unproblematic ontology in the naive version of the report, in that all we seem to have to take account of other than people are discourses and discursive conventions. But then how do *these* beings exist? And where do the people come into the story? It is people who talk and write, and who know or believe in rules and conventions. The social entity frying pan having proved too hot, are we any better off in the fire of a discursive ontology?

### *Some useful analytical concepts*

Psychology is currently undergoing one of its major convulsions, the third in the twentieth century. Social psychologists, it must be admitted very reluctantly, are coming to realize that social interaction is a dynamic affair. Static concepts like 'attitudes', 'personality traits', 'self-esteem' and so on are giving way to dynamic concepts like 'positioning', 'conversation' and 'narrative'. In the context of this discussion we could say that a corresponding insight might be that social phenomena are not there to be encountered but are continuously produced by people actively engaged in all sorts of projects. We talk in the former way, in phrases like 'join a club', 'matriculating at the university', 'managing the economy' and so on. But clubs, universities and economies are continuously produced by those who continuously produce themselves as members. How does it come about that Wimbledon,

Oxford University and the British Economy look like permanent entities which we might come across? The illusion is fostered by the reproduction, time after time, of certain types of phenomena, such as tennis tournaments, degree givings and monetary transactions. How is this dynamic stability achieved?

Since the late 1960s a growing number of authors, joined by Searle (1996), but pioneered by the ethnomethodologists among others (Garfinkel 1967) have argued that the answer must be found, somehow, in the development of concepts like 'rules', 'scripts', 'customs' and 'conventions', by means of which the reproduction of similar practices can be explained. What is stable is what people believe they should do or are habituated to do. In Wittgenstein's (1953) distinction between patterns of action explained by people following explicit rules and patterns of action explained by people acting in accordance with rules, by training for example, we have a near exhaustive account of social reproduction, if this exhaustive distinction can be coupled in a satisfactory way with an account of human development. It is now widely believed that such an account can be found in the developmental psychology of the great Russian psychologist, Lev Vygotsky (1978).

The standing conditions for that degree of social reproduction in the production of institutions are to be found in people's beliefs, and in the public practices by which shared beliefs are coordinated in collective action. Using the 'rule' metaphor for items of social knowledge enables a useful distinction between two functionally distinct kinds of rules to be brought into the analysis. There is a distinction between constitutive and regulative rules, a distinction with a long history. A constitutive rule determines that A shall count as B (saying 'Guilty' counts as the pronouncing of a judicial verdict), while a regulative rule determines what it is proper to do with As thus constituted as Bs (send those pronounced to be guilty of murder to the electric chair). So long as people believe that these rules are in place, just so long do the activities that display 'institutions' continue to exist. In a paper of more than twenty years ago I used the example of the fall of the Haitian 'Emperor' Christophe, as described by his Scottish physician, to illustrate the internal relation between belief in A as a B, and being a B. When the Haitians ceased to believe in Christophe as Emperor he had that role no longer. Just as when the leaders of the abortive coup against Gorbachev failed to get people to believe that they were in charge, they were not. Authority and power are constituted by beliefs, not vice versa.

But the fact that the members of a population share certain beliefs, that is each has a qualitatively similar belief to every other, goes nowhere, by itself, to explain how collective action productive of a social 'reality' is possible. I must deploy my constitutive and regulative beliefs concerning, say what to play next in the Mendelssohn violin concerto at the same moment as you do. We manage this by looking at the conductor and listening to each other, that is by some public, institutionalized medium of coordination. The nature of this necessity was addressed by Vico (1968[1744]). The question has been revived by Shotter (1993: 63–7, 203–6). What is it that plays the role of the orchestral conductor in everyday life?

Shotter endorses the answer that Vico gave to this question. Mental life as interpersonal discourse is made possible by two conditions. There is a 'sensory topic', a public matter to which all members attend, for instance a clap of thunder. But only when this becomes meaningful through the attachment of an 'imaginary universal', as the voice of Jove, does a social institution come to be. In this way people create a common world of meanings within which to act. There must be a public source of coordination made effective by the endowment of it with meaning. Like Vico, Shotter gives only dynamic stability to persisting sensory topics.

### *Criteria of identity*

When faced with questions of ontology, philosophers are accustomed to turn to a study of criteria of identity that are characteristic of discourses in the domain in question to give their work a robust foundation. The ways we decide whether there is one or there are many of a class of beings, and the ways we decide whether something has persisted as itself through all sorts of changes, are indicative of what sorts of beings constitute the domain of our inquiry. A *catalogue raisonné* of these matters is an ontology. In order to answer the question 'How do we know whether there is one or many beings in a domain?' we must already have a means of individuating and identifying (and where appropriate, reidentifying) such beings. No epistemology is possible without at least a tacit adherence to some ontology.

Having given notice of the question of criteria of identity, I propose to bypass it for the moment, to return with a richer armoury in hand as our investigations proceed.

## Mapping the production of social reality as a mode of knowing

### *Bringing an institution and its constitutive practices into being*

Knowing something is greatly facilitated by studying how it is produced. The final product may have a surface that quite conceals what is within. I believe this to be particularly true of social productions. We bring institutions into being, and they have all the air of something robust existing alongside of the physical supports, the 'plant' so to say, which is needed to sustain them. There are the greens, the fairways, the clubs, the clubhouse, visible as robust material things, and there too, at the end of the road and through the gates, there is the golf club. Clearly the mode of being of a golf club is different from but internally related to that of a fairway. But a strip of grass is a fairway only in the territory of a golf club. As a general rule we should start to answer ontological questions by asking how something is brought into being, and that may be all we need to discern its nature. What did people do that there should be a golf club and what do they have to keep on doing that the club should continue to exist?

We can imagine a group of people getting together to *discuss* setting up a golf club. The preliminary discussions might have been managed by local rules of politeness, though at some point certain people might have been tentatively assigned more formal roles. Perhaps a vote was taken and the group resolved to constitute themselves a club. Perhaps they debated and chose a name. And then came the crucial step: they agreed on a set of rules. So here we have a discursive process by which certain beliefs were inculcated in these people, that embodied constitutive and regulative rules. Perhaps such a club needed to be registered, a matter of writing certain documents. And so on.

It is all very well to set up the Iffley Golf Club, but what then? Golf must be played. To understand how this is possible we need a concept from Wittgenstein, the concept of 'language game'. Drawing on a variety of homely images Wittgenstein (1953) borrowed the expression 'language game' to capture what was most characteristic about human life. On the one hand we generally, though not always, do things for some purpose or other, and in accordance with certain local norms or conventions. There is usually a right and a wrong way of doing something, though occasionally we just idle. Human beings very often manage their activities in ways which intimately involve the uses of words and similarly functioning symbolic devices. Most human collective activities are thus language games. This is the ground work of the turn to a discursive psychology and away from a psychology based on the idea of people as passive and individual responders to external stimuli. The crucial point is not only do people act intentionally, but what they do is normatively constrained. To play golf, to discuss amending the membership criteria, etc., etc., are all activities that must be done correctly to be effective, to be activities of that sort. There is some latitude in practice, but not much. How could this insight be expressed? Wittgenstein used the word 'grammar' for the normative constraints on action. Grammars, so he said, are constitutive of forms of life. Golf is not only a game but also a language game. It is played in a context of norms including ways of scoring, involving esoteric classifications such as 'birdies', 'eagles', 'par' and so on. Mastering golf is a matter of not only getting one's back swing right, but also becoming competent in the jargon. And, of course, one goes on hitting the ball with a purpose.

### *Grammar and custom*

To understand a form of life, a pattern of social practices, of language games, we need to get a grasp of the local grammar. This thought takes us back to the question of rules, broached above. In discussing normative constraints on action, the application of paired concepts such as 'correct/incorrect', 'right/wrong', 'competent/incompetent' and so on it seems natural to have recourse to the notion of 'rule'. But great care is needed, since there are pitfalls in its use that can easily lead us astray.

1 'Rule' seems to be most commonly used to refer to a written or spoken form of norm. Yet, in many cases, we pay attention to the correctness of an action without adverting to anything verbal.
2 This is connected to another caution. In some cases we do the correct thing by paying conscious attention to an explicit instruction, for instance in wiring an electric plug or in playing an orchestral part. In other cases, and these are much the most common, we do things correctly, perhaps guided by what others are doing, or perhaps because we have been trained into good habits, or in a myriad of other ways, which we might lump together as 'acting in accordance with a rule'. The word 'rule' draws our attention to the ways we might have learned to act properly, any one time by attention to explicit instruction or injunction. Or to the ways that people comment upon the doings of others by inventing or citing rules, and so on.
3 We must, above all, beware of slipping into thinking that because we are not consciously following a rule when we are acting as described in (2) above, we must be unconsciously doing what we do consciously as in (1) above. This trap has caught out many of those who have tried to develop a cognitive psychology sufficiently powerful to display behaviourism as the main paradigm of research.

Nevertheless, the notion of 'rule', and the idea of a loosely bounded set of rules that we could call a 'grammar' are valuable heuristic concepts for keeping order in social inquiry. For example one can use these notions to classify the fine structure of a set of social rules in terms of the situations in which this group of language games is appropriate and not that. Furthermore, the notion of 'rule' lends itself very naturally to the task of distinguishing between those constraints that are mandatory, and those that are advisory or permissive. Still there is one final caution that must be entered.

4 The notion of 'rule' tends to be read by many people as implying a strict, well bounded constraint on action. Perhaps it should always be used in tandem with the notion of 'custom' to serve as polar opposite to set up a continuum of normative constraints between the stricter and the looser.

At this point one might enunciate the first 'theorem' concerning 'knowing the social world'.

To the extent that we can formulate a grammar for a pattern of social practices, that makes those patterns intelligible as normatively constrained, to that extent we have knowledge of that the form of life constituted by those practices.

Does this stand because we know how that form of life is constituted? No, because the necessary cautions on taking the concept of 'rule' literally lock in. At most we can say this is how it might have been. To carry this thought a step further we need to turn our attention to a different topic, the role of models in social analysis and explanation.

## Model making as a means of knowing

The concept of 'model' has played an increasingly large part in the understanding of the methods of the physical sciences. But in this usage 'model' is a more strictly bounded concept than that conveyed by the word 'model' in psychology. In the latter usage it is roughly synonymous with 'theory' or sometimes merely 'concept of'. In medicine and physics, models make up a definite hierarchy of classes of entities. In general models are real or imagined beings standing in some set of locally relevant similarity and difference relations to their targets or subjects. One class of such models are those derived by idealization from a certain source. So a map is an idealized model of a countryside, derived by idealization of the features of that very countryside that are relevant to the purposes of the map maker. In the case of these models subject and source are identical. But another, and in many contexts, more important class of models, they are analogues of their targets or subjects, but are drawn from an independent source. Darwin's model of natural selection is offered first as an analogue of the evolutionary processes in nature, derived, as Darwin takes pains to explain, from the breeding procedures of farm and garden. Much of what we know about the physical world we know through models. It is also instructive to realize that a piece of experimental apparatus is most easily understood when it is seen as a model of some process in Nature. For example William Crookes's gas discharge tubes are functionally models of the upper atmosphere when it is acted on by a stream of electrons shaped by the effect of the earth's magnetic field on the solar wind. We say that the Aurora Borealis is like, that is analogous to, the discharge in a Crookes tube.

We need another distinction before turning to apply these ideas in the human sciences. I shall distinguish between 'inner' models, which are themselves examples of the very things and processes they model, and 'outer' models, which are not. For example a Darwinian farm is part of the biosphere as well as a model of it. It is thus an inner model. But the kinetic model of gases, based on a picture of moving and colliding molecules, is not itself a gas. It is thus an outer model. The distinction is not so clear cut in many cases, partly because, as in the case of the molecular model of gases, after a while we begin to think of gases just as swarms of moving molecules, though this was not its original status.

In many ways the use of models is the most powerful way of coming to know the social world, or at least research relevant aspects of it. It is worth emphasizing that since models are analogues of their subjects any subject might attract a variety of models, each revealing a different aspect of it. There are lots of examples of idealizing models in human studies, but one which has proved of enduring popularity is the kinship diagram, a species of genealogy. Anthropologists of the generation of Evans Pritchard made great use of these, since knowing a society was for many best achieved by knowing the kinship relations that obtained in this or that culture. These models became quite complicated in that it was necessary to distinguish between an ideal kinship model (perhaps presented discursively in terms of a kinship nomenclature) and the relations to be found in everyday life.

Among the many analogue models that have been used, two stand out as of dominant influence and importance. One way of knowing the social world is to see it on analogy with a stage play or a movie. The 'dramaturgical model', as analysed by Burke (1945) and deployed by Goffman (1959), has played a central role in 'new paradigm' social psychology. It lends itself to the expression of the dynamics of social episodes, not least because a stage play presents an unfolding plot. We do not go to the theatre or watch a film to see paint drying (*pace* Mr Warhol). One way of loosening up the strictness of the social rule concept is to adjoin such dramaturgical notions as 'script'. It has been suggested that the stage-play model could be taken a step further by including the techniques of improvised theatre as an extension of the original model, which would take it closer to the openness and indeterminacy of the dramas of everyday life. Still, in all these applications, the dramaturgical model is an 'outer model', since only for a tiny fraction of the population is working on the stage their everyday life.

The second way of knowing through models is to adopt an easily observed form of social interaction as an 'inner' model of social process in general. One of the most fruitful and popular is the conversation as a model of social life in general. It has many advantages as a working model for this purpose, since it brings features of social reality to the light that are often overlooked.

1 Any conversation, even a soliloquy, is a colloquium among many voices. More than one might expect, close analysis shows that the number of voices can exceed the number of speaking persons. A speaker may speak in more than one voice. A judge can speak, from the bench, both with the voice of authority and with the voice of compassion. Multivoiced conversations are very common, and their dynamics are sometimes made clear by the overlay of another model on the basic conversational one, namely the idea of a person as having a speaking 'position'. Perhaps 'position'

would best be thought of as a metaphor rather than concretely as a model. A speaking position is a loose and open and contestable set of rights, duties and obligations as a contributor to a conversation, particularly with respect to the kinds of social acts one is recognized as legitimately deploying.

2 The speech actions, utterances, performed by the contributors to a conversation are often indeterminate as speech acts. They almost always could, if challenged, be revised to be heard as the expression of a different social act. Insults become jokes, queries become pleas, orders become requests, boasting becomes prideful self-expression, displays of jealousy become anger and so on.
3 Conversations ramify out far from the core speakers, and at the same time, there is a wider conversation which influences the most small scale exchange. It is in conversations that power is constituted. It is by conversational means that constitutive rules, treat A as a B, are instituted.

The point of the deployment of a model is to permit us to see features of a phenomenon we would have missed, by getting us to pay attention to the ways the phenomenon is similar to the model and the ways it is dissimilar. There are surprises on both fronts. The conversational model has alerted us to the many parts a person plays in social interactions, and to the indeterminacy of most social interaction. It means this to Jack and something else to Jill, but both are satisfied with what they think they see. Since there is no further reality to conversation, both are right and both are satisfied or not. We come to know the social world in coming to see it as if it were brought into being in ways similar to the ways conversations come to be. And conversations *are* social interactions.

## Political correctness in knowings of the social world

In accordance with everything said above it can hardly be disputed that the social world is made, not found. But it can also hardly be disputed that for individuals it has the character of a world that is found not made. Individual contributions to the making of social worlds are rarely of significance, yet it is in the waves of novelty that pervade the discursive activities of a collective that change often comes. Different discourses, different social worlds. This can not be quite right. Indeed it may be seriously misleading to draw this consequence in an unqualified way from what has been said heretofore. The reason is deep and comes, at least for me, from Wittgenstein's Private Language Argument (Wittgenstein 1953: 201). In this famous argument Wittgenstein asks how it is possible for people to understand one another when they are discussing their private feelings, phenomena like itches and stabs of pain that only I can feel. If we thought that words could gain a meaning only by reference to the entities to which we use them to refer, then no one could ever teach nor be taught words for private feelings, since there would be no common public exemplar to anchor the meanings of such words. The solution, introduced by Wittgenstein almost as an aside, is that there must be a repertoire of natural expressions of feeling upon which, by substitution of verbal forms of self-expression, a thoroughgoing language of feeling can be built. The same must be true for the colours, the hues we see. There must be a public expression of our colour discriminations. That is found, for instance, in our ability to agree on how coloured things should be sorted. Violations of our way of sorting are used as a diagnostic criterion for colour blindness. If no such public expression existed, since we cannot compare our individual private experiences of hues, no colour vocabulary could ever be learned.

This is a very deep point, and infects all sorts of socially significant matters, such as the expression of emotion, the displays of personhood as a singular being in the uses of pronominal grammars, and so on. It means that the Sapir-Whorf hypothesis, that thought patterns derive from learned linguistic patterns, while true in respect of some features of our lives, cannot be true for all. Without a common ethology, an inherited basis of fixed action patterns, our languages could consist of little but names for public objects. Human sociality is partly constituted by a common ethology. It follows that extreme versions of politically correct (PC) policing of language cannot hope to succeed,[1] since some socially relevant matters will be settled in advance by the necessary ethological conditions for having a psychologically relevant language at all. Coupled with PC observations on language reform, one often finds reference to postmodernist criticisms of the very possibility of a 'scientific' mode of knowing the social world.

Drawing on the observation that social worlds are made not found, it is sometimes argued by postmodernists, that the enterprise of trying to find out true things about the social worlds we live in is a futile exercise. Versions, socially constructed accounts of the social world are themselves in the social world, and are, so to speak, of the very same substance. The social world, so it is alleged, just is the open set of versions so far constructed. But that conclusion is flawed in two respects. Versions can indeed differ and in differing transform social reality, since they are social reality. But this is not a matter of thrilling significance provided we take time into account. Today's common version is today's social world. And it is not made any less today's world by the realization that another version of today's world might be constructed tomorrow, nor that tomorrow's world is also a social construction and probably a different one at that. Why is this? It is because the way people live their lives is by reference to the rules, models and indeed versions, with which their everyday world is currently constructed. The point that new paradigm social theorists ought to be hammering home is that the social world is reconstructible by creating new narratives, rules and so on.

True in principle, but why is it so difficult to achieve? Why is the post-revolutionary society so similar to the society it purported to displace? Why were Stalin and the KGB so similar to the Tsar and the OGPU? Why is the regime of the Ayatollahs so similar to the regime of the Shah? Why was Napoleon so like Louis XIV? (Moghaddam and Harré 1995). To find an answer we look again to the account I have presented here of 'knowing the social world'. What do spectators like Harré and Moghaddam know that the actors do not know? What do these models, when explicitly and knowing deployed, reveal that is hidden from those who are caught up in revolution? The social world is constructed above all by the innumerable repetitions of small scale social interactions, constrained by all sorts of almost unnoticed normative constraints. Doing the everyday things, such as walking down the street, greeting people, serving the dinner, hanging up the coats on a rainy day, greeting among men and women, and so on, and so on, call out unattended normative constraints, *immanent in which is the old social order, and also the new!* But couldn't these too be changed? Perhaps, but we have seen how hopeless such efforts by managed microtransformation have proved. The architects of the French Revolution saw this clearly and tried to change these very 'reductons', micropractices. Terms of address were changed by law, as were the names of the days, the months and the metrical systems. Even the preferred side of the road for driving carts and carriages was changed, from the aristocratic left to the proletarian right. For the most part the French people could hardly wait to get back to the old practices, though some survived the Imperial revival under Napoleon. The Red Guards in Mao's China were attacking reductons too, but we have seen how little long term effect their enthusiasm achieved. The idea that knowing the mechanisms of production of social orders enables those who do so to act effectively to make the world a better place, according to their lights (forbear to quote Marx's aphorism yet again!) is, it seems, naive. Social orders do change but I do not think we have much idea how or why. Perhaps a social, discursive analysis on the model of gene selection theory might offer useful insights in which practices correspond to organisms and rules to genes (Harré 1993: ch. 9).

## The basic distinctions in knowing once again

I began with a distinction between knowledge by acquaintance, knowing something by living it so to speak, and knowledge by description. Since we all live in social worlds, we do indeed, and must have first hand acquaintance with the minutiae of social life. But this knowledge, as I have argued, is largely procedural, it is knowledge of practices, and it is largely habitual and trained and ingrained. We can step back, but it is only by adopting a model to throw light on what we and the others are doing, that anyone is able to produce the other kind of knowledge, knowledge by description. That will above all be expressed in lists of rules and catalogues of customs. But this is not procedural knowledge. It is a 'rule hounds' version. I pointed out that the other distinction, knowing how and knowing that, cuts across the first one. Its crosscutting is clearly visible in this summing up. Competence in social life is a species of knowing how, procedural knowledge and skill. Social science demands a written report, and what can we offer but once again lists of rules and catalogues of customs. But these are not the active ingredients in the mix that creates social orders. They are descriptions of models of them. At best we can hope for a well described 'inner' model in which something we all know how to do becomes the device by which we can come to know that the world, is for the nonce, wagging this way.

## Note

1 For example the use of a plethora of '. . . challenged' as unoffensive synonyms for such words as 'blind' or 'fat' have rightly been ridiculed, since, in no time, they take on all the pejorative implications of the expressions they replace.

# 4 | Social properties and their basis

**David-Hillel Ruben**

There is an old Russian proverb, quoted in Vladimir Medem's autobiography (1979), that says: 'An individual in Russia was composed of three parts: a body, a soul, and a passport'. Although the saying speaks of three kinds of entities, I shall speak of three kinds of properties: physical, mental and social. I do not think that these three types of properties are exhaustive of the types of properties that there are. For example, I think that there are moral and mathematical properties. But these three are the only types of properties that will concern me here, and so I shall write as if the three types were exhaustive.

Except in the case of social properties, I rely on readers' intuitions about which specific properties are of one or another kind, and why this might be so. I know of no condition C such that all and only properties meeting condition C count as mental (or physical) properties. Intentionality is a mark of the mental, but there are properties, intuitively mental, that do not exhibit intentionality (like having an itch).[1]

Having such and such mass is a physical property; desiring something is a mental property; voting and purchasing are social properties. It is not my intention to discuss, or to beg any questions about, the relation between mental and physical properties. The question of social properties is more than enough to deal with here. In what follows, I speak of physical and mental properties as if these were different kinds of properties. For those who think that physical and mental properties are irreducibly different, my terminology will pose no difficulty. But my way of speaking is meant only as a terminological convenience, not as the result of a philosophical decision. For those who think that mental properties are a species of physical property, let them in what follows read the contrast between mental and physical properties as a contrast between a specific subset of physical properties and all the other physical properties not in that subset. Indeed, if there are those who think that physical properties are a species of mental property, let them in what follows read the contrast between physical and mental properties as a contrast between a specific subset of mental properties and all the other mental properties not in that subset. Nothing whatever hangs on this in what follows.

The question I wish to answer in this chapter is this: can social properties be reductively identified with mental properties (perhaps with mental properties in combination with physical properties)? The thought may seem plausible that they can be so reductively identified. What is it, after all, to be an alderman, or a mayor, or an army officer, but for certain beliefs and attitudes to be generally true? Where shall we understand the social to be but in the realms of the mind? Of course, the beliefs and attitudes must be widely held, for a person's believing that they are an army officer does not make them one. But there is certainly some sort of affinity between the social and the mental, and might it not be that being an army officer can be understood as a general system of beliefs and attitudes widely held? Isn't the reality of the social characteristics of persons connected with the ways in which they think about and consider things (including one another)?

Since I limit my sights to the physical, the mental and the social, it would be sufficient, in order to demonstrate the irreducibility of social properties, to demonstrate their irreducibility to physical and mental properties. In fact, my effort will go into showing their irreducibility to mental properties, for I do not think it would really be plausible to suggest either that their reduction to the physical alone could be adequate, or, that if they were irreducible to the mental, adding the physical would alter that irreducibility. Since I argue that the identification of a particularly characteristic social property with mental properties would be circular and hence not reductive at all, I take myself to have given reasons for thinking that social properties (of that type) are irreducible to mental properties and therefore irreducible to combinations of physical and mental properties.

The question of the reduction of social properties, as I have expressed it, is a problem of philosophy. Hopefully, it will have some bearing on the question of the relationship between institutional and agent analyses in sociological thought, and the validity of structuration theory. But these are not the same question.

Certainly some sociologists, Giddens for example, speak of structural properties (Giddens 1981a; 1984); social systems, says Giddens, 'exhibit structural properties'. Structural properties (or, sometimes, 'structuring properties'), on this account, seem to be a proper subset of social properties, since social properties can be properties of things other than social systems. It would not do to try to characterize a property as social in virtue of the type of entity having that property, since mental, social and physical entities can have social properties. Even if a person were an embodied mental entity, as Descartes thought, that person could still be a mayor. A piece of plastic, a physical thing, can be a credit card. A nation, a social entity, can join a confederation. Yet the properties asserted of these three different kinds of things are all social properties. That a property is social has something to do with the property itself, rather than that to which it applies, whereas Giddens's structural properties are, it seems, *only* properties of social systems.

## What makes a property a social property?

In attempting to provide an answer to the question about the reducibility of any F to some G, we need a perspicuous account of what F and G are. To answer the question about the reducibility of social properties to mental properties, we should have some such account of what makes a property mental or social. The former is beyond the scope of this discussion; it is my intention to provide just such an account for social properties. We need to know what makes a property social, before we can have any confidence in our answer to the reducibility question.

There is a tendency, especially in some of the literature critical of individualism, to locate this special feature of social properties in their relationality. On a different but not unrelated topic, Alan Garfinkel (1981) argues for the irreducibility of social explanations to individualistic ones. In the following quotation, he uses 'atomistically' to mean 'unrelated' and 'structural relations' to mean 'irreducible social relations' (or 'macro-level', as he calls them): 'The essence of this critique of the market lies in insisting on the structural relations that hold among individuals. The classical conception of the market sees individuals atomistically' (Garfinkel 1981: 85). Garfinkel begins with the perfectly sound point that one cannot understand human economic activity apart from the relations that exist between the economic agents. However, Garfinkel, without further argument, refers to such relations as 'structural', by which he intends that the relations are irreducibly social. He overlooks the possibility that all the relations that exist between persons are non-social, or reducible to non-social, relations. Since there certainly are at least some non-social relations between persons, we still need to know in virtue of what a property is social, if not simply in virtue of its relationality.

Let us start by contrasting two relational properties, the first intuitively non-social and the second intuitively social: the property of jointly bearing the weight of a stone, and the property of paying for a stone. The property of jointly bearing the weight of a stone might be true of two or more inanimate objects, but it also might be true of two or more persons. Still, even when this relational property is true of persons, it does not ascribe a social relation to them. The two individuals might jointly bear the weight of a stone as a matter of fact of which they were completely unaware, and of which anyone else was unaware. What is the difference between these two relational properties which accounts for the fact that only one of them is a social relational property?

Unlike what might be the case when $x$ and $y$ jointly bear the weight of a stone, if $x$ pays for a stone, there is a characteristic system of interlocking beliefs and expectations whose existence is entailed by the social property's applicability. It would not damage my argument if I were forced to concede the possibility of non-standard, odd cases in which the specific individuals related by the social relation fail to have any of these beliefs and expectations, so that I might unintentionally pay you for a stone while we were briefly visiting Borneo, both of us being completely unaware that what we were doing counted, in Borneo, as paying someone for a stone. In such a case, there is still a nested system of beliefs involved, though the beliefs are not located in the standard place, namely the participants to the transaction. The characteristic system of interlocking beliefs and expectations will exist, because our Borneian observers will certainly have them. In claiming that the applicability of a social relation between $x$ and $y$ entails the existence of an interlocking system of beliefs and expectations, it does not necessarily follow that in all cases $x$ and $y$ must share those beliefs and expectations, although I think that the cases in which they fail to share them are necessarily parasitic on the standard cases in which they do (nothing in my argument depends on my belief that these non-standard cases are parasitic on the standard ones). In what follows, I consider only the standard case in which the agents related by the social relation share in the system of beliefs and expectations, but all of what follows must be understood so as to permit the possibility of non-standard cases.

A rather different sort of problem is this. To use an example that I will be employing in a moment, normally paying someone for something involves expectations that the person will surrender it in exchange for what I am to give that person and will not try to regain it without my consent. On a specific occasion, I may be paying Al Capone for something, knowing full well that he will refuse to deliver the goods as expected, or, if he does deliver, that he will creep back when I am unaware and repossess what I bought from him. Let's even suppose that Capone is himself aware that I fail to have the normal expectations about what he will do. Indeed, suppose no one in the whole society expects Capone to surrender what he is meant to surrender, or not to retake what he surrenders if he does so. I do not know if this would still be a case of my paying Capone for something in our legal system, because failure of intent might be important in determining whether I have paid him for something. But whether or not it is true in our legal system that, in such a case, I have paid Capone for something, there is no difficulty in supposing a 'strict liability' legal system (perhaps ours is like this) in which intention plays no part in the definition of some act like a sale. If this is so, then if Capone and I go through certain recognized acts, then I have paid him for something, in spite of the complete breakdown in the normal expectations and beliefs about purchase and sale in the particular case.

But this too leaves our claim undisturbed. If I pay Capone for a stone, it follows that there is a system of beliefs and expectations of the kind I shall describe, even if those beliefs and expectations do not attach to our specific acts on this particular occasion. And this is surely correct. It is essential to the case of purchasing something from Capone that there is this general system of beliefs and expectations that attach to purchase and sale; if this were not so, whatever we were doing could not be a *paying* by me, to Capone, for something. In what follows, for ease of exposition, the examples I discuss are ones in which the beliefs and expectations attach not only generally to acts of that kind, but to the specific acts of the agents of whom the social relation is true. Again, nothing depends on this, and all of what follows must be understood to permit the possibility of these non-standard cases.

## Nested systems: the first and second components

What is such a system of interlocking beliefs and expectations like? I will claim that a necessary and sufficient condition for a relational property *P* being a social relational property is that, if *x* and *y* stand or were to stand in the relation *P*, then it follows that a nested system of interlocking beliefs and expectations exists. I use 'nested system' in a technical sense. Thus, to assess my contention, it is essential to be precise about in what such a nested system consists. I shall argue that there are four parts or components of a nested system that can be distinguished, each part being necessary and the four being jointly sufficient for the existence of a nested system.

I begin, then, by singling out only two of the four conditions for the existence of a nested system. My strategy is to uncover the final two by seeing why it is that the presence of these two parts alone is insufficient for the obtaining of any social relation. The first condition for the existence of a nested system is this: if there are any social relations between *x* and *y*, *x* and *y* will have interlocking beliefs and expectations about actions (where this category must be taken sufficiently widely so as to permit mental actions, and also forbearances or omissions). In the case of *x* paying *y* for a stone, *x* will expect *y* to surrender the stone in return for something that *x* gives *y*, and *x* will expect that *y* will not try and regain control of the stone unless in return for something *x* willingly accepts from *y*. Matching and interlocking beliefs and expectations are held by *y* about *x*: *y* will expect *x* to be given something in return for the stone and *y* will not expect to regain control of the stone with *x*'s consent unless in return for something *x* willingly accepts from *y*.

But these beliefs and expectations are insufficient. The second condition for the existence of the required system of interlocking beliefs and expectations are beliefs and expectations about beliefs and expectations (or second-order beliefs and expectations). In the standard case, *x* believes that *y* has the beliefs and expectations attributed above to *y*; and *y* believes that *x* has the beliefs and expectations attributed above to *x*; *x* believes that *y* believes that *x* has them; *y* believes that *x* believes that *y* has them; and so on. The 'and so on' is not intended to generate a vicious regress. The regress is limited by the natural ability of agents to form third or fourth order beliefs and expectations, so wherever the reader believes these limits fall, there it may be thought that the regress is brought to an end. The beliefs in question will typically only be dispositional rather than occurrent.

Even though these first two components, beliefs and expectations about actions and beliefs and expectations about beliefs and expectations, are insufficient for composing a nested system of beliefs and expectations in the technical sense I want that will help us get at the idea of a social relation, they are certainly sufficient for distinguishing between jointly bearing the weight of a stone and paying for a stone, and sufficient for seeing why the former is not a social relation. When *x* and *y* jointly bear the weight of a stone, such beliefs and expectations may or may not exist, so their existence does not follow from the ascription of the relational property, jointly bearing the weight of a stone. But their existence does follow in the case of the application of the social relational property, purchasing a stone from. Still, although these first two components of a nested system are sufficient for distinguishing between the non-social relational property, jointly bearing the weight of a stone, and the social relational property, purchasing a stone, they are insufficient for distinguishing between all cases of non-social and social relational properties, as we shall soon see.

## Nested systems: the third and fourth components

Anthony Quinton says that 'What is characteristic of the relations studied by the social sciences is that they involve consciousness of each other by the people related (Quinton 1976: 2–3). Quinton's claim is on the right lines, but too weak. In thinking about why Quinton's claim is too weak, we shall see why the first two components of a nested system – beliefs and expectations about actions, second order (perhaps even higher order) beliefs and expectations – are insufficient for the existence of a nested system, in the sufficiently full technical sense to permit the latter idea to distinguish between all social and non-social relational properties.

The insufficiency of Quinton's proposed criterion for 'What is characteristic of the social sciences' can be brought out by means of the following example. Suppose that there were two tribes, *A* and *B*, on either side of a mountain, both tribes having strong taboos which prevent them from crossing the mountain. The two tribes thus lack any awareness of each other's existence. We introduce young Marco Polo into our story. On his travels, he first visits tribe *A*. He then crosses the mountain and discovers tribe *B*. He tells tribe *B* about tribe *A* and tells *B* that he will tell *A* about *B*'s existence on his return trip. This he does, and neither tribe have any contact with, or learn anything further about, the other after Marco Polo's departure. Intuitively, there are no social relations between the two tribes, in spite of the fact that they are fully aware of each other's existence. So consciousness of one another may be necessary, but it is not sufficient, for the existence of social relations (perhaps Quinton did not intend to be giving a sufficient condition in saying what he thought was 'characteristic' of the relations studied by the social sciences).

We can use this same story to show why the first two components of a nested system that I have so far mentioned are insufficient, if we are to use nested systems to distinguish between social and non-social relations. Consider the relation that holds between the two tribes, *A* and *B*. *A* has beliefs about the existence of *B*, and *B* believes that *A* has these beliefs. *B* has beliefs about the existence of *A*, and *A* believes that *B* has these beliefs. But of course the first order beliefs are not about actions, which was a requirement of our account.

It would not be difficult to amend our story so that this requirement was met. Suppose Marco Polo leaves each tribe with a very powerful and tall periscope-like instrument, so that they can minutely observe each other's behaviour and activity. Being curious, they begin to amass a great deal of information about one another's doings. They develop an intimate knowledge of each other's social tribe. Moreover, suppose Marco Polo has told both tribes that the other would have an instrument identical to theirs, and has told each tribe that the other was capable of perfecting a knowledge as complete as it itself could.

If we presume all this, it may well happen that all the beliefs and expectations we have discussed as forming part of a nested set might grow up. They will be conscious not only that one another exists, but also that each will be conscious of the activities of the other. Moreover, the second order beliefs and expectations may occur. Tribe *A* believes that tribe *B* will do certain things, and tribe *B* believes that tribe *A* has these beliefs about it. Tribe *B* believes that tribe *A* will do certain things, and tribe *A* believes that tribe *B* has these beliefs about it. We can imagine this developing to whatever degree of nestedness we care to hypothesize, and still, I think, it will be admitted that something essential for there being a social relation has been omitted. What more is needed?

In the story so far, there are certainly relations between actions on the one hand and beliefs and expectations on the other. What tribe *B* does can be a reason for what tribe *A* believes, because tribe *A* believes that tribe *B* is doing something partly because *B* is doing that thing. The beliefs of tribe *A* (e.g. the belief that *B* is doing something) can themselves *be* reasons as well as *being held for* reasons, because tribe *B* believes that tribe *A* believes that *B* is doing something, in part because tribe *A* does believe that *B* is doing it.

That is, one of the reasons for tribe *B*'s believing that tribe *A* believes that *B* is doing something is that tribe *A* does in fact believe that *B* is doing that thing. But note that these beliefs and expectations are ascending, in this sense: an action can be a reason for a belief or expectation about an action, and a belief or expectation of order $n$ can be a reason for a belief or expectation of order $n + 1$. But no belief or expectation of order $n$ is a reason for a belief or expectation of order $n - 1$, nor is a belief or expectation about an action a reason for acting in some way. There is no descent, only ascent.

No one likes to be the subject of scientific observation unwillingly. Suppose tribe *A*, believing that *B* believes that it will do something, decides to do something else as a way of falsifying *B*'s belief. Both tribes might start altering their activities as a strategy for defeating the expectations of the other. That is, the role of the beliefs and expectations alter, so that they begin to play what I refer to as a descending role; one of the reasons for *A*'s altering its behaviour is *A*'s belief about what *B* expects that *A* will do. Social actors not only react to what each other do, because physical objects can do this, but also react to what they believe others believe that they will do. Let us require, then, for the existence of a nested set of beliefs and expectations, not only the two conditions already mentioned (beliefs and expectations about action; higher order beliefs and expectations about beliefs and expectations), but *also* a third condition, namely that some descending reason-relations exist among them. Descending reason-relations exist among such beliefs, expectations and actions if some belief or expectation about how others believe or expect an agent to act is at least part of that agent's reason for acting in some way.

An analogous requirement to that of descending 'reason' relations is built in by Schwayder to his analysis of community rules by the condition that one acts in some way because one *believes* that others believe that one's acts will arise from the belief that there is an expectation that one will act in some way (Schwayder 1965: 250–2; Lewis 1977). The similarity between my account and Schwayder's resides in the fact that he too requires that one's actions are sometimes partly motivated by beliefs about what others expect or believe.

Of course, I am not saying that social relations exist only when social actors alter their behaviour in order to outwit one another by falsifying beliefs about what they will do. More often than not, I do something partly because it is what I believe that others believe or expect that I will do. Social cooperation assumes that this happens. So what is crucial for the existence of social relations between people is that they sometimes do what they do (and this includes altering what they are doing to defeat those expectations as a special case), whether to achieve cooperation or deception, partly as a consequence of the beliefs they have about the beliefs or expectations others have about what they will do. If we add this third requirement, that of descending reason-relations, to what is needed for a system of nested beliefs to exist, is the fact that the existence of a nested system (with only these three components) follows from the obtaining of a relation *P* a necessary and sufficient condition for *P*'s being a social relation?

There is, alas, a final complication. Suppose tribe *A* alters what it does because of its beliefs about what tribe *B* expects it to do, and suppose tribe *B* alters what it does because of its beliefs about what tribe *A* expects it to do. But suppose tribe *B* is not aware that tribe *A* is altering its behaviour for these reasons, and similarly that tribe *A* is not aware that tribe *B* is altering its behaviour for these reasons. If so, they may simply think of their expectations and beliefs about the behaviour of the other as falsified because based on insufficient or faulty empirical data about the other's activities. The fourth condition which is necessary, in order for there to be social relations between them, is that *A* believes that *B* sometimes does what it does for these reasons (i.e. *A* believes that sometimes *B* does what it does because of its, *B*'s, belief about what *A* believes that *B* will do), and that *B* believes that *A* sometimes does what it does for these reasons (i.e. *B* believes that sometimes *A* does what it does because of its, *A*'s, belief about what *B* believes that *A* will do). Note that this fourth requirement is again one of an 'ascending' relation. In social life, agents respond to the beliefs and expectations of others (the third requirement), and this is generally believed to be the case (the fourth requirement).

To sum up, then, a relation *P* is a social relation if and only if it follows from the fact that *P* obtains that a system of nested beliefs and expectations exists. A nested system of beliefs and expectations exist if and only if (1) there is an interlocking set of beliefs and expectations about the actions of agents; (2) there is an interlocking set of higher order beliefs and expectations about beliefs and expectations; (3) there are some descending reason-relations among these beliefs, expectations and actions, so that sometimes what agents do is a consequence of their beliefs or expectations about what other agents believe or expect that they will do; (4) it is generally believed that (3) is true. When conditions (1)–(4) obtain, it seems to me intuitive that a point has been reached at which we are willing to concede that specifically *social* relations obtain between the agents mentioned in the four conditions.

My confidence in this analysis has been strengthened by the fact that subsequent writers have tended to quote or rely on it with little objection. Raimo Tuomela (1995), for example, says: 'The result of my analysis tallies with Schwayder's . . . and Ruben's mentioned analyses, even if my argumentation has been different' (Tuomela 1995: 50). It might still be helpful if I add several points by way of explanation and clarification.

First, as previously mentioned, 'activity' and 'behaviour' should be understood widely, so as to include mental acts (and omissions). In the descending reason-chains, the ultimate stopping places need not be physical actions. There could be social relations between mathematicians who had nested beliefs about the proofs each other were working on in their heads, and who sometimes changed their mental activity in the light of the beliefs they held about what others believed about their mental activity. Even more dramatically, I cannot see why there could not be social relations between disembodied minds (if it is logically possible that there be disembodied minds), as long as such beings could form the requisite nested beliefs and expectations about one another's mental activity with the requisite direction of reasons between them. It seems to be a point in favour of my analysis that it does not make impossible the idea of social relations between disembodied minds.

Second, it is no requirement of my analysis of *P*'s being a social relation that *P* itself turn up in the description of the behaviour or activity which the nested beliefs or expectations are ultimately about. For example, the social relation between *x* and *y* might be one of economic exploitation, and both *x* and *y*, and indeed even social agents generally, might be quite unaware of this exploitation and what it means to their lives. Social actors, even whole communities, do not always understand their social life, which may remain opaque to them. They may be victims of false consciousness, as it is sometimes called. Yet, it may still be true that social relations of exploitation exist among members of that community. If so, from the fact that *x* exploits *y*, it follows that there is *some* set of nested beliefs and expectations in the sense that I have explained, but the beliefs and expectations in the required set might not be about exploitation, because the concept of exploitation may not be available to *x* or *y* or to anyone else in the community. The beliefs and expectations which are necessary for the social relation of exploitation holding between any two agents may be beliefs and expectations about the rights and duties of the employer and the employee, or other beliefs that embody common sense ideas that are available to the social agents.

Third, the analysis of a property's being a social property that I have offered shows why all social properties are relational. The reason is this: if any social property is true of anything, it follows that an appropriately nested system of interlocking beliefs and expectations exists. But a nested system of these beliefs and expectations can only exist if at least two persons exist. Therefore, if any social property is true of anything, at least two persons exist; no social property can be true of anything in a universe in which there is only one person and a *fortiori* no social property can be true of anything in a universe in which there is only one object. All social properties are therefore relational properties.

Rajeev Bhargava (1992) argues that my requirement of interlocking beliefs and expectations is too weak to entail the existence of at least two people: 'I do not see how the presence of an interlocking system of beliefs and desires [this last is Bhargava's addition] implies the existence of a collectivity. Why cannot the system exist in the head of each individual, indeed in the head of one superhuman individual being? (1992: 202–3). But his supposition comes to nothing. If A=B, then there are no interlocking beliefs at all. If we rewrite some of the above, substituting 'A' for 'B' throughout, we obtain, for example: (a) Tribe *A* believes that tribe *A* will do certain things, and tribe *A* believes that tribe *A* has these beliefs about itself. (b) Tribe *A* believes that tribe *A* will do certain things, and tribe *A* believes that tribe *A* has these beliefs about itself. (a) and (b) are the same belief, no longer interlocking beliefs at all! We obtain beliefs and beliefs about beliefs, but no interlocking beliefs at all. So the requirement of interlocking beliefs does, after all, entail the existence of at least two distinct persons.

Fourth, I have spoken in terms of the existence of the nested system following from the obtaining of the relations property, not from its mere existence. This is to *allow* for the possibility that uninstantiated social properties exist (I expect intuitions to differ about this, perhaps even more so than intuitions about the existence of uninstantiated properties generally). Margaret Mead might wrongly identify some social institution in a primitive society as one of engaging in kitchiboo. It may be that, in fact, no person anywhere has ever engaged in this practice that she wrongly locates in this primitive society. If so, it may be that the social property of engaging in kitchiboo exists (Margaret Mead might have given us a very precise account of what is involved in this property of engaging in kitchiboo, in spite of the fact that it has never been true of anyone), and yet no system of nested beliefs has ever existed anywhere. On our criterion, engaging in kitchiboo still counts as a social property, because a certain counterfactual is true: if it were to hold of some individual, then it would follow that a nested system of beliefs existed.

Fifth, the account of social properties that I offer here is similar in some respects to one given by David Schwayder, in *The Stratification of Social Behaviour* (1965), with one difference of special importance. His account is not of a social property, but of a social rule: 'Community rules are systems of expectations', 'The rule is, as it were, a system of community, mutual expectations' (Schwayder 1965: 252–63). I think that an account in terms of nested systems, although strong enough to capture the idea of a social property, is not strong enough to capture the idea of a social rule (Ruben 1972: 349–54). Consider for example a situation in which a customary practice has grown up between two people to meet at the tennis court on a certain day of the week. There may well be a nested system of interlocking beliefs and expectations between them about these meetings, and it certainly does seem right to say that there is a social relation between them, for they share a practice to meet in this way. But what they may not share is a rule to do so. The idea of a rule is a stronger idea; in my view it includes the idea of 'pressures for conformity', for one has rules about what one must do willy-nilly. And they may not regard their practice or custom of meeting in this light. Since social relations so commonly take a coercive form, it is easy to confuse the idea of the social generally with the more specific idea of a social rule. These are, though, quite distinct ideas, and I offer an account, similar in content to Schwayder's, but of the idea of a social property rather than that of a social rule.

Finally, social relations can hold between persons and persons (e.g. being the godfather of), between persons and objects (e.g. renting), and objects and objects (e.g. costing more than). In my account, I considered cases in which the social relations relate persons and persons. This is the simplest case, and the analysis can easily be extended for the other cases. Nothing in my analysis depends on restricting the applicability of social relations to persons in any way; on the other hand, I confess to the Marxian belief that cases of social relations obtaining between persons and objects or between objects and objects are entirely parasitic on the cases in which they obtain between persons and persons. The denial of this belief is what Marx calls 'fetishism' (Marx 1965: 71–83).

## The irreducibility of social to mental properties

Now that we have some grasp of what makes a property a social property, it will be easier, I think, to return to our main question concerning the reducibility of social to mental properties. My claim is: a property *P* is a social property if and only if from the fact that *P* applies to anything, it follows that a nested system of beliefs and expectations exists. It might seem an easy step to conclude from this that social properties were themselves mental properties, or sets thereof. Cannot social property *P* be reductively identified with the set of mental properties which go into making up the nested system in question (plus perhaps the requisite ascending and descending reason-relations between them)?

Specific analyses of social properties in terms of parts of the nest might be suggested. Would such analyses be reductive? For example, can the social property of paying *y* for a stone just *be* the mental properties of expecting *y* to surrender the stone in return for something given to *y*, expecting *y* will not try to regain control of the stone unless in return for something willingly accepted from *y*, and so on? It might seem that, from the description of the beliefs and expectations in the nested system, one should be able to extract sufficient mental properties, like the properties of believing or expecting certain things, with which reductively to identify social properties.

There are two sorts of reasons that I should like to discuss for thinking that this apparently natural development of my analysis of what it is for a property to be a social property is not acceptable. That is, these are reasons for thinking that the analyses of social properties in terms of mental properties are either unavailable or, if available, not reductive. I would not wish to overstate the degree of conclusiveness I take my reasons, or argument sketches, to possess. I do not think that I can *demonstrate* the unavailability of reductive analyses in terms of mental properties for social properties generally. Rather, I select certain important subsets of social properties. Even for the subsets, my anti-reductive arguments are not conclusive. The first argument appeals to a certain amount of empirical hypothesis. I think that my second argument is more powerful than the first. Still, even the second rests on a premise which I regard as overwhelmingly likely, but for which I advance no independent argument.

## The first anti-reductive argument

I argued that a property *P* is a social property if and only if it follows from the fact that *P* is true of something that there is *some* nested system of beliefs and expectations. One can distinguish two sorts of social properties: variable and non-variable. A social property is non-variable if there is some specific system of beliefs and expectations that must exist whenever the property is true of something. For example, consider the social property, participating in the (British) custom of drinking tea at breakfast. If this property is true of a person, it follows that there is a *specific* system of beliefs and expectations that must exist, for in general we will expect one another to drink tea at breakfast. Since this is so, I call the social property of participating in the custom of drinking tea at breakfast 'a non-variable social property'.

Most social properties are not like this; most social properties are variable. If a variable social property obtains, it follows that some nested system or other must exist, but there is no nested system whose existence is entailed by the obtaining of the variable social property. Suppose *P* is a variable social property. Then, if *P* is true of $x$, nested system $s_1$ might exist. If *P* is true of $y$ (who may live in another society at a different time than $x$), nested system $s_2$ might exist. The applicability of these social properties requires only that *a* nested system exists, but that requirement might be filled at one time by one system and at another time by another.

As an example of a variable social property, consider first the property of being a mayor. What nested system of beliefs and expectations must exist when it is true of some person that she or he is a mayor? What the mayor or other people believe or expect of one another when the person is a mayor will depend on the duties and responsibilities that attach to that office. These depend on social convention and can vary indefinitely. When someone is a mayor, there must be some nested system of beliefs and expectations, held both by the mayor and by a section of the people for whom that person is the mayor. But there are almost no restrictions on which beliefs and expectations can go to make up the system, and therefore almost no restrictions on the range of systems which might exist when someone is a mayor. There is no specific system of beliefs and expectations whose existence is necessary for someone's being a mayor. To put it in terms familiar from a similar argument in the philosophy of mind, there seem to be indefinitely many sets of mental properties, all of which can alternatively 'realize' the social property.

Human beings have a part in choosing what the material and mental world must be like, such that being that way makes it true that someone is a mayor. It is not just in virtue of the laws of nature that certain arrangements of mind and matter are sufficient for the realization of social properties. It is also in virtue of how we decide to construct the social world.

I would say that this first argument, or reason, suggests the irreducibility of at least one important kind of social property, but that it is far from decisive. It 'suggests' that there are no mental properties or disjunctions of mental properties nomologically necessary and sufficient for social properties of a certain kind. The argument suggests that such analyses are unavailable. However, it owes far too much to intuition and empirical speculation. It invites the reader to think of a mental property or disjunction of such properties necessary and sufficient as a matter of natural law for a variable social property like being a mayor, and assumes that the invitation cannot be met.

The use of this argument in this context does not seem to me to be any weaker than its use in the philosophy of mind, where some anti-reductivists of the mental to the physical similarly state or assume that for no mental property is there a physical property or disjunction of physical properties nomologically necessary and sufficient for it. Indeed, its use in the case of social science seems to me to be stronger, since it is more plausible to believe that there are nomological restrictions on which physical properties can realize a given mental property than it is to believe that there are nomological restrictions on which mental properties can realize a variable social property. Still, even if the use of this kind of argument is no weaker when used against the alleged reduction of the social to the mental than it is when used against the alleged reduction of the mental to the physical, it is too weak for comfort. It would be better to find another argument that convinces those not already convinced.

## The second anti-reductive argument

The second argument does not attempt to show, like the first, that no analyses of the social in terms of the mental are available. The second argument tries to show that, even if available, analyses of the social in terms of the mental would not be reductive. Such analyses would, I claim, be circular, at least in the case of one important kind of social property. I argue that, for one sort of social property, indeed the most characteristic sort, mental properties adequate for their identification (if any) would themselves presuppose the existence of other social properties. Any such identification would be circular, and hence non-reductive. However, even this second argument, though I think stronger than the first, rests on an unargued premise, which I state but for which I offer no independent argument.

We should note the kind of circularity being alleged. One idea of circularity is that you end up with the same token item with which you started. Another idea of circularity is that you end up with the same sort of thing with which you started. It is the second idea of circularity that I am interested in. The reduction we are considering does not just aim at eliminating specific social properties. It aims to show that the very category of a social property is ontologically redundant, since all such properties are in reality nothing more than mental properties or disjunctions of mental properties. Therefore, in an identification of a social property *P* with a mental property *M*, in order to sustain the charge of circularity, I do not need to show that, in an analysis of *M*, the property *P* itself rearises. It is enough to show that in the analysis of *M*, some social property *P′* occurs, where *P′* may or may not be the same as *P*.

I now turn to the argument. We can again distinguish between two kinds of social properties, weakly social and strongly social properties. I do not wish to commit myself on how this distinction fits with the earlier distinction between non-variable and variable social properties. However, as my example of a weakly social property, I would like to consider the same social property that I used as an example of a non-variable social property: participating in the *custom* of drinking tea at breakfast. This is a social property, even though the property of drinking tea at breakfast is not a social property.

Of course, we might say of someone that they drink tea at breakfast, its being understood from context that we mean that the person participates in the custom of doing this. But simply to say of someone that they drink tea at breakfast, even when there is a social custom to do this and when that person drinks tea because it is a custom, is not to *say* that some social property is true of that person.

On the other hand, the property of participating in the *custom* of drinking tea at breakfast is a social property, because if it is true of someone, it follows that a nested system of interlocking beliefs and expectations exists. As I have already claimed, the property is a non-variable social property, because specifically a nested system of interlocking beliefs and expectations about tea drinking at breakfast *is* necessary for the property's applicability.

These beliefs and expectations have propositional objects. What are they? They are or include: that some token action of the type, tea drinking at breakfast, will be performed. The beliefs and expectations in the nested systems are characteristically about specific action types, not specific action tokens. What is believed or expected is that some action token or other of a specific type will be done. Although I have said that it is logically possible for there to be social relations between disembodied persons (if it is logically possible for there to be disembodied persons), in fact social relations hold between embodied persons like ourselves.

Even so, the propositional objects of the beliefs and expectations which go to make up the nested system can sometimes be: that some mental action token of some specific mental action type will be done. For example, as I suggested earlier, there may be a club of mathematicians which has as one of its rules that between meetings each member will think about some especially important proof. But, this kind of example would be atypical. Characteristically, the beliefs and expectations are about non-mental actions. In the case of tea drinking at breakfast, the object of belief or expectation is: that some token of the action type, tea drinking at breakfast, will be performed. Note that the action type (or property?)[2] which the belief is about is itself non-social, in the sense I have already indicated.

So, in the example of participating in the custom of tea drinking at breakfast, the associated beliefs and expectations are about non-social action types. I call a social property 'weakly social' when *all* of the beliefs or expectations in the associated nested system have propositional objects of the form, 'Someone will *F*', where '*F*' specifies a non-social action type.

On the other hand, a social property is strongly social when some of the associated beliefs and expectations have propositional objects involving a *social* action type. Consider, again, the social property of being a mayor. I have already argued that this is a variable social property, so it makes no sense to ask that one consider all of the beliefs and expectations that may be associated with any instance of the property. But consider some plausible examples. I expect the mayor to attend certain civic functions and to sign executive orders. I expect the mayor to offer the keys of the city to selected visiting dignitaries. And so on. That is, what I believe or expect of the mayor is to perform some action token of a specific *social* action type. Some propositional objects of my beliefs and expectations will have the form: 'Someone will *G*', where '*G*' specifies a social action type. Action types are a special sort of property, and social action types are a special sort of social property.

Reference to social action types will re-arise in unpacking the idea of strongly social properties. I may expect the mayor to sign an executive order, and yet have no beliefs or expectations about the physical actions that must be undertaken by the mayor in order to sign the order. I may expect the mayor to sign the order, and this may be done by etching the mayor's name with a laser beam, but I may not expect the mayor to have done this. Even in those instances in which I do also have beliefs and expectations about the physical actions of this person (perhaps I do expect the mayor to etch his or her name with a laser), this is insufficient for believing that an executive order will be signed by the mayor, since someone completely ignorant of the society may form the first belief or expectation while failing to have the second.

The property of believing or expecting that some token of a social action type will be done is a psychological property (or, mental property). Belief and expectation contexts are non-extensional, in the sense that in general there is no inference from '*A* believes that *x* is *P*' to 'There is an *x* such that

*A* believes that it is *P*'. From the fact that I have expectations that the mayor will sign an executive order, it does not follow that there are any executive orders, or even that there are any mayors. I might be as misled as the Margaret Mead of my earlier story, with her theory of kitchiboo. Thus, by my criterion, although the property of signing an executive order is a social property, believing that someone will perform some token action of the social action type, a signing of an executive order, is not a social property (it is a mental property), since the existence of a nested system of beliefs and expectations is not entailed by its correct application.

However, although beliefs and expectations are non-extensional with regard to objects or token acts or events, they are not non-extensional with regard to properties or action types. If I have an intelligible belief that *x* is *P*, it does not follow that there is an *x*, but it does follow that there is a property *P* such that I believe that *x* has it. This is, of course, compatible with believing that properties are only sets, or concepts, or anything else one might like. Whatever properties are, if there is an intelligible belief that *x* is *P*, there must be the property of being *P*.[3]

In the case of a strongly social property *S*, believing that someone will perform a token action of the social action type *S* is a mental and not a social property, but if there is this mental property, it follows that there is some social action type *S*, or some social property, namely engaging in an *S*-type act. These last *are* social properties on the criterion I have given: *if* instantiated, it follows that some nested system of beliefs and expectations exists. The mental believings and expectings that form the nested systems associated with strongly social properties themselves presuppose, in turn, the existence of social properties (but do not of course presuppose that the social properties are instantiated).

My second argument has, so far, merely unpacked what is involved in the definition of a strongly social property, namely, that a strongly social property is a property such that in its analysis in terms of beliefs and expectations, a further social property will reappear in the analysans. Can we conclude that such analyses, even if available, will be circular? This will not yet follow. Weakly social properties can (by definition) be given social-property-free analyses. Suppose, then, that the first phase of the reduction is from strongly social properties to beliefs and expectations about the instantiation of (only) weakly social properties or weakly social action types. Then there will be a further, second reduction that analyses the weakly social properties or weakly social action types in terms of beliefs and expectations about the instantiation of (only) non-social properties or non-social action types. We cannot hope to have convincingly argued for the irreducibility of strongly social properties unless we can block this possibility.

In order to block this move, I need something stronger than just the definition of a strongly social property:

(A) In the analysis of any strongly social property in terms of beliefs and expectations, a further social property will reappear in the analysans.

I need the stronger claim:

(B) There are at least some strongly social properties such that no analysis of them, however remote,[4] in terms of beliefs and expectations about the instantiation of only weakly social properties can be adequate.

I think that (B) is true. I do not assert that there could not be a recognisably human social life unless there were social properties of the kind mentioned in (B). On the contrary, one can imagine a social life such that only weakly social properties were instantiated, or only strongly social properties which had no further strongly social properties in their analysans. All such social properties could finally be 'reduced' to beliefs and expectations about the instantiation of non-social properties or action types. Such a social life would allow for the ascription of such social properties as: following a public rule to do *G*, cooperating in *G*-ing, playing a game that involves doing *G* (where '*G*' specifies a non-social action type).

One could conceive of such a social life, and social life may take this form in very primitive and rudimentary societies. But our social life is not like that, for our social life allows for the ascription of strongly social properties concerning which (*B*) is true. Indeed, it is these social properties that strike us as *most characteristic* of what social life is like. My examples in the discussion of strongly social properties were of this kind. Consider again the strongly social property of being a mayor. What I expect of the mayor is to sign executive orders, attend certain state functions, and so on. The instantiations which I expect are *of* further social action types themselves strongly social. I could not set out the beliefs and expectations I have when someone signs an executive order or attends a state function without employing further (strongly) social properties or action types. (B), I hold, is true of the social properties that we ascribe and which we take to be most characteristic of what sociality is like.

Since (B) is true, there is a whole range of social properties that we ascribe in the course of our lives, like being a mayor, opening a session of Parliament, voting, cashing a cheque, being a prison (a social property true of some buildings), for which no *reductive* analysis in terms of mental properties like believing and expecting is possible, since mental properties adequate for the analysis (if any; this is a moot point, given my first argument about variability) will themselves presuppose the existence of social properties of the same sort. I think that there is an important class of social properties which could not be reductively identified with the mental, even if it could be identified with it, because the mental properties associated with the application of the social property must themselves be beliefs or expectations about the instancing of strongly social action types. No commitment to social properties is thereby escaped by the identification; hence, it cannot be reductive.

J.W.N. Watkins describes approvingly Keynes's theory: 'At the heart of his *General Theory* Keynes placed 'three fundamental psychological factors, namely, the psychological propensity to consume, the psychological attitude to liquidity and the psychological expectation of future yield from capital-assets' (Watkins 1973: 159). Whatever form of individualism this is, it is certainly consistent with the existence of irreducible social properties, since some of the mental properties Keynes mentions themselves presuppose the existence of strongly social properties.

## Notes

1 Crane and Mellor (1990) present a good discussion of the problems of finding any non-circular criterion of the physical.

2 I begin by distinguishing between act-types and act-tokens. 'An act-type is simply an act-property. . . . To perform an act, then, is to exemplify a property' (Goldman 1970: 10–11).

3 But why suppose that there *are* properties at all? Can't we simply refuse to quantify over properties? This will hardly do in the context of this discussion, since we are discussing whether one property is identical with another. The whole discussion is predicated on the assumption that it makes perfectly good sense to speak of the existence of properties. On the other hand, suppose there are properties, but that they are only sets (or whatever else one's favourite reductive candidate might be). Since any such reduction will have to provide parsing of talk about properties and their identities, the contents of this paper will apply *mutatis mutandis*, to whatever reduces properties and the identities of these.

4 If '*q*' is an analysis of '*p*', and if '*r*' is an analysis of '*q*', then '*r*' is a remote analysis of '*p*'.

# 5 | Social theory and the analysis of society

**Margaret S. Archer**

In the beginning, theory and practice were conjoined. The Comtean promise of positivism was one where sociology as queen of the sciences would predict, correct and direct social development. Yet positivism rested foursquare upon empiricism and as the foundational premisses of the latter were progressively undermined there were basically three positions which social theorists adopted. Which was taken up depended upon how the impossibility of naturalism, that is of an empiricist science of society, was received. In turn this was immediately related to the practical utility assigned to, or assumed by, social theorists, which ranged from 'everything' to 'something' to 'nothing' for the three different positions.

The rejection of empiricism rested on the following denials:

1 That there were no 'hard facts' out there which were directly registered as sense-data. Instead, because there is no theory neutral language, no vantage point for the 'pure visitor' (Gellner 1979), we select and shape our 'facts' (and findings) as filtered through the linguistic concepts used. In short all knowledge (natural and social) is conceptually formed. Note that this denial has no implications concerning the nature of social reality: it is an epistemological matter about obtaining access to it and not a judgement about its status.
2 Even law-like generalizations could never approximate to naturalistic predictions because the nature of sociological subject matter, which includes reflexive/creative human beings, served to preclude any approximation to conditions of laboratory closure. Societies were necessarily open systems where correlation was always at the mercy of contingency.
3 That the Humean model of seeking constant conjunctions between observables was both quintessentially non-explanatory, since it could only adduce associations and not the mechanisms accounting for them, and necessarily incomplete, because non-observable properties could never figure in it.

The implications of (1), that all knowledge was conceptually formed, was the necessary variety of social theories. Since theories are statements which link concepts, then the inevitable plurality in conceptualization meant that theory itself would also be plural (except under the condition of complete conceptual agreement). Theoretical pluralism in turn raises the question of evaluation and the appropriate context of justification (for warranted assertability). Depending upon how seriously the denials of (2) and (3) were taken as a rejection of naturalism, the three basic positions mentioned at the start emerged and now roughly divide the literature between them.

First, at one extreme there is rearguard positivism which takes instrumentalism as its context of justification and thus not only does but must sustain its engagement with practical social problems. Basically, providing data and (generally) guidance on major contemporary social issues is its *raison d'être*. However, instrumentalism is a value which evaluates in terms of what works best (meaning what predicts more accurately or correlates most closely). So, for example, we could ask 'what best predicts school achievement?' Some objective concept of social class or a subjective one (both suitably operationalized)? Now it is possible to answer the question empirically (at a given time, *T1*, and place, *S1*), but this is not the end of the matter for instrumentalism. Pragmatic utility as the criterion of justification hoists instrumentalism with its own petard. It takes on board unquestioningly the ontological premisses of whatever concept works best for problems *x* and *y* – neatly epitomized in Deng's maxim, 'It doesn't matter whether a cat is black or white, as long as it catches mice'. But the amorality of practical utility as a criterion quickly rebounds. Suppose what 'works best' for predicting *x* (house buying) is a subjectively assigned concept of class, whereas what 'works best' for problem *y* (incidence of strikes) is some objective concept (income, relations to production or market life chances), then instrumentalists are condemned to accept two disparate/divergent premisses about class. This also has the practical implication that different people 'belong' to different classes depending on the problem in hand! Here, practical utility necessarily generates theoretical inconsistency, for there is no guarantor of mutual coherence among the multiple rules of thumb. Theoretical fragmentation then follows; that is the multiplication of incompatible concepts retained because of their workability. In the end instrumentalism becomes the supreme exemplar of theory being underdetermined by the 'facts', even though its credo is exactly the opposite. Most national journals still prominently display this Humean heritage in articles which correlate numerous variables and, with increasing statistical sophistication, 'account' for variance in 'development', 'voting patterns', 'employment rates' and so on.

Second, at the other extreme, discontent with positivism progressively induced disenchantment with the entire scientific enterprise, entailing the disengagement of sociology from any practical contribution to major social problems whatsoever. The necessity of this entailment was not fully evident in the bridging work of Kuhn (1962), who still entertained a notion of scientific progress, but its origins were there in the epistemic slide from 'progress' in science to the scientific community's paradigmatic view of progress. It grew within ethnomethodology and became blatant with the development of postmodernism and its radical reactions to the three main deficiencies of positivism. From (1), 'all knowledge being conceptually formed' was derived the reverse, namely, that knowledge dissolved into discourse. Since discourses were untrammelled by ontological limitations then the discursive swung free from any source of evaluation beyond community consensus – where rhetorical persuasion replaced arbitration. From (2), 'the impossibility of generating social laws', came the obverse, a celebration of contingency based on the assertion of the radical indeterminacy of things social. With this went not only the end of any quest for law-like (quasi-naturalistic) generalizations but also the condemnation of explanatory grand narratives. The Enlightenment project had relied upon instrumental rationality to construct its totalizing accounts. Contingency defied such theorization and was held to reveal the authoritarian nature of Rationality in overriding it to produce such narratives. From (3), the doubts cast on 'the Humean model', came a radical rejection of any notion of social science, of explanation or of understanding. Since there was no context of justification beyond the community and because communities were various, then their different discourses, lacking a grounding in common rationality, were held to be radically incommensurable and untranslatable. Science gave way to sitting in on a multiplicity of local language games, which lacked common measure and thus were only amenable to aesthetic appreciation and never to practical evaluation. Hence the postmodernist response to (1) had been to relativize discourse, to (2) to relativize reason, and to (3) to relativize truth. Such full blown relativism necessarily severed postmodernism from making a contribution to major social issues, since the very designation of such (as topics) was now up for discursive grabs, while any methodology for approaching them (explanatory tools) had been displaced by the aestheticization of social life.

Finally, it is the position (or rather positions) which lie between these extremes with which the remainder of this chapter is concerned, namely those who, in shorthand, no longer believed that the facts spoke for themselves yet refused to conclude that this licences us to say anything we please regardless of the way things are in the social world. In longhand, these are the theorists whose response to (1), that 'all knowledge is conceptually formed' is to maintain that some concepts are better than others for portraying reality and that the nature of social reality itself imposes limits on its conceptualization. Their response to (2), 'society as an open system', is indeed to abandon hope of predictive laws but not to jettison retrodictive explanation of why things are so and not otherwise at any given *T1*, *S1*. Their response to (3), 'the empiricist Humean model', is certainly to reject the notion of constant conjunctions as central to the sociological enterprise: regularities are important but less so than the generative mechanisms which produce them because if these can be identified we can basically account for both the systematic effects they do produce but also for the contingencies which intervene to mask them or even to suspend their powers.

One of the most important distinctive features of those taking up this middle ground is their acknowledgement that the constituent elements of social theorizing are threefold, that none is dispensable and that each exerts a regulatory role on others as follows:

| Social Ontology (SO) | ⇒ | Explanatory Methodology (EM) | ⇒ | Practical social Theory (PST) |
|---|---|---|---|---|

In contrast, instrumentalism uncouples the last element from the other two. There is no working backwards from the empirical connections found between social problems and related properties or conditions because the composition of the EM is merely that collection of indices which have demonstrated their workability. Such concepts, whose only common denominator is their predictive utility (i.e. the capacity to account for some variance in phenomena), prevents the distillation of a social ontology from this diverse cluster, since nothing can preclude their mutual inconsistency.

On the other hand, postmodernism proceeds in the opposite direction, detaching social ontology from EM and PST. Because social reality is defined as being discursive, but discourses themselves are held to be incommensurable and untranslatable, this cannot lead to an EM. It governs it only in the sense of condemning the explanatory enterprise as such and replacing it by aesthetic appreciation. In consequence, postmodernism then represents a principled refusal to move forward to PST, and substitutes for it various notions of 'playing with the pieces' (Baudrillard 1984: 38–9) and practices of 'self-enrichment' (Rorty 1989) which effectively enjoin muteness on major contemporary social issues.

What differentiates theorists occupying the middle ground are the mutual connections which they emphasize between SO, EM and PST, as in the above sketch. Where the relationship between SO and EM is concerned, the connection consists in maintaining that what is held to exist must exert an influence upon how it should be explained. It is certainly not the case that the relationship between the two is one of logical implication. This cannot be so because it must remain possible to hold that some things exist socially which carry no particular implications about how we should study them or what importance should be assigned to them in explanations. For example, because both pleasure and pain are undeniably part of our social lot, this does not commit us all to being Utilitarians.

Nevertheless, the social ontology endorsed does play a powerful regulatory role *vis-à-vis* the explanatory methodology for the basic reason that it conceptualizes social reality in certain terms, thus identifying what there is to be explained and also ruling out explanations in terms of entities or properties which are deemed non-existent. Social ontologies thus govern those concepts which are deemed admissible in explanation as in description. Because the ontology contains judgements about the 'ultimate constituents' (and non-constituents) of social reality, it thus governs what sort of concepts may properly be countenanced for any purpose whatsoever. To regulate is not to dictate: there can be a lively debate about the most useful concepts to employ within a given view of what social reality is, but equally that view of what exists (and thus constitutes our subject matter) does serve to rule out certain concepts from explanations, just as atheists cannot attribute their well being to divine providence. No explanation is acceptable to any group of theorists if it contains terms whose referents misconstrue social reality as they see it – whether such misconstruction is due to sins of conceptual omission or commission.

Practical social theorists addressing substantive social issues do not directly derive their propositions from either the SO or its congruent EMs, for a plurality of the latter can be fully compatible with the former. However the shaping of PSTs is profound in terms of their scope. The nature of different social ontologies and their associated methods of explanation are manifestly stronger at a particular level of PST or with specific time spans. Thus, for example, Individualists, insisting that the ultimate constituents of the social world were individual people (Watkins 1968: 270), next adduced related explanatory injunctions (methodological individualism) which worked more convincingly (though by no means unproblematically) at the level of interpersonal relations, confined to those taking place between contemporary individuals. By contrast, Collectivists, insisting that the ultimate constituents of social life embraced societal facts (Mandelbaum 1973: 223), irreducible to individual terms, and their explanatory programme (methodological collectivism) fared better with structural or cultural problems with a historical dimension. As the long running debate between these two schools illustrated, since the nature of social reality is a matter of fact which is independent of the prior commitments of any theorists about what exists, then if and when an incongruous method of explanation gives evidence of working, or the congruent methodological programme breaks down in practice, this should result in a reinspection of those commitments themselves. What we think social reality is cannot be a separate matter from what we find it to be. The relationship between SO and PST is one of reciprocal regulation, as indicated by the feedback arrow in the diagram. Now the reason for introducing and stressing the tripartite connections between SO $\Rightarrow$ EM $\Rightarrow$ PST is to underline why we cannot simply gather up the fruits (the PST findings) which stem from different ontological assumptions as transmitted through their cognate explanatory methodologies. Some textbook writers have been tempted to uncouple PST from its underpinnings and to suggest an eclectic pragmatism which seemingly allows us to have the best of all theoretical worlds. However, such 'perspectivism' simultaneously denies that there are serious underlying reasons for theoretical variety and thus again slides, via eclecticism, into a marriage of inconveniently inconsistent premisses.

## The conflation of structure and agency in social theory

Although there are important differences between the various social ontologies occupying the middle ground, nevertheless I regard the fundamental issues raised, i.e. 'individual and society', 'voluntarism and determinism', 'subjectivism and objectivism', the 'micro versus the macro', as being variations on the basic problem of 'structure and agency'. Discussion in the UK has tended to use the latter term, accepting it (Giddens 1979; Layder 1994; Mouzelis 1995) as an umbrella for the rest, while in the USA the major ontological problem has been highlighted as the 'micro–macro link'. Yet, as Alexander (1987) emphasizes, it is the same debate: 'The perennial conflict between individualistic and collectivist theories has been re-worked as a conflict between micro-sociology and macro-sociology' (1987: 289). Moreover, although reference will be largely confined to the Anglo-Saxon world, the 'problem of structure and agency' has the same centrality throughout Europe (see the works of Boudon, Bourdieu, Touraine, Crespi, Donati, Elster, Habermas, Mtiller, Offe and Sztompka).

Originally the dispute concerned ontological epiphenomenalism (the assertion of the primacy of either structure or agency as the ultimate constituents of society) and methodological reductionism as the means of explanation in terms of whichever of the two was held to be primary. Thus, the old division described as 'the two sociologies' (Dawe 1970) reflected this difference. In downwards reductionism, systemic features like the (later) Parsonian central value system served to orchestrate lower order institutional compatibility and a congruent socialization of agency. In upwards reductionism the opposite assumption was made, namely that society was simply the small group writ large. This led interpretative sociologists in particular to place a 'big etc.' (Wagner 1964) against their microsociological expositions in the expectation that the explanation of the social system could be derived by a process of aggregation.

Therefore in both cases agency and structure have been linked by making one dependent on the other, which automatically precludes a twoway interplay between them. This, it will be argued, blocks any satisfactory theorization of stability and change, since this needs to be based on the interplay between structure and agency, which in turn is predicated upon relative autonomy being assigned to both elements. However, epiphenomenalism is not the only way in which either structure or agency are deprived of independent, irreducible properties, and thus their interplay is denied. Any form of what I have termed 'conflation' (Archer 1989; 1995) has the same consequence for theorizing social issues. In other words, conflation is the more basic error and epiphenomenalism represents two directions in which it can occur – downwards and upwards. However, there is another possibility, namely 'central conflation', where elision occurs in the 'middle'. This directional approach instead withholds relative autonomy from both levels because structure and agency are conceptualized as being tightly mutually constitutive. Here their ontological inseparability has the common effect of conflationism, namely that of precluding any examination of their interplay.

### *Downwards conflation*

Downwards conflation where structure and agency are conflated because action is treated as fundamentally epiphenomenal has many variants, but is encountered today in any uncompromising version of technological determinism, economism, structuralism or normative functionalism. Despite their differences, the bottom line is always that agents may be indispensable for energizing the social system (no people: no society) but it is not they whose actions give it direction by shaping structural properties. They cannot, for on this view there are no reflective, promotive and innovative human beings as such, but only social agents, formed from Durkheim's famous 'indeterminate material', who energize the system after appropriate socialization. Since agency is unidirectionally shaped by structure, a passive agent (Hollis 1977) is advanced because social determinism is endorsed rather than social conditioning (which would allow relative autonomy to agency). Therefore it is granted that agency constitutes the motor-power but agents themselves are never admitted to touch the steering wheel. So the course of social change is never pictured as a wild zigzag, as social groups struggle to wrest the wheel from one another. Often taking us all where no one wants to go, with the result that society become something which nobody wants, in its precise form, at any given time. Instead here, at most, it might be allowed that social interaction is a sort of white noise or Brownian motion in the system, but one whose very randomness deprives it of any decisive effect upon the state of society. This apart, we are presented with either the 'oversocialized view of humans' or the 'overdetermined view of humans' depending on whether the epiphenomenal character of agency is grounded in idealism or materialism, which are the twin fountainheads of downwards conflation.

Consequently to any downward conflationist, action leads nowhere except where structure guides it. Hence, there is never anything to examine other than the imprint of structure upon agency. Since people are literally the agents of structure – its embodiments-cum-executors – then sociocultural change results from some autonomous unfurling process which is operative at the structural level, meaning that human agents are never granted the autonomy to have any independent effect upon it. Since social interaction is not credited with the capacity to generate intended, unintended, aggregate or emergent properties which are of structural magnitude or consequence, then 'the future' is the unfolding of immanent structural tendencies which are already present in the system. (At most they might be considered to develop in adaptation to an external environment, often a purely physical one, but even if it is made up of other structures, these of course are held to have the same relationship to their own agents.)

Looking backwards instead, if action is epiphenomenal then logically structure must predate it. Yet because action is not held to create it, then the sources of structure are located elsewhere since they have to come from somewhere. Social systems thus become the progeny of holistic or psychologistic factors. The explanation of how things got to be the way they are is handed over to impersonal forces or factors – the hidden hand of evolutionary adaptation, the iron grip of economic progression, the unseen grasp of a destiny ideal or architectonic principle.

However, what this means about the development of any particular social structure is that it is not by examining prior group interaction that we can arrive at an explanation of it. On the contrary, social structures are never admitted to have social origins (in contradistinction, social agents are always assumed to be structural products). Hence the PSTs which are advanced to explain major social issues or configurations show a strong common tendency to work in coarse grained terms delineating stages or phases of structural development or to deal with fairly gross dichotomies in social progression (underdeveloped/developed; segmented/cooperative; cold/hot; preindustrial/industrial; modernity/postmodernity; etc.). It does not seem unjust that these have sometimes been dubbed as 'steamroller' theories of social transformation.

### *Upwards conflation*

Upwards conflation represents the exact opposite since structure is held to be the creature of agency. Thus approaches like Rational Choice Theory present a model of humankind, an idealized human being standing for the social agent, who alone with others of the same kind generate the entirety of the social structure from their inbuilt dispositions to be rational (in this case) agents. The social context of action may not look that way to the investigator, upon first inspection, and it may never feel that way to the agent, because of lasting objectification. Nevertheless, to upwards conflationists it is always a major descriptive error to treat structural properties as having the ontological status of facts rather than facticity, and it is equally erroneous to allow them to figure in explanatory statements as external conditioners of action. Thus, for instance, the neo-phenomenological school asserts the primacy of agency by reducing the structural context of action to a series of intersubjectively negotiated constructs. However the basic charter of all versions of upward conflation, of which interpretative sociology is only one variant, is methodological individualism. Its prime injunction is to view so-called structural properties as reducible to the effects of other agents, which are in their turn always recoverable by agency.

Essentially structure becomes epiphenomenal in methodological individualism because the social context is defined as made up of nothing more than other people. Hence to Watkins, the

> central assumption of the individualist position – an assumption which is admittedly counter-factual and metaphysical – is that no social tendency exists which could not be altered if the individuals concerned both wanted to alter it and possessed the appropriate information.
>
> (Watkins 1968: 271)

For this strategy of 'personalization' to work its protagonists have to show that all structural properties (every aspect of the social environment), which figure in explanations, refer to nothing more than the activities and attitudes of other people.

Note here that the structural properties and the constraints they exert have now become the effects of contemporary action. For it follows that what constitutes our social context are things that the 'people concerned' do not want to change/do not know how to change/do not think about changing. This is one of the problems with viewing society from the bottom up, namely it constitutes an underconstrained picture of 'humans' (or an underenabled one for that matter) because it makes no allowance for inherited structures, their resistance to change, the influence they exert on attitudes to change and, crucially, the delineation of agents capable of seeking change, and endowed with a heritage of vested interests which prompt them to do so. Thus whatever the origins of the structural tendencies and characteristics we observe, their present existence is due in some way to the people present. Yet the 'central assumption' upon which this is based is undoubtedly counterfactual for there appear to be some structural properties which cannot be eliminated at will (given any amount of information, thought or desire) by contemporary agents – at least not for a considerable period of time.

This would be the case for demographic structures, for levels of literacy or class, gender or ethnic privileges. Such structural influences are the unintended consequences of past actions but their conditioning and constraining effects in the present cannot be reduced to or made the responsibility of contemporary agents who quite literally inherit them. The fact that such structural properties are ultimately reversible by human action is not at issue, the point is that they exert constraints until they can be changed. There are then some aspects of our social environment which obstruct us (e.g. certain kinds of military recruitment or pension policies are impossible with a particular kind of demographic structure) but these cannot be attributed to the sustaining behaviour of contemporary agents (who may be concertively seeking their transformation).

Yet if the bedrock of any acceptable explanation of a social phenomenon is individual dispositions, then this presupposes the possibility of always isolating more elementary dispositions

> as they are prior to their manifestations in a social context. The real oddity of the reductionist case is that it seems to preclude a priori the possibility of human dispositions being the dependent variable in an historical explanation – when in fact they often or always are.
>
> (Gellner, 1968: 260)

In other words upwards conflationists cannot accept that unintended consequences from past action, may become consequential in their own right – as emergent properties or aggregate effects which represent new structural influences upon subsequent action. For structural factors are inefficacious without the sanction, as it were, of contemporary other people. Consequently methodological individualists endorse a perpetual 'autonomy of the present tense' in order for agency to explain the very existence of structures but also their maintenance and influence.

However, further difficulties attach to practical efforts to derive complex structures directly from some 'model of the human', i.e. from some property pertaining to the (idealized) human being. Thus the first contender was the 'rational man [*sic*]' of classical economics, whose calculus, consistency and selfishness organized his desires, resulting in choices which summed to produce social reality (Sen 1985). The fact that this model of the 'rational man' could not cope with phenomena like voluntary collective behaviour or the voluntary creation of public goods, led some to complement him with an inner running mate. Enter the 'normative man', who shifts to a different logic of action under circumstances in which he realizes he is dependent upon others for his own welfare ( Etzioni 1988). Yet again, inexplicable macro-level effects remained, and the 'emotional man' (Flam 1990) joined the team to mop up structural and cultural properties based on expressive solidarity or willingness to share.

The trouble with this multiplication of 'inner complements', all inhabiting the same being, is that it eventually comes full circle ending up with the 'multiple self' (Elster 1986) and his suggestion that we treat humankind like an organization. Yet this is a completely vicious circle: some sort of 'man' was wanted to explain that which was problematic, namely social organization, but now we are enjoined to use social organization in order to conceptualize the nature of humankind! What is going wrong here is the desperate incorporation of all emergent and aggregate social properties into the individual. Deficiencies in PST are directly attributable to the underlying social ontology of individualism.

*Central conflation*

Central conflation is an approach based upon the conviction that structure and agency form an inseparable duality and finds its most sophisticated expression in modern 'structuration theory'. The latter rests upon an 'ontology of praxis' where structure and culture have to be drawn upon in the routine production of action, which in turn instantiates structural properties, thus recursively reproducing structure itself. Hence the core ontological notion of 'structure as the medium and outcome of the reproduction of practices' (Giddens 1979: 69): thus structure is not only activity dependent, but has no independence from the practices constituting it. To construe social reality solely in terms of social practices presents us with highly 'knowledgeable' agents (who must know a great deal about their society) and an omnipresent structure (necessarily drawn upon in each practical act) (Archer 1982; 1989; 1995). It can be criticized for three things: the excessive knowledgeability accorded to agency, the excessive mutability attributed to social structure, and the difficulties for explanation which derive from the inseparability of the two. Here I will begin with the last point. For the insistence upon the inseparability of structure and agency is also a denial that distinctive emergent properties and powers pertain to each. This sets 'structuration theory' firmly apart from an ontology in which 'structures' and 'agents' are held to be distinct strata of social reality, as is the case for realists. Despite considerable confusion in the literature between these two positions, their divergence stems from this crucial ontological difference and continues through their respective approaches to EM and PST (for a full discussion, see Archer 1995: ch. 5).

Endorsement of inseparability results in an inability to examine the interplay between structure and agency because the two presuppose one another so closely – this ontological supposition being directly transmitted to the methodology adopted and enjoined (Craib 1992: 3–4). The intimacy of mutual constitution thus means that the only way in which structure and agency can be examined 'independently' is through an artificial exercise of 'methodological bracketing'. On the one hand, institutional analysis brackets strategic action and treats structural properties as 'chronically reproduced features of social systems'. This image of recursiveness figures prominently, but many would deny that these features necessarily are 'chronic': though they might be long lasting, they are nevertheless temporary (e.g. feudalism) or may change frequently (e.g. interest rates). Here the capacity to differentiate between them and to explain their differential durability is lost. On the other hand, to examine the constitution of social systems as strategic conduct, institutional analysis is bracketed and what is studied is the mobilization of rules and resources by agents in their social relations. This leads immediately to the reverse image: 'Change, or its potentiality, is thus inherent in all moments of social reproduction' (Giddens

1979: 114). Here an equally spurious changeability appears as a product of this methodological device – structural malleability is not only high but also constant over time. On the contrary many would argue that it is variable and that its variations are partially independent of strategic action, however intensely it is mobilized or knowledgeably it is conducted. Both elements of the model may be challenged (and are) within social realism, as follows:

First, agents cannot have 'discursive penetration' of the unacknowledged conditions of action (some things do go on behind their backs, though these are no more sinister than the results of past interaction); agents have differential knowledgeability according to social position; and some agents have defective, deficient and distorted knowledge owing to the cultural manipulation of others. Second, different structural features have to be seen as differentially malleable, or resistant to change, because of what they themselves are rather than solely due to the practices adopted towards them – which in any case are conditioned by them. However, this methodological bracketing produces a pendular swing between contradictory images – of chronic recursiveness and total transformation.

It might be replied in defence that no contradiction is involved as social reality is inherently Janus faced. Insistence upon this entails a principled refusal to unravel the interrelations between structure and agency since this would be an unacceptable lapse into dualistic theorizing. Yet, ironically, what does the bracketing device do other than traduce this very principle, since it merely transposes dualism from the ontological to the methodological level, thus conceding its analytical indispensability. However, since what is bracketed are the two aspects of the 'duality of structure', then structural properties and strategic conduct are being separated out by placing a 'methodological *époche*' upon each in turn. But because these are the two sides of the same thing, the pocketed elements must thus be coterminous in time (the coexistence of the époches confines analysis to the same *époque*); and it follows from this that the historical interplay between structure and agency logically cannot be examined.

Thus the central notion of 'duality' precludes any specification of the conditions under which agency can most readily induce change, versus circumstances under which the stringency of constraints confines agents to reproduction of the status quo. It follows that instead of being able to generate PSTs which would explain in terms of the relative stringency of structure/cultural constraints in combination with the strategic use made of agential degrees of freedom, the theory then retreats into broad generalizations about the 'essential importance of tradition and routinization in social life' (Giddens 1979: 7) to account for recursiveness. Where transformation is concerned, Giddens allows at most that there are 'critical situations' or 'critical phases' where the drastic disruption of routine corrodes the customary behaviour of agents and heightens susceptibility to alternatives. Then 'there is established a kind of "spot welding" of institutions that forms modes of integration which may subsequently become resistant to further change' (Giddens 1979: 229). Not only is the concept of a 'critical situation' dubious because of its *post hoc* designation, but also this formulation begs more questions than it answers. What makes a phase 'critical' – are structural factors not only always germane? What produces a particular crisis – do specific systemic features not generate distinctive crises?

The limitations of central conflationism as far as PST is concerned are conceded within structuration theory. Because of the kaleidoscopic permutations on structural properties to which knowledgeable agents can give rise, Giddens himself bows out, accepting that there is 'little point in looking for an overall theory of stability and change in social systems, since the conditions of reproduction vary so widely between different types of society' (1979: 215). Indeed, later on he goes further in acknowledging the gulf between structuration theory's social 'ontology of praxis' and practical social theorizing. Thus, at the level of EM, Giddens accepts that he has merely supplied a 'sensitization device' because he does 'not think it useful, as some others have tried to do, to "apply" structuration theory as a whole in research projects' (Giddens 1990: 310–11). Since PST is quintessentially propositional, then such practical work as has been done on this basis (and many reproach it for paucity in this respect) has substantially depended upon independent contributions injected by research workers, rather than representing outworkings directly attributable to this theoretical framework.

## The prospects of non-conflationary theorizing

With the steady development of social realism in the philosophy of social science came a genuine alternative to positivism and its defects. At the ontological level this basically consisted in the defence of a stratified view of social reality such that different strata (and particularly here 'the individual' and 'social structures') were maintained to have their own irreducible emergent properties, possessed of relative autonomy, pro-existence and causal efficacy (see Bhaskar 1979), which could be known by virtue of their generative causal powers rather than by their observability. (Emergence itself, upon which autonomy, pre-existence and causal efficacy depend, is explicitly disavowed by structuration theory, given the flattened nature of its 'ontology of praxis', compared with the robustly stratified social ontology of realism.) The emergent properties and powers attaching respectively to structures and agents are relational (therefore not reified) and defined by necessary internal relationships which exert influences on their components (landlords and tenants presuppose one another and will cease to exist as such if they do not respectively extract and pay rent), and beyond them (rent increases investment income) (Sayer 1992). Since emergence characterized both agency (emergent from psychology) and structures (emergent from interaction) then projects of reductionism and conflation are set aside because of the need 'to distinguish sharply, then between the genesis of human actions, lying in the reasons and plans of human beings, on the one hand; and the structures governing the reproduction and transformation of social activities, on the other' (Bhaskar 1979: 79). Nothing could be further removed from the notion of their inseparable mutual constitution, and, in social realism, this distinction leads on to methodological dualism – diametrically opposed to the 'bracketing device' entailed by commitment to 'duality' in structuration theory.

Thus analytical dualism is enjoined in social sciences as the basis of explanatory methodology – analytical because the two elements are interdependent and any social form is always activity dependent, but necessarily examined dualistically because the irreducibility of their properties entails investigation of their interplay. Methodologically this is possible, as Lockwood's (1964) early distinction between 'social' and 'system' integration maintained, because the two operate over different tracts of time, they can be out of synch with one another, and therefore it is possible to talk about relations of priority and posteriority between specific agents and determinate parts of social structure. Indeed temporality constitutes the methodological bridge making it possible to examine the interplay between structure and agency and thus explain changes in both – over time – in contradistinction to every version of conflationary social theorizing.

Thus at the level of EM, analytical dualism is based on two simple propositions: that structure necessarily predates the actions which transform it; and that structural elaboration necessarily postdates those actions. These can be pictured as shown in the diagram which pictures the 'tensed' nature of structure/agency relations, distinctive of social realism.

Structural conditioning
*TI*
Interaction
*T2* *T3*
Structural elaboration
*T4*

In *structural conditioning*, systemic properties are viewed as the emergent or aggregate consequences of past actions. Once they have been elaborated over time they are held to exert a causal influence upon subsequent interaction. Fundamentally they do so by shaping the situations in which later 'generations'of agents find themselves and by endowing various agents with different vested interests according to the positions they occupy in the structures they 'inherit' (in the class structure, in the social distribution of resources or in the educational system, for example). In short, when we talk about structural properties and their effects from a realist perspective we accept that the results of past actions (often of those long dead) have effects in their own rights later on, as constraining or facilitating influences upon agents, which are not attributable or reducible to the practices of other contemporary agents. They are in no sense dependent upon contemporary agential 'instantiation', since their active dependence is past tense. In present time, the only question is what agents will do with their problematic heritage.

Social interaction is seen as being structurally conditioned but never as structurally determined (since agents possess their own irreducible emergent powers). On the one hand, the mediatory mechanism which transmits structural influences to human agents consists in the former moulding frustrating or rewarding contexts for different groups of agents, depending upon the social positions they occupy. In turn it is argued that these experiences of frustrations or benefits condition different situational interpretations and dissimilar action patterns: groups experiencing exigencies seek to eradicate them (thus pursuing structural change) and those experiencing rewards try to retain them (thus defending structural stability). Regularities of this kind, detectable in subsequent patterns of interaction, are reflections of these objective opportunity costs. Nonetheless their effect is only conditional: they force no one, but simply set a price on acting against one's self-declared interests and a premium on following them (consequently detectable regularities do not even approximate to constant conjunctures). On the other hand, since conditioning is not determinism, the middle element of the cycle also recognizes the promotive creativity of interest groups and incorporates their capacity for innovative responses in the face of contextual constraints. Equally, it accommodates the possibility of reflective self-sacrifice of inherited vested interests on the part of individuals or groups.

The *structural elaboration* which then ensues is interpreted as being a largely unintended consequence. The modification of previous structural properties and the introduction of new ones is the combined product of the different outcomes pursued simultaneously by various social groups. The unintended element largely results from group conflict and concession, which together mean that the consequential elaboration is often what no one sought or wanted; it is also what supplies the motivation to keep vested interest groups struggling on against one another to elaborate more optimal arrangements. (This reflects the realist assertion about the non-predictability of change in open systems.) The endpoint and the whole point of examining any particular cycle is that we will then have provided an analytical history of emergence of the problematic properties under investigation. At this stage, which is also the start of another cycle, the elaborated structure constitutes new conditional influences upon subsequent interaction, and the concepts and theories we employ to deal with this next cycle may well have to alter in order to cope with the transformation which our subject matter has undergone. Reconceptualization has to be transitive because transitivity is the nature of social reality. The transforming of theory is necessary to capture the radical and unpredictable reshaping of society which is referred to as morphogenesis (Buckley 1967; Archer 1995) – society has no inbuilt preferred state but is shaped and reshaped over time, assuming unpredictable forms.

All three lines in the diagram are in fact continuous. The task of the practical social theorist consists in breaking up the flows into intervals determined by the problem in hand. Given any problem and accompanying periodization, the projection of the three lines backwards and forwards would connect up with the anterior and posterior morphogenetic cycles. This represents the bedrock of an understanding of systemic properties, of structuring over time, which enables explanations of specific forms of structural elaboration to be advanced (or of morphostasis generating reproduction). It is of course up to practical social analysts to delineate the three phases in terms of their substantive interests (see Archer 1979).

## Conclusion

All that there is space to indicate here is that this generic non-conflationary approach can be applied equally at macro, meso or micro level; over large historical time tracts as well as small time intervals; and most important of all, is not confined to structural or cultural forms but can also be used to account for the (double) morphogenesis of agency itself – namely how agents transform themselves in the selfsame process of seeking to bring about social transformations. In short, such non-conflationary theorizing holds considerable promise for dealing with major social issues, past and present, but it is not an open sesame which can dispense with the need for considerable work of theoretical application from the substantive specialist.

This commitment to investigating why things are so and not otherwise, in the (past, present and future) development of societies, is predicated upon abandoning all traditional analogies – of society being like a mechanism, organism, simple cybernetic system, a language, or any other kind of system but itself. In the twentieth century, the 'linguistic turn' has substituted rhetorical persuasion for investigative work. Sociology can indeed catch its 'second wind', but this depends upon acknowledging that all such analogical shortcuts are misleading since they cannot capture the ontological uniqueness of society. The constitution of social reality can be expressed in the following riddle: what is it that depends on human intentionality but never conforms to human intentions? What is it that relies upon people's concepts but which they never fully know? What is it that depends upon action but never corresponds to the actions of even the most powerful? What is it that has no form without us, yet which forms us even as we seek its transformation? And what is it that never satisfies the precise designs of anyone yet because of this always motivates its attempted reconstitution?

The suggestion in this chapter is that the riddle can be solved ontologically in transcendental realism, that it has fostered a progressive explanatory methodology in the morphogenetic approach, and that this should indeed yield fruit in the form of practical social theorizing which addresses the range of substantive areas in sociology – on a non-conflationary basis in the next millennium.

# 6 | The reality of social domains: implications for theory and method

**Derek Layder**

My primary aim in this chapter is to delineate in a broad sense the nature of social-scientific concepts as they relate to the social world which they attempt to depict. In so doing it will be necessary to say something about the explanatory forms that are implied by this analysis and this in turn involves some discussion of the role of reasons and causes in the explanation of social phenomena. This will occupy the bulk of the discussion even though the analysis must be regarded as necessarily brief and preliminary in nature. The final section will attempt to spell out some of the methodological implications of this position for social research.

The basic starting point for this analysis is the premise that the social world is variegated and stratified. This insists that social reality should not and cannot be understood as a unitary whole which is susceptible only to one kind of explanatory principle, theoretical assumption, or methodological approach. Such a starting point runs counter to a number of approaches – many of which compete with each other for explanatory prominence – and which insist that the social world is constituted by a unimodal ontology. Such alternative positions come in various guises: for example in the claim that the social world is exclusively about doing and being (and thus is primarily concerned with actor's reasons and motives) or that that social life is entirely discursive in nature. Other variants suggest that 'local practices', 'intersubjective relations', 'relational figurations' or 'social systems' are in themselves exhaustive ontological characterizations of the social world.

The eclectic and synthetic position which I adopt suggests that taken singly these characterizations of social reality are, at best, partial and thus eventuate in a misleadingly constricted view of the nature of the social world – and of the theoretical and methodological means of studying it. Such one dimensional approaches should be abandoned because they fail to provide a fully comprehensive coverage of the diversity and complexity of the social world. Rather, as I have indicated, the social world must be understood as ontologically multidimensional and as constituted by a number of domains which are interrelated in a complex manner. This ontological differentiation must be conceived in conjunction with an epistemological pluralism which is able to embrace, and incorporate the multifaceted nature of social reality within its explanatory terms of reference. Let me elaborate on some of the implications of these general points before commenting in detail on the nature of social scientific concepts.

## The nature of social science

Conceptual appropriations of the social world must attend to the way that world is – its form and nature – the sort of reality it is. In this sense we need to know the kind of social scientific viewpoint that has to be adopted in order to appreciate the variegated nature of the social world. In this respect it is important not to indulge in a wholesale rejection of objectivism or naturalism as do most humanist positions. That is, it is unwise to simply reject the idea that the social world is in any respect like the natural world since this simply precludes the possibility of perceiving any overlaps and similarities that may exist between the natural and social worlds, while at the same time appreciating that there are profound differences between them. The social world is unlike the natural world in the sense that much of the subject matter of the social world consists of intentional human beings who act as agents on that world and confer meaning on it. However, the social world is analogous to the natural world in the sense that it possesses objective features (in parallel with its subjective ones).

It is this sense of externality and objectivity which is lost to analysis in those approaches which centralize meaning, doing and being and intersubjectivity as the exclusive media of social reality. Conversely those traditional positivist positions which (over)emphasize the continuities between the natural and social sciences focus on the external world of social facts including objective and systemic features and thereby lose sight of subjective meaning, and so on. Both these positions are profoundly inadequate in so far as they do not work to fashion a connection between subjective and objective aspects of the social world, they simply serve to perpetuate a sterile debate and reinforce a false gap between the respective 'all-or-nothing' positions. While I do not in any sense want to deny the importance of the humanist ontology (intersubjectivity and so on), it is even more important not to lose sight of the objective moments of society in the clamour to vilify positivism.

It is quite wrong and insufficient to suppose that because human subjectivity is important that therefore any notion of objectivism and the 'externality' of social reality are illicit reifications. It is also wrong to suggest that any form of objectivism is bound up with a 'false dualism' in which subjective and objective aspects are thought to be opposed and unconnected. As I have already said we do not want to perpetuate a false separation and therefore it is important to understand that I am proposing a subjective–objective duality – not a disconnected dualism – when I refer to objective and external aspects of social life. The notion of a duality here refers to two continuously interrelated aspects of social life. First, it indicates that society exists simultaneously both inside and outside individuals in the sense that while individuals deeply internalize the social world in order to become social beings, society is, of necessity, a system of reproduced social relations which stretches beyond the power and influence of specific individuals and groups and so on. The manner in which the canopy of social life includes at the same time as it reaches beyond the domain of intersubjectivity requires that some sense of the objectivity and externality of social phenomena be registered in our theories and methods. (See Layder (1997) for a discussion of 'moderate objectivism' and also Popper's (1972) notion of a 'Third World' of objective knowledge – including culture, language and institutions.)

The second aspect of the duality between objectivism and subjectivism concerns the interconnections between aspects of agency and structure (or system) which are variously but continuously fashioned in over time and space. These represent the sites at which different ontological domains and temporal modalities of the social intersect and mutually influence one another. On the one hand, forms of agency represent the transformative capacities of individuals and groups as they come to terms with and alter the social circumstances they encounter in their everyday lives. On the other hand, systemic or structural aspects represent the historically formed standing conditions transmitted and inherited from the past (see Marx and Engels 1968: 96) which confront people as constraints and (enablements). The intersection of these two domains signifies a melding of very different time frames: that of the unfolding of situated activity – and the grand sweep of history as it manifests itself in the emergent institutional forms of whole societies. In this sense there is a convergence and continuous dialectic between objective, intersubjective and subjective facets of social life.

## Ontological domains and epistemological space

As I have just indicated the basic duality between subjective and objective facets of social life generates two broad domains of social life which need to be registered. However, what I have been referring to as the subjective domain, can in fact be divided into two distinct subdomains: the intersubjective domain and the individual–subjective domain (or the 'psychobiographical domain': Layder 1997). The intersubjective domain represents an intermediary domain which mediates between objective and subjective aspects (in other words the continuous middle ground of interrelations between agency and structure). Overall then there are three distinct ontological domains that need recognition in relation to the sorts of concepts we use. (Elsewhere – Layder 1997 – I distinguish four social domains by subdividing the 'objective' side of the duality into 'social settings' and 'contextual resources'. However, for present purposes my main arguments are served by treating both areas as aspects of social systems.)

In saying that these are distinct ontological domains, I am elaborating on and extending what Archer (1995) calls 'analytic dualism' – while retaining the idea of a basic distinction between agency and structure (system). I am suggesting that the social world possesses a varying array of characteristics and properties which cluster at various points or sites in the social order and represent different dimensions of social reality. At the same time there is no implication that the differing domains are separate and opposed and thus in analytic competition with each other (as implied in the critique of dualism); rather they are parallel features of social reality which bear complementary relations. Thus although not separated from each other the domains are different in both analytic and real senses. That is they are real (not virtual) aspects of social life as well as useful analytic categories which can be employed in social research. However, while distinct in their own right, the domains also overlap, interpenetrate and diffusely influence each other. This characterization of the relations between the domains connects with what Archer (1995) terms 'emergentism' and which calls attention to the fact that different aspects or dimensions of social reality have their own 'emergent' properties. Thus emergentism indicates that particular domains are endowed with specific properties or characteristics allowing them to be distinguished from others. It is in this sense that they are different but connected features of social reality.

Another consequence of emergentism and the acknowledgement of the existence of a multidimensional social reality concerns the epistemological problem of the kind of framework that is appropriate and adequate to the task of explanation. The most important consideration in this respect is the idea of the non-reducibility of levels of explanation with respect to the different domains. This means that with regard to the tripartite ontology (subjective – intersubjective – objective) it is important that each domain is accounted for in its own right and is not understood as the effect or influence of some other level. Thus objective-systemic aspects cannot be thought to be the result of the aggregation of micro episodes nor can intersubjective properties be viewed simply as an effect or reflection of allegedly more important and far reaching objective (systemic or macro social) phenomena. Each domain has to be conceptualized as possessing its own internally distinct properties and effects and should not be understood as residues or epiphenomena of other domains. Only when this point in the analysis has been reached is it then possible to begin to impute causal or acausal effects (ones of mere influence or affinity) in terms of the relationships between the domains.

The question of exactly how they relate to each other is complex but it suffices to say at this juncture that this is not simply a 'theoretical' problem; in my view the domains also relate to each other variably according to different empirical cirumstances (Layder 1993; 1997). The important point is that their independent effects and properties must not be lost to analysis by any form of explanatory reduction. This is a problem that besets many of the principal schools of thought and theoretical frameworks. For instance by prioritizing the lived experience of social actors, interactionism and phenomenology tend to confine (and thus reduce) social reality to the domain of intersubjectivity thereby occluding objective aspects of society (systemic phenomena like markets and bureaucracies) and also treating individual psychobiographies as mere epiphenomena of the intersubjective world. Conversely structural, functional and systems theories typically view interaction and subjectivity as residues or effects of macro phenomena.

The position is slightly different for those other schools of thought which attempt to occupy a synthetic middle ground (such as structuration theory, Foucauldian analysis, poststructuralism and postmodernism) since they manage to do so only by conflating the properties and effects of different domains. The result of this is to lose hold of any of the distinctive features and formative effects of specific domains by treating them as a diffuse amalgam. In this manner 'underground' forms of reduction take place 'behind the scenes' so to speak: for example, structuration theory rejects all forms of objectivism outright and thus favours intersubjectivity, while Foucault rejects individualism and intersubjectivity in favour of objective discourses and practices. It is important not to entertain these forms of conflation (see Chapter 5) since they divert attention away from important aspects of social reality, confuse the effects of different domains and at best they can only offer partial and inadequate explanatory schemas.

Thus instead of offering a differentiated ontology which adequately captures the multifaceted nature of social reality these approaches opt for oversimplified one dimensional versions. As a result the epistemological infrastructures of these approaches reflect their unitary ontological basis by clinging to and insisting upon some narrow explanatory underpinning. Examples of such would be that all social scientific statements must have a hermeneutic character, or must make reference to the socially constructed rule structure from which people fashion reasons and motives that allow them to operate in certain social milieux or to make social encounters happen. Conversely to take the classical positivist (or macro sociological) viewpoint requires analysts to divest themselves of any subjective engagement with the subject matter of their investigations.

Instead of a narrow and partial epistemological approach which is blind (and thus indifferent) to integral aspects of the social world we need to endorse an epistemological pluralism which is sufficiently flexible to accommodate the nuanced character of social reality. Pluralism here indicates an explanatory openness, flexibility and adaptability in the face of the heterogeneity of social reality. In short it points to an epistemological capacity and readiness to represent (and adequately 'fit') the multifaceted nature of the social world. However this notion of epistemological pluralism must not be misunderstood as a relativistic anarchism in which 'anything goes' (Feyerabend 1978). Such a viewpoint would overlook the disciplined and limited character of the pluralism advocated here. Pluralism in this latter sense refers to a general epistemological approach which can throw light on the internal operation of, and external relations between social domains – a plural ontology whose shape and contours are, to some extent already 'known'. What counts therefore is not an *ad hoc* and arbitrary set of interventions and/or explanatory schemas, rather, what is required is the ability to systematically service the needs of an ontology of distinct but interconnected domains.

There are many implications of this kind of pluralism with regard to the kinds of concepts and explanatory resources required for social scientific analysis some of which I shall explore in more detail later. In particular this includes both the ability to refer to and underwrite aspects of lived experience as well as to represent relatively impersonal social forces which are only *indirectly* related to human consciousness and lived experience – in short to depict both intersubjective and systemic aspects of social reality. Thus elements of humanist/phenomenological and objectivist epistemology need to be welded together in such a way as to connect these domains of social reality. In order to do this properly it is necessary to plumb the depths of epistemological discourse to enjoin and engage with the debate between empiricism and rationalism.

As I have pointed out elsewhere (Layder 1990) there is a need to avoid the extremes of these theories of knowledge since they both have debilitating consequences for the possibilities of our knowledge of the social. Thus some versions of empiricism which are deeply wedded to correspondence theories of truth unhelpfully restrict the parameters of knowledge to that which is available to experience and sensory data in general. As consequence they place rational forms of argument and discourse – including theories and theoretical models informed by them – out of bounds as legitimate arenas of social explanation. Conversely, some strains of rationalism, particularly those associated with strict coherence theories of truth, place in jeopardy the whole enterprise of empirical social research by denying the notion of an empirical world relatively independent of discourse about it. Clearly both options are deeply flawed in that they ignore whole tracts of the social universe and thus offer adulterated representations of, and thus knowledge about social reality.

Also the idea that the unique human being in a certain sense can, and routinely does, stand apart from the play of social forces (including reproduced discourses and social practices) must be built into the overall scenario. This is because although it is often convenient and plausible to treat the individual as if she or he were simply part of the continuous flow of interactional traffic that constitutes the main business of social life, as a rounded or comprehensive picture of psychobiography and individual (social) agency it falls far short of the mark. Perhaps the clearest, most subtle (and therefore most acceptable) example of this 'cramping' of psychology to suit the sociological study 'of conversation, track-meets, banquets, jury trials and street loitering' is portrayed by Goffman (1967). However Goffman's insistence 'that the proper study of interaction is not the individual and his psychology, but rather the syntactical relations among different acts of persons mutually present to one another' (Goffman 1967: 2) needs to be considerably amended if we are indeed to do justice to individual psychology and the unique psychobiographical careers that are conjoined with them.

But at least Goffman was intimately aware of the subtleties of face-to-face encounters and the vicissitudes of the interaction order which informs it. Not the least of these are the interrelations between self-identity, meaning and the moral implications of co-presence. Other social constructionist positions are much less subtle than Goffman here when it comes to recognizing the delicate interlacing between self-identity and other aspects of subjectivity. Poststructuralists and postmodernists alike simply do not recognize either the interaction order or the nature and consequences of individual social agency as they are implicated in the notion of psychobiography. Instead they tend to view human subjects and their subjectivity as if they were simply nodal points at the intersection of the array of available discursive influences. Now while it is undeniable that discursive practices play some considerable role in forming individual subjectivities, they can be nothing more than contextual and generalized in their effects. Crucial mediating aspects of situated activity and individual psychobiography are simply obscured and denied by insisting on a direct, determinative role for discourse. Such crude behaviouristic models of the person and social being must be replaced in any schema that hopes to do justice to the subtlety of social behaviour and the complexity of the social world. The epistemological problems that arise from understanding the link between psychological and social worlds have to be rethought in the context of a pluralistic approach which also endorses the notion of emergence and a differentiated ontology of domains.

## The nature of social scientific concepts

It follows from what has been said that the concepts of social analysis must be attentive to the ontological and epistemological issues already raised.

That is in some sense they must reflect a plurality of domains and explanatory premises without lapsing into an unprincipled eclecticism. But this does not imply that such concepts are wholly determined by these prior considerations; it simply means that they must underpin concepts in a general sense. In terms of the development and discovery of concepts and theoretical ideas through the process of empirical research we must adopt a position which allows for their construction via the confrontation between theorizing and empirical evidence. Nevertheless, it is absolutely essential that the background presuppositions concerning the properties of social domains is incorporated as a constant accompaniment to the development and refinement of theory and knowledge, since otherwise they will be subject to the flaws and omissions already considered.

In this section I want to discuss some of these issues by introducing a preliminary classification of social scientific concepts which corresponds to the distinctions I have made in previous sections. This entails making various claims about the object references of concepts – the sorts of phenomena to which they refer and making distinctions among them. Before embarking on this task let me make it clear that by so doing I am not claiming that these distinctions are pure and clean cut. The main concern is with the relative weighting of referential foci in relation to the nature of the objects to which they are attached. That is to say that both the concepts themselves and the phenomena to which they refer contain varying 'mixtures' or combinations of the different characteristics which distinguish them from others. The point of classification is to concentrate attention on the relative weighting of these combinations in order to highlight their consequences for our understanding of various aspects of social life.

This point is especially important in relation to one of the overarching considerations and thematics connected with the sort of schema presented here. This concerns the agency structure (or system) distinction in social analysis. Giddens has forcefully argued that these two facets of social life (represented respectively by interpretative and institutional schools of analysis in sociology) are mutually implicated in each other and should not be conceived of as separately constituted or as standing in some opposed or antagonistic relation. Now I am entirely in agreement that both action and structural (or system) elements must be understood as directly implicated in each other. But it is the nature of this implication and the consequences that flow for social analysis that gives cause for disagreement because in Giddens's schema action and structure are replaced by the 'duality of structure' and this has the effect of dissolving the formerly distinct domains into one another and thereby obscuring their different forms and effects.

As I stressed before, this will not do if we are to retain hold on the ontological distinctions that are an intrinsic and pivotal feature of social reality. Thus although I would want to stress that action and structural or system elements are always implicated in each other this does not mean that the ontological features which they subsume are simply collapsed together into a diffuse duality of structure. This is contrary to Giddens's position since he is clear that structuration theory does not recognize the partial independence of the interaction order as a domain with its own features, characteristics and effects (Giddens 1987). Neither does he recognize the partly independent, asocial and anti-social effects of individual psychobiography. In this respect his schema conflates all three domains (intersubjective, institutional and psychological) into a synthetic but falsely unified and undifferentiated amalgam. By contrast if we understand the domains to be implicated in each other in the sense of interacting, comingling, overlapping while retaining their integrity as relatively autonomous ontological features then this comes close to the kind of model I have in mind.

The upshot of this is that while I want to distinguish between what I term behavioural (or action) concepts and systemic (social-structural) concepts, I want to say that they are never entirely 'free' or separable from each other and consequently they always bear each other's imprint. This means that while it is possible to distinguish behavioural concepts from systemic concepts this is primarily a matter of weighting since systemic phenomena provide the contextual environment of social behaviour and thus both elements of social reality always impress themselves upon each other to a greater or lesser degree. While systemic concepts deal with and point to relatively impersonal phenomena – at some remove from particular instances of co-present activity – they are also related to these phenomena in that they are continually reproduced by virtue of the activity and behaviour of those people who are subject to their influence. Thus the distinction between these concepts is primarily a matter of emphasis.

## Behavioural concepts

For the purposes of this discussion and because of the limited space at my disposal I am grouping together what I have otherwise referred to as the psychobiographical and intersubjective domains and treating them both as the source of behavioural concepts. This is because generically behavioural concepts directly pinpoint some aspect of a person or people's 'behaviour' or their psychological predispositions or attitudes. In addition they typically include some reference to an individual's self-identity or the quality and meaning of the relationships and the social environment in which they are embedded. Thus this type of concept covers a broad range of phenomena. By grouping psychobiographical and intersubjective phenomena together it is undoubtedly true that the differences between them are rather lost but my main purpose here is to focus on the larger contrast between behavioural and systemic concepts and phenomena.

Nonetheless it is important to bear in mind that although the psychobiographical and intersubjective types overlap considerably they are not interchangeable. In this respect the primary focus of psychobiographical concepts is on the individual's involvements with social arrangements and settings (as reflected for example in the concept of 'subjective career': Stebbins 1970) whereas the intersubjective types tend to focus on the quality and nature of the interactional resources that are at the disposal of various groups, such as the identification of different types of vocabularies (skills, fatalism and routinization) used by members of the Royal Ulster Constabulary (RUC) for dealing with threatening situations (Brewer 1990). Of course some concepts straddle the two such as concepts describing participants, such as types of women prisoners (Giallombardo 1966).

In principle these concepts may be member defined or observer defined but in all cases they must conform in some way with the notion of 'subjective adequacy' which Bruyn (1966) believes marks out the validity and adequacy of *all* concepts associated with social analysis. Leaving aside this latter highly contentious claim, 'subjective adequacy' involves a number of factors including the soundness of the methodological procedures of the research which inform these concepts and the extent to which the researcher is familiar with the language of the people who are being studied. Glaser and Strauss (1967) also insist that concepts should 'fit' and be relevant to the people to whom they are meant to apply indicating that they should directly represent their experiences, behaviour and meaningful worlds.

However, my position here is very different from Bruyn, Glaser and Strauss and others (such as Rock or Becker: in Rock 1979) in that while I agree that subjective adequacy is a necessary hallmark of behavioural concepts, this does not and should not apply across the board to all social scientific concepts.This is where an epistemological (and ontological) pluralism makes a crucial difference in approach. Those who insist on criteria of subjective adequacy as the sole arbiters of the validity of concepts are locked into a view of social reality as 'all of a piece' and this has the effect of limiting the applicability and scope of their analyses. In particular their commitment to an exclusively interpretivist (humanist or phenomenological) conception of the nature of social analysis prevents them from tracing the much more inclusive interconnections between agency and structure. In order to map such pivotal aspects of social reality it is necessary for social analysts and researchers to draw upon both systemic concepts as well as those that represent 'bridges' or ligatures between behavioural and systemic phenomena.

The broadly realist position I am advocating insists that social reality is not simply composed of people's meanings, experiences and subjective understandings, but that it is in large part constituted by systemic features that are relatively impersonal, inert and which represent the standing conditions confronting people in their everyday lives – and representing what Marx and Engels describe as circumstances transmitted and inherited from the past. Behavioural and systemic phenomena (such as bureaucracies and markets), as I have already indicated are deeply intertwined with one another. On the one hand, the continued existence of systemic factors depends upon the routine reproductive activities of social actors, while on the other behavioural phenomena and subjective experience are strongly influenced and shaped by the systemic factors which compose the social environment. The position I want to press for here assumes that social analysis and research should therefore attempt to trace the modes in which both subjective and objective factors interpenetrate and mutually influence each other.

Thus on these grounds all social science or analytic concepts imply and contain references to both behavioural (agency) and systems aspects of social life but differ in terms of their relative emphasis on one or the other types of phenomena. Behavioural concepts concentrate their referential focus on depicting (inter) subjective meaning and behavioural worlds while systemic concepts tend to concentrate on the contextual conditions of social behaviour (organizational, cultural, distributive factors on a society-wide basis). Thus while subjective adequacy is a necessary and perhaps 'primary' arbiter of the validity of behavioural concepts, other criteria are more relevant to systemic concepts. I say 'primary' here because again it is a matter of degree or weighting of emphasis. Just as systemic concepts are connected at some level to the behaviour of people, so too behavioural concepts are always touched (even if only in a minimal way) by the impress of systemic phenomena.

In this respect there must always be some sort of convergence with the more formal analytic criteria relating to the validity of systemic (and 'bridging') concepts. This means that the truth content and validity of such concepts is never completely determined by fit between the concept and the subjective experience of those to whom it refers. Thus although a behavioural concept may closely mirror or faithfully depict the intersubjective world as it is expressed by particular people (say an oppressed or exploited group) this version of the truth may be flatly contradicted by even the most cursory examination of the social conditions of this group made by an external observer (Habermas 1984; 1987). Although of necessity behavioural concepts will accord primacy to criteria of subjective adequacy, the overall validity of the concept must be judged by its ability to fashion a concordance between subjective and objective adequacy.

## Systemic or social-structural concepts

Bearing in mind the qualifications in relation to questions of degree and relativity mentioned above it is possible to say that systemic concepts can be defined negatively as non-behavioural concepts which depict relatively impersonal and inert features of social organization (both the immediate settings of interaction and the wider contextual resources – cultural, material and dominative: see Layder 1997). Specifically they refer to the historically reproduced social relations, practices and powers which stand as the already formed social circumstances that confront people in their everyday lives but which have a relative independence from the activities they undoubtedly influence. In this sense although they represent a 'depth' ontology (partly composed of relatively inert social mechanisms) they are also intrinsically involved in ongoing, social processes of change at several different levels through the transformative activities of people (see Layder 1993).

Although, as I have stressed, the link between systemic phenomena and the reproductive activities of people, their reproduced nature and thus their historically emergent character as prior conditions of ongoing activities also ensures their relative autonomy from particular instances of activity (although not activity in a general sense). This is a crucial factor in arbitrating the validity and adequacy of such concepts. The reproduced character of relations, powers and practices refers to the fact that they have been stretched through time and space away from the face-to-face activities which ultimately feed into their continuity and reproduction. On these grounds the validity of the concepts that denote such phenomena cannot be arbitrated by reference to the motives, reasons or intersubjective (lived) experiences of people. Instead they have to be understood as part of the contextual conditions which form the wider social environment. This view is completely at odds with those principles enshrined in structuration theory, interactionism, phenomenology and grounded theory which either deny the existence or suppress the importance of these aspects of social life.

An essential component of systemic elements (and thus of the concepts which denote them) is their inherent tie with relations of power, control and domination. In so far as all reproduced social relations are embedded in the settings and contexts of social activity they are also interwoven with the powers and practices which underpin them in various ways and thereby allow for a variety of modes of power and power relationship. Habermas (1984; 1987) has underlined the power dimension of system phenomena in drawing attention to markets and bureaucracy as principal systemic foci. Also the work of many scholars has unearthed a plethora of system concepts associated with these areas. For example Etzioni (1961) distinguishes between 'normative', 'coercive' and 'remunerative' types of power in organizations, while Foucault (1970; 1980) distinguishes between 'sovereign', 'disciplinary' and 'bio-power' (although it is not clear whether he would have agreed with the label 'systemic' to decribe these concepts and the phenomena to which they refer).

The primary reference point of these concepts is not social behaviour in itself (although it is indirectly related) but rather the reproduced relations and powers that underpin them that form the settings and context in which social activity is enacted. Epistemologically therefore it follows that criteria of subjective adequacy play a very subordinate role as arbiters of the validity of such concepts. Other criteria of validity and adequacy are far more important. These include the logical and rational connections between a particular concept and other systemic concepts (or even clusterings of them), or the ability to derive or deduce empirical propositions from them (see Merton 1967), concerning say the behaviour of people or the functioning of labour markets or bureaucratic organizations. Validity and adequacy are therefore sought within connected chains of reasoning as the analyst seeks to place the empirical phenomenon in a wider, more generalized and abstract context of ideas and research. In this sense systemic concepts are primarily observer defined because they require more precise, consistent and technical definitions which are typically not available in lay or colloquial usage (this is so even where the colloquial and technical terms are formally the same – as in the concept of 'bureaucracy').

Finally in that the validity or otherwise of systemic concepts has far more to do with the criteria and issues just outlined, then it follows that criteria of 'relevance', 'fit' and 'understandability' to participants becomes less and less important. The question of whether systemic concepts make subjective sense to participants or whether they believe such entities to be real or not is of little moment in deciding upon their validity and usefulness since they do not purport to represent or characterize these aspects of social life. Systemic concepts focus on the social organizational context that surrounds particular arenas or pockets of situated activity and although it has implications for social behaviour it must not be confused with an attempt to depict social behaviour itself.

For instance the usefulness or otherwise of concepts such as 'coercive power' or 'disciplinary regimes of power' is not dependent upon whether people working or held within such organizations recognize or believe that these concepts refer to their lived experience. Rather the utility, validity and adequacy of systemic concepts revolve around their connectedness with other related concepts and their capacity to explain or throw light on the particular areas of social life to which they refer. In this sense it is unwise to adopt a wholesale policy which suggests that the only valid concepts in social analysis are those which conform rigorously to criteria of subjective adequacy – as several phenomenologically oriented writers have suggested. Of course it goes almost without saying that to pursue such a course would be to limit social analysis in a wholly arbitrary manner by precluding vast areas of social life from the purview of legitimate social inquiry.

## Implications for methodology and research strategy

The foregoing discussion has been primarily concerned with specifying what I take to be some of the most important features of a social ontology which recognizes the variegated nature of social life and social reality. This is a view which strongly resists the idea that social reality can be reduced to some basic unifying 'domain' or principle which then functions as the most important and fundamental explanatory bedrock. Such exclusive and exclusionary strategies can be seen in the call to adopt various versions of reductionism in social analysis. The two most common of these are, first, the idea of reducing what are variously termed system, structural or macro analyses to aggregates of small scale patterns of social life. The second is the assimilation (and hence reduction) of micro-events to macro phenomena whereby the micro-events are then understood as epiphenomenal. Both these strategies are profoundly insufficient since they subserve a reductionist agenda which can offer only a partial, simplifed and misleading model of social ontology.

These reductionist strategies miss out on the opportunity to bring both interpretative and institutional forms of analysis together and thus they perpetuate what Giddens (1984) calls the 'phoney war' between them. However the analysis I have presented here is also wary of many of those attempts to transcend dualism in social analysis which opt for a synthetic unity or principle which purports to present a more comprehensive and synthetic approach. Social theory and analysis is replete with these sorts of devices which compete with each other for explanatory pre-eminence and which are also more often than not, mutually exclusive. Examples of these concepts or devices are 'social practices' (combined with the 'duality of structure' as in Giddens's (1984), or with the 'social habitus' in Bourdieu (1977) or 'discourse and power' (Foucault 1980) or 'figurations' (Elias 1978)). Although some examples of this kind of approach are more likely to formally acknowledge the existence of different social domains their practical effect is to compact, dissolve or conflate them and thus to fail to account for their distinct and partly autonomous effects.

The main methodological implication that follows from the kind of differentiated ontology that I present here is that social analysis and research cannot afford to concentrate exclusively on one aspect of social reality or methodological framework. A multidimensional approach which grasps the variegated nature of social reality and the necessity for a plural epistemological basis is the only viable approach for the job at hand. I have stressed that it is absolutely essential to regard the domains as both different, but connected, aspects of social reality. Methodologically, therefore, it is necessary to find ways of weaving them together while preserving their integrity as distinct, but relatively autonomous, from each other. One thematic possibility which could inform analysis in this regard is the idea of tracing the continuous but variable interrelatedness of agency and structure (although I think Habermas's distinction between 'lifeworld' and 'system' is a better characterization of these aspects of social life) as it manifests itself in the topic or area of investigation.

Let me unpack some of the implications of this by comparing it with, and examining it against the background of what Giddens (1984) calls 'methodological bracketing'. Giddens developed this idea in the context of the wider framework of structuration theory and offered it as the solution to what he took to be some of the problems faced by the theory when applied to practical matters of social research. One of the central axioms of the theory concerns what Giddens terms the 'duality of structure' and this points to the deep mutual implication of agency and structure in social life. In Giddens's terms structures are both medium and outcome of social activities and in this sense they reflect the dual nature of social practices. Importantly for Giddens this is a duality – a unity with a dual nature – not a dualism, which implies separation and lack of connection between agency and structure. As I have already said the attempt to join what I would prefer to call lifeworld and system aspects of social life is laudable, although I think the the idea of collapsing them into a unity (albeit with a dual nature) is misplaced and actually hinders the attempt to trace the connections between these fundamental elements of social life.

However, Giddens's schema is doubly disadvantaged in this respect because in trying to overcome the practical problems posed by the duality of the structure principle, he adopts the notion of methodological bracketing. This has the paradoxical effect of enforcing an artificial separation between lifeworld and system elements and this, of course, is an outcome which is directly counter to the explicit objectives of struturation theory. Thus Giddens suggests that it is often not practically feasible to concentrate analytic attention on both the analysis of 'strategic conduct' at the same time as engaging in 'institutional analysis'. As a way around this dilemma Giddens proposes that the researcher brackets off one side of the equation in order to concentrate on the other, although he recognizes that the dividing line between them is not clear cut and that in principle each 'has to be rounded out by a concentration on the duality of structure' (Giddens 1984: 288). This, to me, is a very unsatisfactory methodological solution which seems to undercut the intention of bringing the continuous and 'inseparable' interrelation between agency and structure directly into social analysis and research. This unhelpful move has as much, if not more, to do with the inherent weaknesses in structuration theory as it has to do with problems of a practical or methodological nature.

In this respect the crux of the problem concerns the manner in which the duality of structure poses insuperable problems for both the analytic and methodological grasp of the important features of social reality. Through the concept of the duality of structure Giddens proposes a diffuse amalgam of both agency and structure which prevents the analyst from understanding the separate or relative contributions of either in particular circumstances. Thus the analyst is unable to properly separate out institutional analysis from that of strategic conduct since the dissolution of the elements of agency and structure into a unified 'duality of structure' means that they no longer have any recognizably distinct characteristics or properties. Of course this is not very satisfactory from a social research point of view and thus the 'methodological bracketing' caveat is adopted in order to generate conventionally recognizable research results. Unfortunately by adopting this principle Giddens reconstitutes the very dualism between agency and structure (strategic conduct versus institutional analysis) that structuration theory is designed to avoid. Thus for particular research purposes the analysis of either strategic conduct or institutional analysis are assumed to be 'methodologically given' and thus by implication they are treated as analytically separable aspects of social reality.

By adopting the alternative ontological and epistemological vision that I have outlined in earlier sections, I think it is possible to find ways of coming to terms with the problem of the unwitting reaffirmation of a dualism in which lifeworld and system elements are treated methodologically as if they were separate and independently given aspects of the social world. First of all, we have to recognize the need to decompose lifeworld and system elements (agency and structure) into important subdomains. In this chapter I have distinguished (but only in a very sketchy manner) between psychobiography and situated activity which represent different aspects of agency or the lifeworld. Similarly a full and proper treatment of these issues would require that system elements be also subdivided into social settings and contextual resources (see Layder 1997). Since these ontological features and distinctions are defined in terms of, and pinpoint particular phases or modalities of agency and structure (or lifeworld and system) elements, it is then possible to envisage forms of multistrategy research which are able to target empirical data and identify them as relevant to particular domain characteristics.

The above has the clear advantage that empirical data are understood as implicated in lifeworld and system characteristics at different and empirically discernible levels of social reality. As a result, the contributions of their different aspects and modalities may be more easily registered in methodological strategies. It also encourages the idea of pursuing as many different analytic angles and making as many methodological 'cuts' into the data as possible and feasible at any one time – including qualitative and quantitative forms of analysis – since this provides a denser empirical coverage of the domains and their interpenetrations (Layder 1993). Of course it is also recognized that maximum coverage in this respect is not always possible and thus it is sometimes necessary to engage in 'selective methodological focusing' whereby the researcher tends to concentrate on empirical data which reflect only one or two domains rather than a comprehensive coverage.

This is simply a matter of focus and emphasis since it must always be assumed that all the domains are interdependent and mutually influential. By understanding the social domains as distinct but interconnected facets of social reality the analyst is shunted away from the idea that any of the domains can be treated as methodologically given. Rather, in the light of the ontological model she or he is thereby encouraged to think of them as representing different levels and modalities in terms of which the different aspects of lifeworld and system intersect and influence each other. Thus analytic attention is trained on the continuous interweaving of these facets of social reality. Most importantly such analyses have to be understood against the background assumption of the variegated or multifaceted nature of social reality rather than one which is assumed to be 'all of a piece' – as falsely unified and unimodal. In turn, the acknowledgement of a variegated (stratified) ontology demands an open (rather than a prematurely closed) attitude of epistemological pluralism. This indicates the multifaceted nature of social reality, rather than an 'anything goes' epistemological anarchism, or unthinking eclecticism.

# 7 | Relationism, cubism, and reality: beyond relativism

John Scott

Recent interest in postmodernist theories has renewed the drift towards relativism in social theory. The positivist orthodoxy, of course, only really held sway in a particular corner of the philosophy of science. It has, however, long been in retreat. The challenge to Popper's (1959) sophisticated empiricism – he described his own position as a 'realist' one – from such writers as Kuhn (1962) and then Feyerabend (1978) was received with much enthusiasm within sociology, not least because they wrote from a background within natural scientific empiricism itself. As sociology expanded as a discipline in the 1960s and 1970s, there was a growing enthusiasm and willingness to recognize diversity in theoretical positions. Friedrich's famous book *A Sociology of Sociology* (1970) became a manifesto for plurality, and a climate of, in Cole Porter's words, 'anything goes' began to establish itself. All knowledge was held to be relative to particular theoretical standpoints. The choice between standpoints was seen as a matter of interests and values, not a matter of objectivity. In and around these claims there have arisen philosophical defences of relativism that have echoed earlier traditions of thought. Rorty (1980), for example, has returned to the pragmatist works of James and Dewey (not, unfortunately, to the rather different ideas of Peirce) to defend the idea that while some kind of progress or advance in knowledge might be possible, this can occur only within specific theoretical traditions. Gouldner, who had once invoked Weber in defence of an assertion of the need for value commitment in sociology (1962), recoiled at what he felt he had unleashed (Gouldner 1968). His belated defence of objectivity, however, seemed regressive and did little to stem the tide of relativism.

Debates within feminism have reinforced this same trajectory. The Enlightenment model of absolutist, objective science was rejected by feminist standpoint epistemologists (Hartsock 1983; see also Hartsock 1984) that were built around an explicit awareness of the grounded character of all human activity. Science, as a human activity, was inescapably gendered.

There could be no impartial or neutral standpoint, only gendered standpoints. Women's activities in the home and its domestic sphere involve them in experiences and concerns that differ radically from those of men and are the basis of their distinctive standpoint or perspective on the world in which we live. Feminist scholarship, then, had to stand opposed to the masculine scholarship of the scientific orthodoxy.

Feminist standpoint epistemology, however, embodied an ambiguity. While recognizing the relativity of standpoints, it sought to sustain the idea that one of these standpoints – the feminist one – was privileged. This is, of course, a familiar position. Lukács (1923) had recognized the need for a proletarian standpoint to challenge the bourgeois standpoint, while also asserting that the proletarian standpoint did, indeed, offer a properly scientific basis for understanding the world. In feminist standpoint epistemology, it is not the lived experiences of social classes but those of men and women that are the bases of their differing perspectives on the world. The successor science to the masculine, bourgeois science of the Enlightenment is not a proletarian science but a feminist science.

Postmodernist and poststructuralist arguments about the end of the grand narratives (Lyotard 1979) have reinforced the idea that 'objectivity', along with 'science', should be jettisoned into the dustbin of history. These arguments suggested, in a far more radical way than Kuhn had done, that the idea of 'progress' or 'growth' in scientific knowledge could no longer be sustained. In feminist writing, postmodernism destroyed not only the attempt to privilege a feminist standpoint but also the very idea that there could be a single feminist standpoint. 'Women', it was argued, did not form a universal, essential category. People are constituted as women (or as men) through specific social practices, and this occurs in the context of other social practices that constitute them as members of particular classes, ethnic groups, and so on. Women are divided by class and ethnicity and there are a variety of women's standpoints that can be adopted on the world, each of which is appropriate to the interests and concerns of a particular group (Stanley and Wise 1983; Harding 1986).

Relativism has not, of course, had everything its own way. One of the success stories of recent philosophical discussion has been the rise of a truly critical realism, inspired by the work of Harré (Harré 1970; Harré and Madden 1975) and Bhaskar (1975; 1979; 1993). This critical realism has gained a small, but significant following in sociology, but it has yet to dethrone the advocates of relativism. Like positivism, critical realism reaffirms the possibility of objectivity. Where empiricism held that this objectivity involved the adoption of an impartial standpoint, independent of all perspectives and valid for all observers, realism remained sceptical. Recognizing the 'intransitive' foundation of knowledge in real objects that exist outside of knowledge, the realists also recognized the 'transitive' dimension of shifting conceptual frameworks. This recognition has proved particularly problematic when realism is invoked in social science. Realism has a very poor account of the nature of a distinctively *social* reality, and this has made it difficult for it to establish its claims against those of relativism.

In this chapter, I will use the arguments of Max Weber and Karl Mannheim to provide some of the missing elements in a realist account of social science. Only if a proper account of the nature of social reality is built can the claims of realism be made effective in sociology. Weber's great essay on '"Objectivity" in social science and social policy' (Weber 1904) and Mannheim's reflections on this in *Ideology and Utopia* (Mannheim 1929; 1931) and other works from the mid-1920s to the mid-1930s comprise a powerful basis for future development. Mannheim sought explicitly to transcend the opposition between relativism and absolutism (see also Elias 1971; 1983). He took his central assumptions from Max Weber and explored the ways in which our knowledge of the social world is, itself, shaped by our social position. Mannheim points the way out of our current impasse.

## The Weberian starting point

The specific purpose behind Weber's great essay was to set out an editorial policy for the *Archiv für Sozialwissenschaft und Socialpolitik*. The broad outlines of this policy had been jointly agreed by Weber, Werner Sombart and Edgar Jaffé. In fact, Weber turned the article into a far more wide ranging set of reflections on the nature of knowledge in social science. Central to his argument was a concern to show that the 'value relevance' of social and historical knowledge did not mean that social scientists had to become mere purveyors of value judgements. All knowledge is, indeed, relative to the values of the investigator, but it can still embody 'objective', 'factual' statements about historical situations.

Weber sets out with a simple assertion of the logical distinction between the value judgements that form 'normative knowledge' and the factual statements that form 'existential knowledge'. Value judgements, Weber said, reflect 'warring gods', ultimate values that claim final authority but that can sustain no claim on grounds other than the faith or emotional commitment of their believers. Value judgements are, therefore, inherently pluralistic and contestable. Policy proposals and programmes of action derive from value judgements and so share their contestable status. They can never be justified in terms of the purely factual, existential knowledge that is produced by scientists. It is, Weber holds, axiomatic that 'it can never be the task of an empirical science to provide binding norms and ideals from which directives for immediate practical activity can be derived' (Weber 1904: 52). Scientists may, of course, contribute to the criticism of value judgements and policy proposals by showing what their consequences would be, by examining their logical consistency, or by suggesting alternative ways of achieving the policy goals. They cannot, however, pre-empt the actual making of policy decisions. All such decisions are acts of *will*. They involve weighing and choosing from among various possible value standpoints according to the decision makers' 'conscience' and 'personal view of the world' (Weber 1904: 53). All moral agents are, in principle, equal participants in decision making. The scientist has no more right to be considered or heard than does anyone else.

Weber concludes that policy preferences may be stated in a scientific journal, and they should not be suppressed. It must always be made clear, however, that they *are* value judgements and that they do not follow from a scientific analysis. Scientists need not be 'morally indifferent', but they must make it clear whenever they step beyond the realm of factual, empirical knowledge (see also Weber 1919: 20–1).

Having clarified this distinction between value judgements and factual knowledge, Weber went on to set out the nature of factual knowledge itself. His views echoed the neo-Kantian ideas of Windelband, Simmel and, above all, Rickert. His position starts out from the separation between the sphere of values, which Weber has already described, and the external reality that exists completely independently of the human mind. The question of knowledge is the question of how these two spheres are to be brought together. Kant held that there can be no 'presuppositionless' knowledge. We acquire our knowledge of the 'nuomenal' reality of 'things in themselves' only through the employment of categories and concepts that are intrinsic to our mind and so are not a part of that reality. For the neo-Kantians, these categories and concepts derived from values. Human beings acquire a knowledge of the world by relating it to their values. Our cognitive interest towards the world involves a value orientation through which we give a 'cultural significance' to reality. Something 'is significant because it reveals relationships which are important to us due to their connection with our values' (Weber 1904: 76) The objects that comprise our knowledge of the world are, therefore, 'value relevant'.

If this position is accepted, it merely pushes the fundamental question back one step. If factual knowledge is value relevant knowledge of an external reality, what is the nature of this reality itself? This question cannot, of course, be answered with any certainty. Because our knowledge of reality is always value related, we can say nothing about reality that is not, already, organized in terms of value relevant concepts. If the nuomenal reality is impossible to describe, however, it can be alluded to. That is, the features that it must necessarily have by virtue of its independence of values can, at least, be sketched out in relation to the way that it presents itself to us. This is the task that Weber set for himself. He characterizes this external reality as being devoid of any intrinsic meaning and, therefore, as being chaotic. The word that he uses most frequently is 'infinite'. This external reality – the 'world process' (Weber 1904: 81) – is variously termed an 'absolute infinitude', an 'infinite reality', an 'infinitely manifold stream of events' (Weber 1904: 72), and a 'vast chaotic stream of events' (1904: 111). It is, in short, an inexhaustibly chaotic source of experiences:

> Now, as soon as we attempt to reflect about the way in which life confronts us in immediate concrete situations, it presents an infinite multiplicity of successively and co-existently emerging and disappearing events, both 'within' and 'outside' ourselves.
>
> (Weber 1904: 72)

What Weber seems to be saying is that our experience – in so far as we can disentangle this from our concepts – is that of our own body and its physical environment as these are embedded in an 'infinite' flux of occurrences. Weber refused to speculate any further than this. Any further questions about reality, he held, could be raised only within a *scientific* frame of reference, and science, of course, is a cultural activity that grasps reality in and through value relevant concepts. It is not sensible to ask whether the findings of science properly reflect or correspond to the structure of reality. The validity of scientific knowledge is something that must be judged from within science itself.

Weber does make the point, however, that reality is not uniform. In their attempts to understand the external reality that they encounter, human beings create a secondary layer of reality. By relating the nuomenal reality to our values, we create cultural objects. Words, concepts, values and propositions together comprise the sphere of 'culture', a part of reality that is, in crucial respects, distinct from non-cultural reality. Culture, Weber says, is 'a finite segment of the meaningless infinity' (1904: 81). Human beings, in their attempts to make sense of their world, carve out discrete and bounded aspects of infinity and so give them form, meaning, and significance. This they do by employing concepts that are related to their values: 'Empirical reality becomes "culture" to us because and insofar as we relate it to value ideas' (Weber 1904: 76).

Human beings create 'culture' from the physical reality in which they live by giving meaning to physical events and processes in terms of their values. They also do this, however, by giving meaning to pre-existing *cultural* entities and processes. We never act in a cultural vacuum, creating our ideas from nothing. We are born into a world that has already been interpreted and signified by others, and in our own actions we contribute to the transformation of these inherited cultural forms. Human beings try to make sense of the 'infinity of discrete and diffuse human actions' (Weber 1904: 98) in which they find themselves by relating them together, or synthesizing them, in terms of particular value relevant conceptions: the state, the church, the entrepreneur, and so on. Weber developed this insight in his introduction to *Economy and Society* (Weber 1920). Social action and social relations, he held, involve the mutual interpenetration and imputation of meaning: each participant in a social relationship has to infer what the other participants intend to do. In so doing, they give solidity to the cultural representations on which they draw. The cultural forms under which they act come to seem every bit as real to them as the physical conditions of their actions. Cultural reality is itself multilayered. While physical reality might be said to be laterally infinite, cultural reality can be said to be both laterally and vertically infinite.[1] This additional dimension of 'infinity' is a result of the reverberating reflection and interpretation of cultural meanings in the mutual acts of interpretation that constitute social interaction.

Cultural reality is every bit as chaotic as the larger nuomenal reality of which it forms a part. There is a multiplicity of value standpoints from which cultural meanings can be constructed, and so there is no 'overall', absolute or 'objective' meaning for culture as a whole. While particular cultural items have meaning for those who construct them, the cultural sphere as a whole is the kaleidoscopic tessellation of these individually meaningful items – it has no pattern or purpose that can be grasped independently of the standpoints of the individual human beings who constitute it. The sciences of culture, therefore, must have a different character from the sciences of 'nature'. The natural sciences involve only first order concepts that aim to grasp an independent non-conceptual reality. The cultural sciences, on the other hand, must employ second order concepts that refer to a pre-existing conceptual reality. Each type of science stands in a different relationship to its object of study. The cultural scientist is involved in a cultural activity that aims at grasping culture itself. The cultural sciences are concerned with *understanding* a cultural reality, while the natural sciences are concerned with *explaining* a physical reality.

The understanding at which the cultural sciences aim is undertaken from a particular value relevant point of view. There is a specific 'focus of attention on reality under the guidance of values which lend it significance' (Weber 1904: 77). 'All knowledge of cultural reality . . . is always knowledge from particular points of view' (1904: 81, emphasis removed). From the particular point of view that is adopted, the cultural scientist constructs value relevant concepts that attempt to synthesize 'the unclear syntheses which are found in the minds of human beings' (1904: 98). For example, the social science concept of the state is an attempt to make sense of the idea of the state that is held by all of those who are involved in a particular political process that the scientist has identified as being significant for his or her values.

Weber's position seems to lead him to an extreme relativism. If he has successfully separated factual statements from value judgements, has he not delivered them into the chaotic plurality of value relevance? Weber did not think that this was the case. While there was, indeed, a relativity of standpoints, the very point of his paper was to establish the sense in which it was possible to talk about 'objectivity' in the social sciences. He explored this question, however, only in relation to the concerns of different social sciences. The various social sciences, he argued, differ in their 'cognitive interest', the particular point of view from which they select, analyse and organize an aspect of social reality in terms of its specific 'cultural significance' for them. Economic science, for example, identifies the material aspects of the struggle for existence as culturally significant and so defines these specifically 'economic' phenomena for investigation. Political scientists, on the other hand, identify specifically political phenomena in relation to the struggle for power in a 'state'. Each social science, therefore, adopts a 'one sided' point of view. The various one sided points of view are not, however, merely arbitrary and subjective constructions of the social scientist. They have an objectivity as well as a subjectivity. The guarantee of objectivity is to be found in the methods of science itself. The disciplined use of the conceptual and methodological apparatus of a science produces insights that are valuable in the causal explanation of concrete historical events, then the science has a general significance (Weber 1904: 66–71).

## Mannheim's position

Mannheim accepted much of Weber's argument, but he pushed it in a very different, and more satisfactory direction. In doing so, he gave a firmer foundation for Weber's claims for the objectivity of science and the role of scientific method in achieving this. Mannheim saw that the implications of Weber's viewpoint concern much more than just disciplinary differences between economists, political scientists, and other cultural scientists. Weber's general position recognized, of course, that there are contending, value relevant theoretical positions *within* disciplines, but he did not properly follow through the implications of this for the objectivity of social scientific investigations. Mannheim made the diversity of value standpoints his own point of reference, and he set himself the interdependent tasks of explaining their origins and exploring their consequences. He approached his task by recapping and enlarging Weber's arguments. Weber had said little about the origins of cultural values, seeing them simply as arbitrary and irrational conditions for practical action. Mannheim, on the other hand, saw that values arise as an integral element in the whole way of life that a person follows. They are social facts that can be understood in relation to a person's *social location*. It was this insight that Mannheim developed into his 'sociology of knowledge' (Mannheim 1929; 1931).

The sociology of knowledge was developed by considering the shifting meanings that have been given to the concept of ideology. Machiavelli and Pareto had employed what Mannheim called the 'particular' concept of ideology. According to this point of view, ideas are mere masks that obscure and distort the expression of interests and power. Mannheim contrasted this with the 'total concept' of ideology, which he traced back to German idealism. This conception of ideology has its roots in the philosophy of Kant and was given its definitive historical form in Hegel. Mannheim's work began with an exploration of the development of these ideas in the hermeneutic tradition of Droysen and Dilthey (Mannheim 1922; 1923; 1924). According to Hegel, it was the continuous historical transformation of consciousness that determines the form in which the 'world' appears to human beings (Mannheim 1929: 59). It was this insight, Mannheim says, that Marx took up in his analysis of ideology as the form taken by class consciousness. Mannheim locates his own development of the sociology of knowledge firmly in this tradition. According to the sociology of knowledge, all thought, including that of scientists, is 'ideological' in the total sense. Ideology is no longer a term that can be applied only to particular political opponents. It becomes a general and inescapable feature of human consciousness and knowledge (Mannheim 1929: 68–9).

The diversity of values, then, is an inescapable consequence of the historical character of human existence. It is impossible for people to escape the values and concepts that are reproduced and transformed in their historically situated actions. The diversity of historical action is the basis of a diversity of historical experience and perception. This argument might appear to lead to a complete *relativism*. If knowledge is grounded in historically conditioned standpoints, then is it possible to regard any knowledge as 'true', as valid for all members of a society? Hegel, of course, held that the standpoint of the nation or people as a whole, as it emerged in the course of history, provided a firm standpoint for true knowledge. Lukács (1923), on the other hand, took the Marxian view that social classes were the carriers of knowledge, and he saw the standpoint of the proletariat as providing a foundation for true knowledge. Mannheim could not accept this privileging of particular standpoints. True knowledge is 'objective', not 'subjective', and it is not possible to establish objective knowledge by the arbitrary privileging of a particular standpoint. It would appear that the sociology of knowledge must end in a relativism in which all standpoints and intellectual positions are equally illusory. Mannheim rejected this implication of the sociology of knowledge. His argument was that the apparent choice between a historical relativism and an arbitrary absolutism rests on an inadequate epistemology.

Mannheim saw the emergence of epistemological debate as a feature of the 'disenchantment' that Weber had seen as characterizing the modern world. The disappearance of traditional religious certainties in the face of Enlightenment ideals of science and rationality meant that epistemology became necessary as a way of arbitrating between the competing forms of human knowledge (Scott 1987).

Conventional epistemology, he argues, has seen all knowledge as founded in the subject, the isolated and self-sufficient individual *cogito*. This epistemology saw knowledge as something that is to be judged in relation to abstract and eternal truths such as the mathematical formula '2 × 2 = 4'. Mannheim accepts that some purely formal mathematical ideas may have an absolute truth, but no attempt to conceptualize an external reality can be seen in this way. He holds that 'there are spheres of thought in which it is impossible to conceive of absolute truth existing independently of the values and position of the subject and unrelated to social context' (Mannheim 1929: 70–1).

Mannheim is rather ambivalent about the possibility of absolute truth in relation to the physical world, but he is clear that the idea of a sphere of truth that is independent of the knowing subject cannot be extended to the sociohistorical world. The subject is not an isolated *cogito* but is historically located. Social phenomena are meaningful, in the sense that they are constituted by and can be understood only through meaningful concepts (Mannheim 1931: 264). This means that 'what is intelligible in history can be formulated only with reference to problems and conceptual constructions which themselves arise in the flux of historical experience' (1929: 71). These problems and conceptual constructions reflect the distinct 'perspectives' that must be taken by subjects within specific and concrete sociohistorical locations.

Mannheim rejects the traditional epistemology, which he believes Kant to have demolished. With the rejection of this traditional epistemology, he believed that he could also abandon the dilemma of absolutism *versus* relativism. The alternative, historical epistemology that Mannheim attempts to build is based around the principle that he calls *relationism*. Relativism and relationism are very different principles. The distinction between them is a subtle, but fundamental one. Where relativism holds that all knowledge is 'illusion', relationism holds that all knowledge is, in part, 'true'. These truths are partial and limited, resting on more or less narrow points of view, but they must figure as elements in any more comprehensive account. Mannheim did, in fact, believe that a relational epistemology would allow the possibility of knowledge that went, in crucial respects, beyond the socially located partial truths. All knowledge has a *relational truth*. It may be genuine or sincere, cynical or manipulative, but it is an authentic expression of the interests, experiences, concerns and circumstances of those in a particular social location.

Relationally true bodies of knowledge do not grasp the whole truth of a historical situation. Historical situations are the result of actions that are based on the knowledge possessed by participants, and this knowledge is rooted in their varying perspectives. Their varying knowledges enter into the constitution of the very historical situations that they attempt to describe. This is why all perspectival knowledge has, to a greater or lesser extent, a historical truth. Mannheim would accept the dictum that when people define situations in particular ways, their definitions have real consequences for the development of that situation. A historical situation itself is a fragmented interplay of actions based on various partial, relational truths, and a more comprehensive truth is achieved by transcending the relational truths and synthesizing them into a broader historical truth. This involves 'the assimilation and transcendence of the limitations of particular points of view', allowing 'the broadest possible extension of our horizon of vision' (Mannheim 1929: 94, 95). Mannheim holds that a synthesis of these partial views gives a more comprehensive view of the historical reality than does any one on its own:

> All points of view in politics are but partial points of view because historical totality is always too comprehensive to be grasped by any one of the individual points of view which emerge out of it. Since, however, all these points of view emerge out of the same social and historical current, and since their partiality exists in the matrix of an emerging whole, it is possible to see them in juxtaposition, and their synthesis becomes a problem which must continually be reformulated and resolved.
>
> (Mannheim 1929: 134)

The final phrase is crucial. No synthesis can ever be absolute and final: reality is constantly changing, and so there can only be a 'dynamic' synthesis that is constantly being reformulated.

Mannheim's position is difficult to grasp, and unless its details are understood it may appear too simplistic. He is not, for example, making the claim that objectivity consists in avoiding the extremes of the various positions. This argument was quite rightly repudiated by Weber in his 1904 essay. Weber held that his journal 'will struggle relentlessly against the self-deception which asserts that through the synthesis of several party points of view . . . practical norms of scientific validity can be arrived at' (Weber 1904: 58). Weber was here opposing the naive idea that simply because policy positions differ from one another, a 'midpoint' synthesis that steers a line among them is somehow more objective and less partisan. In the realm of cognitive judgements this would involve the absurd idea that the statements 'This box weighs 10 kilos' and 'This box weighs 20 kilos' could be 'synthesized' into the statement 'This box weighs 15 kilos'. Weber rightly shows that this procedure has no place in relation to either normative judgements or factual judgements.

Nor is Mannheim's claim that a more comprehensive truth is produced by adding up the various partial truths and forging them into a consensus. This would run quite counter to his argument. The dynamic synthesis that Mannheim advocates can be achieved only if the relativity of the partial truths is recognized, appreciated and incorporated into the more comprehensive account. This requires particular skills on the part of the sociologist, and I will discuss his views on this in the next section of the chapter. Meanwhile, the nature of his relationism must be spelled out more fully. The view of *physical* reality taken by Mannheim can usefully be described as 'cubist' in the sense that this term has been used in art. The cubist movement in art originated in Paris between the years 1907 and 1925. Its main characteristics were the abandonment of the idea that one single vantage point and source of light should be used in a painting. Although some early suggestions can be found in Cézanne, who tried to depict multiple perceptions of an object from several points of view, the truly pioneering work was Picasso's *Demoiselles d'Avignon* (1907), which broke completely with nineteenth century ideas of space and perspective. Cubism recognizes the existence of multiple perspectives on the same reality, and attempts to synthesize these different perspectives into a single picture. In such painters as Picasso and Braque, aesthetic representations became completely detached from any idea of a real object that could be accurately grasped in a single image.[2]

The cubist holds that various observers all see the same object, but they see it differently because they occupy different positions relative to it. An object or situation might be seen from the left, from the right, from above, from below, and so on. Each of these standpoints provides a different perspective from which perfectly valid views of the object (for example a violin) can be derived. None of them corresponds to the object as it is 'in itself', independently of all standpoints, but each of them can convey a true and accurate image of it from the particular standpoint occupied. For this reason, a cubist representation of the object attempts to present it simultaneously from all possible standpoints, taking account of how each of these positions stands in relation to all others. This point of view is compatible with contemporary epistemological realism, which sees the objects of the natural sciences as 'intransitive', as existing independently of any theories that are held about them. These objects continue to exist and to exercise their powers even when no one attempts to observe or to explain them.

A first approximation to Mannheim's position on *social* reality would be a simple cubist claim that the social scientist synthesizes the various perspectives that can be adopted towards the social structure in which people live. The social scientist's image does not correspond to the social structure as it exists in itself; it remains separate from the object that it describes, but is more comprehensive than any of the individual perspectives adopted by the participants. In fact, however, Mannheim adopts a far more radical cubist position.

In the case of cultural, historical objects such as social structures, there is no independently existing thing-in-itself in quite the same sense as there is in the physical world. Cultural reality, as a secondary layer imposed upon the physical world, is already a synthesis. The social scientist is dealing with individual perspectives on a cultural reality that already has the character of a cubist image. It has this character because it is the outcome of the interplay of actions grounded in competing perspectival meanings. The task of a dynamic synthesis, then, is to synthesize the varying perspectives on the already 'cubist' cultural reality that is the social structure.[3] While all knowledge has a relational truth, Mannheim wanted to retain the possibility of showing that some forms of knowledge may be 'false'. Having rejected the idea that the falsity of knowledge can be assessed by comparing it with a fixed and independently existing reality, Mannheim has to adopt a view that is compatible with his relationist epistemology. He finds the answer in the concept of practice. This provides an important advance for Mannheim's image of historical reality. Historical situations involve more than just knowledge and meanings; they also involve practices. Knowledge, he argues, has to be seen as 'an instrument for dealing with life-situations at the disposal of a certain kind of vital being under certain conditions of life' (Mannheim 1931: 268). That is, knowledge has the practical function of allowing people to engage in successful action. If their knowledge is an inappropriate guide to successful action, it can be seen as false. It remains an authentic expression of group interests and concerns, a 'true' expression of their worldview, but it does not actually allow their interests to be successfully realized and so is false to them. A false consciousness fails to comprehend the actualities of the 'dynamic reality' that results from the interplay of the meanings and actions of social groups:

> A theory . . . is wrong if in a given practical situation it uses concepts and categories which, if taken seriously, would prevent man [*sic*] from adjusting himself at that historical stage.
>
> (Mannheim 1929: 84–5)

In formulating a dynamic synthesis, bodies of knowledge must also be compared in terms of their relative success for participants in practical settings. Mannheim points to parallels between his ideas on practical action and the 'pragmatism' of Peirce, but he does not develop these in any detail. This incorporation of the idea of practice alongside perspective is crucial for linking Mannheim's relationism with recent statements of realism. This can be seen through a simple example. Consider, first, the attempt by friends and colleagues to describe a particular individual. Each is likely to offer a different description, concerned with those particular attributes that they regard as salient or significant. Thus, we might be offered the following descriptions:

- He has short fair hair and blue eyes.
- He is tall and well built.
- He is solid and reliable.
- He is a good lover.

At one level, of course, these descriptions compete with one another, simply by virtue of the fact that they are different. They are incomparable, however, only on the assumption that just one description can be true. If this absolutist epistemology is rejected, as it was by Mannheim, then all the statements can be accepted as true, or authentic descriptions of how the individual is seen by particular others. Mannheim's relationism, then, is perfectly compatible with an ordinary, commonsense understanding of description. An individual can be perceived in various partial ways, and it is only by putting together the separate descriptions that it is possible to gain a better, more rounded view of what the individual is really like.

Now consider what would follow if we were offered a further description:

- He has short fair hair and green eyes.

This statement introduces a new kind of incompatibility that cannot so easily be resolved. The person cannot have both blue eyes and green eyes (unless he has one of each!). If the person were suspected of a crime, the police would seek a comprehensive description that would help in their practical attempts to find him and arrest him. This can be produced only if it is assumed that the various descriptions connect with the real person in some way. Whether a particular description helps or hinders the police would, in this situation, provide a criterion for deciding the practical truth or falsity of a description. In other contexts, different criteria would apply. The case of physical attributes might be thought too simple to bear the weight of the argument, but it is used solely to illustrate the point that it is only by assuming that normal objects do, in fact, have certain characteristics, intransitively, that it makes any sense to attempt to compare alternative descriptions. Exactly the same considerations arise with cultural attributes. The person may be described, for example, as both 'a good lover' and 'an inconsiderate brute'. These contested judgements can be reconciled only by relating them to the actual behaviour of the person in particular situations.

Scientific statements have the same descriptive characteristics as everyday judgements. They are partial views and give incomplete pictures of the external world. They connect with this nuomenal world through attempts to intervene or to alter it in certain practical ways. Social science does not, however, simply reproduce the reflexive understandings of participants: it attempts to understand the understandings of participants. It does not simply adjudicate between different viewpoints, it assesses their partial truth and aims to reconcile them in a larger picture that must itself be tested through its practical relevance (see the discussion in May 1998).

## The intellectuals and genuine discussion

A crucial question that Mannheim must answer is that of how the sociologist can escape from her or his own social location and produce a synthesis that is not simply one more socially relative partial truth? To answer this question, Mannheim stressed the role of the sociologist as an intellectual rather than a partisan. Certain intellectuals, by virtue of their social location and social origins, are especially well placed to avoid undue partisan entanglements and to achieve the broader, more comprehensive outlook that Mannheim advocates. These intellectuals are, he holds, 'a relatively classless stratum which is not too firmly situated in the social order' (Mannheim 1929: 136). They are recruited from a variety of classes and social groups. They are relatively detached from the immediate clash of interests and so are better able to synthesize rival social perspectives.

Mannheim's view of the intellectuals has been much misunderstood. In essays written a few years after *Ideology and Utopia*, he expanded and clarified his ideas on the intellectuals and their social location (Mannheim 1932–3b; see also Mannheim 1932–3c).[4] He makes it clear that his argument was not concerned with all intellectuals, but only with those who, following Alfred Weber, he describes as 'relatively unattached'. The common attribute of those groups that can be designated as 'intellectuals' is their high degree of exposure to culture and education. However, this describes a wide range of groups, including many that are involved in practical economic and political activities. At the same time, many intellectuals are partisan spokespersons for the class or sectional programmes of political parties and social movements. Such advocates for partisan alignment, Mannheim makes clear, are no more likely to seek a broad and comprehensive perspective than any other actively involved participant. The 'relatively impartial intellectuals', on the other hand, are not entirely free from social liaisons, but they have cross-cutting attachments and a detachment from political participation that gives them a considerable autonomy from practical concerns (Mannheim 1932–3b: 105–6). The term that Mannheim used to describe them was '*relativ freischwebende Intelligenz*'. The best translation of this phrase is not the widely used 'free floating intellectuals', though this is one of its literal translations. A much better translation of '*freischwebende*' is 'freely balanced' or 'impartial', the whole phrase translating as the 'relatively impartial intellectuals'.

The relatively impartial intellectuals are drawn from a diverse range of social strata, not only from a single class. They are, then, an 'interstitial' category, existing 'between' strata. Their solidarity derives *solely* from their intellectual interests and concerns and not from any pre-existing class interests. They do not, therefore, align themselves collectively with any particular class-based party or political programme. The relatively impartial intellectuals are fundamentally different from Gramsci's 'organic intellectuals', who are committed to partisan movements (1971). The relatively detached intellectuals' lack of direct involvement in partisan causes means that they do not react to practical issues in the same way as employers, factory workers, and others who are directly involved in the material struggles of everyday life. They have a relative detachment and so can take a broader outlook and make a more considered and better thought out response that takes account of a wide range of issues. They are peculiarly well placed to consider matters from several perspectives. The claim, then, is that 'certain types of intellectuals have a maximum opportunity to test and employ the socially available vistas and to experience their inconsistencies' (Mannheim 1932–3b: 106):

> His [*sic*] acquired equipment makes him potentially more labile than others. He can more easily change his point of view and he is less rigidly committed to one side of the contest, for he is capable of experiencing concomitantly several conflicting approaches to the same thing.
>
> (Mannheim 1932–3b: 105)

The 'contemporary intellectual' is a member of a formally open and secular social group that is committed to the 'intellectual process' rather than to specific political programmes. They are, to use the terms of Bauman (1987), not the authoritative *legislators* but the *interpreters* of culture. The contemporary intellectual is aware that there can no longer be any talk of absolute truth, and that partial truths must be recognized and synthesized:

> The modern intellectual . . . does not intend to reconcile or to ignore the alternative views which are potential in the order of things around him, but he seeks out the tensions and participates in the polarities of his society.
>
> (Mannheim 1932–3b: 117)

The intellectual who is capable of achieving a dynamic synthesis, then, is one whose commitment is to the life of the mind and the autonomy of science, rather than to specific, practical interests and programmes. The relatively impartial intellectual is one who participates in a diverse intellectual community whose members struggle to establish and maintain the intellectual autonomy that allows them to compare and to synthesize the perspectives of those who participate in the practical struggles that they study. It is in such an intellectual community that it is possible to establish what Mannheim refers to as 'genuine discussion'. The phrase 'genuine discussion' is central to Mannheim's essay on the democratization of culture (Mannheim 1932–3a).[5] In this essay, Mannheim discusses what Habermas was later to describe as the 'ideal speech situation', though he does so in a more concrete and more achievable form. An intellectual community must be formed, he holds, in which 'genuine discussion' is the principal concern of all involved. In these circumstances, cultural matters are pursued in a 'democratic mode', reflecting the fact that scientific truth does not depend upon the authority or power of a particular theorist, but on the exercise of reason:

> The essential feature of genuine discussion is that no argument from authority and no dogmatic assertion based upon mere intuition is admitted.
>
> (Mannheim 1932–3b: 192)

'Truth' is that 'which can be ascertained by everybody in ordinary experience', or 'which can be cogently proved by steps that everybody can reproduce' (Mannheim 1932–3a: 185). Thus, 'all initial positions have some right to be considered' and 'all participants are equally and jointly responsible for the conclusion reached' (1932–3a: 192, 194). The relatively impartial intellectuals are involved in an attempt to establish or to maintain the social conditions that allow intellectual detachment and autonomy. They are not involved in practical affairs, they avoid partisan involvement, and they maintain a critical stance towards all political programmes. This does not mean, however, that the relatively impartial intellectual must be morally neutral. As Weber showed, value judgements orientate scientific work and may be expressed in scientific publications, so long as their distinction from factual judgements is kept firmly in view. The relatively impartial intellectual pursues science as a vocation, valuing the scientific role above all others, and is constantly struggling to prevent the subversion of rational, critical discussion by the dictates of power and practical interests. It is in these conditions that the principles of scientific objectivity stressed by Weber can thrive.[6]

Mannheim's discussion of the 'detachment' of the contemporary intellectual was more of a beginning than an end. His main concern was with the question of the class origins of intellectuals and their relative autonomy from class interests. He gave far less consideration to other forms of social division and their impact on the possibility of genuine discussion and scientific objectivity. He gives some considerable attention to generational differences (Mannheim 1927), seeing the post-1880 generation of intellectuals – of which, of course, he was a part – as having been the first to move forward the prospects of a scientific investigation of social affairs. He also mentions differences of ethnicity and gender, though these remarks are not at all developed. Mannheim, as a Hungarian Jew, working in Germany and forced into exile in Britain, ought, perhaps, to have been particularly aware of the need to ensure that the intellectual community recruited from all ethnic groups and took no account of ethnic differences in considering the validity of intellectual positions.

The question of gender differences, unfortunately, is the least considered part of his own work. As his own language makes clear, Mannheim did not seem to be aware of the implications of the fact that the contemporary intellectuals about whom he wrote were almost exclusively male. As has been made clear by feminist writers in recent decades, the prospects for scientific truth and objectivity are undermined by the exclusion of women from science, the patriarchal structure of universities, and the consequent failure to incorporate the authentic truths of women's experiences into the framework of genuine discussion. Mannheim's argument certainly needs to be modified to make this matter explicit. A proper inclusion of female standpoints – alongside class, ethnic, generational and other standpoints – must be central to a relational epistemology and the establishment of dynamic synthesis.

Mannheim's position might appear to be hopelessly idealistic. The difficulties of establishing 'genuine discussion' in our universities, let alone in the political sphere, are immense. This should not , however, be made a reason for rejecting his aspiration for a genuinely free and open discussion of scientific differences. Mannheim's advocacy of genuine discussion is a call for sociologists and other social scientists to be involved in the maintenance and enhancement of the conditions of academic freedom and intellectual autonomy. It is only by striving to protect what genuine discussion there is and by trying to expand its reach that the irrationalism of the present chaos of relativism can be avoided. Mannheim points out the only way in which we can truly know the social world.

## Notes

1 These are my terms and not Weber's, but they grasp the distinction that he tried to make.
2 Cézanne's ideas on art have been linked to Bergson's philosophy of mind. Bergson held that human beings accumulate information about different aspects of objects and then synthesize these into a conceptual knowledge of the object itself (Fry 1966). Picasso linked his own work with Husserl's views on comprehending the essence of an object.
3 Mannheim says relatively little about natural science, but a very brief discussion of the arguments of Heisenberg and Einstein suggests that a fully relational view could be extended to the natural world (Mannheim 1931: 275).
4 These essays were written in 1932–3, but were not published until after his death. There is a possibility that some of the language may have been altered by his editor and translator.
5 The essay translated as 'The democratization of culture' might more appropriately be rendered as 'The democratization of spirit'.
6 In his later work, Mannheim became disillusioned with contemporary politics and moved closer to an elitist stress on expertise and rational planning that runs counter to some of his earlier remarks.

# 8 | Feminists' knowledge and the knowledge of feminisms: epistemology, theory, methodology and method

**Mary Maynard**

Since the mid-1960s feminism has provided some major challenges to our understanding of how the social world is constructed and the processes through which our knowledge about this might be obtained. Certainly, the significance of gender in an empirical context is now widely accepted. Women's lives have been rescued from their previous invisibility, necessitating the generation of new concepts in order to encapsulate the gendered specificities of their experiences. Since the 1980s work has also begun on the gendering of men and the analysis of masculinities. However, while the exploration and analysis of the substantive aspects of gender are now deemed to be sociologically legitimate, the potential contribution of feminists to debates of a more theoretical and methodological nature have been treated in a much more tangential fashion. In fact, a glance through most publications and syllabi in these areas indicates the marginalization of feminist ideas in relation to mainstream (or malestream) thought.

This chapter is concerned with the contributions made by feminists to debates about knowledge construction and the nature and possibilities of feminism in this process. It is divided into a number of sections, the first four of which consider issues of epistemology, theory, research methods and methodology respectively. Each will briefly trace how the arguments have developed and assess the current 'state of the art' in the area. It will be seen that, although feminism has a lot to contribute to our understanding of how we should 'know' the social world, feminist thinking in this regard is not some kind of uniform and linear affair. There are healthy and vibrant disputes between feminists about these matters, just as there are between other philosophers, social theorists, methodologists and empirical researchers. It is part of the intention of this chapter to explore some of the tensions and contradictions which have arisen.

The fifth section of the chapter focuses on some of the currently pressing issues for feminists, and for other social scientists, which have arisen from the previous four. It draws on my own collaborative research on older women and widowhood in order to explore some of the problems and possibilities which emerge when adopting a feminist perspective. The chapter concludes with some comments on the overall significance of feminists' contribution to 'knowing the social world' and on the future direction for feminism in the creation of knowledge.

## Feminism, epistemology and the critique of male knowledge

Most contemporary accounts of feminism's engagement with epistemological concerns focus on the heated exchanges that have taken place on the role of postmodern and poststructuralist thinking.[1] This conveniently ignores the fact that early second wave feminism included critiques of scholarly activity and the academic disciplines as part of its overall appraisal of patriarchal institutions. It was argued that the construction of knowledge was not exempt from the exploitative and oppressive processes which characterized other aspects of social phenomena. The introduction of feminism into the academy, therefore, had two major aims. One was to provide analyses of, and explanations for, women's inequality in order to locate those mechanisms that might be most effectively employed to bring about change. The other was to provide a rigorously intellectual evaluation of existing knowledge forms which would demonstrate how and why women's perspectives had been marginalized and their experiences, where they were considered at all, treated as deviant.

For example, writers such as Callaway and Bernard drew attention not only to what might have been ignored or omitted in the knowledge creating process, when looked at from a woman's point of view, but also to the priority which had been given to issues derived from male interests and male ways of seeing (Bernard 1973; Callaway 1984). Because the social world has been studied from the perspective of a male universe, this has had a profound influence on what has been regarded as significant for study and how it has been structured and ordered (Smith 1988). In short, the male perspective has been afforded a privileged epistemological position. Referring to what she calls 'the male epistemological stance', Mackinnon writes that:

> men create the world from their own point of view, which then becomes the truth to be described. . . . Power to create the world from one's point of view is power in the male form. The male epistemological stance, which corresponds to the world it creates, is objectivity: the

> ostensibly noninvolved stance, the view from a distance and from no particular perspective, apparently transparent to its reality. It does not comprehend its own perspectivity, does not recognise what it sees as subjects like itself, or that the way it apprehends its world is a form of its subjection and presupposes it.
>
> (Mackinnon 1982: 23–4)

For feminists such as Mackinnon, although objectivity and scientific practice are supposedly neutral positions, they are, in fact, gendered and partial. Notwithstanding the current postmodern hypercriticism of Enlightenment thinking and the normative views of science which grew out of it, feminists were criticizing the notion that reason, employed philosophically and scientifically, could provide an objective, reliable and universal foundation for knowledge, well before it became part of received wisdom (Smith 1974; Rose 1983; Stanley and Wise 1983; Harding 1986). For instance, Mackinnon (1982) claims that objectivity is the methodological stance of which objectification is the social practice. By this she means that a position of value neutrality makes the focus of any research fraudulently appear as if it is independent of the social relations which both create and require it. For these reasons feminists more generally have argued that to objectify social phenomena and present them as external to their observer is in itself a social practice which should be subjected to critical scrutiny (Smith 1974). Harding (1991) refers to this as strong, as opposed to weak, objectivity. She argues that objectivity is not some kind of complete state that can be ultimately and definitively achieved. Rather, it involves a process in which all the evidence marshalled in knowledge creation, including the hidden and unexplicated cultural agendas and assumptions of the knower/researcher should be called to account. Strong objectivity includes the systematic examination of such background beliefs, thereby transforming 'the reflexivity of research from a problem to a resource' (Harding 1991: 164). Strong objectivity is an improvement on the more conventional, weaker, versions precisely because it includes the cultural and biographical aspects of 'knowing' which other forms ignore. It, thus, 'maximizes' the possibilities of objectivity by making these visible and part of the equation in assessing knowledge claims.

Concern over the status of objectivity is one way of identifying the differences between two current major positions in feminist epistemology, the idea of a feminist standpoint and that of feminist postmodernism. Taking a feminist standpoint combines both a commitment to a realist acceptance of the existence of social processes and mechanisms which are potentially 'knowable', with the general feminist axiom on the importance of experience in producing more representative accounts of women's lives (Harding 1986, 1991; Hartsock 1987a; Smith 1988; Ramazanoglu 1989; Haraway 1991; Rose 1994). Drawing on the Marxist idea concerning the epistemic privilege of oppressed groups, Harding has argued, for example, that understanding women's lives from a committed feminist exploration of their experiences constructs more complete and less distorted knowledge than that produced through male science (Harding 1986; 1991). Women and men lead lives that have significantly different contours and boundaries. It is the material oppression experienced in women's daily lives which gives them a different standpoint from that of men, and so access to different knowledge of the relations involved in their subordination. Thus, adopting a feminist standpoint can reveal the existence of forms of human relationships which may not be visible from the position of the 'ruling gender'. It, therefore, offers the possibility of more reliable and less perverse understandings, along with the possibility of extension to a range of other subordinate and underprivileged groups.

The standpoint approach has been criticized from a number of positions, the silencing of Black feminist and lesbian standpoints, the potential existence of a multiplicity of incommensurable standpoints, the dangers of essentialism and relativism (Stanley and Wise 1990). An example of how it might be operationalized is given in the fifth section of this chapter. However, it is most often contrasted with postmodern accounts.

Feminist postmodernism shares most of the major characteristics of other variants. It is critical of grand theorizing, of universal categories, of the existence of a stable and coherent self, of the transparency of language and of the ability of reason and scientific rationality to produce 'truth' (Nicholson 1990; Braidotti 1991; Alcoff and Potter 1993; Lennon and Whitford 1994). It focuses, instead, on discourse, textuality, fragmentation, multiple subjectivities and flux. Of course, it is not difficult to see why such ideas might be attractive to feminists in their pursuit of alternatives to the 'male epistemological stance'. However, whereas the standpoint approach acknowledges that accounts are selective constructions, while retaining the possibility that they are also able to represent independent phenomena with some degree of rigorousness and reliability, feminist postmodernism eschews any such thing. Instead, it is in agreement with postmodern views more generally that due to the impossibilities of apprehending social phenomena without invoking discourse, and since the very practising of discourse serves to invoke forms of sociality, it is, therefore, impossible to understand the social without also simultaneously constructing it. This latter, then, becomes the task of what it means to 'know'. The focus switches in most accounts from trying to identify and analyse what gives rise to inequality and oppression to the discourse and texts through which things come to be 'known' (Barrett 1992). As others have remarked, such an emphasis causes major problems for any feminist project designed to make social interventions which foster change, either through political action or social research (Hartsock 1987b; Stefano 1990; Walby 1992). It also poses difficulties for feminist theory. It is this latter issue to which I now turn.

## Feminist theory: beyond the 'big three'[2]

If feminist epistemology has been directed towards the questions 'who knows what about what and how is this knowledge legitimized?', then the purpose of feminist theory can be identified as that of exploring the nature of women's experiences, with a view to explaining the mechanisms through which inequalities are generated and reproduced. Again, the intention behind this was both social and political in the desire to locate key aspects of power relations, the identification of which might lead to the challenging of oppression. It has been customary to characterize feminist theory in terms of three major approaches: liberal feminism, Marxist feminism and radical feminism. Indeed, a glance at those contemporary sociology textbooks which bother to include any discussion of feminist theory confirms the extent to which it is still described in this way.

Briefly,[3] liberal feminism is usually regarded as focusing on individual rights and on the concepts of equality, justice and equal opportunities, where legal and social policy changes are seen as tools for engineering women's equality with men. Marxist feminism is seen as being concerned with women's oppression as it is tied to forms of capitalist exploitation of labour and where women's paid and unpaid labour is analysed in relation to its function within the capitalist economy. Radical feminism is 'radical' because of its attempts to formulate new ways of theorizing women's relationship to men. There is particular focus on the 'personal being political', that is on the ways in which power is located in everyday experiences and relationships and is not just a prerogative of a government or state. Men's social control of women through various mechanisms is emphasized, especially violence, heterosexism and reproduction and men as a group are seen as responsible for women's continued oppression in a system of patriarchy.

A more careful analysis of the history of second wave feminist theorizing, however, indicates that it never fitted neatly into these labels and was always more diverse than the stereotypes indicated. For instance, as early as 1984 McFadden published an analytical framework positioning feminist analyses in terms of a wide spectrum of arguments (McFadden 1984). In some accounts, that of Jaggar's (1983) for example, socialist and Marxist feminism are regarded as being distinct from each other, thus giving four categories in all, with socialist feminism regarded as being less economistically determinist than the Marxist variant. Others, such as Walby (1990), have developed dual sysems theory as a fourth perspective, attempting to marry Marxist and radical feminist analyses. More recently, there have been attempts to go beyond 'the big three', with the introduction of psychoanalytic, materialist, postmodern, Black, lesbian and various other forms of feminist thought.

The problems faced by feminists in labelling theories and presenting them as distinct and relatively homogeneous ways of knowing is not unique to them alone and remains an issue for all the social sciences when trying to get to grips with knowledge construction. For a start, there is little consensus as to which labels are the most meaningful, how many there are and which theorists are to be located to each, leading to theorists and their work being treated in different ways by different commentators (Maynard 1995). Another difficulty is the implication that there is some degree of unity in approach, assumptions and intention between those writers assigned to a particular category and a corresponding incommensurability with those placed in others. Yet, despite the stereotypes, radical feminists have been concerned, for example, with how women's material circumstances effect their experiences of events such as violence and abuse, Marxist feminists have focused on phenomena such as sexuality and both have been prepared to theorize the need for social policies and political reform in such areas as abortion, gay parenthood and workplace sexual harassment. A further problem is the existence of those whose work defies classification in the available terms. The ideas of those such as Stanley and Wise (1983), Gayatri Chakravorty Spivak (1988), Iris Marion Young (1990) and Tania Modleski (1991), along with many others, all lie outside the conventional feminist theoretical classificatory schema.

Another reason why the usual formats for thinking about feminist theory might be problematic relates to the ways in which they have been derived from white, western and, mainly, Anglo-American perspectives. Some very distinctive tendencies which are located in countries such as France and Italy are absent.[4] Further, the writings of Black and Third World women tend to be ignored. Despite the fact that Black feminist writers have challengingly drawn attention to the racist and exclusionary nature of much white feminist theory (as well as practice), the frameworks employed to describe theory tend to remain immune to their concerns.

A final difficulty with the penchant for classifying feminist theoretical knowledge is that this tends to be presented in an ahistorical fashion, as if the categories are unchanging, whereas, as with other forms of social thought, it is continually developing. Worrying also is how this portrays coming to terms with theory as a rather sterile business. Using theory is made to seem as if it is simply the application of pregiven labels which can be 'mugged up' and learnt parrot fashion, in advance, before being applied to the problem at hand. The emphasis is on the product, theory, rather than on the process and benefits of theorizing. This is an issue to which I will return.

Social and political trends have now contrived to turn feminist theory into something much more pluralistic than was previously acknowledged. The challenge from Black and Third World women, as well as from other groups, to the undifferentiated and homogenized use of the concept 'woman' has led to the recognition of diversity of experiences, of hierarchical power relations between women and to the problems associated with a unified notion of women's oppression. At the same time, feminist theory is increasingly produced in universities, rather than in activist groups, and the demise of Marxism has hastened the search for alternative theoretical frameworks. In such circumstances it is hardly surprising that feminists interested in theory, like those involved in epistemology, should be heavily influenced by the ideas of poststructuralism and postmodernism.

This has led to some important developments (Maynard 1995). For instance, there has been a move away from foundationalism and associated claims that there can be a specific cause of oppression for women. It has been acknowledged that the language of systems theory creates problems for feminism because its connotations of passivity, determinism and mechanization deny women agency and the ability to resist. Thus, concepts, such as that of patriarchy, have given way to more pluralistic notions, such as patriarchal relations, signifying that gender relations are not uniform and can be contradictory. The emphasis on situated relations, rather than holistic systems, also makes it easier to theorize the interconnections between gender and other forms of oppressive power. There is also an awareness of the unevenness of power, that not all experiences are necessarily negatively oppressive and related to relations of power and that it is important to analyse how women are variously positioned in specific contexts.

The problem, however, is that, as has already been seen, the 'posts' tend to ask questions about the ways in which knowledge is constructed and how it operates, rather than about what is actually known. This means that a lot of feminist postmodern writing is concerned with epistemological matters rather than strictly theoretical ones or that it focuses on issues related to 'knowing', such as the self, identity and subjectivity (Braidotti 1991; Brodribb 1993; Griffiths 1995). There has been a blurring of the boundaries between disciplines and increasing interest, by feminists among others, in fields such as psychoanalysis, linguistics and literary theory (Mouzelis 1991). In such circumstances feminist theory ceases to be theory about the gendered nature of the social world, becoming, instead, theory about theory. It runs the risk of focusing only on epistemological, philosophical or, paradoxically, metatheoretical issues, rather than on how gender operates to construct life chances differently for women and for men, and the subordinations which result from this. Now, of course, every social theory, in addition to a concern for/explication of the nature of social reality, entails epistemological assumptions and problems which should not be ignored (Mouzelis 1991). However, as Mouzelis points out, whatever continuities might exist between 'epistemological issues and socio-theoretical problems proper, there are also marked discontinuities' (Mouzelis 1991: 3). As he argues, the conflation and abolition of the distinction between what constitutes epistemology and what constitutes theory 'destroys the latter's specificity and relative autonomy – resulting in analyses which, despite the numerous insights and brilliant comments they provide on particular theories, often lead to misleading or inadequate conclusions' (Mouzelis 1991: 13).

To take just one example from feminism, the deconstructing of categories, such as occurs in Butler's accounts of 'performative gender' is important in making visible the contradictions, mystifications, silences and hidden possibilities through which individuals are 'made up' (Butler 1990; 1993). However, this is not the same as destroying or rendering obsolete the categories themselves, since notions of woman and man, as well as of race and ethnicity, still play a significant part in how the social world is organized on a global scale. Thinking through the construction of and imagining beyond labels, such as those of race and gender, for those in the privileged position to be able to do so, is one important part of challenging both their legitimacy and their efficacy. A reworking of the discourses alone, however, does not make them go away. Rather, it removes the referrents which have constituted feminist theories' subject matter. As a result, what passes as theory in feminism, as with sociology more generally, is becoming increasingly more abstract and even more divorced from the practice of empirical investigation.

## Doing feminist research

The construction of feminist knowledge has always focused, in part, on conducting empirical research. This has been particularly necessary given the extent to which the parameters and characteristics of women's lives have been rendered invisible in masculinist projects. Much discussion has taken place as to whether there is, or should be, a specifically feminist approach to doing social research (Harding 1987b; and see the debate in the journal, *Sociology*: Gelsthorpe 1992; Hammersley 1992b, 1994; Ramazanoglu 1992). Yet, despite the fact that such an aim has been attributed to feminists' work, the claim has more legitimacy in relation to methodology than it does to methods *per se*. While discussing the characteristics which might make feminist work different from non-feminist kinds, feminist writers have frequently railed against forcing researchers to adopt one particular position or set strategy (Cook 1983; Stanley and Wise 1983). In fact, it was precisely because of their criticisms that the academic disciplines had preferred methods, and regarded these as the only legitimate investigative techniques, that early feminist discussions about the nature of research originated in the first place. As Kelly (1988) has commented:

> Many of the methods used by feminist researchers are not original. What is new are the questions we have asked, the way we locate ourselves within our questions, and the purposes of our work. Given the short history of feminist research, perhaps we should shift our attention

> from discussions of 'feminist methods' to what I now call 'feminist research practice'.
>
> (Kelly 1988: 6)

Given this, it is somewhat ironic that an orthodoxy, privileging qualitative methods and especially the in-depth face-to-face interview, seems gradually to have developed (Kelly *et al.* 1992; 1994).

The debate about the uses and benefits of qualitative versus quantitative methods of social research is a long term one which is certainly not the sole prerogative of feminists. Nevertheless, since the 1970s, feminists have added their own particular dimension to the arguments. Because quantification has been associated with scientific notions of measurement, objectivity, control and detachment many have argued that it is inappropriate for the purposes of feminist study (Graham 1983; Nielsen 1990). Following the work of phenomenological sociologists, feminists have argued that the assumptions as to how social actors structure their everyday worlds, to be found in the questionnaires or highly structured interview schedules on which statistical or numerical analysis is largely based, produce a falsely concrete body of data, which distort rather than reflect actors' meanings. Similarly, the production of atomistic facts and figures fractures people's lives (Graham 1983; 1984). Only one part of experience is abstracted for the focus of attention and this is done in a static and atemporal fashion. Further, research practices which utilize either precoded or preclosed categories are often of limited use when trying to understand women's lives or those of other subordinated groups. This is because they are based on assumptions, often at an unrecognized and commonsense level, that researchers are already significantly familiar with the topic under investigation to be able to specify, in advance, the full range of issues which need to be included. Anything which is not already part of the research schedule cannot be recorded and, therefore, cannot be studied, resulting in the silencing of women's own voices. Social research which is based on such assumptions can be neither exploratory nor investigatory. Rather, it assesses the extent, distribution and intensity of something which has been defined in advance of the research. Feminists have argued that there are aspects to the lives of oppressed groups which cannot be preknown or predefined in such a way.

In contrast, qualitative studies maximize understandings of women's activities and beliefs and the processes through which these are structured. Such research tends to be oriented towards the interior of women's lives, focusing on the meanings and interpretations of those being researched (Graham 1984; Stanley and Wise 1983; 1993; Roseneil 1993). Qualitative work enables researchers to see the world through their subjects' eyes and, because the associated techniques are less structured than in quantitative approaches, it can be made more responsive to the needs of respondents and the nature of the subject matter. Much feminist writing on this topic has tended to imply, somewhat cosily, that developing good rapport with the researched produces 'rich', 'deep', more holistic and less exploitative material due to the various degrees of sustained contact with those being studied, although this is not uncontested (Stacey 1988; Kelly *et al.* 1992). In comparison, quantitative research is depicted as providing only superficial and surface information, as insensitive to change and as tearing individuals from their social context (Graham 1984).

For all these reasons, then, many feminists, whatever their theoretical persuasion, have found methods such as in-depth and ethnographic interviewing, life and oral histories particularly attractive in coming to 'know' the social worlds of women. Some, however, have continued to advocate the utility of methods which produce numerical information (Jayaratne 1983; Sprague and Zimmerman 1989; Jayaratne and Stewart 1991; Risman 1993). One major reason for this is the political potential and necessity of being able to demonstrate degrees of inequality and the intensity of patriarchal oppression. The significance of violence in women's lives or the feminization of poverty, for example, are underlined by studies that show the extent and severity of their existence. Further, some feminists have argued that the negative characteristics attributed to quantitative research techniques are not necessarily intrinsic to them. Not all researchers using such methods see themselves as neutral and as producing objective and value free 'facts' and it is possible to devise sensitive and sensitizing forms. For instance, the British feminist and researcher on sexual violence, Liz Kelly (1992), has described her 'journey in reverse', during which she moved from face-to-face interviews to using large scale self-report questionnaires, the very method of which she had earlier been most critical. Together with her collaborators, she has considered how such an approach can remain sensitive to feminist principles, particularly in terms of how to treat participants and how to use the information to which their testimonies give rise (Kelly *et al.* 1992; 1994). Arguing that participants might find it easier to disclose and talk about sexual abuse by responding to a questionnaire than by being interviewed, they point out that, although feminists say they take the unintended consequences of participation in research seriously, few have investigated the harm that might be involved in practice (Kelly *et al.* 1994). They quote approvingly an earlier observation that 'a well crafted quantitative study may be more use to policy makers and cause less harm to women than a poorly crafted qualitative one' (Fonow and Cook 1991b: 8). Further, rather than asserting the primacy of one particular research method, it makes more sense to adopt a pragmatic position of flexibility, combining and comparing methods in order to ascertain the limitations and possibilities of each in relation to a particular research project. Currently, then, feminists are beginning to move towards mixing methods in their empirical work. They have moved away from the previously entrenched, and unfortunately dualist, disputes about which methods and techniques are 'best'.

These are being replaced by attitudes which are more phlegmatic and behaviour which is more pragmatic in nature.

## Methodology and research practice[5]

Methodology refers to the theory and analysis of how research should proceed and the processes through which research questions might best be addressed. Feminist methodology has been less informed by reference to particular theories (Marxist, radical, dual systems, etc.) and more influenced by a diffuse and general theoretical commitment to understanding gendered and other social divisions, women's oppression and patriarchal control. This means that there has been little concern with fitting research questions derived from a specific theoretical perspective to commensurate field practice. Indeed, the assumed orthodoxy of qualitative methods, along with the tendency of theorists and researchers to move in divergent directions, has ensured that the lack of dialogue between theory and empirical work, to be found in much of the social sciences, is paralleled in feminism. Instead, feminist debates about methodology, broadly speaking, have centred on how to ensure that the research process takes place in non-exploitative and ethically responsible ways. A central issue here has been the existence of possible structural inequalities between researcher and researched and the extent to which these might be minimized. It is argued that it is hypocritical, and undermining of the knowledge produced, for feminists to replicate, during their research, the kind of power relations of which they are critical elsewhere (Stanley and Wise 1983; 1993).

As is well known, the debate about power and research practice originally took hold with the publication of Ann Oakley's (1981) landmark article on interviewing in which she was critical of its standard textbook forms. Exhortations against developing any kind of rapport or relationship with respondents, lest this contaminate the interview, present research as a one way process, with interviewees allocated a narrow and objectified function as mere sources of data. According to Oakley, this creates an unequal, hierarchical and exploitative situation, where the all powerful researcher invests nothing of herself but expects other women to speak freely and frankly about their experiences. Such forms of research conduct contravene the basic principles of feminist knowledge creation and politics, which are designed to counter practices of subordination. They also lead to poor research by failing to acknowledge how good communications with respondents can enhance the depth and richness of the feelings they are prepared to reveal.

As a result of such concerns, feminist researchers turned their attention to the ways in which hierarchies might be broken down and exploitation minimized when conducting research (Stanley and Wise 1983, 1993; Bell and

Roberts 1984; Warren 1988; Fonow and Cook 1991b). Such strategies might involve, for example, explaining as much as possible about the nature of the research, obtaining participants' feedback on interpretations and analysis of research materials, and the dissemination of findings to them. It is also advocated that, rather than deflecting respondents' questions, these should be dealt with seriously, information given and experiences shared.

One way in which feminists have suggested that it might be possible to reduce 'social distance' between the researched and themselves encourages the telling of stories (Graham 1984; Roseneil 1993). Roseneil, for instance, used what she calls 'dialogic interviews' when researching women activists at Greenham Common, a place where she had also been politically involved. Describing these as the 'mutual exchange of stories', she writes that this was

> not only ethically and politically desirable for me as a feminist, but I believe it added to the richness of the interview material. . . . However, none of this is standard interview practice, and would be frowned upon by those adhering to methodologies that emphasize objectivity, intersubjective reliability, replicability, and which do not seek to locate the researcher on the same critical plane as the researched.
>
> (Roseneil 1993: 199)

Roseneil's reference to locating 'the researcher on the same critical plane as the researched' draws attention to a further feature of feminists' attempts to counter relations of power and exploitation in research. This is a commitment to reflexivity. The idea of reflexivity is a response to the recognition that the cultural beliefs and behaviours of researchers shape the results of their analyses, the ignoring of which leads to weak objectivity. As Harding puts it, these behaviours are 'part of the empirical evidence for (or against) the claims advanced in the results of the research' (1987b: 9). It is, therefore, necessary for the researcher to locate herself in relation to the research in two ways. One is to make explicit the grounds for conducting the research, clearly setting out the procedures used and explaining why things have been done in certain ways (Edwards 1990). The second is for researchers to explore their 'intellectual autobiographies' by reflecting on the likely effect of their class, race, gender and other assumptions on the research and its analysis (Stanley 1985). Reflexively acknowledging the role of subjectivity in the construction and conduct of research challenges the idea of the researcher as an invisible and anonymous voice of authority. It, thus, contributes towards making the relationship between the researcher and researched more transparent and, thereby, to the feminist notion of strong objectivity.

However, although some feminist researchers appear to assume that it is possible to eliminate most aspects of power dynamics from the research process, many are less sanguine (Stacey 1988; Skeggs 1994). An educated female researcher may find it all too easy to encourage women to talk about aspects of their lives, concerning which, on reflection, they may have preferred to remain silent. It is also easy for any researcher to deny their privileges, in terms of knowledge and skills, in order to minimize the differences between themselves and their research participants. Focusing on the influence of 'race' in the conduct of research, for instance, immediately challenges the assumption that feminist interviewing comprises a cosy enterprise during which women enjoy talking intimately with each other. For example, Black women may feel inhibited by and suspicious of the intentions of a white researcher, while white women can display visible consternation when a Black interviewer appears on their doorstep, albeit a comparatively unlikely occurrence (Edwards 1990; Phoenix 1994). Even when a certain degree of rapport between women is achieved, this may well be more the result of shared social class and/or shared colour or culture than gender. Riessman (1991), for instance, has compared the shared assumptions about the social world which framed her successful interview with a white middle class American woman, with the barriers created by class and cultural divisions when interviewing a Puerto Rican woman. Clearly, then, 'simply being women discussing "women's issues" in the context of a research interview is not sufficient for the establishment of rapport and the seamless flow of an interview' (Phoenix 1994: 50). Differences of gender, race, class, age and sexuality can all impinge on the research process and it is not always easy to ascertain which are exerting an influence at any one moment in time and what the precise nature of this influence might be. Overall, then, shared gender characteristics are not sufficient to promote shared understandings and it cannot be assumed that trust can easily be established on the basis of gender alone.

The debates about these issues are continuing, with some writers objecting to the ways in which the power of the researcher can be overstated and those being researched ascribed a passive victimized status in which they have no space for resistance (Skeggs 1994). However, there is some general acceptance that, while a concern for reflexivity must be a central component of any research project, awareness of this kind does not, of itself, eliminate relations of power and control. Ultimately, it may be the case that, despite the best endeavours of feminists, research inevitably involves some degree of power imbalance. This results both from what goes on in the research process itself and what is derived from more general social divisions and inequalities. Feminism forces the researcher to confront such issues, rather than ignore them. Thus egalitarianism in research is best regarded as something to be worked towards rather than fully achieved (Skeggs 1994).

## Creating feminist knowledge

So far this chapter has reviewed some of the arguments and debates which have taken place in the process of feminists' creating knowledge in terms of epistemology, theory, research methods and methodology. This section will focus more specifically on some of the more significant issues to which these discussions give rise. Clearly, what follows is by no means definitive and is, necessarily, selective in its focus. By means of illustration, the section draws on my collaborative research on the experiences of older widows.[6]

As with other feminist research, we chose to base our study in widows' own experiences of bereavement and loss. Although it is the case for many women that their experience of advancing years is influenced, in part, by their lives as widows, scant attention has been paid to a status which increases in likelihood the older that married women get. Further, little of what exists has been informed by feminist perspectives. There was, therefore, no large extant literature to use as a basis from which to develop hypotheses or structured questions to 'test'. As for many social researchers our project was exploratory and investigatory in nature.

The decision to use focus groups in the research stemmed from the ways in which they facilitate interaction between participants, allowing them to share experiences and perspectives and signalling where they might agree or disagree. Although the agenda is, in part, set by the researcher (this is always the case in any research project, even in-depth interviewing, and it is naive to assume otherwise), focus groups are inductive in that they give participants opportunities to introduce new themes and ideas. Focus groups also create quasi-naturalistic settings which resemble the contexts in which most people negotiate the recounting of their opinions and the remembering of experiences. In this, they are are more akin to what goes on in social life than one-to-one interviews and the knowledge produced is shown to be partial and changing, rather than definitive. Finally, focus groups offer a setting which can be mutually supportive and constructive as opposed to threatening. This was important for research on widows, where the subject matter is sensitive and potentially very emotionally stressful. For all these reasons, then, focus groups seemed to be the most appropriate method for researching the experience of widowhood.

However, the experience of conducting the research and analysing the material arising from it subsequently raised a number of issues for the construction of feminist knowledge. To begin with there was the problem of how to treat the widow's accounts. While it had already been accepted that these were historical constructions and did not represent some ultimate 'truth', there remained the issue of whether the widows' voices should be left to speak for themselves, since to do otherwise ran the risk of being accused of violation. The problem with the latter strategy, however, is that it overlooks the fact that all feminist work is theoretically grounded in a framework concerned with gender divisions, women's oppression or patriarchal control. It can, therefore, never be politically neutral, completely inductive or solely based in grounded theory. This means that interpretation has to be intrinsic to feminist research and has implications, for example, for what taking a feminist standpoint might mean. For although the experience of research participants, however mediated, might provide the starting point for the construction of feminist knowledge, this is not sufficient for understanding the processes and practices through which such experience is structured and organized. The latter requires those experiences to be positioned within a wider understanding of their location in society. As Maureen Cain (1986) has argued, we need 'to take our own theory seriously' and 'use the theory to make sense of . . . the experience' (1986: 265). Dorothy Smith (1986) explains this further when she writes that feminist knowledge:

> must be able to disclose for women how their own social situation, their everyday world is organized and determined by social processes which are not knowable through the ordinary means through which we find our everyday world.
>
> (Smith 1986: 6)

What is involved, then, is an interpretative and synthesizing process in which taking a feminist standpoint connects experience to understanding. In the widowhood project it involved locating women's accounts within the framework of a gendered analysis of marriage, family/household, domestic career and ideas about ageing. It also meant that the researchers had to be reflexive about the assumptions which they themselves were bringing to the research, particularly the autobiographies of the project leaders, both of whom have widowed mothers. All of this led to further considerations about the relationship between theory and empirical investigation in knowledge production.

First, as has previously been argued, the current emphasis on theorizing about theory, with its emphasis on philosophical and epistemological issues, has led to an ever widening gap between theory and research. The effects of an increasing academic division of labour within the social sciences, together with the development of subareas of the disciplines devoted solely to something called theory, means that when we think about what the latter involves we focus on theories with a capital T. The emphasis is on work which has adopted a 'grand' or abstract approach and which is 'lofty' in conception, execution or expression. Yet, in order to restore its resonance with social and political issues, perhaps a different conception of theory is required.

In the research on widowhood we aimed to generate theoretical understandings, in a previously poorly theorized area, from empirically grounded research. More specifically, we refined existing concepts, such as independency, interdependency, autonomy and the notion of the domestic environment in the context of our investigations. These could then be translated into a wider theoretical framework for understanding widowhood, at the same time as helping us make sense of the substantive findings. Our intention was to formulate sets of conceptual tools, without either reifying social reality, as tends to happen with more abstract formulations, or reducing complex phenomena to the mere aggregate of its constituent parts, as with empiricism (Mouzelis 1991). The idea of such a middle order approach is, of course, borrowed from the American sociologist, Robert Merton (1968). His conception of 'middle range' theory sees it as lying between grand theory, which he describes as being remote from real life, and detailed descriptions of particulars that are not generalizable at all. Mouzelis, arguing that it is not necessary to agree with Merton's ideas about sociology or functionalist explanations to find his ways of theorizing useful, describes the latter as 'more a style of concept-building, a type of intellectual craftsmanship rather than any specific theoretical position on the nature of the social and the way of knowing it' (Mouzelis 1991: 5).

These ideas were extremely useful in the widowhood project. For instance, they enabled us to distinguish between universalizations, untenable because they deal with totalities and closed explications which are held to be universally applicable, and generalizations. The latter address, albeit in qualified terms, general properties and highlight, through comparison, similarities and differences, where these clearly arise from substantive material. In the research on widows, for example, it was possible to generalize about the relationship between the sexual division of labour between spouses prior to bereavement and subsequent meanings of independence and autonomy. Such generalizations involve what might be regarded as pattern perception and are significant in developing the ideas of theoretical contextualization involved in taking a feminist standpoint (Frye 1990). Frye suggests that patterns are important because they enable us to sketch a schema within which certain meanings are sustained. Their significance is in terms of rendering intelligible those repetitions in social life which may be invisible or perceived in purely isolated and personal terms by the individual. Yet, this does not mean that they are either statistical or universal generalizations. Patterns may change as new fields of meaning open up. They are important, however, because (as with the traveller in new geographical territory) they offer a map, however partial, of knowledge so far attained and future directions which it might be prudent to peruse. Such generalizations do not provide a summing up, thereby foreclosing further discussion (Frye 1990). Rather, they can open up new fields of meaning and generate new understandings and political possibilities.

Such a realistic position on knowledge creation is, however, possible only if the postmodern stance concerning the decentred self and lack of a unified subject to be a 'knower' is rejected. Here the work of Jane Flax (1990) is extremely helpful in pointing towards the confusion which exists between the idea of a 'unitary' homogeneous self and a 'core' one. Drawing on her work as a therapist with people suffering from borderline syndrome, a condition defined in terms of lack of a core self, she argues that, without the latter, such individuals are unable to register their own experiences, those of others or the world around them more generally. Flax suggests that it is only when a core self begins to cohere that exploration of the spaces between self and other, inner and outer, reality and illusion become possible. Although the self may change, have its own inner world and be affected by emotion and desire, it still maintains some sense of continuity. Yet, this is so much part of the background to our lives that it tends to be taken for granted. Flax writes that:

> those who celebrate or call for a 'de-centred' self seem deceptively naive and unaware of the basic cohesion within themselves that makes the fragmentation of experience something other than a terrifying psychosis. . . . Persons who have a core self find the experiences of those who lack or who have lacked it almost unimaginable.
>
> (Flax 1990: 218–19)

The idea of a core self posits an alternative concept of subjectivity to that offered by modernist notions of the unified self or postmodern denials that the self exists at all. It reinstates the possibility of the 'knowing' individual and that there is 'knowledge' to be 'known', although the outcomes, of course, may be contested or modified.

## Concluding remarks

This chapter has reviewed a variety of issues in relation to the construction of feminist knowledge, demonstrating the richness and detailed nature of the debates that have taken place. It has advocated a reconception of the relationship between theory and research, a reconception which is as pertinent to other forms of knowledge constituting practices as it is to feminism. One of the reasons why a middle order approach proves so attractive is in the ways in which it invites us to rethink what is meant by theory. In the widowhood project this encouraged an emphasis on the creative process of theorizing in relation to specific empirical concerns, rather than the simple application of ideas from pregiven theories.

It could be argued, however, that, in many ways, feminists, along with other social researchers, are already involved in middle order projects. A good case can be made for claiming that more is understood about patriarchal, or other unequal and oppressive, relations from empirical studies, such as those on the workplace, male violence and welfare provision, than from theories about patriarchy *per se*. Unfortunately, though, such empirical work is often not associated with 'doing theory' and is treated as low status in comparison with more rarefied kinds. For the future, feminists need to challenge the unfortunate bifurcation in knowledge creation that such dualism supports. Drawing from, and slightly adapting, Mouzelis's work, I argue that, in order to push forward the frontiers of knowledge, we need less exhaustive exposition and mugging up of theories, together with their philosophical foundations and epistemological underpinnings. Instead, what is required is more middle order concern for better ways of understanding how the social world is 'constructed, reproduced and transformed' (Mouzelis 1991: 5).

## Notes

1 This is not the place to engage in semantic discussion over possible divergence or convergence between postmodern and poststructural thought. Suffice it to acknowledge here that there is widespread disagreement as to what the terms mean, who is to be allocated to which and how great an epistemological break has been created from the previous 'modern' era or theoretical emphasis on structures.
2 For a more detailed discussion of these arguments, see Maynard (1995).
3 There is no space to do other than provide very caricatured synopsis of what each perspective is taken to involve. Obviously, the picture is much more varied and complex than indicated here.
4 For example, Psycho et Po in France and the Milan Women's Bookstore.
5 This is an abbreviated discussion of the issues covered in my forthcoming book for UCL Press, *Feminists and Social Research: Pragmatics, Politics and Power*.
6 The research was designed and directed by myself and Lesley Hicks. It was carried out by Lesley Archer, Lesley Hicks and Wendy Mitchell and funded by a grant from the University of York Innovation and Priming Fund. Focus group interviews were carried out with recently bereaved able-bodied women aged between 60 and 75 years. They were designed to explore the effect of loss on women's experiences of daily living and the kinds of coping strategies which are adopted. Analyses made by the researchers were discussed for consistency and reliability with participants at subsequent focus group meetings.

# 9 | Quantitative and qualitative research strategies in knowing the social world

**Alan Bryman**

The distinction between quantitative and qualitative research occupies a somewhat ambiguous status in current discussions of research methodology in that it is simultaneously being treated as a basic, taken-for-granted means of differentiating approaches to social research and as a limited contrast that has had its day. On the one hand, one often hears despairing remarks to the effect that the distinction is tired, no longer a useful means of classifying research methods or the practices of social researchers, or simply 'false' (Layder 1993: 110). On the other hand, there is ample evidence of its continued, even growing, currency. It is frequently used in advertisements and job descriptions for research assistantships. It is often referred to in textbooks and in research methods courses. Indeed, the large general research methods text has increasingly given way to texts specializing in aspects of either quantitative or qualitative research. Sage Publications has two extensive series of books devoted to 'Quantitative Applications in the Social Sciences' and to 'Qualitative Research Methods'. Separate journals devoted to qualitative research issues are proliferating. A growing number of articles seem to be being published which proudly proclaim that they incorporate both approaches. The distinction seems to resonate with social science professionals: the editor of the *American Sociological Review* in his 1997 'Editor's Comment' noted that the journal is often accused of being biased against *both* quantitative and qualitative research (Firebaugh 1997: vi). The editor of the *Academy of Management Journal* made a similar comment in the last issue of 1996 (DeNisi 1996). These remarks by journal editors probably reflect a widespread feeling among many qualitative researchers that their work is discriminated against in favour of quantitative research in mainstream journals (Sutton 1997). More and more fields are incorporating the distinction into their basic research vocabularies and/or are calling for more qualitative research in domains dominated by quantitative research.

At the same time, there is still widespread discussion about what quantitative and qualitative research actually *are* and whether they really are all that different (e.g. Hammersley 1992a; 1996).

In spite of some disillusionment with the distinction, its use seems to show few signs of abating. Whatever one's doubts about its meaning or validity, it seems to resonate as a useful means of construing the nature of social research for many writers and students. In a number of places, I have tried to suggest that there are two different versions of the quantitative–qualitative distinction – the technical and the epistemological – and that a failure to recognize this demarcation means that many writers shuttle uneasily back and forth between them (Bryman 1984; 1988; 1992; 1996; 1998).

## Epistemological and technical arguments

According to the epistemological argument, quantitative and qualitative research are located in different ways of knowing the social world. Quantitative research is seen as implacably wedded to a natural science version (and in particular to a positivist version) of both the character of the social world and how it ought to be studied. By 'character of the social world' I simply mean that social reality is seen as having an 'out there' quality; it is an objective reality waiting to be revealed by social scientists and their tools of investigation. In line with the image of the social world as an external, objective reality and with a natural science model of the research process, quantitative research exhibits certain distinctive characteristics, in particular emphases on precise measurement, causality, generalization, replication (or more precisely, replicability) and individualism.

By contrast, qualitative research is typically depicted as subscribing to an epistemological position that rejects the natural science model, along with its assumptions and its image of the nature of the social world. Drawing substantially on a number of anti-positivist intellectual traditions (most notably, phenomenology, symbolic interactionism, *verstehen* and naturalism), the social world is viewed as socially constructed, that is, as a subjectively meaningful reality that is in a constant state of revision. This orientation has resulted in a distinctive cluster of characteristics: an emphasis on taking the perspective of those being studied, on detailed description of social settings, on understanding in context, on a processual view of social life, on flexible research approaches, and on a preference for theory and concepts to emerge out of data (rather than being posited in advance of data collection as in quantitative research). While this list has been criticized for being too general (Silverman 1993), it serves as a reasonably helpful heuristic, particularly when juxtaposed against the list of distinctive features of quantitative research.

For many writers, this depiction of quantitative and qualitative research resembles a contrast between competing paradigms in a Kuhnian sense (Hammersley 1996), to the extent that Shadish (1995) writes about the need for 'deKuhnifying' the debate. Such a position has many implications of which two stand out. First, there will be a close interpenetration of epistemological features and research practice. This is often taken to mean that only certain methods of data collection and analysis are acceptable mechanisms for generating valid and acceptable knowledge and that vice versa those very methods of data collection and analysis carry with them a cluster of epistemological presuppositions. Thus, methods of research and analysis are not neutral devices for gaining leverage on the social world, but different approaches to knowing that world. Accordingly, the use of a structured interview or a self-administered questionnaire is *ipso facto* evidence of a commitment to positivist assumptions, just as ethnographic evidence is in tune with anti-positivist streams of thought like phenomenology. A second implication is that quantitative and qualitative research are incommensurable, that is, they are based on such divergent and incompatible assumptions and presuppositions that they are incapable of resolution or of combination.

The technical version of the debate about quantitative and qualitative research takes a somewhat looser view of the connections between methods and each of the two research traditions. It recognizes that research methods and approaches to analysis may have been developed with a particular view of social reality in mind, but that this does not tie them exclusively and ineluctably to particular epistemological viewpoints. Methods of data collection and analytic approaches are therefore more 'free floating' than in the epistemological version. The crucial question according to the technical version of the debate is not whether there is an appropriate fit between epistemological position and method but whether there is an appropriate fit between the research problem and the method. Accordingly, quantitative and qualitative research are simply different general approaches to data collection.

## Combining quantitative and qualitative research

One important implication of the distinction between epistemological and technical versions of the debate concerns the issue of combining quantitative and qualitative research. In the technical version of the debate, there are no intellectual barriers to an integrated approach. To simplify matters somewhat, if a researcher feels that a particular research question or set of related questions is not likely to be answered adequately through the use of a single method or of (say) quantitative research alone, there are no obvious impediments to introducing a qualitative research element, other than the usual considerations of cost, time and competence. Some issues relating to integrative research will be examined below.

In the epistemological version, reconciliation and integration are much more problematic. Precisely because methods are located in divergent assumptions associated with incommensurable paradigms, integration is essentially impossible. This argument is most strongly associated with the educational researcher, John K. Smith (1983; Smith and Heshusius 1986). His work is often cited in this context (Bryman 1996; Hammersley 1996) and there is a risk that he is being used as a 'straw man [*sic*]'. He writes, for example, that each 'approach sponsors different procedures and has different epistemological implications' and warns us not to 'accept the unfounded assumption that the methods are complementary' (Smith 1983: 12, 13). And again: 'the claim of compatibility, let alone one of synthesis, cannot be sustained' (Smith and Heshusius 1986: 4). Smith is not alone in holding such a view about the possibilities of integration (e.g. Guba 1985; Buchanan 1992), but other writers also argue that methods are firmly rooted in particular positions about what passes as warrantable knowledge (e.g. Hughes 1990). Proponents of the epistemological version do not deny that methods associated with quantitative and qualitative research can be and have been combined in research, but argue that a genuine *rapprochement* is not attained at the paradigmatic level; instead, qualitative research is typically used as an adjunct to what is essentially an exercise in quantitative research.

Thus, while the technical version of the debate about quantitative and qualitative research readily allows for the possibility of integration, the epistemological version is much more sceptical, even to the point of denying its viability at anything other than a superficial level. The chief problem with the epistemological version is that it is difficult to demonstrate that the connection between epistemology and research method is anything other than a convention. Platt's (1985; 1986; 1996) historical researches lead us to question the connections between methods and their supposed epistemological assumptions, while a close examination of classic and other ethnographic texts leads one to query the inevitability of such links.

In view of the adoption by many writers and researchers of a technical version of the debate about quantitative and qualitative research, along with the largely realist form of writing in both traditions, it is not surprising that a considerable number of investigations combine the two. Indeed, it is difficult not to get the impression that the incidence of integrative research is growing. I suggested in 1988 that ten different approaches to blending quantitative and qualitative research could be discerned, along with a residual category of hybrids (Bryman 1988: 131–52). Hammersley (1996) adopted a somewhat more parsimonious threefold classification: *triangulation*, which was one of my ten types; *facilitation*, which effectively combines two of my types (qualitative research facilitates quantitative research and quantitative research facilitates qualitative research); and *complementarity*, which essentially includes the rest.

Of all the different ways of conceptualizing the ways in which quantitative and qualitative research can be combined, triangulation represents the one in which the differences between the two traditions are least prominent. Sechrest and Sidani (1995) provide a fairly typical view in their programmatic argument that the differences tend to be exaggerated and that 'both approaches may be used at the same points with the additional benefit of permitting triangulation on a closer approximation to the truth' (1995: 77). The commitment to a realist position is readily apparent here, but so too is a sense of irritation with academic debates about methodological divisions.

## Quantitative and qualitative research as rhetorics of persuasion

It is common for writers on the differences between quantitative and qualitative research to draw up lists of divergent attributes of the two traditions (e.g. Halfpenny 1979: 799; Reichardt and Cook 1979: 10; Bryman 1988: 94). One aspect of the possible differences between them that is less frequently remarked upon by these and other writers on the debate is that to a significant extent they represent different rhetorics of persuasion. In other words, quantitative and qualitative research can be viewed as entailing *inter alia*, or perhaps even above all, contrasting ways of persuading audiences of the cogency of their truth claims. I hinted at this possibility some years ago:

> To a very large extent, these two research traditions (be they indicative of epistemological or technical positions) may be thought of as divergent *genres*, especially in regard to their modes of presenting research findings and programmatic statements. Of course, they are more than merely literary devices; but it is difficult not to be struck by the different styles of exposition that practitioners of the two traditions espouse.
> (Bryman 1988: 5)

I gave a few illustrations of the contrasting styles, but did not pursue this line in the rest of the book.

In the rest of this chapter, I intend to explore this idea in greater detail. In other words, I want to pursue the notion that quantitative and qualitative research represent in large part different rhetorics of persuasion and see how far it takes us. The issue is fundamental to both the debate about quantitative and qualitative research and to the question of knowing the social world. As regards the former, it suggests that if different rhetorics of persuasion are in evidence, it may be necessary to reassess the current *entente cordiale* which suggests either that the differences between them are exaggerated or that they can be combined; and in relation to the latter, the question is raised about the extent to which 'knowing the social world' is inseparable from how that social world is rhetorically presented. However, in arguing that quantitative and qualitative research may fruitfully be examined in terms of the possibility that they reflect different rhetorics of persuasion, an important caveat has to be acknowledged at the outset, because as Billig (1994) and Potter (1996: 106–8) have observed, writing practices are not just methods of persuasion: they are part of the very act of forging ideas. Therefore, while the emphasis in what follows will be upon persuasion, it needs to be recognized that the importance of rhetoric is more extensive than such a focus might suggest.

## Rhetoric and the natural sciences

The view that rhetorical conventions are important features of knowledge is by no means a new concept in the context of research on the natural sciences. A few illustrations will allow this general point to be established. Law and Williams (1982) examined the discussions between two groups of scientists in the course of preparing a paper on polymers that was to be jointly published. They show that the scientists' concern was not just with their findings as such, but also with the best ways to make the paper attractive to referees and peers. Three factors stood out in their discussions as mechanisms for enhancing the appeal of their paper. First, an important consideration is who should be cited, as this affects how the domain is construed, and how citations should be presented. Citation is not a simple question of mapping the domain to which the findings relate, but one of deciding how best to market the paper's relevance and attractiveness. Gilbert (1977) has also argued that referencing is a means of persuasion, for example, as a way of backing up the author's own arguments and as a means of demonstrating the novelty of research findings. Second, how the findings are best presented, especially their juxtaposition in terms of existing findings and theories in the field, was a focus of considerable discussion. The third factor is particularly relevant to the present discussion in that Law and Williams argue that what they call 'literary conventions' are about how best to establish linkages between key figures in the field and findings. In seeking to forge connections between their findings and particular past findings considerable debate focused on the appropriate literary devices for expressing the desired associations.

Gilbert and Mulkay's (1984) examination of a paper prepared for an audience of biochemists notes the commonly observed tendency for agency to be marginalized through textual conventions like 'results suggest'. Woolgar (1988) calls this kind of gambit an *externalizing device*, a tactic for creating a sense of the phenomenon in question being 'out there' and consequently not the product of human agency. Gilbert and Mulkay also show how the paper's opening sentences are devised to create a sense of uncertainty about the current status of an issue within the field and of the need to welcome the authors' soundly based experimental findings.

However, when the same scientists are interviewed a different picture comes across. Whereas the papers give an impression of inevitable conclusions being drawn from evidence based on neutral techniques, in interviews the scientists' views and actions sometimes come across as 'more personal, open to debate and generally contingent' (Gilbert and Mulkay 1984: 46). The papers suppress precisely those elements of the scientific process that are frequently referred to in interviews: the significance of theoretical speculation, experimenters' theoretical positions, and the impact of social relationships in the scientific community on actions and beliefs. When explaining in articles the methods used in their experiments, authors seek to get across the fact that experimental protocol was rigorously followed; in interviews, the same scientists emphasized 'craft skills, subtle judgements and intuitive understanding' (Gilbert and Mulkay 1984: 53). The contrast between the style of the research paper and scientists' own accounts (a contrast of which they are themselves typically aware) are summarized by Gilbert and Mulkay as one between *empiricist* and *contingent* 'repertoires'.

These examples, which derive from research by sociologists on scientific accounts, draw attention to the ways in which scientists in their writings draw on a range of rhetorical and literary devices to persuade their peers of the cogency of their claims. This is apparent in the empiricist repertoire in the ways in which scientists' own actions are absent from formal accounts, in the prominence given to data as the basis for their reasoning, and in the following of rules in arriving at the evidence. Knowing the natural world is in large part a function of the textual strategies employed by scientists in convincing others of the importance of their work.

## Rhetoric and quantitative research in the social sciences

There are clear signs of the operation of the empiricist repertoire in the rhetoric of persuasion employed by quantitative researchers in the social sciences. Many of the tactics just described can be seen in Gusfield's (1976) examination of an article on people who drive while under the influence of alcohol (Waller 1967). He points to the linear approach in the article in which the 'centrality of method and externality of the data' are the key elements (Gusfield 1976: 19). The researcher is absent from the text to demonstrate the primacy of the methods used and hence the scientific probity of the approach taken and the findings generated. The style is impersonal so that no impression of Waller's beliefs affecting the findings or their interpretation could be gleaned. As Gusfield puts it:

> The language . . . informs the reader that the persuasion is to come from an external reality not from the author or his use of language. . . . The agent is minimized and the drama of the paper is presented as flowing

> from the unfolding of the procedures of method, not from the interests, biases or language of the author.
>
> (Gusfield 1976: 21)

Gusfield is at pains to make clear that he is not accusing Waller of being a bad scientist; rather, he sees Waller's writing as 'normal' and as 'unavoidable' (1976: 31).

McCloskey (1985) has conducted a similar exercise in relation to a branch of the social sciences in which quantitative research has a vice-like grip – economics. He examined a paper by Paul Samuelson and notes that its persuasive appeal lies in such features as the prominence of its mathematical form and the use of key figures as authorities. Similar features are detected in an article by John Muth in which rhetorical devices which are designed to make 'an appeal to his character as a Scientist and to the self-image of his audience as fellow scientists' (McCloskey 1985: 97–8).

Bazerman (1987) has noted how the *Publication Manual* of the American Psychological Association (APA) over successive editions has sought to develop the impression that good writing resided in the application of rules regarding what should be reported in an article and to a large extent how it should be done. Bazerman depicts the growing routinization of writing as a product of the growth of behaviourism (by which he means a focus on behaviour rather than the workings of the mind), which is itself strongly associated with the rise of empiricism. Articles written after the early 1930s developed a similarity of style in which the authors, their subjects and the literature became more 'objectlike', as Bazerman (1987: 137) puts it. Individual behaviour disappeared from view and raw scores gave way to statistical calculations (see also Billig 1994). The standard gambit is to refer to an area of behaviour that has not been adequately addressed by psychologists and then to demonstrate that one has carefully designed an experiment to redress the situation. While the methods section occupies a prominent position, it is reduced to smaller print. This section is meant to make clear that the writer has conformed to the appropriate standards, rather than to demonstrate an aspect of the researcher's reasoning, hence its apparent relegation to a smaller font. Bazerman's work suggests that rhetorics of persuasion are enshrined in the APA's dictates to which prospective writers more or less have to conform. How far the various developments he describes are due to APA guidelines or to incremental changes in conventions is not entirely clear, but his suggestions bring out once again the important role played by rhetorical devices in knowing the social world through quantitative research.

Bazerman has also examined rhetorical strategies in political science, where he again notes the growing prominence of 'a form of scientific presentation relying heavily on mathematics for both evidence and argument' (1988: 280). Like writers on rhetoric in the natural sciences, he notes the importance of citations, but argues that their use in political science is different: in the latter discipline citing is both more extensive and less codified than in the natural sciences. The aim is to offer a number of interpretations of the literature which establish the credentials and credibility of the writer's own research and the results. The research by Law and Williams (1982) cited earlier suggests that the role of referencing is not as different from the natural sciences as Bazerman argues. In spite of the identification of certain general tendencies, Bazerman argues that there is considerable variety in the forms of political science writing, suggesting that the field 'has yet to forge a consistent rhetoric' (1988: 288).

Like Bazerman, John (1992) has noted the rhetorical use of statistics in psychology. He argues that in a contested field like psychology, statistics fill an important function in research because their apparent association with science bestows legitimacy and credibility on the field. One of the chief grounds for John's view is that there is widespread misuse of statistical significance testing and occasional recognition of its limitations in the field. Why then does the practice survive? John's answer is that it helps to justify knowledge claims and what he calls the 'epistemic authority' of the field and its practitioners. A similar point was made many years earlier in relation to sociology when McCartney (1970) argued that a major reason for the growing use of statistics was its association with scientific method and the greater likelihood that research based on statistics will receive external funding and be published in major journals. Indeed, McCartney provided statistical evidence to show with respect to the period 1895–1964 the decline of case study research, the growth of articles reporting statistics, and the rise of articles mentioning funding.

One further rhetorical device in quantitative research is the frequent recourse to a *management* metaphor (Shapiro 1985; Richardson 1990). This feature can be discerned in the mention of such devices as 'designing' research, 'controlling' variables, 'managing' data and 'generating' tables. The metaphor brings out the researcher's ingenuity and conformity with good practice. Indeed, the originality of an article often resides in precisely this element, such as controlling for a variable that has not previously been taken into consideration.

This account seems to suggest (note this and many other rhetorical flourishes in the presentation of the argument) that natural science writing and that found in quantitative research in the social sciences exhibit certain rhetorical styles which are the product of practitioners' writing strategies to convince others of the cogency of their findings. However, it should also be noted that there is some variation in certain issues, most notably the insertion of the author in the text. As pointed out earlier, Gusfield (1976) observed that Waller was largely absent from the text he produced and that this was a deliberate device to establish a sense of externality and a sense of the researcher being a carrier of scientific methods. However, in the context of quantitative research in political science, Bazerman makes an almost opposite point:

> In political science papers, as in natural science papers, the first person frequently is used to express the author's active role in constructing ideas and collecting data as well as to claim credit for the research process and results.
>
> (Bazerman 1988: 287)

He quotes extensively from an article (Page and Jones 1979) in which such phrases are employed as 'we intend to specify and estimate', 'we first consider', 'we measured reactions', 'we can with some confidence specify' and 'perhaps the theoretically most important of all our estimates'. The suggestion that the active role of the author can also be found in natural science papers seems to clash with Gilbert and Mulkay's (1984) view, though the latter did find occasional instances of the use of the first person in each of the two articles they examined in detail: 'we report', 'we describe' and 'we conclude' (Gilbert and Mulkay 1984: 41, 44). However, this point aside, it would seem that it is not straightforward to characterize the style of reporting as impersonal to convey a sense of externality. Bazerman's point is almost the opposite of Gusfield's. The latter wants us to believe that authors *remove* themselves from the text to inject a sense of facticity; Bazerman suggests that they *insert* themselves into the text to demonstrate their role and ingenuity. Nor can this divergence be quickly written off in terms of the choice of article by these two writers: Gusfield (1976: 18) suggests that his choice 'represents' other papers on drinking driving; Bazerman examined other political science articles in 1979 and observes that the authors 'also represent themselves as the doers, interpreters, and owners of the research' (1988: 287). Thus, while we can accept the general principles of rhetoric being integral to our knowledge of the social world and of the notion that quantitative research exhibits a distinctive mode of rhetorical persuasion, the characterization of the forms of the strategies involved warrants further examination.

As an illustration of some of these general ideas, I will use an article taken from one of the premier journals in sociology. The choice is possibly perverse because it is a quantitative research approach to qualitative findings. Hodson (1996) examined the well known field of research concerned with worker alienation under different technologies. His 'data' are book-length ethnographic studies in the field. A sifting process that is fully explicated yielded 108 cases which derive from 86 ethnographies.

The first several pages provide the customary extensive citations and summary of the literature in order to develop a new typology of forms of workplace organization and to demonstrate that one aspect of this literature – workers' strategies of independence – 'remains conceptually underdeveloped' (Hodson 1996: 719), as a result of which a new model of the 'active worker' is developed. Much of the time, the voice is active: 'the model of worklife I develop here', 'the model I use here', 'my model', 'I use this typology', 'by worker strategies I mean' and 'I divide worker experiences'. But occasionally, there is an externalizing approach: when discussing each of the two aspects of the model of the active worker, the phrase 'the workplace literature identifies' is used. When we move to the discussion of the ways in which the cases were generated, we find even more oscillation between the two modes of writing. In fact, there is a third, because a new subject emerges – 'we'. This 'we' is not a euphemism for 'I', because as will be seen, it tends to occur specifically when referring to the data selection process in which a footnote on the first page tells us who were involved: 'staff and students of the 1992 Sociological Research Practicum at Indiana University who helped collect the data for this study' (Hodson 1996: 719). In the discussion of the selection of cases, there is a general oscillation between active and passive voice; relevant phrases are: 'likely titles were generated by computer-assisted searches', 'we excluded cases', 'we examined each selected book', 'workplace characteristics that I hypothesize', 'about 200 books were rejected', and when summarizing the process he writes 'application of the above criteria generated'. The discussion of the coding of the ethnographies is mainly in the active voice: 'the researchers discussed', 'our goal was' and 'the ethnographies were read and coded by the same team of four researchers', but again when summarizing the process, the researchers are suppressed – 'an underlying assumption of this analysis is that the ethnographic data constitute a realist account'. In the results section, both styles can be found: 'I use ordinary least squares regression', 'missing values for these variables were replaced with mean values', 'Table 4 presents results', 'the pattern for these variables would be better described' and 'we examine passages from the ethnographies'. When we come to the Discussion and Conclusion sections, the author and his researchers disappear: 'the results presented here do not support' and 'the findings reported here do not represent'.

The strategies depicted by Gusfield and Bazerman seem to be represented in this article in almost equal measure. The presence of both authorial voice and third person account in the same sections makes it difficult to identify general patterns, though there does seem to be a tendency toward externalizing in the Discussion and Conclusion. Other features of the rhetorical strategies of writers working within a quantitative research approach can be identified in Hodson's article. The citations are employed in such a way as to establish a link with well known authorities in the field, such as Blauner, but also to establish the need for a new slant on the areas because of changes in technology since they wrote and because they have typically neglected precisely the issue that is to be emphasized, namely strategies of autonomous activity. Although some quotations from ethnographic evidence are provided, the emphasis in the bulk of the results is upon the quantitative findings. Moreover, we see a feature that John (1992) highlighted: an inappropriate (albeit self-confessed) use of significance testing. Since the ethnographies generated represent a population, the application of significance testing of the regression coefficients is unnecessary but 'should be interpreted as suggestive' (Hodson 1996: 726). The methods section has pride of place and serves to establish the rigorous nature of the data collection and coding processes. People as such disappear from view, but resurface very briefly in a couple of quotations from the workplace ethnographies that are employed 'to better understand the meaning' of the statistical patterns (Hodson 1996: 729).

The management metaphor is evident in a number of places, but perhaps most notably in the section on 'control variables' in which we are informed: 'Variables measuring worker skill and autonomy are included in parts of the analysis as intervening variables'. Similarly, in the preamble to the results, we are told that 'missing values for . . . variables were replaced with mean values' (Hodson 1996: 726, 728). It is striking that in both these instances of a management metaphor an externalizing mode of presentation is employed.

## Rhetoric and qualitative research in the social sciences

Qualitative researchers have probably displayed, especially since the mid-1980s, a greater awareness of and reflexivity about the rhetorical character of fieldwork than their counterparts in quantitative research. In large part, this is a product of the immense surge of interest in the nature of ethnographic writing within anthropology (e.g. Clifford and Marcus 1986). Such writers show that writing an ethnography entails a strategy for convincing the reader that the ethnographer has a special warrant to convey a culture to others, or, as Clifford (1983: 120) puts it, how to transform 'unruly experience' into an 'authoritative written account'. At the same time, the very fact that a rhetorical strategy is being deployed is suppressed in the course of writing (Crapanzano 1986). This emphasis has gradually been taken up by qualitative researchers in sociology in particular (e.g. Van Maanen 1988; Atkinson 1990). Knowing the social world is no longer a simple matter of considering what procedures are followed in generating knowledge, but how that knowledge is conveyed and indeed how the procedures leading to it are conveyed become integral elements. In fact, 'findings' and the modes of their rhetorical transmission become inseparable elements in knowledge of the social world.

But are the rhetorical tropes devised by qualitative researchers fundamentally different from those of quantitative researchers? If the notion of quantitative and qualitative research being different rhetorics of persuasion has any veracity we would expect to encounter essentially different persuasive tactics. When the literature on ethnographic writing is examined, it is difficult not to be struck by the fact that in both quantitative and qualitative research there is a pronounced realism. The characterization of the debate about quantitative and qualitative research being in large part about a clash between realism and idealism cannot be sustained in practice. It is true that it is more difficult to demonstrate that quantitative research is not imbued with realism than it is to show that qualitative research is drenched in a realist view of the world. Hammersley (1992a: 170–1) has shown that George Lundberg, a writer typically viewed as an unforgiving spokesman for a scientistic programme for the study of social reality, sometimes wrote in a way that suggested that he was sensitive to the effects of prior conceptions upon findings. However, the comment Hammersley quotes is difficult to assess because it was a general statement about the implications of a shift from a Copernican to a Ptolemaic conception of the universe. It is not clear how such a view linked with Lundberg's notion of research practice with respect to the study of social reality. In fact, it is difficult to demonstrate at the level of research practice that quantitative social researchers are not fundamentally realists. Their general approach tends to be one of uncovering a pre-existing reality. They may pay lip service, since most have at least a passing acquaintance with Kuhn, to a recognition that research results are at least in part a function of prior conceptions, but when carrying out research and particularly when presenting findings, their attachment to realism seems inescapable. The criteria associated with good quantitative research – such as, measurement validity and reliability, internal validity, external validity – also betray this realism.

But realism is also a feature of much, if not most, ethnographic writing. Van Maanen (1988) has demonstrated the realism in much ethnographic writing. This realism reveals itself in a number of ways, but is particularly evident in the presentation of third person accounts of a representation of reality that ethnographers present as having been deciphered by them. The reader is presented with an account that any reasonable person conducting a study of a culture would have arrived at. Readers are presented with an avalanche of contextual detail, which serves to reinforce the ethnographer's indepth understanding of a culture. The ethnographer takes the native point of view that he or she by dint of hard work and expertise has fathomed out and which is now presented for the reader's consumption. Of course, ethnographers do not simply act as conduits for this native point of view: they conceptualize, theorize and draw conclusions that will be of interest to readers. Research which is qualitative but only loosely ethnographic, in the sense of being derived from such techniques as unstructured interviewing, focus groups, textual analysis and oral history rather than participant observation, is also likely to be found in realist form. Disputes between ethnographers about who has accurately interpreted and understood a culture are invariably underpinned by an explicit realism (Bryman 1994).

Van Maanen (1988) distinguished two forms of ethnographic writing that are not 'realist tales'. First, there are 'confessional tales', which are personalized accounts in which the ethnographer is fully implicated in the data gathering and writing up processes; they are warts and all accounts of the trials and tribulations of doing ethnography. By and large, however, the confessional and the realist tale are not really comparable: the realist tale is a form of presenting an ethnographic account of culture; the confessional tale is invariably a form of presenting accounts of the methodology involved in an ethnographic account of a culture. As Van Maanen notes: 'Collections of autobiographical reflections on past projects represent the most common outlet for confessional tales of the field' (1988: 82). So too are methodological appendices to ethnographic monographs. Whyte's (1955 [1943]) candid reflections on his methods in *Street Corner Society* provide an illustration of this genre. In his case, a confessional tale is tacked onto an essentially realist ethnography, but the realist tenor of the ethnography is not compromised in any way.

The other major form of ethnographic writing distinguished by Van Maanen is 'impressionist tales' which place a heavy emphasis on 'words, metaphors, phrasings, and . . . the expansive recall of fieldwork experience' (1988: 102) and in which there is a heavy emphasis on dramatic events. However, as Van Maanen also notes, such tales are 'typically enclosed within realist, or perhaps more frequently, confessional tales' (1988: 106). Thus, the essentially realist essence of much ethnographic writing has been largely unmoved by the impressionist style which prospered after the 'discovery' of the poetics of ethnographic reporting. If the impressionist tale is usually found either in the context of realist tales or of confessional tales, which are themselves often offshoots of realist tales, it is difficult to deny the fundamentally realist nature of ethnographic writing. There is no doubt that some writers, particularly those influenced by postmodernism, have sought to promote anti-realist accounts (e.g. Rosaldo 1986; Tyler 1986) and their suggestions have found some adherents, but most ethnographic reporting continues largely untouched by these ideas.

However, the suggestion that quantitative and qualitative research generally share a realist view of the world does not *ipso facto* mean that they do not differ in terms of rhetorical strategies. As a counterpoint to the analysis of Hodson (1996), a similar examination is given of a study, also in the area of the sociology of work and occupations, by Fine (1996). Like Hodson's article, Fine's paper was published in a bastion of quantitative research – the *Administrative Science Quarterly*. The research is concerned with restaurant cooks and in particular their 'rhetorical strategies' which define their work and their identities. This choice too might appear perverse since we are searching for the rhetorical strategies involved in writing up research on rhetorical strategies!

It barely requires stating that one rhetorical device employed in quantitative research is absent from Fine (1996) – statistical reasoning. Instead, Fine makes use of the familiar device of extensive quotations from interviews or from field notes to attest to the validity of his findings. In some respects, the quotations are not necessary: they do little more than illustrate the general points that he is making. However, they serve the important function of attesting to Fine's grip on his evidence and the force of his analytical reasoning.

Fine's article is similar to Hodson in the use of citations: there is a review of the relevant literature on work and identity along with a distinctive 'take' on how the issue should be tackled. There is very little externalizing; indeed, the author seems to be at pains, most notably in his account of his research methods, to place himself at the centre of the presentation. He writes:

> I focus on four sets of rhetorical strategies that cooks rely on. . . . I argue that cooks can rely on images of being professionals, artists, businessmen, or manual labourers. . . . I do not contend that these are the only rhetorical resources that are available. . . . I conducted participant observation in four restaurants in the Twin Cities metropolitan area. . . . I spent, on average, 50–85 hours in each. . . . In each restaurant, I interviewed all full-time cooks, a total of thirty interviews. . . . The four restaurants represent a range of professional cooking environments in the Twin Cities. . . . I do not claim that these four restaurants form a representative sample; clearly they do not. They represent the upper portion of Minnesota restaurants in status.
>
> (Fine 1996: 93)

And again:

> In each restaurant, I first received the approval of the head chef and then the owners. On my first day in the restaurant kitchen, I explained my interest in understanding the world of cooks and assured them that I was not an agent of the owners. I emphasized that I wished to watch them work and subsequently to interview them. At no time did I 'cook', but occasionally, when a need existed, I served as an extra pair of hands.
>
> (Fine 1996: 94)

Fine places himself at the centre of the research process, pointing to the details of his research. The theorization and his close involvement in the life-worlds of cooks are unmistakably and unashamedly attributed to him. In this way, he uses the standard devices for attributing ethnographic authority to himself. His defensiveness about the representativeness at the end of the first of the two extended quotations is striking: after years of case study research, ethnographers should hardly need to establish that they are not claiming that their sites are representative in this routine way, but in the context of a journal strongly associated with the quantitative research tradition, such a qualification appears to be deemed necessary.

Fine's presentation of his findings are broadly realist in tone and barely differ from Hodson's or those of other quantitative researchers. The findings have a fixed, 'out there' quality that is routinely found in quantitative research reports. For example, in his concluding section Fine writes:

> Cooks use a range of occupational rhetorics as resources to provide a sense of self worth. In this they are not alone. . . . Cooks, situated within an occupation that is cross-cut by numerous conflicting strains, represent a compelling example of how a range of identities can define a worker.
>
> (Fine 1996: 111–12)

This general style of characterizing his findings barely differs from Hodson's. In both articles, the reader is left with the sense of a definitive account of an external reality. Missing from Fine's account, compared to that of Hodson and most quantitative researchers, are intimations of the management of data collection process or of the handling of data. Indeed, in place of a management metaphor we are confronted with what might best be called a naturalistic metaphor. Fine is at pains to get across the notion that he endeavoured to preserve the naturalness of the research setting. Moreover, while the characterization of the four occupational rhetorics is unmistakably his gloss on cooks' identity formation strategies, there is a clear implication that they are very much rooted in his subjects' own perspective, as when Fine writes just before presenting the details of his classification:

> The diversity of images embedded in being a chef are in part a function of his or her deeper, richer, and more complex conceptualizations, a consequence of long-term involvement in the industry.
>
> (Fine 1996: 96)

Thus, while the data collection is presented in terms of a metaphor of naturalism, conceptualization and analysis are presented in terms preserving the naturalness of cooks' accounts. Ironically, the latter means that just like natural scientists and quantitative social researchers, Fine probably has to play down the role of 'craft skills, subtle judgements and intuitive understanding' (Gilbert and Mulkay 1984: 53) in the interests of displaying his retention of the integrity of the worldview of cooks.

## Comparing the rhetorical devices of quantitative and qualitative research

To what extent, then, do the foregoing analyses imply that quantitative and qualitative research represent different rhetorics of persuasion? The answer seems to be that they do, but only in some respects. The similarities will be examined initially. First, both articles are imbued with a pronounced realism; each writer presents his results in terms of a definitive picture of an objective, external reality. There is, of course, an interesting tension here, for in recognizing that both quantitative and qualitative research rhetorically construct a realist account of the world one is taking an anti-realist position, because the knowledge of the social world that Hodson and Fine report is being construed as a representation. Second, both authors place themselves at the centre of the research process, but whereas Fine adopts this stance more or less unremittingly, Hodson does so intermittently. Externalizing was most evident in the latter's Discussion and Conclusion. Third, and linked to the second point, both authors seem to play down their craft skills in the analysis of their data, but for different reasons: Hodson seems to want to show that he followed strictly the correct procedures associated with quantitative research; Fine wants to demonstrate that in conceptualizing his data he has not overstepped the mark and lost sight of his subjects' experiences. Fourth, both authors deploy citations in the manner suggested by Gilbert (1977) and Law and Williams (1982).

However, there are differences as well. First, and most obviously, there is a contrast between the use of a statistical rhetoric of persuasion in Hodson and detailed quotations in Fine's article. Second, there is a clear contrast between the presence of a management metaphor in Hodson's article and the indications of fidelity to the naturalness of the research setting in Fine's work. Third, there is much greater use of externalizing in Hodson's than in Fine's article.

This examination suggests that there is evidence to suggest that quantitative and qualitative research represent different rhetorics of persuasion, but that there are important similarities as well. To a certain extent, the similarities may be a product of the need to conform to journals' writing conventions, particularly in connection with the use of citations. However, the finding that there are important similarities with respect to rhetorics of persuasion is very much in tune with those writers who have sought to play down the differences between quantitative and qualitative research (e.g. Hammersley 1992a) and with those writers who have sought to draw attention to their compatibility in connection with the possibility of integrating them in research (e.g. Bryman 1988). But the significance of the differences in rhetorics of persuasion should not be ignored and may provide a spur to further textual analyses of articles representative of quantitative and qualitative research.

Mention was made earlier of the growing trend toward studies that integrate quantitative and qualitative research and in this respect it would be interesting to know how far different rhetorics can be discerned within a single report. My best guess is that differences will be even less pronounced than in the Hodson/Fine contrast because most cases of integration operate within a frame in which one tradition predominates. Thus, we tend to find either that the quantitative research is the dominant mode and that the qualitative evidence is written up in a very similar way; or that qualitative research is the dominant frame and that the quantitative research is simply deployed within that frame. It is rather uncommon for investigations to allocate more or less equal weight to quantitative and qualitative research; it is striking that when Brannen (1992: 28–31) discussed this possibility, she drew entirely upon her own research.

## Conclusion

Discussions of quantitative and qualitative research have tended to emphasize the epistemological foundations of the two traditions or have explored them as essentially data collection and handling strategies, though many writers undoubtedly conflate these two levels of conceptualization. This issue has implications for the question of whether quantitative and qualitative research can be integrated because arguments that stress their epistemological bases do not readily admit the possibility of combined research.

Another way of addressing the nature of quantitative and qualitative research and the differences between them is to examine the possibility that they represent different rhetorics of persuasion. An analysis of two articles which exemplify both forms of research proved somewhat inconclusive: the similarities were as striking (and perhaps as surprising) as the differences. The outcome of the exercise was sufficiently interesting to warrant similar exercises being conducted on other articles. One of the most striking aspects of the comparison was the extent to which published quantitative and qualitative research seem to be imbued with realism. While the growth of reflection about the nature of ethnographic writing has undoubtedly spawned new modes of presenting findings, much of it is still suffused with realism or with a form with which it is closely related.

It must also be recognized that the very question of whether quantitative and qualitative research share or differ in rhetorics of persuasion presumes a non-realist position. The question itself implies that knowing the social world is not a simple matter of generating 'valid' research findings because an essential ingredient of that knowledge is rendering one's findings in a compelling way. This should not be taken to mean that social scientists are being duped by the use of rhetorical conventions, since these are an essential ingredient of all writing and indeed of all argument. Instead, it entails a recognition of the integral role played by such tropes in social science writing.

A further implication of the present discussion is that the examination of quantitative and qualitative research – their differences and similarities and the prospects for their integration – has to encapsulate the question of how far they are constituted by the rhetorics of persuasion deployed by their practitioners. This is not to say that there is nothing more to quantitative and qualitative research than the employment of different rhetorics (especially since this piece has suggested that the similarities may be just as striking as the differences), but that they represent an important component of our knowledge of the social world. In other words, to the extent that quantitative and qualitative research represent different forms of knowledge of the social world, this may only partly be a function of such considerations as different epistemological foundations, different methods of data collection and different data analytic strategies. Instead, contrasting writing tropes need to be included in any examination of the significance of differences between quantitative and qualitative research strategies in knowing the social world.

# 10 | Reflections and reflexivity

**Tim May**

In this final chapter, I would like to look back over the contents of the various chapters in order to draw out their implications for questions about how we know the social world. In the process, I will consider how these discussions relate to the place of reflexivity in the practices of the social sciences and social life.

## Reflexivity: role and dimensions

Before considering the issues raised in this volume, it is first necessary to clarify how I will be using the term 'reflexivity'. I have argued that in order to understand the role of social science in society and how it is implicated in the constitution of social life, it is necessary to consider reflexivity as having two dimensions: endogenous and referential (May 1998). These two senses are difficult to separate in practice. Nevertheless, it is my argument that attention to either dimension without due consideration to the other, leads to a limited understanding of social science and its relevance for understanding and informing social life.

Endogenous reflexivity refers to the ways in which the actions of members of a given community contribute to social reality itself. This encompasses not only an understanding of how interpretations and actions within the lifeworld contribute to the constitution of social reality, but also those same aspects within the social scientific community itself. Endogenous reflexivity thus relates to the knowledge we have of our immediate social and cultural milieux. This knowledge then informs our practical actions which are oriented to those localities.

To the above we have to add the dimension of referential reflexivity. This refers to the consequences which arise from a meeting between the reflexivity exhibited by actors within the social world and that exhibited by the researcher as part of a social scientific community. Referential reflexivity thus refers to the knowledge which is gained via an encounter with ways of life and ways of viewing the social world that are different from our own. The constitution of this discursive knowledge and its implications for social practice, enables an understanding of the conditions under which action takes place. As such, through this meeting, how and under what circumstances reflexivity itself is heightened may be open to examination in the relationship between knowledge, action and social circumstances.

To focus upon endogenous reflexivity alone means that the varying conditions under which reflexivity may be generated within the lifeworld and the social scientific community is not examined as a topic, but assumed as a given resource that is available to all, regardless of the social conditions under and through which they act. Reflexivity is then given *within* actions, but not *upon* actions. To exclusively examine endogenous reflexivity brackets consideration of the following issues which are fundamental for understanding the role of social science in social life. These are: the interactions between lay and scientific communities, how these are negotiated, under what conditions and with what effects? How social scientific knowledge is interpreted and acted upon (or not) when disseminated and with what consequences for the study of the phenomena itself and those who are part of the study? How an understanding of these issues feeds back into research practice and relates to how social science is evaluated in terms of its knowledge base and what it may offer for understanding and explanation in general? Finally, what is the nature of the relationship between reflexivity within actions and reflexivity upon actions in terms of social change and how does social scientific knowledge contribute to this process and with what effects?

With these two dimensions to reflexivity in mind, I now wish to consider how these relate to the contributions within this volume. In the process I will be not only summarizing the main points in each chapter, but also elaborating upon them in terms of the above discussions on reflexivity.

### *Reflexive questioning*

The contributions in this book have examined fundamental issues concerning the nature of social science, the ontological properties of the phenomena with which it is concerned and its theory and practice. This is part of a healthy and ongoing debate that should not only enable clarification and improvements in precision, but also aim to question the conventions upon which practices are based in order that common pre-reflexive assumptions are open to critical scrutiny. However, there is a basic tension in these aims for the very act of raising such issues may itself threaten established procedures and beliefs. The question then becomes: at what point does this become 'unproductive' for research purposes and part of a philosophical game without end? Indeed, David Silverman recounts a story to illustrate his resistance to taking reflexive questioning too far:

> Many years ago, I remember a research student who used to make visiting speakers flounder by asking them: 'how would you apply your own analysis to the text you have just presented?' As they wriggled, I wriggled too – not from intellectual difficulty but rather from distaste for this sort of wordplay which appeared to make a not very articulate student into a profound thinker.
>
> (Silverman 1997b: 240)

His is an aesthetic resistance to a certain form of reflexivity, but these comments reflect a trend in contemporary methodological discussions. This is apparent in concerns with the play of words in textual representations of reality, rather than a discussion of results in relation to the process of their production *and* reception. Although it is of clear importance to examine how texts are implicated in representations of social reality, there is a clear tendency within these discussions to focus upon the endogenous dimension of reflexivity.

Reflexive questioning should not only involve an examination of the grounds upon which we may claim to know the social world, but also point to the limitations of our knowledge. In this sense it acts as a corrective to the instrumentalism informed by the desire to control, rather than understand, the social world. Nevertheless, there are those who are dismissive of such debates and carry on regardless. Others, proud to be relativists in the age of apparent uncertainty, tell their stories about social life and are able to justify their practices through reference to the collapse of science into literature and the retreat of objectivism.

In this climate it is possible to form the distinct impression that methodological discussions are trapped within a descending interpretative circle. A reputation for astute methodological reflections is then left to be forged through interpretations of interpretations. Yet, referentially speaking, how are the interpreters authorized to make such pronouncements? Is it something to do with the institutional authority that is bestowed upon individuals that affords them a distance from the process and possible repercussions of investigations into the social world itself? Academic commentators may well fall into this group. That said, they do not enjoy a monopoly on reflexive questioning and also find themselves increasingly subject to the very forces which act as a counter to reflexivity: for example, funds have to be won from external agencies who expect results within a given time, according to certain specifications. In a methodologically post-positivist/empiricist/modernist age, therefore, the quiet revenge of 'instrumental positivism' (Bryant 1985) may be marching onwards. Practical and discursive knowledge then lie in an increasing disjuncture to one another.

None of this is to suggest that issues about research practice are not of fundamental importance. Nor is it to suggest that researchers are not able to exercise differing degrees of latitude in the decisions they make during their research, or regarding how and what they report as a result. However, it is to suggest that a failure to understand the forces which act upon the process of social research and the conditions under which it is enacted, leads to a limited understanding of its place and value in social life. Furthermore, the limits of these understandings may then be replicated in the studies of social life itself through the invoking of prereflexive assumptions. These assumptions can be seen in terms of the consequences which arise from different ontological, theoretical and methodological allegiances. It is to a consideration of these and their implications for the two dimensions of reflexivity that I now turn.

## Issues in knowing the social world

My point in drawing attention to the relationship between research decisions and funding agencies, is that what is often called 'practical' in the research process can so easily lapse into the instrumental. At this point, theoretical and philosophical discourse can assist in the process of gaining a critical distance from everyday exigencies in order to reflect upon such decisions, the results of which feed back into practice itself. However, in considering this possibility, some basic questions need to be considered. These are: what is the relationship between thought, action and reality? This, in turn, raises the question: how do we conceive of reality itself? These are of central importance to what it is to 'know' the social world.

### *Making connections: ontology, language and social properties*

In terms of the relationship between thought, action and social conditions, social phenomena are often held to produce regular effects that exhibit clear patterns within social life which lead to particular consequences. Belonging to a social class, for instance, is said to affect life chances. On the other hand, if we admit of considerable diversity due to an absence of *any* structural effects to social life, what is there left for the social scientist to do but to describe fleeting cultural configurations that have disappeared before their descriptions are disseminated to a wider audience? Caught in a vortex of symbolism without referents, the time would come for the social scientist to seek alternative employment and for the potential of reflexivity to finally disappear without trace.

In Malcolm Williams's contribution to this volume, we find an account of a journey from politics to philosophy and from there back to methodology and method in the study of a political, social and economic phenomenon – homelessness. His overall point is that in order to produce meaningful results, it is necessary to start at the experiential level of 'being homeless'. However, if the results themselves are to have any impact, from a policy point of view, there must be some generalizations, albeit *moderatum*, that result from the research. From a pragmatic point of view, policy makers are in the business of macrostructuring reality. With this in mind, research techniques then combine in the overall desire to have some 'impact' on the construction of social issues and policies through positing particular effects on the lifestyles of people.

This argument combines elements of both endogenous and referential reflexivity. The overall aim, while one of impact on policy decision making is not, however, separate from theory construction in order to be able to make *moderatum* generalizations in the first place. In this respect, Pawson's secondary analysis of the writings of Goldthorpe, Boudin and Wright on class, as Malcolm Williams notes, finds a high degree of consistency in their explanatory and measurement strategies, but not in their generative models of class itself. This does not imply that class does not exist, simply that these approaches might seek to explain different aspects of the experience of 'being' classed. That noted, problems then arise in the two dimensions of reflexivity. If there are different meanings attributed to a phenomenon, then surely such models are incommensurable? Further, if these are incommensurable it is because the phenomenon to which they refer does not possess any properties which can be attributed with producing effects on the constitution of social life itself.

The effect of this line of reasoning is twofold. First, it can relieve the reader of the burden of engaging with and thinking through ideas about class (endogenous), and second, to ignore the impact of such discussions on the social climate as a whole and their more immediate effects on people's everyday lives (referential). Politics, theory and practice then mingle in an ideological terrain that becomes closed to examination (class belonging determines life chances and experiences), or presumed to be open to such a multiplicity of perspectives that the phenomenon itself no longer has any explanatory purchase on social reality (class is 'dead'). These issues arise in the separation between endogenous and referential reflexivity.

We might admit that ideas about class are socially produced and in that sense do not simply reflect an independently given reality. However, does this admission of 'epistemic relativism' necessarily commit us to 'judgemental relativism'? Judgemental relativism being the position: 'that all beliefs are equally valid in the sense that there are no rational grounds for preferring one to another' (Bhaskar 1986: 72). Relativists would hold that epistemic relativism does imply judgemental relativism; a situation of incommensurability between different explanatory frameworks necessarily being the outcome.

In the first instance what is required is a distinction between two aspects of a theory that parallel the two dimensions of reflexivity: its sense and referent (Bhaskar 1986). The sense of a theory is concerned with an examination of the meanings and definitions used within a theory. Reference is concerned with the object or phenomena to which the theory refers in its explanations and understandings. For those who argue that the social scientist is so caught up in the 'sense' of their theory that there are no shared meanings with other, competing theories, incommensurability is inevitable. Yet incommensurability is without interest unless it implies that there is a clash over common referents. After all: 'Nobody bothers to say that astronomy is incommensurable with monetarism or generative grammar with acupuncture' (Collier 1994: 91).

The ontology of incommensurability thereby assumes a common referent. From this we can say that there will be an overlap of meanings within different theories (Bhaskar 1986). The question remains as to whether this constitutes grounds for agreement over which theory explains more of the phenomena in question? This requires an examination of effects within the social world that are produced by the results of research, along with an understanding of the hermeneutic mediation of language games:

> The process of learning a paradigm or language-game as the expression of a form of life is also a process of learning what a paradigm is not: that is to say, learning to mediate it with other, rejected, alternatives, by contrast to which the claims of the paradigm in question are clarified.
> (Giddens 1976: 144)

In thinking about the referential dimension of reflexivity in terms of the practices of the social sciences, once a regulative, not prescriptive, concept of some type is abandoned, the possibility that 'anything goes' (Feyerabend 1978) can be embraced. In the process a relativistic focus for reflexivity is given at the endogenous level. Different lifeworlds are then assumed to be hermetically sealed off from one another and the social sciences stand in clear danger of losing their relevance for contributing to a greater understanding of social life. This understanding has the potential not only to contribute to a greater tolerance between what appear to be incommensurable worldviews, but equally importantly, where consensus appears to exist, to examine it in terms of that which is forced in the name of particular interests. In so doing, it does not seek to legislate, but contribute to interpretation (Bauman 1987).

The suggestion here is that difference should not be ignored in the name of universality, nor overemphasized without due regard to existing commonalities. The social world routinely confronts us as an objective reality that produces a set of constraints or enablements to our actions. How these constraints are themselves manifested is of practical, theoretical and political concern. After all, the realities that we inhabit inform our actions and ideas about ourselves. Thus, in relation to class, Beverley Skeggs (1997) concludes her study on the relationships between class, gender and identity, with the following observations on the women with whom she conducted her research:

> They do not produce themselves in relation to individualistic narratives. They feel their lives are very public, very social and hence open to scrutiny. They can only authorize their place in public narratives at the local level. This book is not an account of how individuals make themselves but how they cannot fail to make themselves in particular ways. . . . There are limitations on how they can *be*. Within these constraints they deploy many constructive and creative strategies to generate a sense of themselves with value.
>
> (Skeggs 1997: 162; original emphasis)

Admitting that we are all capable of endogenous reflexivity does not mean an absence of objective constraints to individual self-fashioning. There is more to identity politics than 'being', there is also the capacity to 'do'. Of course being and practice are linked. Nevertheless, one might be forgiven in reading those accounts that collapse the cultural and social, that individual self-fashioning holds infinite possibilities for all – regardless of the means that may, or may not, be utilized in their actions.

The issue now arises as to the connection between the thought processes of individuals and the social and physical realities that they inhabit. The referential question of how knowledge production relates to social practice is a complicated one – philosophically speaking. It is not such a difficult issue for those who feel themselves to be routinely subject to ruling interests that are not in accord with their own. Nevertheless, this suggestion itself is an act of interpretation that is both practical and theoretical. Our ability to understand derives from the opportunities that are presented to us that help to explain the events and conditions that we encounter and/or are implicated in. Providing such a discursive understanding is no guarantor of changing those conditions, but it is part of seeing the possibilities for transformation. In examining these possibilities, the relationship between what we see, what we think and what we do requires examination. In this, we find the meeting between endogenous and referential reflexivity, but with different answers being given to these relations by naturalism and anti-naturalism.

As William Outhwaite clearly demonstrates in his chapter, there is more to life and knowing the social world than naturalistic ideas permit. There is an ontological dimension to knowing in terms of being located or situated within the sociocultural milieux that we inhabit. This ontologically grounded form of knowing can be traced through the anti-naturalistic strands evident in the works of those such as Dilthey, Weber, Mead, Schutz, Winch, Gadamer, Garfinkel and Harré. Once there is a focus upon the idea of knowing the social world in this way, epistemology still has its place, but its concerns are focused in a different manner and the implications for the practices of the social sciences change. For instance, we need to recognize, as both William Outhwaite and Rom Harré note in their respective contributions, that the 'discoveries' of the social sciences will never be regarded as 'revelatory' in the sense that is often attributed to those of the natural sciences.

Ideas of knowledge being interpreted according to social situations raises questions about the appropriate method or means through which to know the social world. Rom Harré thus refers to interpretative issues in astronomy, but points out that galaxies are not made up of astronomers, unlike social institutions which are made up of human beings! From this it follows that knowledge about the social world must be both a practical and a representational endeavour. The ontological focus of knowing then moves attention towards the creative means through which social reproduction occurs within the sociocultural milieux that we inhabit (see Shotter 1993).

As epistemology in this model rests upon some idea of ontology, then the starting point to answering our questions about 'knowing' will be with how things are brought into being and reproduced in the social world. With this in mind Rom Harré's social constructionism is clear in its orientation. As he has stated before: 'That language encodes social orders in the rules of their grammar is one of the central tenets of the social constructionist approach' (Harré 1988: 157). In his contribution here, we find his return to Vico is via Wittgenstein. As such, in the absence of linguistic meanings being derived from a correspondence between language and the objects it describes, the focus shifts towards linguistic conventions, publicly available, through which feelings are expressed in a regularized and recognizable manner.

In terms of understanding the potential for social transformation, does it then follow that the social world can be changed simply through the creation of different narratives through which we view it? In his work *Social Being* (1993), Rom Harré distinguishes between what he calls 'primary' and 'secondary' revolutions. The former concentrate on, for example, the distribution of wealth in society and the latter on changes in the moral order of society:

> It seems clear to me that primary revolutions can occur with little effect on the expressive order of society. Is the reverse true? Could there be a secondary revolution, a drastic change in the personas people project, in the moral careers open to categories of person and so on, which had no real effect on the practical order? I think not.
>
> (Harré 1993: 272)

This is a position in which macrosocial concepts, such as class, are seen as rhetorical, not referential. Therefore, their properties cannot be 'known' (see Harré 1981). However, if social conditions are intransigent to change, despite apparent alterations in linguistic conventions, might we reasonably suspect that there is more to social life than language? Perhaps this is what Michel Foucault (1991) had in mind when he spoke of the need to study the limits of appropriation to discourse?

In thinking through the relations between choice, necessity and social change, the ontology that is adopted in relation to social reality is of fundamental importance. Roy Bhaskar (1989; 1993), having argued that there are structures and mechanisms that are relatively enduring for science to be possible in the first place, seeks to avoid any accompanying determinism by employing a 'transformational' model of social action in which structure and praxis combine. This is in a similar manner to Anthony Giddens's (1984) ontologically based social theory, but without what Bhaskar (1993) calls his 'tendential voluntarism'. Despite this possibility, Giddens (1984) usefully distinguishes between two approaches in the social sciences. First, there are those who seek generalizations within the linguistic lifeworlds of actors via an explication of interactional rules. In terms of knowing the social world, the focus is upon how people 'know how' to get on in their sociocultural milieux in some skilled, reflexive and accomplished sense. Second, there are those who do not refer to the actions of agents themselves and instead speak of conditions or circumstances about which agents may be ignorant, but which nevertheless inform their actions. This is referential in the sense of 'knowing that' certain conditions or systems produce certain outcomes.

These two approaches have tended to polarize debates in philosophy and social theory, particularly in relation to the types of social properties that are attributed to various social phenomena. In the first instance the linguistic turn, influenced by the work of Wittgenstein and Austin, was to concentrate on the production of society through meaningful exchanges between people within the lifeworld. This may be seen in the arguments of not only Rom Harré, but also Harold Garfinkel (1967). The idea of an unmediated access to the world is replaced by attention to how it is that the world itself is ordered. Post-Wittgenstein, the social sciences are urged to move from the study of truth and falsity in terms of a correspondence with reality, towards the study of language whose usage, as correct or incorrect in terms of convention and/or rules, replaces truth as correspondence with truth as coherence.

The second approach, on the other hand, tends to gloss over endogenous reflexivity in favour of a limited reading of referential reflexivity. This refers to the conditions under which action takes place 'behind the back' of social actors. This does not adequately consider the relations between social science and society in terms of knowledge production and fails to understand the conditions under which reflexivity upon actions may be enhanced. The debate between these positions then polarizes via attention being devoted to a celebration of lifeworld reflexivity on the one hand and a focus upon its limitations due to structural constraints, on the other. This may be illuminated in the differences that each attributes to the nature of social properties and how these relate to everyday practices.

In his contribution to this volume, David-Hillel Ruben considers the nature of social properties. Starting with the simple act of paying for a stone, he then notes that this is based upon a complicated system of interlocking beliefs and expectations. Consciousness of other persons is a component that is required in order to establish such a relation, but is not a sufficient condition, for there must be some kind of contact, or interaction, that anticipates the beliefs or expectations of others as being consistent in some way. What is particularly significant in this discussion is the interaction of elements of both social constructionism *and* realism: that is, while social properties are not taken to be reducible to mental properties, there is an acknowledgement of choice in the constitution of the material and mental worlds.

This argument allows for the possibility, *contra* Giddens, that uninstantiated social properties exist. Going back to what was said earlier about class as a system of relations that produces constraints in which choices are still made, parallels are evident here with the work of Pierre Bourdieu. For Bourdieu: 'An adequate science of society must encompass both objective regularities and the process of internalization of objectivity' (Wacquant 1992: 13). His work differs from both linguistic *and* structuralist approaches to knowing the social world for they bracket not only history, but also an explanation of the conditions under which utterances are produced and heard (Bourdieu 1992a; 1992b). In order to understand these conditions he employs the idea of 'fields'. While this idea should be seen in terms of his general 'tools for thinking' (Bourdieu and Wacquant 1992) – habitus, capital, strategy and field – fields are spaces of positions, whose properties depend on those very positions (see Robbins 1991; May 1996).

Bourdieu's fields, while ultimately dependent upon the actions of those within them, can also be analysed separately from those actions. In terms of social transformation, therefore: 'This structure, which governs the strategies aimed at transforming it, is itself always at stake' (Bourdieu 1993: 73). Linking this into previous discussions about relations that are not reducible to mental properties, allows the researcher to analyse the constitution of the social world in a different way. Structure, while ultimately reliant upon agency in terms of reproduction, can also exist in the sense of being relatively enduring separate from the actions of those who seek to transform it. Linguistic utterances are not then seen as free floating separate from power, but are linked to institutional conditions which provide the utterance with authority (Bourdieu 1992b). In terms of the relations between choice, necessity and social change, this does not deny freedom of action, merely approaches it in a different manner:

> It is through the illusion of freedom from social determinants (an illusion which I have said a hundred times is the specific determination of intellectuals) that social determinations win the freedom to exercise their full power. . . . Freedom is not something given: it is something you conquer – collectively.
>
> (Bourdieu 1990: 15)

*Justification and application: positioning, belonging and persuading*

In an illuminating discussion in a collection dedicated to the work of Pierre Bourdieu, Aaron Cicourel raises issues concerning the interconnections between structural and processual epistemologies. Noting that Bourdieu is unique among leading theorists in his methodological preoccupations and empirical projects, a gap in his work nevertheless remains. This refers to 'the local ways in which a habitus reproduces dominant beliefs, values, and norms through the exercise of symbolic power' (Cicourel 1993: 111).

This gap appears to be filled by processual approaches to the study of social life, such as ethnomethodology, that focus upon the role of practical reasoning in daily interaction. However, this takes place without due regard to how structures, in terms of an ontology of already existing properties, are implicated in daily life. Thus, in returning to the issues concerned with social transformation, we can say that structural theories tend towards abstraction and determinism in respect to phenomena such as class, whereas processual theories overlook the institutional contexts of locally produced verbal and non-verbal interactions.

In their respective contributions, both Margaret Archer and Derek Layder examine the gap between these epistemologies. This is seen as indicative of a problem of theoretical conflation that rests upon problematic ontological assumptions. These, in turn, feed into the research process itself. Margaret Archer argues that conflation takes three broad forms in social theory: the upward conflation of individualistic theories; the downward conflation of collectivist or holist theories and the central conflation of theories that see action and structure as inseparable. The problems with upward or downward conflation have been noted. Central conflation, however, translates its ontological suppositions into methodological prescriptions that, paradoxically, accord relative autonomy to agency in the desire to overcome the determinism of structuralist approaches.

Returning to the theme of social transformation, Anthony Giddens's duality of structure allows for agency to ' "make a difference" to a pre-existing state of affairs or course of events' (Giddens 1984: 14). For Margaret Archer, however, this precludes not only an understanding of how and under what conditions people can make a difference, but relatedly how it is that agency and structure interact in particular ways. Her preference for 'analytic dualism' is said to allow for a more adequate study of the relations between agency and structure. The social sciences are then accorded the role of examining the social conditions which either enable or constrain the realm of intentional activities. In this way the social and psychological are viewed as autonomous and not conflated. As Roy Bhaskar puts it:

> people, in their conscious human activity, for the most part unconsciously reproduce (or occasionally, transform) the structures that

> govern their substantive activities of production. Thus people do not marry to reproduce the nuclear family, or work to reproduce the capitalist economy. But it is nevertheless the unintended consequence (and inexorable result) of, as it is also the necessary condition for, their activity.
>
> (Bhaskar 1989: 80)

What is being employed here is an ontology that permits practical theorizing, along with a methodology that provides for the separate study of the social and psychological without resort to determinism. As Margaret Archer argues, it then becomes possible to understand how social change is brought about in interactions between the elements of what David Lockwood (1976) has called social and system integration.

Taking this discussion into the realm of explanatory frameworks, Derek Layder argues that unimodal ontologies are inadequate as depictions of the social world. Opting for ontological differentiation and epistemological pluralism can provide for an examination of the interactions between, say, the work of the Annales historians and the ethnomethodologists, but as ontologically distinct domains of inquiry. Once again, the subjective, intersubjective and objective aspects of social life may be examined not only as realms in their own right, but also as ones which are seen to mediate and influence one another.

The call to examine the interplay between processual and structural features of society as dualisms, rather than a duality, is seen to render justice to each domain and enhance the validity of the research process itself. The referential dimension of reflexivity may then be seen to inform the endogenous dimension through a movement from practical to discursive reasoning. This encompasses a movement from reflexivity within actions towards reflexivity upon actions in terms of an understanding, via an encounter with social scientific explanation, of the conditions which either enable or constrain those actions. This process often occurs in periods of upheaval and transformation when the generative structures of action become more visible to people (Bhaskar 1989: 84).

An issue that relates to the referential dimension of reflexivity still remains. This concerns the relations between the researcher and the researched. The classic Platonic view is of a person detached and unsituated who casts an objective gaze upon the social landscape. For the social sciences to be accorded the role of laying out the structural conditions for conscious actions, must the analysts be able to free themselves, to some degree, from the sociocultural milieux of which they are a part? If so, how is this to occur?

In noting that the idea of knowing the social world must take on board being situated within the lifeworlds of which we are a part, attention needs to be turned towards thinking through the relations between positioning and the process of research itself. In Pierre Bourdieu's concept of the habitus we find a link between history and being in terms of a 'socialized subjectivity' (Bourdieu and Wacquant 1992: 126). This is seen as embodied in human beings and manifested in ways of talking, walking and making sense of one's environment. Parallels are evident with this and Mannheim's idea of *Weltanschauung* (worldview). Therefore, although situated within our everyday lives, what we find is a mediated sphere that provides the grounds for the development of a sociology of knowledge. How we can claim to know the social world in terms of the relations between referential and endogenous reflexivity then takes on a very different form from the Platonic 'view from nowhere'.

This sphere is one in which an investigation of the relationship between thought, social conditions and action takes place. In the process of discovery, the criteria for understanding their interrelationships is then made more manifest, not in order to escape from social conditions, but to create the space for reflections upon them in order that new possibilities for social existence then emerge. An emphasis on an analysis of relations within the social world in terms of how they bear upon knowledge and action also allows for a justification of the ways in which the social world can be known. In his project Mannheim thus hoped:

> to develop a theory, appropriate to the contemporary situation, concerning the significance of the *non-theoretical conditioning factors* in knowledge. . . . Only in this way can we hope to overcome the vague, ill-considered, and sterile form of relativism with regard to scientific knowledge.
>
> (Mannheim 1970: 109, emphasis added)

Mannheim's answer to the question as to whether it is possible to go beyond objectivism and relativism is novel. To admit of the difficulty of speaking of an external reality beyond particular standpoints does not mean surrendering to relativism. As John Scott argues in his chapter, through the employment of 'relationalism', we can see how all knowledge is at least partially true. Furthermore, the adequacy of knowledge should be seen in terms of its abilities to inform practical action. The link between knowledge produced by social scientific work and practical action then appears in terms of rendering intelligible what might otherwise appear to be an impediment to understanding.

As John Scott notes, the direction in which the popularity of contemporary ways of thinking goes can mean a bracketing of a whole perspective within a tradition of thought – in particular, Richard Rorty's (1979; 1982) use of James and Dewey to the exclusion of the 'other' pragmatism of Peirce. Peirce, although critical of Cartesian thought, did not surrender truth to instrumentalism and empiricism (Mounce 1997). The links between Mannheim's sociology of knowledge and the work of Peirce actually provide for a different way of looking at truth in relation to referential reflexivity. Take Peirce's Pragmatic Maxim. It is stated as follows:

> For the maxim of Pragmatism is that a conception can have no logical effect or import differing from that of a second conception except so far as, taken in connection with other conceptions and intentions, it might conceivably modify our practical conduct differently from that second conception.
>
> (Peirce quoted in Mounce 1997: 33)

This allows us to bring these two thinkers together to see two criteria existing side by side. First, the constitution of the social object itself and/or the problem to which the scientists turn their attention is intersubjectively validated within the scientific community (endogenous dimension). Second, however, to see the resulting knowledge acting as a mirror that reflects upon practice. It is then appraised in terms of its abilities to inform practical actions within the lifeworld (referential dimension). Here I must add the potential for the creation of dialogic communities in which the possibility exists for moving beyond relativism and objectivism. This is a practical task that has informed the work of such divergent thinkers as Rorty, Gadamer, Habermas, Arendt and Foucault (see Bernstein 1983).

The regulative framework to social scientific inquiry may now shift from the possibility of the existence of intransitive objects that furnish the conditions for agreement in the shared meanings of different theories (Bhaskar), to that of communicative reason (Habermas 1984; 1987; 1992). I take these two positions as being concerned with what John Shotter has called an 'ontology of already existing things' and an 'ontology of ethically significant, developmental activities' (1993: 100). Despite the different theories of truth – coherence and consensus respectively – they are ultimately reconcilable (Outhwaite 1987a). Whichever path is taken, however, the endpoint is still the same: that is, to understand the role of the social sciences in social life, we need to attend not only to the endogenous, but also referential dimensions of reflexivity in democratic ways if we are to see the potential for informing practical actions within the lifeworld.

Despite this clear possibility, an important issue still remains in terms of endogenous reflexivity and its effects on the referential dimension. This relates to the ability of intellectuals to 'free float' when considering Mannheim's idea on 'free discussion'. As noted, ideas of positioning in relation to belonging and how this relates to social scientific practice need to be taken on board. This is where we encounter a central omission in respect to gender and its place in knowing the social world.

Mary Maynard's chapter clearly demonstrates that no account of knowing the social world can ignore the critiques and reconstructions that come from feminist thought as a whole. In terms of reflexivity, a number of issues from her comprehensive discussion require exploration; the starting point being standpoint feminism.

Standpoint feminism is as an important landmark in the history of reflexivity. This is because an examination of the relationship between subject and object takes place without a simple separation of the knower from the known. In addition, any interest the researcher possesses in the subject of her work comes not from some idea of the disinterested pursuit of knowledge, but from actually 'being engaged' (Hartsock 1987a). Finally, in terms of positioning, belonging and the production of social scientific knowledge, the ontological exclusion of women in social life is employed in the service of methodological application and epistemological justification:

> women's lives make available a particular and privileged vantage point on male supremacy, a vantage point that can ground a powerful critique of the phallocentric institutions and ideology that constitute the capitalist form of patriarchy . . . a feminist standpoint can allow us to understand patriarchal institutions and ideologies as perverse inversions of more human social relations.
>
> (Hartsock 1987a: 159)

Dorothy Smith (1988; 1993) takes an absence of women's experiences in the findings of the social sciences as symptomatic of the very 'relations of ruling' which exclude women within society and relegate their experiences in terms of knowing the social world. Her aim is to create a forum of referential reflexivity, employing the social sciences, through which the lost voices of women may be recovered in terms of making links between women's experiences in a more public, rather than private, forum. This activity of empowerment overcomes the tendency to see women as not possessing: 'an autonomous source of knowledge, experience, relevance and imagination' (Smith 1988: 51). In the process, women's endogenous reflexivity is also revealed, rather than concealed in the partial perspectives of male 'scientific' findings.

What emerges from this programme is a 'strong objectivity' in which those processes and structures that appear natural from a male viewpoint necessitate explanation from a feminist standpoint. This 'double vision of reality' (Cook and Fonow 1990) generates a concern with the macro tendencies of exclusion. This focus is argued to permit 'a more robust notion of reflexivity than is currently available in the sociology of knowledge or the philosophy of science' (Harding 1991: 149). It is also said to value, rather than exclude, differences between women:

> To enact or operationalize the directive of strong objectivity is to value the Other's perspective and to pass over in thought into the social condition that creates it – not in order to stay there, to 'go native' or merge

> the self with the Other, but in order to look back at the self in all its cultural particularity from a more distant, critical, objectifying location.
> (Harding 1991: 151)

As Mary Maynard argues in her contribution to this volume, this is harnessed towards the achievement of two aims. First, an investigation into existing knowledge systems and how women have been excluded from these, and second, to examine topics such as women's inequality in order to bring about social change. The programme of research is then evaluated in terms of its abilities to bring about particular outcomes.

In terms of these outcomes and who are advantaged by them, critiques of standpoint feminism from Black and lesbian perspectives criticize this idea of 'woman' as somehow universal and thus, in the process, question the ontological basis upon which standpoint feminism is constructed. Critiques from postmodern feminists, however, add another dimension to this issue in terms of the celebration of fragmentation and relativism. The result, however, is to focus attention towards endogenous critiques of knowledge systems, as opposed to building upon the referential findings concerning women's positions and experiences within the social world (see Walby 1997).

As with any one dimensional approach to reflexivity, the result of this last move is to collapse theory into epistemology and displace the very terms of reference which constituted the uniqueness and power of feminist approaches to knowing the social world. The history of an intellectual and political struggle to get women's studies recognized within educational institutions thus runs the danger of being assumed by those who now enjoy the benefits, albeit small but significant, afforded by earlier generations of women. A 'postfeminist' political standpoint then emerges via a theoretical concern with discourse deconstruction to the exclusion of a focus on the institutional arrangements under which knowledge production, dissemination and reception take place.

This move runs the clear risk of abandoning a referential component to feminist practice. Here, the practice and dissemination of research findings is explicitly designed to improve the position of women in different societies and groups through contributing to a dialogic community that is designed to enhance understanding. In the need to recognize, but not reify difference and in the name of improving women's position within societies, feminist scholars have noted the need for a balance between the potential arrogant complacency of universalism and the nihilism of perspectivism (Martin 1994). Arguments have therefore emerged for 'strategic essentialism' (Grosz 1990), 'fractured foundationalism' (Stanley and Wise 1993) and 'interactive universalism' (Benhabib 1992).

With this background in mind, Mary Maynard presents her case for *moderatum* generalizations employing middle range theory. This is seen not only as a strategy that incorporates feminist aims within a viable theoretical programme, but also one which acts as a necessary condition for practical interventions within social life. What, however, of the means for attaining such knowledge? The process of knowledge production (means), must itself be related to the end (improvement in the position of women in society). Thus, as Mary Maynard notes, feminist approaches to research do not reflect new methods of social investigation as such, but new questions for different purposes.

Referentially speaking, it follows that feminist research should not seek to appropriate and objectify women's experiences, but conduct itself along different lines from mainstream research in terms of both process and dissemination. Dialogic retrospection is a core component of this, being defined as: 'an open and active exchange between the researcher and participant in a partnership of co-research' (Humm 1995: 63). Expressed in these interactive and interpretative terms, this might explain the reason why many feminist researchers seem to prefer qualitative methods. However, there is no necessary reason for this outcome. As Anne Pugh (1990) puts it:

> it is important not to be frightened by statistics, to let them intimidate you, or naïvely to believe that 'statistics' = bad. Counting is an everyday action basic to many activities. Statistics need to be demystified. Yet their power remains: '75 per cent' sound stronger, more assertive than saying 'most' or even 'three-quarters'. Numbers have an impact, but they are no more scientific or objective or correct than anything else. Their actual status depends on their context and the frames of reference of those who construct them.
>
> (Pugh 1990: 110)

In considering the impact of social research, we necessarily move away from the preoccupations of an epistemology of production (endogenous), to an epistemology of reception (referential): that is, how and under what circumstances social scientific knowledge is received, evaluated and acted upon and with what consequences? As I have argued, all too often discussions of reflexivity omit this dimension in the practice of the social sciences and so appear inward looking and sometimes even indulgent. Yet it is in the domain of reception, a domain that is not simply separate from production, that the social sciences are also accorded their legitimacy and upon which their survival depends.

One way in which it is possible to make some separation between production and reception is in relation to rhetorical persuasion. A good performance in front of an audience by a researcher can hide many of the inadequacies and failures of the research itself. In addition, it should be admitted that it is often rhetorical persuasion, rather than the production of systematic findings on a particular social phenomenon, that influences decision makers. From a political point of view, it may be advantageous to omit considerations of data, particularly that which contradicts the desired ends (Hammersley 1995: 117).

Our attention is now focused upon issues of interpretation in relation to its ability to convince and persuade, without ever proving. As Hans-Georg Gadamer writes:

> The ubiquity of rhetoric, indeed, is unlimited. Only through it is science a sociological factor of life, for all the representations of science that are directed beyond the mere narrow circle of specialists (and, perhaps one should say, insofar as they are not limited in their impact to a very small circle of initiates) owe their effectiveness to the rhetorical element they contain.
>
> (Gadamer 1977: 24)

In the politics of persuasion and allusions to social scientific findings, the power of numbers within texts cannot be doubted. In terms of writing on science itself, it is frequently held that quantification is concerned with justification, while qualitative research is about discovery. When it comes to reception, one method is often seen as being able to 'prove', while the other acts as underlabourer in the name of uncovering areas which can then be subject to the 'rigours' of quantification. In the politics of implementation, one can be seen to orientate in the name of discovery, the other to control in the name of certainty. Yet the dichotomy which is produced between the two – one that obscures more than it clarifies – so often focuses upon the process of production. From this point of view, what is novel about Alan Bryman's contribution is an examination of these issues in terms of the rhetoric of their respective practitioners in acts of disseminating their research findings.

Returning to ideas about strategic essentialism in feminist research, it is possible to see how, to use Alan Bryman's distinction between the epistemological and technical, this programme would tend towards the latter. Much the same has been said in relation to critical theory (Brunkhorst 1996). In this case, as systems become more abstract and complicated and yet are implicated in power relations which have effects on everyday life, quantitative analysis may be the only means to reveal their workings and consequences (Calhoun 1995). Yet the epistemological sceptics persist in producing this dichotomy, while historical researchers excavate the terrain of common assumptions in order to debunk the idea that epistemological allegiances actually inform the choice to adopt different research methods (J. Platt 1996). However, the tendency is then to reproduce a separation between theory and methods by invoking the rational exigencies of situated decisions that appear free from assumptions and/or consequences (May 1997).

Turning away from the epistemological debates to explain the persistence of the differences between quantitative and qualitative methods, Alan Bryman undertakes an analysis of the rhetorics of persuasion in relation to the respective truth claims that each method entails. Finding that the 'distancing techniques' of reports on quantitative research vary in terms of the active and passive modes of reporting, it is also clear that control/management of data metaphors prevail in the texts themselves. The resort to justification in terms of the control of variables is thus evident. However, there are clear similarities in terms of a reproduced realism in both quantitative and qualitative accounts, albeit that they employ different means for this purpose. This is seen, in part, as indicative of the types of journals in which the articles are published. I would add that it should also be seen in terms of the status of the author in the academic hierarchy itself. Following Pierre Bourdieu (Bourdieu and Wacquant 1992), we need to turn the tools which we use upon others back onto ourselves. This focus would be upon who are the gatekeepers of knowledge, why they act in the way that they do and with what consequences for what is then read and disseminated to a wider public?

These questions link reception and production. Yet they seem difficult to address for they question that which is so often assumed at the level of production: for example, the hierarchies in research communities and how they work to structure fields of interest and the research field itself. These are the 'debunking' aspects of reflexivity to which I alluded at the beginning of this chapter. Those wielding power in the academic hierarchy will be genuinely mystified by any attention called to its exercise. After all: 'Misrecognition . . . enables objectivity to become subjectivized by agents of power' (Cicourel 1993: 102).

An examination of the interactions between social research communities and those which they study, assist in making the prereflexive assumptions of the social scientific community more clear. This should not mean, however, that we lose sight of the ways in which the results of research are interpreted, used and with what consequences? To do so is to translate the need to study the rhetoric of research texts themselves into the endogenous dimension which then ends up being self-referential. This is what tends to happen in methodological reflections that focus upon how language and reality are inextricably linked within an apparent homogenous particularity of world-views.

The consequence of this form of analysis is to bracket the referential dimension. It is argued, for example, that continual acts of textual dissemination undermine any such attempts. Consider the following:

> The idea that textual dissemination creates a polysemic universe in which terms are infinitely substitutable breaches the Hegelian notion of infinity as the thinking of totality. The infinite substitutability of terms and of texts makes conclusions undecidable.
>
> (R. Platt 1989: 649)

It is the works of those such as Jacques Derrida (1978) that are often seen to have enabled such an outcome. However, this is paradoxical given the neo-Kantian twist in Derrida's writings (Norris 1987). As Derrida himself puts it:

> the value of truth (and all those values associated with it) is never contested nor destroyed in my writings, but only reinscribed in more powerful, larger, more stratified contexts. . . . And within those contexts . . . it should be possible to invoke rules of competence, criteria of discussion and of consensus, good faith, lucidity, rigour, criticism, and pedagogy.
>
> (quoted in Norris 1993: 300)

Why, given this, has this movement towards textual introspection occurred? According to Norris (1987; 1993) it represents a limited reading of Derrida. In the terms employed here it represents the same elements, whether it be modernist or postmodernist, to speak in the name of the truth(s) from a one sided viewpoint. It is to focus upon the dimensions of referential *or* endogenous reflexivity as if one can unproblematically speak in the name of the other. This is to forget the context and process in which research is conducted, the consequences which arise in the study of social life by social science in terms of the knowledge it produces, how that knowledge is to be negotiated upon, for what purposes and with what end in mind?

## Summary

Social research is not interesting for what it tells us about the practices of the people who perform it, but what it reveals about the social world itself. In that statement lies its justification and a basis upon which to assess its application. In that statement also lies a basic tension: between situated and universal knowledge. In this respect it should not be doubted that the belief in the 'philosopher king' as the bearer of absolute knowledge should be uncrowned: 'this kingly, divine ambition is a tremendous cause of error' (Bourdieu 1990: 33). At the same time, some belief in the absolute, as regulative, remains important as a strategy for doing social research. Communities of researchers who, collectively and supportively, conduct themselves in the manner that feminists have suggested, are then required in order to exercise continual vigilance over how fields of interest are constructed and with what effects.

To this must be added, as I have suggested, the dimension of referential reflexivity which does not simply act as a check upon endogenous reflexivity within the social sciences, but also as a means through which its knowledge is evaluated, used and acted upon. Therefore, the relations between social science and civic discourse constitute a fundamental aspect of this dimension (Brown 1992). It is within such an understanding, in terms of the relations between the social sciences and social life and the knowledges which are produced, that the potential to see under what conditions and utilizing what resources, reflexivity may be enhanced. By reflecting upon social circumstances, it is not held that we can simply escape from our sociocultural milieux, but it is suggested we can more satisfactorily reflect on the relations between freedom and necessity. In knowing the social world in this manner, transformation is possible alongside a greater understanding and tolerance of the differences, as well as commonalities, in our lived experiences.

# References


Abell, P. (1990) Methodological achievements in sociology with special reference to the interplay of quantitative and qualitative methods, in C.G. Bryant and H. Becker (eds) *What has Sociology Achieved?* London: Macmillan.

Adorno, T.W. (1969) *Der Positivismusstreit in der deutschen Soziologie*. Neuwied and Berlin: Luchterhand. Reprinted (1976) *The Positivist Dispute in German Sociology*, trans. G. Adey and D. Frisby. London: Heinemann.

Alcoff, L. and Potter, E. (eds) (1993) *Feminist Epistemologies*. London: Routledge.

Alexander, J. (1987) Action and its environments, in J. Alexander, B. Gieson, R. Munch and N. Smelser (eds) *The Micro–Macro Link*. Berkeley, CA: University of California Press.

Antaki, C. (ed.) (1988) *Analysing Everyday Explanation: A Casebook of Methods*. London: Sage.

Archer, M.S. (1979) *Social Origins of Educational Systems*. London: Sage.

Archer, M.S. (1982) Morphogenesis versus structuration. *British Journal of Sociology*, 33: 455–83.

Archer, M.S. (1989) *Culture and Agency*. Cambridge: Cambridge University Press.

Archer, M.S. (1995) *Realist Social Theory: The Morphogenetic Approach*. Cambridge: Cambridge University Press.

Atkinson, P. (1990) *The Ethnographic Imagination: Textual Constructions of Society*. London: Routledge.

Ayer, A. (1956) *The Problem of Knowledge*. Harmondsworth: Penguin.

Barrett, M. (1992) Words and things: materialism and method in contemporary feminist analysis, in M. Barrett and A. Phillips (eds) *Destabilizing Theory: Contemporary Feminist Debates*. Cambridge: Polity.

Baudrillard, J. (1983) *Simulations*. New York: Semiotext(e).

Baudrillard, J. (1984) On nihilism. *On the Beach*, 6: 38–9.

Bauman, Z. (1987) *Legislators and Interpreters: On Modernity, Post-Modernity and Intellectuals*. Cambridge: Polity.

Bazerman, C. (1987) Codifying the social scientific style: the APA *Publication Manual* as a behaviorist rhetoric, in J.S. Nelson, A. Megill and D.N. McClosky (eds) *The Rhetoric of the Human Sciences*. Madison, WI: University of Wisconsin Press.

Bazerman, C. (1988) *Shaping Written Knowledge: The Genre and Activity of the Experimental Article in Science*. Madison, WI: University of Wisconsin Press.
Beck, U. (1986) *Risikogesellschaft*. Frankfurt: Suhrkamp.
Beck, U., Giddens, A. and Lash, S. (1994) *Reflexive Modernization*. Cambridge: Polity.
Bell, C. and Roberts, H. (eds) (1984) *Social Researching: Problems, Politics, Practice*. London: Routledge and Kegan Paul.
Benhabib, S. (1992) *Situating the Self: Gender, Community and Postmodernism in Contemporary Ethics*. Cambridge: Polity.
Berger, P. and Luckmann, T. (1961) *The Social Construction of Reality*. London: Allen Lane.
Bernard, J. (1973) My four revolutions: an autobiographical history of the ASA. *American Journal of Sociology*, 78: 773–801.
Bernstein, R. (1983) *Beyond Objectivism and Relativism: Science, Hermeneutics and Praxis*. Oxford: Blackwell.
Bhargava, R. (1992) *Individualism in Social Science*. Oxford: Oxford University Press.
Bhaskar, R. (1975) *A Realist Theory of Science*. Leeds: Leeds Books.
Bhaskar, R. (1979) *The Possibility of Naturalism*. Brighton: Harvester.
Bhaskar, R. (1986) *Scientific Realism and Human Emancipation*. London: Verso.
Bhaskar, R. (1989) *Reclaiming Reality: A Critical Introduction to Contemporary Philosophy*. London: Verso.
Bhaskar, R. (1993) *Dialectic: The Pulse of Freedom*. London: Verso.
Billig, M. (1994) Repopulating the depopulated pages of social psychology. *Theory and Psychology*, 4: 307–35.
Blalock, H. and Blalock, A. (1971) *Methodology in Social Research*. New York: McGraw-Hill.
Blumer, H. (1969) *Symbolic Interactionism: Perspective and Method*. Englewood Cliffs, NJ: Prentice Hall.
Bourdieu, P. (1977) *Outline of a Theory of Practice*. Cambridge: Cambridge University Press.
Bourdieu, P. (1990) *In Other Words: Essays Towards a Reflexive Sociology*, trans. M. Adamson. Cambridge: Polity.
Bourdieu, P. (1992a) *The Logic of Practice*, trans. R. Nice. Original edn (1980) *Le Sens pratique*. Cambridge: Polity.
Bourdieu, P. (1992b) *Language and Symbolic Power*, ed. J. Thompson, trans. G. Raymond and M. Adamson. Cambridge: Polity.
Bourdieu, P. (1993) *Sociology in Question*, trans. R. Nice. London: Sage.
Bourdieu, P. and Wacquant, L.J. (1992) *An Invitation to Reflexive Sociology*. Cambridge: Polity.
Braidotti, R. (1991) *Patterns of Dissonance*. Cambridge: Polity.
Bramley, G. (1988) The definition and measurement of homelessness, in G. Bramley (ed.) *Homelessness and the London Housing Market*. Bristol: School for Advanced Urban Studies (SAUS), University of Bristol.
Brannen, J. (1992) Combining qualitative and quantitative approaches: an overview, in J. Brannen (ed.) *Mixing Methods: Theory and Practice in Combining Quantitative and Qualitative Research*. Aldershot: Avebury.

Brewer, J. (1990) Talking about danger: the RUC and the paramilitary threat. *Sociology*, 24: 657–74.

Bridgeman, P. (1959) *The Way Things Are*. Cambridge, MA: Harvard University Press.

Brodribb, S. (1993) *Nothing Mat(t)ers: A Feminist Critique of Postmodernism*. Melbourne: Spinifex.

Brown, R.H. (1992) Social science and society as discourse: towards a sociology for civic competence, in S. Seidman and D. Wagner (eds) *Postmodernism and Social Theory*. Oxford: Blackwell.

Brunkhorst, H. (1996) Critical theory and empirical research, in D. Rasmussen (ed.) *Handbook of Critical Theory*. Oxford: Blackwell.

Bruyn, S. (1966) *The Human Perspective in Sociology*. Englewood Cliffs, NJ: Prentice Hall.

Bryant, C. (1985) *Postivism in Social Theory and Research*. London: Macmillan.

Bryman, A. (1984) The debate about quantitative and qualitative research: a question of method or epistemology? *British Journal of Sociology*, 35: 75–92.

Bryman, A. (1988) *Quantity and Quality in Social Research*. London: Routledge.

Bryman, A. (1992) Quantitative and qualitative research: further reflections on their integration, in J. Brannen (ed.) *Mixing Methods: Theory and Practice in Combining Quantitative and Qualitative Research*. Aldershot: Avebury.

Bryman, A. (1994) The Mead/Freeman controversy: some implications for qualitative researchers, in R.G. Burgess (ed.) *Studies in Qualitative Methodology, Volume 4*. Greenwich, CT: JAI Press.

Bryman, A. (1996) Foreword to M. Williams and T. May, *An Introduction to the Philosophy of Social Research*. London: UCL Press.

Bryman, A. (1998) Quantitative and qualitative research, in R.G. Burgess (ed.) *Encyclopaedia of Social Research Methods*. London: Routledge.

Buchanan, D.R. (1992) An uneasy alliance: combining qualitative and quantitative research methods. *Health Education Quarterly*, 19: 117–35.

Buckley, W. (1967) *Sociology and Modern Systems Theory*. Englewood Cliffs, NJ: Prentice Hall.

Bulmer, M. (ed.) (1978) *Social Policy Research*. London: Macmillan.

Bunge, M. (1996) *Finding Philosophy in Social Science*. New Haven, CT: Yale University Press.

Burchell, G., Gordon, C. and Miller, P. (eds) (1991) *The Foucault Effect: Studies in Governmentality*. London: Harvester Wheatsheaf.

Burke, K. (1945) *A Grammar of Motives*. Englewood Cliffs, NJ: Prentice Hall.

Butler, J. (1990) *Gender Trouble: Feminism and the Subversion of Identity*. London: Routledge.

Butler, J. (1993) *Bodies that Matter: On the Discursive Limits of Sex*. London: Routledge.

Cain, M. (1986) Realism, feminism, methodology and the law. *International Journal of the Sociology of Law*, 14: 255–67.

Calhoun, C. (1995) *Critical Social Theory: Culture, History and the Challenge of Difference*. Oxford: Blackwell.

Calhoun, C., LiPuma, E. and Postone, M. (eds) (1993) *Bourdieu: Critical Perspectives*. Cambridge: Polity.

Callaway, H. (1984) Women's perspectives: research as re-vision, in P. Reason and

J. Rowan (eds) *Human Inquiry: A Sourcebook of New Paradigm Research*. New York: Wiley.

Carnap, R. (1928) *Der Logische Aufbau der Welt*. Berlin.

Cicourel, A.V. (1993) Aspects of structural and processual theories of knowledge, in C. Calhoun, E. LiPuma and M. Postone (eds) *Bourdieu: Critical Perspectives*. Cambridge: Polity.

Clifford, J. (1983) On ethnographic authority. *Representations*, 1: 118–46.

Clifford, J. and Marcus, G.E. (1986) *Writing Culture: The Poetics and Politics of Ethnography*. Berkeley, CA: University of California Press.

Collier, A. (1994) *Critical Realism: An Introduction to Roy Bhaskar's Philosophy*. London: Verso.

Cook, J. (1983) An interdisciplinary look at feminist methodology: ideas and practice in sociology, history and anthropology. *Humboldt Journal of Social Relations*, 10(2): 127–52.

Cook, J. and Fonow, M. (1990) Knowledge and women's interests: issues of epistemology and methodology in sociological research, in J. McCarl Nielsen (ed.) *Feminist Research Methods: Exemplary Readings in the Social Sciences*. London: Westview.

Craib, I. (1992) *Anthony Giddens*. London: Routledge.

Crane, T. and Mellor, H. (1990) There is no question of physicalism. *Mind*, 99: 185–206.

Crapanzano, V. (1986) Hermes dilemma: the masking of subversion in ethnographic description, in J. Clifford and G.E. Marcus (eds) *Writing Culture: The Poetics and Politics of Ethnography*. Berkeley, CA: University of California Press.

Curtis, J. and Petras, J. (eds) (1970) *The Sociology of Knowledge: A Reader*. London: Duckworth.

Dawe, A. (1970) The two sociologies. *British Journal of Sociology*, 21(2): 207–18.

Denzin, N. (1983) Interpretive interactionism, in G. Morgan (ed.) *Beyond Method: Strategies for Social Research*. Beverly Hills, CA: Sage.

Derrida, J. (1978) *Writing and Difference*. London: Routledge.

de Vaus, D. (1991) *Surveys in Social Research*. London: UCL Press.

DeNisi, A. (1996) From the editor. *Academy of Management Journal*, 39: 1477–8.

Durkheim, E. (1952 [1897]) *Suicide*. London: Routledge and Kegan Paul.

Edwards, D. and Potter, J. (1992) *Discursive Psychology*. London: Sage.

Edwards, R. (1990) Connecting method and epistemology: a white woman interviewing black women. *Women's Studies International Forum*, 13(5): 477–90.

Elias, N. (1971) The sociology of knowledge: new perspectives, parts I and II. *Sociology*, 5: 149–68, 355–70.

Elias, N. (1978) *What is Sociology?* London: Hutchinson.

Elias, N. (1983) *Problems of Involvement and Detachment*. Oxford: Blackwell.

Elster, J. (1986) *The Multiple Self*. Cambridge: Cambridge University Press.

Etzioni, A. (1961) *A Comparative Analysis of Complex Organisations*. New York: Free Press.

Etzioni, A. (1988) *The Moral Dimension: Towards a New Economics*. New York: Free Press.

Feyerabend, P. (1978) *Against Method*. London: Verso.

Fine, G.A. (1996) Justifying work: occupational rhetorics as resources in kitchen restaurants. *Administrative Science Quarterly*, 41: 90–115.

Firebaugh, G. (1997) Standards, centripetal forces, and some questions and answers about *ASR*: editor's comment. *American Sociological Review*, 62: v–vi.

Fisher, S. (1993) The pull of the fruit machine: a sociological typology of young players. *Sociological Review*, 41(3): 446–74.

Flam, H. (1990) 'Emotional Man I' and 'Emotional Man II'. *International Sociology*, 5: 39–56, 225–34.

Flax, J. (1990) *Thinking Fragments*. Berkeley, CA: University of California Press.

Føllesdal, D. (1994) Hermeneutics and the hypothetico-deductive method, in M. Martin and L.C. McIntyre (eds) *Readings in the Philosophy of Social Science*. Cambridge, MA: MIT Press.

Fonow, M.M. and Cook, J. (eds) (1991a) *Beyond Methodology*. Bloomington, IN: Indiana University Press.

Fonow, M.M. and Cook, J. (1991b) Back to the future: a look at the second wave feminist epistemology, in M.M. Fonow and J. Cook (eds) *Beyond Methodology*. Bloomington, IN: Indiana University Press.

Foucault, M. (1970) *Discipline and Punish: The Birth of the Prison*. Harmondsworth: Penguin.

Foucault, M. (1980) *Power/Knowledge*. Brighton: Harvester.

Foucault, M. (1991) Questions of method, in G. Burchell, C. Gordon and P. Miller (eds) *The Foucault Effect: Studies in Governmentality*. London: Harvester Wheatsheaf.

Friedrichs, R.W. (1970) *A Sociology of Sociology*. New York: Free Press.

Fry, E.F. (1966) *Cubism*. London: Thames and Hudson.

Frye, M. (1990) The possibility of feminist theory, in D.L. Rhode (ed.) *Theoretical Perspectives on Sexual Difference*. New Haven, CT: Yale University Press.

Fuller, S. (1992) A plague on both your houses: beyond recidivism in the sociological theory debate. *Canadian Journal of Sociology*, 17: 62–8.

Fuller, S. (1998) W(h)ither sociological theory? *European Journal of Sociology*.

Gadamer, H.G. (1960) *Wahrheit und Methode*. Tübingen: Mohr.

Gadamer, H.G. (1977) *Philosophical Hermeneutics*, trans. and ed. D.E. Linge. Berkeley, CA: University of California Press.

Garfinkel, A. (1981) *Forms of Explanation: Rethinking the Questions in Social Theory*. New Haven, CT: Yale University Press.

Garfinkel, H. (1967) *Studies in Ethnomethodology*. Englewood Cliffs, NJ: Prentice Hall.

Gellner, E. (1968) Holism versus individualism, in M. Brodbeck (ed.) *Readings in the Philosophy of the Social Sciences*. New York: Macmillan.

Gellner, E. (1979) Concepts and society, in B.R. Wilson (ed.) *Rationality*. Oxford: Blackwell.

Gelsthorpe, L. (1992) Response to Martin Hammersley's paper 'On feminist methodology'. *Sociology*, 26(2): 213–18.

Giallombardo, R. (1966) Social roles and processes of socialization in the prison community. *Social Problems*, 13: 268–88.

Giddens, A. (1973) *The Class Structure of the Advanced Societies*. London: Hutchinson.

Giddens, A. (1976) *New Rules of Sociological Method: A Positive Critique of Interpretive Sociologies*. London: Hutchinson.

Giddens, A. (1977) *Studies in Social and Political Theory*. London: Hutchinson.

Giddens, A. (1979) *Central Problems in Social Theory*. London: Macmillan.
Giddens, A. (1981a) *A Contemporary Critique of Historical Materialism*. London: Macmillan.
Giddens, A. (1981b) Agency, institution and space–time analysis, in K. Knorr-Cetina and A. Cicourel (eds) *Advances in Social Theory and Methodology: Towards an Integration of Micro and Macro Theories*. London: Routledge and Kegan Paul.
Giddens, A. (1984) *The Constitution of Society: An Outline of the Theory of Structuration*. Cambridge: Polity.
Giddens, A. (1987) *Social Theory and Modern Sociology*. Stanford, CA: Stanford University Press.
Giddens, A. (1990) Structuration theory and sociological analysis, in J. Clark, C. Modgil and S. Modgil (eds) *Anthony Giddens: Consensus and Controversy*. London: Falmer.
Giddens, A. (1991) *Modernity and Self-Identity: Self and Society in the Late Modern Age*. Cambridge: Polity.
Gilbert, G.N. (1977) Referencing as persuasion. *Social Studies of Science*, 7: 113–22.
Gilbert, G.N. and Mulkay, M. (1984) *Opening Pandora's Box: A Sociological Analysis of Scientists' Discourse*. London: Cambridge University Press.
Glaser, B. and Strauss, A. (1967) *The Discovery of Grounded Theory*. Chicago: Aldine.
Goffman, E. (1959) *The Presentation of Self in Everyday Life*. Garden City, NY: Doubleday. Reprinted (1969) London: Allen Lane.
Goffman, E. (1961) *Asylums: Essays on the Social Situation of Mental Patients and Other Inmates*. Garden City, NY: Anchor.
Goffman, E. (1963) *Stigma: Notes on the Management of Spoiled Identity*. Englewood Cliffs, NJ: Prentice Hall.
Goffman, E. (1967) *Interaction Ritual*. New York: Anchor
Goldman, A. (1970) *A Theory of Human Action*. Princeton, NJ: Princeton University Press.
Goodman, N. (1977) *The Structure of Appearance*. Dordrecht: Reidel.
Gouldner, A.W. (1962) Anti-Minotaur: unabridged version, in A. Gouldner (1973) *For Marx*. London: Allen Lane.
Gouldner, A.W. (1968) The sociologist as partisan, in A. Gouldner (1973) *For Marx*. London: Allen Lane.
Graham, H. (1983) Do her answers fit his questions?, in E. Gamarnikow, D. Morgan, J. Purvis and D. Taylorson (eds) *The Public and the Private*. London: Heinemann.
Graham, H. (1984) Surveying through stories, in C. Bell and H. Roberts (eds) *Social Researching: Problems, Politics, Practice*. London: Routledge and Kegan Paul.
Gramsci, A. (1971) *Prison Notebooks: Selections*, trans. Q. Hoare and G.N. Smith. London: Lawrence and Wishart.
Griffiths, M. (1995) *Feminisms and the Self*. London: Routledge.
Grosz, E. (1990) A note on essentialism and difference, in S. Gunew (ed.) *Feminist Knowledge: Critique and Construct*. London: Routledge.
Guba, E.G. (1985) The context of emergent paradigm research, in Y.S. Lincoln (ed.) *Organization Theory and Inquiry: The Paradigm Revolution*. Beverly Hills, CA: Sage.
Guba, E.G. and Lincoln, Y.S. (1982) Epistemological and methodological bases of

naturalistic enquiry. *Educational Communication and Technology Journal*, 30: 233–52.

Gunew, S. (ed.) (1990) *Feminist Knowledge: Critique and Construct*. London: Routledge.

Gusfield, J. (1976) The literary rhetoric of science: comedy and pathos in drinking driving research. *American Sociological Review*, 41: 16–34.

Habermas, J. (1967) *Zur Logik der Sozialwissenschaften*. Frankfurt: Suhrkamp.

Habermas, J. (1968) *Erkenntnis und Interesse*. Frankfurt: Suhrkamp.

Habermas, J. (1982) *Zur Logik der Sozialwissenschaften*, 5th edn. Frankfurt: Suhrkamp.

Habermas, J. (1984) *Theory of Communicative Action. Volume 1: Reason and the Rationalization of Society*, trans. T. McCarthy. London: Heinemann.

Habermas, J. (1987) *Theory of Communicative Action. Volume 2: Lifeworld and System: A Critique of Functionalist Reason*, trans. T. McCarthy. Cambridge: Polity.

Habermas, J. (1990) *Die Nachholende Revolution*. Frankfurt: Suhrkamp.

Habermas, J. (1992) *Postmetaphysical Thinking: Philosophical Essays*, trans. W.M. Hohengarten. Cambridge, MA: MIT Press.

Halfpenny, P. (1979) The analysis of qualitative data. *Sociological Review*, 27: 799–825.

Hall, J. (1996) Measurement and the two cultures of sociology, in S. Turner (ed.) *Social Theory and Sociology: The Classics and Beyond*. Oxford: Blackwell.

Hammersley, M. (1992a) *What's Wrong with Ethnography?* London: Routledge.

Hammersley, M. (1992b) On feminist methodology. *Sociology*, 26(2): 187–206.

Hammersley, M. (1994) On feminist methodology: a response. *Sociology*, 28(1): 293–300.

Hammersley, M. (1995) *The Politics of Social Research*. London: Sage.

Hammersley, M. (1996) The relationship between qualitative and quantitative research: paradigm loyalty versus methodological eclecticism, in J.T.E. Richardson (ed.) *Handbook of Research Methods for Psychology and the Social Sciences*. Leicester: British Psychological Society Books.

Haraway, D. (1991) Situated knowledges: the science question in feminism and the privilege of partial perspective, in D. Haraway, *Simians, Cyborgs, and Women*. London: Free Association Books.

Harding, S. (1986) *The Science Question in Feminism*. Milton Keynes: Open University Press.

Harding, S. (ed.) (1987a) *Feminism and Methodology*. Milton Keynes: Open University Press.

Harding, S. (1987b) Introduction: is there a feminist method?, in S. Harding (ed.) *Feminism and Methodology*. Milton Keynes: Open University Press.

Harding, S. (1991) *Whose Science? Whose Knowledge? Thinking from Women's Lives*. Milton Keynes: Open University Press.

Harré, R. (1970) *The Principles of Scientific Thinking*. London: Macmillan.

Harré, R. (1981) Philosophical aspects of the micro-macro problem, in K. Knorr-Cetina and A. Cicourel (eds) *Advances in Social Theory and Methodology: Towards an Integration of Micro and Macro Theories*. London: Routledge and Kegan Paul.

Harré, R. (1988) Accountability within a social order: the role of pronouns, in

C. Antaki (ed.) *Analysing Everyday Explanation: A Casebook of Methods*. London: Sage.

Harré, R. (1993) *Social Being*, 2nd edn. Oxford: Blackwell.

Harré, R. and Madden, E.H. (1975) *Causal Powers*. Oxford: Oxford University Press.

Harré, R. and Secord, P. (1972) *The Explanation of Social Behaviour*. Oxford: Blackwell.

Hartsock, N. (1983) The feminist standpoint: developing the ground for a specifically feminist historical materialism, in S. Harding and M. Hintikka (eds) *Discovering Reality: Feminist Perspectives on Epistemology, Metaphysics, Methodology and Philosophy of Science*. Dordrecht: D.D. Reidel.

Hartsock, N. (1984) *Money, Sex and Power*. Boston, MA: Northeastern University Press.

Hartsock, N. (1987a) The feminist standpoint: developing the ground for a specifically historical materialism, in S. Harding (ed.) *Feminism and Methodology*. Milton Keynes: Open University Press.

Hartsock, N. (1987b) Rethinking modernism: minority versus majority theories. *Cultural Critique*, 7: 187–206.

Hempel, C.G. and Oppenheim, P. (1936) *Der Typusbegriff im Lichte der neuen Logik*. Leiden: Sijthoff.

Heritage, J. (1984) *Garfinkel and Ethnomethodology*. Cambridge: Polity.

Hodson, R. (1996) Dignity in the workplace under participative management: alienation and freedom revisited. *American Sociological Review*, 61: 719–38.

Hollis, M. (1977) *Models of Man*. Cambridge: Cambridge University Press.

Hughes, J.A. (1990) *The Philosophy of Social Research*, 2nd edn. Harlow: Longman.

Humm, M. (1995) *The Dictionary of Feminist Theory*, 2nd edn. London: Harvester Wheatsheaf.

Jaggar, A. (1983) *Feminist Politics and Human Nature*. Brighton: Harvester.

Jayaratne, T.E. (1983) The value of quantitative methodology for feminist research, in G. Bowles and R. Duelli Klein (eds) *Theories of Women's Studies*. London: Routledge and Kegan Paul.

Jayaratne, T.E. and Stewart, A.J. (1991) Quantitative and qualitative methods in the social sciences, in M.M. Fonow and J. Cook (eds) *Beyond Methodology*. Bloomington, IN: Indiana University Press.

Jencks, C. (1994) *The Homeless*. Cambridge, MA: Harvard University Press.

John, I.D. (1992) Statistics as rhetoric in psychology. *Australian Psychologist* 27: 144–9.

Keat, R. (1971) Positivism, naturalism and anti-naturalism in the social sciences. *Journal for the Theory of Social Behaviour*, 1: 1–17.

Kelly, L. (1988) *Surviving Sexual Violence*. Cambridge: Polity.

Kelly, L. (1992) Journeying in reverse: possibilities and problems in feminist research on sexual violence, in L. Gelsthorpe and A. Morris (eds) *Feminist Perspectives in Criminology*. Buckingham: Open University Press.

Kelly, L., Burton, S. and Regan, L. (1992) Defending the indefensible? Quantitative methods and feminist research, in H. Hinds, A. Phoenix and J. Stacey (eds) *Working Out: New Directions for Women's Studies*. London: Falmer.

Kelly, L., Burton, S. and Regan, L. (1994) Researching women's lives or studying women's oppression? Reflections on what constitutes feminist research, in M. Maynard and J. Purvis (eds) *Researching Women's Lives from a Feminist Perspective*. London: Taylor and Francis.

Knorr-Cetina, K. and Cicourel, A. (eds) (1981) *Advances in Social Theory and Methodology: Towards an Integration of Micro and Macro Theories*. London: Routledge and Kegan Paul.

Kolakowski, L. (1972) *Positivist Philosophy*. Harmondsworth: Penguin.

Kuhn, T.S. (1962) *The Structure of Scientific Revolutions*. Chicago: University of Chicago Press.

Law, J. and Williams, R.J. (1982) Putting facts together: a study of scientific persuasion. *Social Studies of Science*, 12: 535–58.

Layder, D. (1990) *The Realist Image in Social Science*. London: Macmillan.

Layder, D. (1993) *New Strategies in Social Research*. Cambridge: Polity.

Layder, D. (1994) *Understanding Social Theory*. London: Sage.

Layder, D. (1997) *Modern Social Theory: Key Debates and New Directions*. London: UCL Press.

Lennon, K. and Whitford, M. (eds) (1994) *Knowing the Difference: Feminist Perspectives in Epistemology*. London: Routledge.

Lewis, D. (1977) *Convention: A Philosophical Study*. Cambridge, MA: Harvard University Press.

Lockwood, D. (1964) Social integration and system integration, in G.K. Zollschan and W. Hirsch (eds) *Explorations in Social Change*. Boston, MA: Houghton Mifflin.

Lockwood, D. (1976) Social integration and system integration, in G.K. Zollschan and W. Hirsch (eds) *Social Change: Explorations, Diagnoses and Conjectures*. New York: Wiley.

Lukács, G. (1971[1923]) *History and Class Consciousness*. London: Merlin.

Lundberg, G. (1961) *Can Science Save Us?* New York: Longman, Green.

Lyotard, J-F. (1979) *The Postmodern Condition*. Manchester: Manchester University Press.

McCarl Nielsen, J. (ed.) (1990) *Feminist Research Methods: Exemplary Readings in the Social Sciences*. London: Westview.

McCartney, J.L. (1970) On being scientific: changing styles of presentation of sociological research. *American Sociologist*, 1: 30–5.

McCloskey, D.N. (1985) *The Rhetoric of Economics*. Brighton: Wheatsheaf.

McFadden, M. (1984) Anatomy of difference: towards a classification of feminist theory. *Women's Studies International Forum*, 7: 495–504.

Mackinnon, C. (1982) Feminism, Marxism, method and the state: an agenda for theory, in N. Keohane, M. Rosaldo and B. Gelpi (eds) *Feminist Theory*. Brighton: Harvester.

Mandelbaum, M. (1973) Societal facts, in J. O'Neill (ed.) *Modes of Individualism and Collectivism*. London: Heinemann.

Manicas, P. (1987) *A History and Philosophy of the Social Sciences*. Oxford: Blackwell.

Mannheim, K. (1922) The distinctive character of cultural-sociological knowledge, in K. Mannheim (ed.) (1982) *Structures of Thinking*. London: Routledge and Kegan Paul.

Mannheim, K. (1923) On the interpretation of Weltanschauung, in K. Mannheim (ed.) (1952) *Essays on the Sociology of Knowledge*. London: Routledge and Kegan Paul.

Mannheim, K. (1924) A sociological theory of culture and its knowability, in K. Mannheim (ed.) (1982) *Structures of Thinking*. London: Routledge and Kegan Paul.

Mannheim, K. (1927) The problem of generations, in K. Mannheim (ed.) (1952) *Essays on the Sociology of Knowledge*. London: Routledge and Kegan Paul.

Mannheim, K. (1929) Ideology and Utopia, in K. Mannheim (ed.) (1936) *Ideology and Utopia*, Chapters II–IV. London: Routledge and Kegan Paul.

Mannheim, K. (1931) The problem of the sociology of knowledge, in K. Mannheim (ed.) (1936) *Ideology and Utopia*, Chapter V. London: Routledge and Kegan Paul.

Mannheim, K. (1932–3a) The democratisation of culture, in K. Mannheim (ed.) (1956) *Essays on the Sociology of Culture*. London: Routledge and Kegan Paul.

Mannheim, K. (1932–3b) The problem of the intelligentsia, in K. Mannheim (ed.) (1956) *Essays on the Sociology of Culture*. London: Routledge and Kegan Paul.

Mannheim, K. (1932–3c) Towards a sociology of the mind, in K. Mannheim (ed.) (1956) *Essays on the Sociology of Culture*. London: Routledge and Kegan Paul.

Mannheim, K. (1970) The sociology of knowledge, in J. Curtis and J. Petras (eds) *The Sociology of Knowledge: A Reader*. London: Duckworth.

Mannheim, K. (1991) *Ideology and Utopia*. London: Routledge.

Marsh, C. (1992) *The Survey Method: The Contribution of Surveys to Sociological Explanation*. London: George Allen and Unwin.

Martin, J.R. (1994) Methodological essentialism, false difference, and other dangerous traps. *Signs*, 19(3): 630–57.

Marx, K. (1965) *Capital, Volume 1*. Moscow: Progress.

Marx, K. and Engels, F. (1968) *Selected Works*. London: Lawrence and Wishart.

May, T. (1996) *Situating Social Theory*. Buckingham: Open University Press.

May, T. (1997) When theory fails? The history of American sociological research methods. *History of the Human Sciences*, 10(1): 147–56.

May, T. (1998) Reflexivity in the age of reconstructive social science. *International Journal of Social Research Methodology: Theory and Practice*, 1(1): 7–24.

Maynard, M. (1995) Beyond the big three: the development of feminist theory into the 1990s. *Women's History Review*, 4(3): 259–81.

Mead, G.H. (1962) *Mind, Self and Society*. Chicago: University of Chicago Press.

Mead, G.H. (1964) *Selected Writings*. Chicago: University of Chicago Press.

Medem, V. (1979) *The Life and Soul of a Legendary Jewish Socialist*, translated and edited by Samuel A. Portnoy. New York: KTAV.

Merleau-Ponty, M. (1967) What is phenomenology?, in J. Kocckelmans (ed.) *What is Phenomenology?* New York: Anchor.

Merton, R. (1967) *On Theoretical Sociology*. New York: Free Press.

Merton, R. (1968) *Social Theory and Social Structure*. New York: Free Press.

Mesny, A. (1997) 'The appropriation of social science knowledge by "lay people": the emergence of a lay sociological imagination', unpublished PhD thesis. University of Cambridge.

Modleski, T. (1991) *Feminism Without Men*. London: Routledge.

Moghaddam, F. and Harré, R. (1995) But is it science? *World Psychology*, 1.

Mounce, H.O. (1997) *The Two Pragmatisms: From Peirce to Rorty*. London: Routledge.

Mouzelis, N. (1991) *Back to Sociological Theory*. London: Macmillan.
Mouzelis, N. (1995) *Sociological Theory: What Went Wrong?* London: Routledge.
Nagel, T. (1979) *Mortal Questions*. Cambridge: Cambridge University Press.
Nicholson, L. (ed.) (1990) *Feminism/Postmodernism*. London: Routledge.
Nielsen, J.M. (ed.) (1990) *Feminist Research Methods*. Boulder, CO: Westview.
Norris, C. (1987) *Derrida*. London: Fontana.
Norris, C. (1993) *The Truth about Postmodernism*. Oxford: Blackwell.
Oakley, A. (1981) Interviewing women: a contradiction in terms, in H. Roberts (ed.) *Doing Feminist Research*. London: Routledge and Kegan Paul.
Outhwaite, W. (1975) *Understanding Social Life: The Method Called Verstehen*. London: Allen and Unwin.
Outhwaite, W. (1986) *Understanding Social Life: The Method Called Verstehen*, 2nd edn. Lewes: Jean Stroud.
Outhwaite, W. (1987a) *New Philosophies of Social Science*. London: Macmillan.
Outhwaite, W. (1987b) Laws and explanations in sociology, in R.J. Anderson, J.A. Hughes and W.W. Sharrock (eds) *Classic Disputes in Sociology*. London: Allen and Unwin.
Outhwaite, W. (1993) Theorien und Theorieforschung. *Ethik und Sozialwissenschaften*, 8: 1–9.
Page, B.I. and Jones, C.C. (1979) Reciprocal effects of policy preferences, party loyalties and the vote. *American Political Science Review*, 73: 1071–89.
Passmore, J. (1988) *Recent Philosophers*. London: Duckworth.
Pawson, R. (1989) *A Measure for Measures: A Manifesto for Empirical Sociology*. London: Routledge.
Phoenix, A. (1994) Practising feminist research: the intersection of gender and race in the research process, in M. Maynard and J. Purvis (eds) *Researching Women's Lives from a Feminist Perspective*. London: Taylor and Francis.
Platt, J. (1983) The development of the 'participant observation' method in sociology: origin, myth and history. *Journal of the History of the Behavioral Sciences*, 19: 379–93.
Platt, J. (1986) Functionalism and the survey: the relation of theory and method. *Sociological Review*, 34: 501–36.
Platt, J. (1996) *A History of Sociological Research Methods in America 1920–1960*. Cambridge: Cambridge University Press.
Platt, R. (1989) Reflexivity, recursion and social life: elements for a postmodern sociology. *Sociological Review*, 37: 636–67.
Popper, K. (1959) *The Logic of Scientific Discovery*. London: Routledge and Kegan Paul.
Popper, K. (1972) *Objective Knowledge: An Evolutionary Approach*. Oxford: Oxford University Press.
Potter, J. (1996) *Representing Reality: Discourse, Rhetoric and Social Construction*. London: Sage.
Pugh, A. (1990) My statistics and feminism: a true story, in L. Stanley (ed.) *Feminist Praxis: Research, Theory and Epistemology in Feminist Sociology*. London: Routledge.
Quinton, A. (1976) Social objects. *Proceedings of the Aristotelian Society*, 76: 2–3.
Ramazanoglu, C. (1989) Improving on sociology: the problems of taking a feminist standpoint. *Sociology*, 23(3): 427–42.

Ramazanoglu, C. (1992) On feminist methodology: male reason versus feminist empowerment. *Sociology*, 26(2): 207–12.
Rasmussen, D. (ed.) (1996) *Handbook of Critical Theory*. Oxford: Blackwell.
Reichardt, C.S. and Cook, T.D. (1979) Beyond qualitative versus quantitative methods, in T.D. Cook and C.S. Reichardt (eds) *Qualitative and Quantitative Methods in Evaluation Research*. Beverly Hills, CA: Sage.
Richardson, L. (1990) Narrative and sociology. *Journal of Contemporary Ethnography*, 19: 116–35.
Riessman, C.K. (1991) When gender is not enough: women interviewing women, in J. Lorber and S.A. Farrell (eds) *The Social Construction of Gender*. London: Sage.
Risman, B. (1993) Methodological implications of feminist scholarship. *American Sociologist*, 24(3/4): 15–25.
Robbins, D. (1991) *The Work of Pierre Bourdieu: Recognizing Society*. Milton Keynes: Open University Press.
Rock, P. (1979) *The Making of Symbolic Interactionism*. London: Macmillan.
Rorty, R. (1979) *Philosophy and the Mirror of Nature*. Princeton, NJ: Princeton University Press.
Rorty, R. (1980) *Philosophy and the Mirror of Nature*. Oxford: Blackwell.
Rorty, R. (1982) *Consequences of Pragmatism: Essays 1972–1980*. Minneapolis, MN: University of Minneapolis Press.
Rorty, R. (1989) *Contingency, Irony and Solidarity*. Cambridge: Cambridge University Press.
Rosaldo, R. (1986) Ilongot hunting as story and experience, in V.W. Turner and E.M. Bruner (eds) *The Anthropology of Experience*. Urbana, IL: University of Illinois Press.
Rose, H. (1983) Hand, brain and heart: a feminist epistemology for the natural sciences. *Signs*, 9: 73–90.
Rose, H. (1994) *Love, Power and Knowledge*. Cambridge: Polity.
Roseneil, S. (1993) Greenham revisited: researching myself and my sisters, in D. Hobbs and T. May (eds) *Interpreting the Field: Accounts of Ethnography*. Oxford: Oxford University Press.
Ruben, D-H. (1972) Warnock on rules. *The Philosophical Quarterly*, 22(89): 349–54.
Ryle, G. (1949) *The Concept of Mind*. London: Methuen.
Sagan, C. (1996) *The Demon Haunted World: Science as a Candle in the Dark*. London: Headline.
Sayer, A. (1992) *Method in Social Science: A Realist Approach*. London: Routledge.
Schütz, A. (1932) *Der sinnhafte Aufbau der sozialen Welt*. Vienna: Springer.
Schütz, A. (1962–6) *Collected Papers, Volumes 1–3*. The Hague: Nijhoff.
Schütz, A. (1965) The social world and the theory of social action, in D. Braybrooke (ed.) *Philosophical Problems of the Social Sciences*. London: Macmillan.
Schütz, A. (1967) *The Phenomenology of the Social World*. Chicago: Northwestern Press.
Schwayder, D.S. (1965) *The Stratification of Social Behaviour*. London: Routledge and Kegan Paul.
Scott, A. (1987) Politics and method in Mannheim's *Ideology and Utopia*. *Sociology*, 21: 41–54.
Searle, J.R. (1969) *Speech Acts*. Cambridge: Cambridge University Press.

Searle, J.R. (1996) *The Construction of Social Reality*. New York: Free Press.
Sechrest, L. and Sidani, S. (1995) Quantitative and qualitative methods: is there an alternative? *Evaluation and Program Planning*, 18: 77–88.
Seidman, S. and Wagner, D. (eds) (1992) *Postmodernism and Social Theory*. Oxford: Blackwell.
Sen, A. (1985) Rationality and uncertainty. *Theory and Decision*, 18: 109–27.
Shadish, W.R. (1995) The quantitative–qualitative debates: 'deKuhnifying' the conceptual context. *Evaluation and Program Planning*, 18: 47–50.
Shapiro, M. (1985) Metaphor in the philosophy of the social sciences. *Cultural Critique*, 2: 191–214.
Shipman, M. (1988) *The Limitations of Social Research*. Harlow: Longman.
Shotter, J. (1993) *Cultural Politics of Everyday Life: Social Constructionism, Rhetoric and Knowing of the Third Kind*. Buckingham: Open University Press.
Silverman, D. (1993) *Interpreting Qualitative Data: Methods for Analysing Qualitative Data*. London: Sage.
Silverman, D. (ed.) (1997a) *Qualitative Research: Theory, Method and Practice*. London: Sage.
Silverman, D. (1997b) Towards an aesthetics of research, in D. Silverman (ed.) *Qualitative Research: Theory, Method and Practice*. London: Sage.
Simmel, G. (1892) *Die Probleme der Geschichtsphilosophie*. Leipzig: Duncker and Humblot.
Simmel, G. (1900) *Soziologie*. Leipzig: Duncker and Humblot.
Skeggs, B. (1994) Situating the production of feminist ethnography, in M. Maynard and J. Purvis (eds) *Researching Women's Lives from a Feminist Perspective*. London: Taylor and Francis.
Skeggs, B. (1997) *Formations of Class and Gender: Becoming Respectable*. London: Sage.
Smith, D. (1974) Women's perspective as a radical critique of sociology. *Sociological Inquiry*, 44(1): 7–13.
Smith, D. (1986) Institutional ethnography: a feminist method. *Resources for Feminist Research*, 15.
Smith, D. (1988) *The Everyday World as Problematic: A Feminist Sociology*. Milton Keynes: Open University Press.
Smith, D. (1993) *Texts, Facts and Femininity: Exploring the Relations of Ruling*. London: Routledge.
Smith, J.K. (1983) Quantitative versus qualitative research: an attempt to clarify the issue. *Educational Researcher*, 12: 6–13.
Smith, J.K. and Heshusius, L. (1986) Closing down the conversation: the end of the quantitative–qualitative debate among educational enquirers. *Educational Researcher*, 15: 4–12.
Spieler, K-H. (1970) *Droysen*. Berlin: Duncker and Humblot.
Spivak, G.C. (1988) *In Other Worlds*. London: Routledge.
Sprague, J. and Zimmerman, M.K. (1989) Quality and quantity: reconstructing feminist methodology. *American Sociologist*, 20(1): 71–87.
Stacey, J. (1988) Can there be a feminist ethnography? *Women's Studies International Forum*, 11(1): 21–7.
Stanley, L. (1985) Biography as microscope or kaleidoscope?, in D. Farren (ed.)

*Writing Feminist Biography*. Manchester: Department of Sociology, University of Manchester.

Stanley, L. (ed.) (1990) *Feminist Praxis: Research, Theory and Epistemology in Feminist Sociology*. London: Routledge.

Stanley, L. and Wise, S. (1983) *Breaking Out: Feminist Consciousness and Feminist Research*. London: Routledge and Kegan Paul.

Stanley, L. and Wise, S. (1990) Method, methodology and epistemology in feminist research process, in L. Stanley (ed.) *Feminist Praxis*. London: Routledge.

Stanley, L. and Wise, S. (1993) *Breaking Out Again: Feminist Ontology and Epistemology*. London: Routledge.

Stebbins, R. (1970) Career: the subjective approach. *Sociological Quarterly*, 11: 32–49.

Stefano, C.D. (1992) Dilemmas of difference: feminism, modernity and postmodernism, in L. Nicholson (ed.) *Feminism/Postmodernism*. London: Routledge.

Sutton, R.I. (1997) The virtues of closet qualitative research. *Organization Science*, 8: 97–106.

Tarnas, R. (1991) *The Passion of the Western Mind*. London: Random House.

Taylor, C. (1994) Interpretation and the sciences of man, in M. Martin and L.C. McIntyre (eds) *Readings in the Philosophy of Social Science*. Cambridge, MA: MIT Press.

Thomas, W.I. and Znaniecki, F. (1958) *The Polish Peasant in Europe and America*. New York: Dover.

Tönnies, F. (1964) Philosophical terminology. *Mind* (new series), volume 8, p. 322 (first published 1899).

Tudor, A. (1982) *Beyond Empiricism: Philosophy of Science in Sociology*. London: Routledge and Kegan Paul.

Tuomela, R. (1995) *The Importance of Us*. Stanford, CA: Stanford University Press.

Tyler, S.A. (1986) Post-modern ethnography: from document of the occult to occult document, in J. Clifford and G.E. Marcus (eds) *Writing Culture: The Poetics and Politics of Ethnography*. Berkeley, CA: University of California Press.

Van Maanen, J. (1988) *Tales of the Field: On Writing Ethnography*. Chicago: University of Chicago Press.

Vico, G. (1968 [1744]) *The New Science of Giambattista Vico*, trans. T.G. Bergin and M.H. Fisch. Ithaca, NY: Cornell University Press.

Vygotsky, L.S. (1978) *Mind in Society*, ed. M. Cole, V. John-Steiner, S. Scriber and E. Souberman. Cambridge, MA: Harvard University Press.

Wacquant, L. (1992) The structure and logic of Bourdieu's sociology, in P. Bourdieu and L.J. Wacquant, *An Invitation to Reflexive Sociology*. Cambridge: Polity.

Wagner, H.R. (1964) Displacement of scope: a problem of the relationship between small scale and large scale sociological theories. *American Journal of Sociology*, 49(6): 572–94.

Walby, S. (1990) *Theorizing Patriarchy*. Oxford: Blackwell.

Walby, S. (1992) Post-post-modernism? Theorizing social complexity, in M. Barrett and A. Phillips (eds) *Destabilizing Theory*. Cambridge: Polity.

Walby, S. (1997) *Gender Transformations*. London: Routledge.

Waller, J.J. (1967) Identification of problem-drinkers among drunken drivers. *Journal of the American Medical Association*, 200: 124–30.

Ward-Schofield, J. (1993) Increasing the generalizability of quantitative research, in M. Hammersley (ed.) *Social Research, Philosophy, Politics and Practice*. London: Sage.

Warren, C. (1988) *Gender Issues in the Field*. Beverly Hills, CA: Sage.

Watkins, J.W.N. (1968) Methodological individualism and social tendencies, in M. Brodbeck (ed.) *Readings in the Philosophy of the Social Sciences*. New York: Macmillan.

Watkins, J.W.N. (1973) Ideal types and historical explanation, reprinted in J. O'Neill (ed.) *Modes of Individualism and Collectivism*. London: Heinemann.

Weber, M. (1904) 'Objectivity' in social science and social policy, in M. Weber (ed.) (1949) *The Methodology of the Social Sciences*. New York: Free Press.

Weber, M. (1919) Science as a vocation, in P. Lassman and I. Velody (eds) (1989) *Max Weber's Science as a Vocation*. London: Unwin Hyman.

Weber, M. (1920) Conceptual exposition, in G. Roth and C. Wittich (eds) (1968) *Economy and Society: An Outline of Interpretive Sociology*. New York: Bedminster Press.

Weber, M. (1975) *Roscher and Knies*. New York: Free Press.

Weber, M. (1992 [1902]) *The Protestant Ethic and the Spirit of Capitalism*. London: Routledge.

Weingart, P. (1997) Interdisziplinarität: der paradoxe Diskurs. *Ethik und Sozialwissenschaften*, 8: 1–9.

Whyte, W.F. (1955 [1943]) *Street Corner Society*, 2nd edn. Chicago: University of Chicago Press.

Williams, M. (1996) The homeless count in Plymouth: using 'capture-recapture' to estimate the size of the homeless population: evidence from Plymouth, England, in D. Avramov (ed.) *Emergency and Transitory Housing for Homeless People* (collected papers). Brussels: FEANTSA.

Williams, M. and May, T. (1996) *Introduction to the Philosophy of Social Research*. London: UCL Press.

Winch, P. (1958) *The Idea of a Social Science and its Relation to Philosophy*. London: Routledge.

Winch, P. (1964) Understanding a primitive society. *American Philosophical Quarterly*, 1(4): 307–24.

Wittgenstein, L. (1921) *Tractatus Logico-Philosophicus*. London: Routledge.

Wittgenstein, L. (1953) *Philosophical Investigations*, trans. G.E.M. Anscombe. Oxford: Blackwell.

Woolgar, S. (1988) *Science: The Very Idea*. Chichester: Ellis Horwood.

Young, I.M. (1990) *Throwing Like a Girl and Other Essays in Feminist Philosophy and Social Theory*. Bloomington, IN: Indiana University Press.

Zollschan, G.K. and Hirsch, W. (eds) (1976) *Social Change: Explorations, Diagnoses and Conjectures*. New York: Wiley.

# Name index

# Subject index

# Cambridge Studies in Philosophy and Public Policy

General editor: Douglas MacLean, University of North Carolina, Chapel Hill

*Other books in series*

Mark Sagoff: *The Economy of the Earth*
Henry Shue (ed.): *Nuclear Deterrence and Moral Restraint*
Judith Lichtenberg (ed.): *Democracy and Mass Media*
William Galston: *Liberal Purposes*
Elaine Draper: *Risky Business*
R. G. Frey and Christopher W. Morris: *Violence, Terrorism, and Justice*
Douglas Husak: *Drugs and Rights*
Ferdinand Schoeman: *Privacy and Social Freedom*
Dan Brock: *Life and Death*
Paul B. Thompson: *The Ethics of Aid and Trade*
Jeremy Waldron: *Liberal Rights*
Steven Lee: *Morality, Prudence, and Nuclear Weapons*
Robert Goodin: *Utilitarianism as a Public Policy*
Bernard Rollin: *The Frankenstein Syndrome*
Robert K. Fullinwider (ed.): *Public Education in a Multicultural Society*
John Kleinig: *The Ethics of Policing*
Norman Daniels: *Justice and Justification*
James P. Sterba: *Justice for Here and Now*
Erik Nord: *Cost-Value Analysis in Health Care*
David Wasserman and Robert Wachbroit (eds.): *Genetics and Criminal Behavior*
David Boonin: *A Defense of Abortion*
Deen K. Chatterjee and Don E. Scheid (eds.): *Ethics and Foreign Intervention*
Ajume H. Wingo: *Veil Politics in Liberal Democratic States*

*To my partner Glenn, and children Sean, Peter, and Julia, with love.*

# Reconceiving Pregnancy and Childcare

## Ethics, Experience, and Reproductive Labor

AMY MULLIN
University of Toronto

CAMBRIDGE UNIVERSITY PRESS
Cambridge, New York, Melbourne, Madrid, Cape Town, Singapore, São Paulo

Cambridge University Press
40 West 20th Street, New York, NY 10011-4211, USA

www.cambridge.org
Information on this title: www.cambridge.org/9780521844383



First published 2005

Printed in the United States of America

*A catalog record for this publication is available from the British Library.*

*Library of Congress Cataloging in Publication Data*

Mullin, Amy, 1963–
Reconceiving pregnancy and childcare : ethics, experience,
and reproductive labor / Amy Mullin.
p. cm. – (Cambridge studies in philosophy and public policy)
Includes bibliographical references and index.
ISBN 0-521-84438-X – ISBN 0-521-60586-5 (pb.)
1. Pregnancy – Moral and ethical aspects. 2. Pregnancy – Social aspects.
3. Human reproduction – Moral and ethical aspects. 4. Feminism – Moral and
ethical aspects. 5. Children – Care. I. Title. II. Series.

RG560.M827 2005
618.2′001′9 – dc22 2004062883

ISBN-13 978-0-521-84438-3 hardback
ISBN-10 0-521-84438-X hardback

ISBN-13 978-0-521-60586-1 paperback
ISBN-10 0-521-60586-5 paperback

# Contents

# Acknowledgments

It is a mistake to think of a book as solely an individual's project. Even when there is only one author, there are always many people and social groups without whom the work would never have been completed. I would like to thank a small sample of those people. My gratitude goes out to the supportive community of feminist philosophers in the Canadian Society of Women in Philosophy (C-SWIP) to whom I presented talks containing early versions of some of the work that is in this book. My colleague Kathryn Morgan helpfully commented on the proposal that became *Reconceiving Pregnancy and Childcare*. I am indebted to the Social Science and Humanities Research Council (SSHRC) of Canada for a grant that enabled me to hire research assistants, travel to conferences, and purchase books and articles for research. I appreciate the work of my research assistants, Gillian Demeyere, Cheryl Dobinson, Ramona Ilea, Karen Lee Miller, and Marika Warren. Sandra Guzman and the caregivers at Muppets Pre-School Centre shared in the care of my three children; without their caring labor I would not have been able to complete this book. I thank my mother, Mary Mullin, my sister, Gretchen Mullin, and my friend, Regina Olshan, for their companionship and for the models of nurturing that all of them are. Finally, huge thanks go out to my partner, Glenn Cuthbertson, and our three children, Sean, Peter, and Julia, for their patience with my work and their inspiration of much of its content.

# Introduction

Both pregnancy and the provision of childcare are socially valued only (if at all) in relation to the child borne or reared. There is very little interest in the experiences of pregnant women or in the few men and many women who are primary providers of childcare, either paid or unpaid. There is some social interest in questions about how to increase the likelihood of positive outcomes for pregnancy and the provision of childcare, but these positive outcomes are thought of solely in terms of the types of pregnancy and childcare that are most beneficial for the children, either expected or already born.

Very little attention is paid to what these experiences mean to pregnant women or to the men and women providing childcare and to what can make those experiences better or worse. Moreover, these experiences are thought to be of interest only to those who have them. It is assumed that those who are not and never plan to be pregnant and those who do not and never plan to provide childcare have nothing to learn from reflecting on those experiences.

This is so partly because the experiences are misconceived as belonging solely to the natural rather than also to the social realm, and in fact any challenges to the naturalness of these experiences, particularly when the role of biology is separated from the activity of caring for a fetus or a child, are harshly critiqued and presented as undue interferences of the social order with the natural order. Thus, for instance, we hear dire predictions of the social consequences of gestation separate from a biological relation to a child or of keeping those who are genetically related to a child from raising that child.

Pregnant women are assumed both to be the biological mothers of the children they gestate and to go on to raise those children, unless they are radically deficient in some way. Early childcare is thought by many to be best undertaken by mothers or, if the mothers are unfit or unavailable, then by lone individuals who step in to replace (not supplement or coordinate care with) the biological mother. Many forms of alternate childcare arrangements are anxiously examined to see how "mother-like" they are, with a child either having his or her "real mom" replaced or with that child seen as fortunate in having a "second mom" who cares for him or her when the "real mom" is not available. This "second mom" is typically underpaid and temporary and has little control over decisions affecting the child. More collective or collaborative methods of providing childcare are seldom explored or taken seriously.

In this book I look at the impact of pregnancy on pregnant women, and the impact of providing childcare on the caregivers. I seek to correct false assumptions, found in both popular and academic discussions of these topics. I look at these two types of experiences together primarily for three reasons. (1) Some of the same false assumptions are made about both types of kinds of reproductive labor.[1] Both are often overlooked and devalued, taken seriously only insofar as they affect children and babies. In neither case is the work involved in reproductive labor sufficiently recognized or explored. Both pregnancy and childcare are presented as experiences that raise moral questions only when there are competing interests on the part of the different parties involved: the pregnant woman and her fetus, the child and his or her caregivers, or the different caregivers. (2) Both are experiences available only to women or chiefly had by women. Pregnancy happens only to biological females, while providers of childcare, both paid and unpaid, are predominantly but not exclusively female. (3) Finally, both experiences will differ dramatically depending on a number of factors. These include whether or not those who have them are socially approved or socially supported. In both cases, those whose practices differ from societal expectations about pregnancy and childcare, those who cannot conform to expectations about motherhood, in particular, will find their concerns either overlooked or belittled.

Not only do I address issues such as pregnancy and the provision of childcare to young children, which are directly associated with children, either expected or arrived, but I attend also to aspects of those experiences that go beyond concern with the fetus's or child's welfare, for instance, the impact of the disruption of bodily habits on pregnant women or how care providers are seen by other adults who hire them or work with them.

The method I use to examine these questions is informed by work in feminist philosophy. I am a feminist philosopher and engage with other philosophers' work, of feminists and nonfeminists. As a feminist I am committed to paying attention to sex and gender with the goal of ending sexism, whether directed toward women or toward men. I also reflect on my own experiences with pregnancy and childcare, conversations and informal interviews I have had with others who provide childcare in a variety of different contexts, and finally I make use of the work of feminists working in a variety of other disciplines, particularly sociology, anthropology, geography, economics, and nursing. Here I have tried to respond to sociologist Linda Blum's lament that "[p]aradoxically, some feminist philosophers call for such situated knowledges, for research on local or specific subjectivities, yet they pay little (or no) attention to the critical, qualitative sociology that continually tries to produce such knowledge" (Blum 1999, 255).

One way that some feminist theorists have attempted to rethink our understanding of women's reproductive experiences involves reliance on (a suitably revamped, feminist version of) psychoanalytic theory. I do not entirely ignore these works, because some of them, particularly the works of Julia Kristeva (1980, 1986, 1997) on pregnancy and Nancy Chodorow (1999) on parenting, have been important attempts to reconceive these experiences in ways that respect their significance and take women's subjective experiences of them seriously. However, taking a cue from the work of Iris Marion Young, another feminist philosopher whose work on pregnancy has been groundbreaking, I consider Kristeva's work "outside the psychoanalytic framework Kristeva uses" (Young 1984, 48). I made this choice for several reasons. First, I find psychoanalytic thought unpersuasive as a whole, especially when it makes generalizations about the experiences of women, or of men, and in this book I seek to pay attention to the diversity of experiences of engaging in reproductive labor. Second, the vocabulary generally used in these studies is often relatively inaccessible to the uninitiated. Third and finally, although I find the work of many people influenced by psychoanalytic thought to be helpful in thinking through these topics, I have not found the theory itself helpful to my own attempts to think about them.

Instead, somewhat to my initial surprise, I have found throughout the book that much of my thinking about pregnancy and the provision of childcare has been influenced by work done in critical disability studies, particularly the work of feminist disability theorists such as Jenny Morris, Carol Thomas, and Susan Wendell. I found this work very helpful in thinking about the role of illness, impairment, and lack of social accommodation to bodily needs in pregnancy in chapter 2. Disability theorists and feminist philosophers such as Barbara Hillyer (1993), Carol Thomas (1997 and 1999), Eva Feder Kittay (1999), and Jenny Morris (2001) have studied the provision of childcare when either the caregivers or the children involved have mental or physical impairments. I found this work very important to the project of challenging assumptions about what childcare in general should be like, and who should do it, as I discuss in chapters 4 and 5. Finally, disability studies has led me to think about the extent to which discussions of pregnancy and childcare tend to assume that pregnant women and children's caregivers will be without physical and mental impairments. When disability and impairment are discussed, they are typically presented as features of fetuses that should be avoided or that justify abortion, rather than as characteristics of children, caregivers, and the context of providing care that many caregivers must take into account.

Although my focus in this book is on experiences, this does not mean that I believe that we have incorrigible insight into the nature of our experiences or that our experiences can be taken as definitive of the nature of our situations. We can fail to become reflectively aware of aspects of our experience, and our experiences may be distorted by powerful ideologies. It is possible, for instance, to be oppressed even when one does not feel it. Moreover, my focus on the experiences of women who are pregnant and the men and women who provide childcare for very young children does not mean that these experiences are either universally shared or sufficient to constitute a shared identity for those who have them. Instead, there are some aspects of the experiences that are generally shared, others that are very idiosyncratic, and still others that vary with features that are shared by a group of but not by all pregnant women or childcare providers.

Many readers might expect that a book about pregnancy and childcare would devote a great deal of time and attention to questions about birth. I do discuss birth, in a brief chapter, but I do not concentrate on it to the degree that I concentrate on pregnancy and childcare. This is for two reasons. First, probably because of the dramatic nature of birth, women's reflections on and accounts of pregnancy are already focused more on birth than on either the preceding nine months or the transition to becoming a parent. Strikingly, the main form of education and group support that pregnant women are likely to experience comes in the form of childbirth preparation classes. For instance,

I was offered seven weeks of three-hour-long classes to prepare me for childbirth, and one two-hour session to prepare me for caring for my newborn child. Second, feminist attention to reproductive labor has also focused more on birth than on the rest of pregnancy or the provision of childcare.

Many feminists have offered important critiques of the biomedical model of childbirth and have taken an interest in women's experiences of birth, but similar attention has not been directed to women's experiences with pregnancy and the provision of childcare. As a result, rather than devoting a full-length chapter to the topic of birth, I make some brief remarks about it in the short chapter between the part of the book devoted to pregnancy and the part of the book devoted to childcare. I explain why I do not focus more on birth and summarize some of the important feminist work that has been done on women's experiences of birth. I also discuss how to reconcile recognition of the value of feminist critiques of medicalized childbirth with women's ongoing choice of hospitals as a birth setting and with awareness of the need for medical interventions in many births and pregnancies. I seek to avoid what Linda Layne recognizes as the shared feature of both the medicalized and the most common feminist approach, which is emphasis on control and the supposition that birth ends happily when control is properly applied (Layne 2003b).

The first three chapters of the book are devoted to thinking about pregnancy. The first chapter begins by exploring misconceptions of pregnancy by looking at how pregnancy is understood by two philosophers, Plato and Nietzsche, who made frequent use of metaphors of pregnancy. I do not claim that these views of pregnancy have been particularly influential; instead, I suggest that they help to reveal some widespread misconceptions about pregnancy. One widespread misconception is that bodily pregnancies have nothing in common with the kind of intellectual growth and creativity often metaphorically associated with pregnancy. Instead, bodily pregnancies are seen as creative only in the physical sense. Another misconception of pregnancy suggests that pregnancy is to be valued solely because of its product. Next, I discuss some art works as examples of ways in which artists do or do not contest the view of bodily pregnancy traced above in Plato and Nietzsche. I suggest that some art works highlight women's experiences of change during bodily pregnancy, in a way that makes it possible to begin to ask questions about the sharp dichotomy between physical and spiritual pregnancies, the priority given to the latter, and the assumption that the former, at least, are to be valued only because and only when they lead to the birth of children.

In the last section of this chapter, I ask questions raised by my discussion of those art works by turning to some of the recently published narratives of women's experiences with pregnancy. I suggest why we should welcome these narratives and why they should be of interest both to people who are, have been, or are thinking about becoming pregnant, and also to people who will not or cannot become pregnant. However, I also indicate that we should not expect that these narratives on their own will give us clear insight into the many different ways in which women experience pregnancy or into how oppressive cultural understandings of pregnancy affect women's experiences. Instead, these narratives need to be supplemented by philosophical analysis of pregnancy.

As mentioned above, there has been little sustained philosophical attention to pregnancy. Where philosophical attention has been previously directed to pregnancy, the focus is almost always on unwanted pregnancies and questions about abortion. Wanted (or not entirely unwanted) pregnancies have received very little theoretical investigation. While some popular works attending to women's experiences of pregnancy have begun to emerge (such as Cecilia Cancellaro's *Pregnancy Stories: Real Women Share the Joys, Fears, Thrills, and Anxieties of Pregnancy from Conception to Birth* (2001)), there has not been much sustained philosophical attention to what such experiences suggest and reveal. In the second chapter, I give a phenomenology of wanted pregnancies. I briefly define phenomenology as the reflective description of human experience in an attempt to explore the meanings embodied in habit, feeling, and perception. In this chapter I focus primarily on the ways in which wanted pregnancies have elements in common both with other consciously chosen and directed projects and with sudden illnesses or, for some women, suddenly acquired impairments. I distinguish between illness and disability and between impairment and disability along the lines of disability activists such as Liz Crow (1996) and Jenny Morris (2001).

It is only when we take the experiences of pregnant women and childcare providers seriously that we can explore their ethical significance, which is the topic I take up in my third chapter. In this chapter, I argue that attention to pregnant embodiment is an important first step in seeking to understand the ethical significance of pregnancy. I therefore agree with those feminists (Vangie Bergum 1990, Susan Dwyer 1998, Eugenie Gatens-Robinson 1992, and Catriona Mackenzie 1992) who urge us to take the phenomenology of pregnancy seriously in our moral theory. However, we must be sure to do this in a way that, first, pays attention to patterns of difference in women's experiences of pregnancy, seeking to identify which differences are ethically significant. Second, our approach must focus as much on welcome and wanted as unwelcome pregnancies, and not make an overly sharp distinction between the two. Third and finally, our theorizing must attempt to appreciate both what is distinct about experiences of pregnancy and where there are areas of overlap between those experiences and other experiences of reproductive labor. Here we can analyze how ideologies of motherhood affect women who are pregnant or who breastfeed as well as men and women who care for young children.

After the brief chapter on birth, I move in the fifth chapter to the topic of childcare. As with the chapters on pregnancy, I begin by confronting some of the false and dangerous misconceptions about this stage of reproductive labor and then seek to present an alternative understanding of it. I concentrate on the impact of what I term the ideology of motherhood on the provision of childcare. The ideology of motherhood, like all ideological constructions, makes claims both about what its subject is like and what it should be like, often blurring the line between the two. Feminist philosopher Patrice DiQuinzio (1999) labels the ideology of motherhood "essential motherhood" and argues that essential motherhood represents women's mothering as both a natural and a private activity.

I further characterize the ideology of motherhood as committed to a view in which mothers meet all the emotional needs of their young children, care for their bodies, and keep them safe, while fathers provide the material resources required for this mothering work. Neither mothers nor children are expected to have significant disabilities. Mothering work is meant to occur chiefly in private homes, and whenever children enter into more public domains, mothers are expected to continue not only to keep the children safe but also to ensure that the children do not make significant demands on any other adults. This chapter seeks to reconceive the work involved in caring for young children in ways that challenge the false and dangerous assumptions involved in the ideology of motherhood.

First, I summarize one of the most important feminist philosophical challenges to essential motherhood. This challenge involves recognition that the provision of care to children is not natural and instinctive but is instead a social practice requiring specific skills and aiming at specific outcomes. Feminist philosophers Sara Ruddick (1989) and Virginia Held (1993) speak respectively of this work as done by "maternal thinkers" or "mothering persons."

Second, I suggest that asking who counts as maternal thinkers or mothering persons is one useful way to organize our thinking about other important challenges to essential motherhood. Here we need not only to recognize the diverse persons who are actually doing the work, but also to think about how our recognition of this diversity requires us to change our understanding of what is involved in being a maternal thinker. In the process, it will become clear that there are problems in continuing to describe this work in terms that associate it with mothers.

Third and finally, recognition of the variety of different ways in which childcare may be provided needs to be supplemented by an evaluation of those differences. In this evaluation we must pay attention to several factors, some of which might push us in different directions in attempting to rank different forms of care. We must focus attention both on the needs and interests of those who are receiving the care and the needs and interests of those who are providing it. Moreover, we must think about how the benefits and the burdens of childcare work are distributed differently to people of different sexes, social classes, and ethnicities and how the work itself is conceived differently when provided by people with those different social locations.

Throughout this book, I have tried to suggest that experiences of engaging in reproductive labor can have relevance for other aspects of life and that these experiences should be of interest not only to people who have them or plan to have them, but also to people who will never engage in them. In the sixth chapter, I examine the case made for the maternal thinking described in chapter 5 as an ethical paradigm. I argue that some feminist theorists, such as Lorraine Code (1991), Sarah Lucia Hoagland (1991), and Marilyn Friedman (1993), who argue that relations between children and their caregivers are poor models for caring relations more generally, make an overly sharp contrast between friendship and relationships between children and their caregivers. In doing so, they obscure some ethically significant features of each type of relationship. In particular, they miss the extent to which good relations between children and their caregivers may be characterized by mutuality and reciprocity, and they miss the extent to which friendship can be compatible with inequalities in status and resources and with dependence of one person on another or others.

One reason for the sharp dichotomy between the two sorts of relationships has to do with the extent to which the theorists in question understand relations between children and their caregivers in a limited way, conforming to relations involving children and mothers that fit an ideology of motherhood. This was explored in chapter 5. According to this ideology, one person alone meets the needs of a child and makes decisions on his or her behalf. Furthermore, this mother or mother-like person is not expected to seek to meet her or his own needs. Even in contemporary North American society, many children are not cared for in this way. For instance, many of their caregivers are paid, and some of them work collectively. Thinking about a spectrum of relations between children and their caregivers lets us contest some of the assumptions made by theorists who rightly observe differences in the relations that adults have with one another and those they have with dependent children but who miss the continuities between the two sorts of relationship.

In the conclusion to the book, I reflect on my arguments and my findings. Feminist philosopher Christine Overall asks: "Why is the ethics of child care and childrearing not a distinct field within applied ethics?" (Overall 1996, 167). Ethical theory has too often assumed male experience as the norm. As a result, it fails to analyze ethically significant experiences that are available only or chiefly to women. This failure deprives us not only of theoretical reflection on the experiences themselves, but also of the insights that can be gained when those experiences are compared with others of acknowledged ethical significance. In seeking first to explore the phenomena of pregnancy and childcare in all their richness and diversity, and then to think about their ethical significance, this book seeks to begin to redress those failures.

# Chapter 1

# Pregnancy Misconceived

## 1. INTRODUCTION

This book is devoted to rethinking pregnancy and the provision of childcare from a feminist perspective. Representations of these experiences in popular culture and philosophy alike have too often distorted them. As a backdrop to my revisioning of these experiences, I present, in the opening sections of this chapter, some philosophers and artists who have what I see as troubling approaches to pregnancy. I choose these philosophers and artists not because I claim they have had widespread influence on popular culture, but instead because they serve as more extreme, and therefore more obvious, versions of similarly troubling views of pregnancy present in the larger culture.

Feminist theorists have for many years now lamented the absence of accounts of pregnancy from women's own point of view. Writing in 1984, feminist philosopher Iris Marion Young argued: "We should not be surprised to learn that discourse on pregnancy omits subjectivity, for the specific experience of women has been absent from most of our culture's discourse about human experience and history" (1984, 45). More recently, Moira Gatens suggests that experiences such as pregnancy are largely absent from the public arena not only because they are experiences of women, but also because they are bodily or, as she terms it, embodied experiences. She writes that the public arena "will not tolerate an embodied speech" (1996, 26).

Women's stories of their pregnancies have recently entered the public arena, with books aimed at popular audiences (such as the one I discuss below in this chapter) and academic studies alike. However, it will be difficult to get these stories taken seriously if we do not first dispel widespread misconceptions about pregnancy. Some of these misconceptions also shape women's understandings of their own experiences. In this chapter, therefore, I seek to outline some of the most prevalent and dangerous ways of misunderstanding pregnancy.

Attention to philosophical theorizing can make it easier to draw conceptual distinctions between different (but equally troubling) aspects of views implicit or explicit in cultural representations of pregnancy. It can therefore help to point us in the direction I take up in the next two chapters of the book, attempting to come up with a more nuanced view of pregnancy that is attentive to women's actual (divergent) experiences of pregnancy.

Diana Meyers points out that "[m]oral perception and moral imagination are structured to a significant degree by culturally furnished tropes" (Meyers 1998, 49). Meyers argues that cultural tropes about motherhood oscillate between sentimentality and contempt (1998, 53). Catriona Mackenzie labels as the "cultural imaginary" what Meyers refers to as our culturally furnished tropes and argues that cultural images and representations affect our own imaginative self-descriptions in ways that can constrain our autonomy (2000, 139).

Mackenzie argues that the cultural imaginary affects our self-understandings in three ways. First, "the repertoire on which we draw in our imaginary self-representations is mediated by the available cultural repertoire of images and representations (2000, 143). Second, while innovative cultural imagery can open up new options of self understanding, customary and habitual acts of imagining can stymie our self-understanding and self-definition when they draw on oppressive culturally pervasive images (2000, 143). Mackenzie goes on to explain that when "restricted cultural representations grip the imaginations of individuals, the effect is to narrow the range of repertoires on which we can draw in our imaginative projects and so to curtail our imaginative explorations of alternative possibilities of action, emotion, belief, and desire" (2000, 144). Third and finally, despite the oppressive nature of some culturally pervasive images, given the strong connection between one's sense of self-worth and social recognition, we have powerful reasons to understand ourselves in terms of socially recognized cultural representations (2000, 144).

Both Meyers and Mackenzie share an interest in exploring and enhancing our personal autonomy, particularly our capacities to engage in self-reflection, self-understanding, and deliberation about possible courses of action. Their work therefore focuses on the impact that the cultural imaginary has on autonomy, particularly the autonomy of people affected by oppression. I believe that it is worthwhile to outline a variety of other ways in which an oppressive cultural imaginary of pregnancy has undesirable consequences. First, I agree with Meyers and Mackenzie that the cultural imaginary helps to shape our understanding of our own experiences. While neither of these two authors applies their insight to the topic of pregnancy, I believe it certainly is applicable, and the cultural imaginary has an impact on the way pregnant women experience and reflect on their own pregnancies.

This is so for two reasons. As Meyers and Mackenzie argue, the way in which the larger culture thinks about pregnancy invariably shapes the thoughts and feelings of the women within that culture who do become pregnant. However, in the case of pregnancy, assumptions that it is a private and somewhat embarrassing topic encourage dismissal of the idea that women's experiences of pregnancy might be appropriate topics to narrate and to examine critically. This deprives women of access to accounts of other women's experiences. They are therefore likely to begin pregnancy without a clear understanding of what their experiences of it will be and to be discouraged from spending much time thinking about their own experiences or sharing their experiences with others.

Second, the cultural images and representations of pregnancy that do exist encourage the broader public (those who are not pregnant) to neglect or dismiss women's accounts of their experiences with it, when these accounts do emerge. For instance, when I speak below in this chapter about a volume entitled *Pregnancy Stories: Real Women Share the Joys, Fears, Thrills, and Anxieties of Pregnancy from Conception to Birth* (2001), I discuss the assumption that the only people who could possibly be interested in such a book would be currently pregnant women, women thinking about becoming pregnant, and possibly the partners and very close associates of pregnant women. Third, this view discourages us from developing social policies that adequately address women's needs for support during pregnancy, since women are discouraged from speaking of their needs, and the larger public is encouraged to think of pregnancy as a purely private matter. Finally, this view affects individuals' interactions with the particular pregnant women they encounter or withdraw from encountering.

While art and narrations of women's own experiences of pregnancy both can contribute toward the creation of a new cultural imagination of pregnancy, these forms of revisioning are typically the work of individuals, whose works most often reflect their own experiences and those, perhaps, of other women close to them. Because of this, they may well reflect idiosyncratic rather than widespread and common experiences of pregnancy, and they may also reflect the experiences of a small section of women whose relative privilege gives them the resources and the opportunity to reflect on their experiences. Furthermore, because paying public attention to women's experiences of pregnancy is still so relatively rare and new, the artists and the narrators may not always be self-consciously aware of features that structure those experiences and that do so in different ways for women in different social locations and with different life histories.

It is therefore important, I argue, to supplement these individual accounts and expressions of experiences of pregnancy with work done in fields such as sociology, nursing, and anthropology, which seek to discover factors responsible for both commonalities and differences of experience. I will investigate work done in these fields in the next two chapters on pregnancy. Philosophy will also have an important role to play in scrutinizing these factors and developing conceptual accounts of experiences of pregnancy including, but not limited to, the ethical significance of these experiences.

In this first chapter on pregnancy I have three goals. First, I explore how pregnancy is understood in traditional western philosophy, concentrating on two philosophers who made frequent use of metaphors of pregnancy and who held views, implied or explicit, about the nature and philosophical significance of women's bodily pregnancies. I argue that bodily pregnancies are understood to have nothing in common with the kind of intellectual growth and creativity metaphorically associated with pregnancy. Instead, women's pregnancies are seen as events that are only bodily, such that management of these events is limited to exercising the appropriate forms of control over women's bodies. Moreover, this view of pregnancy suggests that either type of pregnancy, physical or mental, is to be valued only because of its product, the physical infant or intellectual or artistic child.

Second, I discuss some art works that depict pregnancy. Some of the artists implicitly share aspects of the understanding of pregnancy traced in Plato and Nietzsche. Others implicitly contest that understanding. I do not offer anything like a historical analysis of shifts in the portrayal of pregnancy[1] or a close contextual analysis of the full meanings of these particular art works. Instead, I suggest that some art works highlight women's experiences of change during bodily pregnancy in a way that makes it possible to begin to ask questions about the sharp dichotomy between physical and spiritual pregnancies, the priority given to the latter, and the assumption that the former, at least, are to be valued only because and only when they lead to the birth of children.

Third and finally, I examine some women's narratives of their own pregnancies and some sociological studies of women's subjective understandings of the nature of their own pregnancies. This leads me into the next chapter, in which I develop an account of factors that shape women's experiences of pregnancy.

## 2. SPIRITUAL AND BODILY PREGNANCY

While feminists will search in vain throughout centuries of western philosophical writings for much interest in the philosophical significance of women's bodily pregnancies, philosophical practice is nonetheless frequently described in language drawn from the female bodily experiences of pregnancy and delivery. Plato and Nietzsche are the two western philosophers who make the most frequent use of this metaphor.[2] Both, moreover, employ the metaphor in different ways throughout their philosophical careers. Philosophy, for each, is associated with spiritual pregnancy and, in the case of Plato, also with the experience of a midwife delivering others' children. Nietzsche writes: "Is there a more holy condition than that of pregnancy? To do all we do in the unspoken belief that it has somehow to benefit that which is coming to be within us? . . . And if what is expected is an idea, a deed – toward every bringing forth we have essentially no other relationship than that of pregnancy" (Nietzsche 1997, 553).[3]

Plato and Nietzsche both draw a radical distinction between spiritual and material pregnancy and give a higher philosophical significance to spiritual pregnancy. Thus Plato has Diotima declare in *The Symposium*:

> Those whose procreancy is of the body turn to woman as the object of their love, and raise a family, in the blessed hope that by doing so they will keep their memory green. . . . But those whose procreancy is of the spirit rather than of the flesh . . . conceive and bear the things of the spirit. . . . Wisdom and all her sister virtues (209a).[4]

In *The Theaetetus* (150d), Plato presents Socrates[5] not as a philosopher who gives birth to ideas, but instead as a midwife who assists others in their philosophizing. He claims here to be barren himself, with no children born to his soul, but he retains the sharp distinction between physical and spiritual pregnancies. Socrates describes midwives who assist women to give birth and then claims: "My art of midwifery is in general like theirs; the only difference is that my patients are men, not women, and my concern is not with the body but with the soul that is in travail of birth. And the highest point of my art is the power to prove by every test whether the offspring of a young man's thought is a false phantom or instinct with life and truth" (855). While Socrates makes a clear distinction between spiritual and physical pregnancy, his use of the metaphor might be thought to evidence respect for both the latter and the midwives who assist in the delivery of children. However, this impression is undercut in another dialogue when Socrates laments the necessity of making reference to the "distasteful topic of the possession of women and procreation of children" (*The Republic*, 502e).

Nietzsche, similarly, draws a sharp distinction between bodily pregnancy and spiritual pregnancy and often speaks of himself as pregnant with his ideas. Nietzsche's references to spiritual pregnancy are particularly prominent in *Thus Spake Zarathustra* (see, among others, Nietzsche 1969, 302), and he also uses this metaphor in his private correspondence.[6]

In *Beyond Good and Evil*, Nietzsche suggests that men turn to forms of spiritual pregnancy, such as that involved in philosophy, because man is "the unfruitful animal." By contrast, "when a woman has scholarly inclinations there is usually something wrong with her sexuality. Unfruitfulness itself disposes one to a certain masculinity of taste" (Nietzsche 1990, 101; see also Nietzsche 1967, 266–267). It is only those who are physically incapable of giving birth who can become spiritually pregnant.

Although the passage quoted from *The Symposium* suggests that Plato recognizes only men's desire for physical or spiritual immortality (since women could not procreate by turning to other women), he does suggest in *The Republic* that a small number of women might be capable of becoming philosophers, and hence spiritually pregnant (*The Republic*, 460b, 541c). Moreover, since he wishes to breed the best men and women together, he also indicates that physical pregnancy by itself does not prevent a woman from developing her philosophical abilities. In fact, he urges that female guardians may nurse their young for a time but should be assisted by wet nurses, writing that then "the trouble of wakeful nights and similar burdens they will devolve upon the nurses, wet and dry" (*The Republic*, 460d, 699). Maternity, then, does not make a woman unsuited to be a philosopher/guardian so long as maternity is ensured to be a "soft job for the women of the guardians"

(*The Republic*, 460d, 699). By contrast, for Nietzsche, a woman who experiences bodily pregnancy fulfills all of her desires and exhausts all her psychic energy, leaving her neither the desire nor the ability to be intellectually or artistically creative (Diethe 1989).

What interests me about these philosophers' use of metaphors drawn from female experiences of pregnancy and the delivery of children is the way that, for both, material, bodily pregnancy, whether or not it is seen to bar a woman from intellectual creativity, is conceived of as devoid of spiritual or philosophical significance and radically distinguished from the kind of mental creativity associated with philosophy. While I think it is relatively rare (although it does still occur) for people in contemporary North American society to claim or believe that women's capacity for pregnancy exhausts their creative potential, it does appear all too common to think of pregnancy as something that happens only to women's bodies. It is held to be something private (and vaguely disgusting) and not something to be discussed in a public context. The other aspect of Plato and Nietzsche's view that remains current is the idea that the significance of pregnancy lies solely in the birth of a child.

In this chapter, I contrast the above understanding of bodily pregnancy with an understanding of pregnancy influenced by female artists' body art,[7] including works by Monica Sjoo, Paula Modersohn-Becker, Alice Neel, and Elizabeth Mackenzie. I am not making anything like a general claim that art can reveal what philosophy cannot. Many art works, including some I discuss here, present pregnancy in ways that are in continuity with Plato and Nietzsche's discussion. Furthermore, although many of these works are by women who had experienced pregnancy, I am not suggesting that either all women or all pregnant women will, as a result of their bodily experiences, contest problematic assumptions about the nature of pregnancy, including misconceptions that pregnancy is only about bodies or only about babies.

Instead, I focus on these particular works because they present, represent, and explore pregnant bodies in ways that contest both the dichotomy between bodily and spiritual pregnancy and the priority given to the latter. In choosing these works, I do not mean to suggest that they are the only art works that manage to do so, but they are still relatively rare. For instance, in a recent article by Rosemary Betterton (2002) entitled "Prima gravida: Reconfiguring the Maternal Body in Visual Representation," I found it striking that the only art works she found to successfully challenge the image of a pregnant woman as a passive container for her fetus were Paula Rego's abortion series (1999) that offer us, as Betterton puts it, "ways of thinking about the pregnant woman, not as a vessel, nor as a thoroughfare for new life, but as an independently embodied subject" (2002, 266). By contrast, in this chapter and throughout this book, I seek to find ways of depicting pregnant women as agents when they both do and do not choose to end their pregnancies.

Most of the works I chose (all but that of Sjoo) refuse to interpret pregnancy as valuable or interesting only for its result, the physical or spiritual child. They therefore represent an advance not only over the understanding of pregnancy found in philosophers such as Plato and Nietzsche, but also over the understanding of pregnancy found in some feminist philosophers such as Mary O'Brien. While O'Brien importantly recognizes that reproductive labor is indeed a form of labor, a human social activity, and not merely natural, her focus, particularly because of her use of Marx's analysis of productive labor, remains on the "product" of birth (O'Brien 1981, 199–200). She specifically notes that she is not interested in what she terms the psychology of pregnancy (1981, 50). Emily Martin, similarly, does significant work analyzing women's bodily experiences as socially and culturally significant, but, as with O'Brien, her account of pregnant women's experiences focuses on the way they understand birth. Martin's work is, however, more relevant to my project than O'Brien's, in that Martin offers an account that does not see birth as meaningful solely because of its issuing in a child (Martin 1987).

By contrast, because Modersohn-Becker, Neel, and Mackenzie do not present pregnancies as significant only or chiefly because they issue in children, they can be interpreted as exploring pregnant embodiment in all its ambivalence and its richness, its vulnerabilities, and its strengths, as they depict women undergoing dramatic physical, emotional, and intellectual transitions. Moreover, they engage in these explorations in a way that I argue avoids two extremes: one extreme suggested by Plato and Nietzsche when they portray physical pregnancy as a solely physical event and the other extreme suggested by Julia Kristeva in her emphasis on the uncanny aspects of pregnancy.[8]

Kristeva's work on pregnancy is extremely valuable for its critique of most systems of representation of maternity, from the medical to the religious. Kristeva interprets pregnancy as replete with philosophical and ethical significance, since she understands pregnancy as a near dissolution of a woman's identity as she comes close to merging with another (Ziarek 1992, 99). This is particularly clear in "Stabat Mater." For Kristeva, pregnancy teaches a woman something about the falseness of supposedly rigid boundaries between persons. It is, as a result, ethically important since we potentially can learn from pregnancy about how open we are to others, and this openness is what Kristeva identifies with love: "[W]hat I call love is openness to the other" (Kristeva 1980, 144).

Moreover, in "Motherhood According to Giovanni Bellini," Kristeva offers a valuable critique of both the scientific discourse that reduces pregnancy to a biological process that happens to a passive woman and the humanistic discourse that seeks to present women as masters of this biological process. She argues, instead, that the pregnant body is a "place of a splitting. . . . a threshold where 'nature' confronts 'culture'" (Kristeva 1997, 304). In "Stabat Mater" Kristeva attempts to give voices to women's experiences of being split by speaking in two different voices about maternity, a poetic lyrical voice and a theoretical voice. However, she continues to maintain that a pregnant woman cannot experience herself as a whole or coherent being and can only alternate between experiences of herself as repressed and experiences of herself as living in a kind of wounded but sensual rapture. Pregnant woman are, for Kristeva, split or even crucified beings (Kristeva 1986).

I find problematic her claims that, if lucid, a woman experiences pregnancy as a kind of delirium (Kristeva 1986, 179). Kristeva finds pregnancy powerful, and for her both the maternal body and poetry have the power to disrupt language as a social code, but she also argues that women can experience wholeness in pregnancy only through the indolence of habit. In "Stabat Mater" she writes: "A mother's identity is maintained only through the well-known closure of consciousness within the indolence of the habit, when a woman protects herself from the borderline that severs her body. . . . Lucidity, on the contrary, would restore her as cut in half, alien to its other – and a ground favorable to delirium" (Kristeva 1986, 179).

Ewa Ziarek cites this passage approvingly, claiming that "any attempt to transform the maternal body into a coherent signifying position is a fraud" (Ziarek 1992, 99). For Kristeva, the only way a woman can reconnect the split aspects of herself, and this only temporarily, is in her relationship with her child once it is born. For both Ziarek and Kristeva, the most important aspect of pregnancy is "the imprint of the other within the same" (Ziarek 1992, 102). There is no acknowledgment that many of a pregnant woman's experiences have to do with changes that occur to her body and in her relationships with others beyond her unborn child. As a result, Kristeva is not interested in exploring many of the changes a woman experiences in what Moira Gatens terms her imaginary body. However, pregnancy is not only about the relationship between a pregnant woman and the fetus she carries. It also involves dramatic transformations of the imaginary body, which involves one's orientation in space and one's relation to other bodies as impacted by socially and historically specific practices (Gatens 1992). It is therefore odd to speak of pregnancy as a time when habits might protect a woman from realizing how split she is, since those habits, as I discuss later in this book, themselves are radically transformed.

## 3. PREGNANCY AND BODY ART

As I have suggested above, I believe that some female artists' body art can counter the extremes represented by Plato and Nietzsche, on the one hand, and Kristeva's work, on the other. Body art itself, however, is often the target of two sorts of criticism. First, it is critiqued, especially by those who are influenced by the feminist psychoanalytic work of Laura Mulvey and Mary Kelly,[9] as participating in the objectification of women's bodies, serving them up to the male gaze. This sort of criticism has been itself criticized for ignoring differences among women and for its heterosexualist assumption that only men can take sexual pleasure in women's bodies (Rich 1978; De Lauretis 1988). Equally seriously, as Andrea Liss observes, prohibitions on portraying women's bodies in art may keep us from discovering "ways of representing that do not continue to allow the patriarchal scheme that divides women's minds from our bodies and desires" (Liss 1994, 87). If we are to seek alternative ways to explore women's experiences of pregnant embodiment in all their significance, we cannot refuse to explore the way those bodies appear to the women themselves and to others (see Partington 1987, 228).

The taboo against the presentation of women's bodies in art is especially unproductive when those women are pregnant. For many women, pregnancy is a time when they are very insistently reminded that they are bodies, bodies in flux. Pregnant women are almost always faced with questions about what it means to be seen differently and what it means to see oneself differently.

One aspect of this phenomenon has to do with the way, in North American society, pregnant women are often seen as unfit subjects for sexual interest, or at least inappropriate objects for a sexual gaze. This attitude stimulated a great deal of controversy when the U.S. actress

Demi Moore appeared as a naked pregnant erotic object on the August 1991 edition of the magazine *Vanity Fair* (Carr 1995 , Matthews and Wexler 2000). The ways in which pregnant women are viewed or not viewed as appropriate subjects for sexual display is a topic I address in the next chapter.

As I discuss in more detail in the next chapter, Iris Marion Young notes that the rapid changes one's body experiences during pregnancy bring one many moments of a sharp awareness of one's body. Young further suggests that being thrown into sharp awareness of the pregnant body, particularly as it changes, means that we cannot take it for granted. This makes it possible to experience the pregnant body in an aesthetic mode, one in which we can become aware of ourselves as body and take an interest in its sensations and limitations for their own sake, experiencing them as a fullness rather than a lack (1984, 51). Art works that portray pregnant bodies in ways that reflect this possibility of women experiencing their own bodies in an aesthetic mode can not only reflect, but also help to stimulate this possibility during pregnant embodiment.

There is a second reason why body art is often criticized, which differs from the claim that it subjects women's bodies to an objectifying male gaze. Body art is frequently misunderstood as depending on essentialist notions either that all women have the same types of experience of their bodies or that women's identities are primarily shaped by bodily experiences open only to women. Female artists do often represent female bodies and bodily experiences. However, these representations often explore mainstream cultural constructions of the body and the possibility of alternative constructions and should not be taken as claims about a universal feminine essence. The artists I discuss explore bodily pregnancy in ways that often call attention both to the different social meanings given to pregnancy by different persons and different cultures and the very different personal significance such bodily experiences have for different individuals (Mackenzie, for instance, explores the impact of the availability and pervasiveness of fetal ultrasound on women's experiences of their pregnancies).

Sjoo, Modersohn-Becker, Neel, and Mackenzie explore the significance of bodily pregnancies through art works, and art works are treated by both Nietzsche and Plato as the products of spiritual pregnancy. This may already lead us to question the rigid distinction between bodily pregnancy and spiritual pregnancy, in that the former is considered a worthy subject of the latter. However, it is important to observe that I am not claiming that it is only the artistic exploration of bodily pregnancy that gives the latter a philosophical[10] and creative significance.

Instead, I argue that bodily pregnancies are only rarely, if ever, experienced by women as solely of bodily significance. This is one of the reasons why artists' depictions of pregnant bodies call forth very strong responses in their audiences. Furthermore, all of the women artists I describe were pregnant at some point in their lives, and the very existence of their art works is evidence that neither being physically pregnant nor being capable of pregnancy disqualifies a person from the kind of intellectual and artistic creativity associated by Nietzsche and Plato with spiritual pregnancy. I wish also to make it clear that despite my claim that bodily pregnancies have significance for women as experiences that are bodily, creative, and replete with mental significance, it would be a rare woman who experienced either her sexuality or her creativity as entirely exhausted by bodily pregnancy. In other words, neither physical nor purely spiritual pregnancies are substitutes for one another.

Because it breaks with only some of the assumptions about pregnancy made by Nietzsche and Plato, I begin my discussion of the art works with an analysis of Monica Sjoo's controversial *God Giving Birth* (1968). Sjoo depicts God as a powerful naked pregnant woman of indeterminate race, her face half black and half white. God's legs are spread wide open and a quite large child emerges from between them. The title of the painting is painted directly below the emerging child. Sjoo wrote that the painting was inspired both by her experiences as a physical mother and of childbirth and by her belief in the Cosmic Mother, a great Goddess[11] who is the creator of all life on earth (Sjoo 1987, 84). Clearly, then, Sjoo rejects the tendency to view the physical and the spiritual as distinct, and, clearly as well, she views women as both spiritually and physically creative. However, Sjoo's God appears only mildly pregnant, and, other than a mildly rounded torso, we see on her body no other evidence of having experienced the sorts of radical changes involved in physical pregnancy.

Sjoo, in choosing to represent the moment of birth, and, more subtly, in her presentation of a God altered very little by her pregnancy, supports rather than undercuts the valorization of pregnancy solely for its product. Pregnancy is valuable, it appears, because it issues in a child, either an individual child or the world. Moreover, given that the pregnant woman depicted is God, it becomes more difficult to imagine a God transformed by her experiences, or challenged by the kinds of physical, emotional, and intellectual change mortal women often associate with pregnancy. Ironically, while her writings on the Goddess make it clear that Sjoo means to suggest that her female God and actual women giving birth share much in common, the way in which she presents God giving birth undercuts this assumption of a common female essence.

In contrast, Paula Modersohn-Becker's *Self-Portrait on Her Sixth Wedding Day* (1906) presents the artist as a woman in the middle of her pregnancy. Modersohn-Becker depicts herself as pregnant on the fifth anniversary of her marriage at a time when she had not yet been pregnant, and when she had temporarily fled her husband and her marriage. She wears a necklace but is otherwise naked from her waist up. Her clothing begins just below her gently pregnant belly, and the belly is cradled by her hands. She looks directly at the audience, but her eyes hold a question, and her head is tilted to one side. Her lower body, draped in a light colored cloth, begins to merge ever so slightly with the background of the portrait, although the upper half of her body is clearly delineated. Her image is cropped at the thighs, which emphasizes her pregnancy.

The self-portrait was painted at a time when the artist felt she was just beginning to explore her creative potential and at a time when she felt that she must abandon marriage and physical motherhood in order to do so (Betterton 1996). It seems that, for a time at least, Modersohn-Becker accepted the disjunction between physical pregnancy and intellectual or artistic creativity. However, due to our knowledge of her biography and the cultural context in which she created, we are aware that she differs from Nietzsche in accepting the disjunction for purely practical reasons, due both to the demands made on bourgeois wives and mothers in Germany at the turn of the century and to the risks inherent in childbirth. At the time the painting was made, the artist frequently used the imagery of birth and fertility to describe the progress of her painting (Betterton 1996, 30). The ambivalence she felt toward physical motherhood is made poignant by the fact that she did choose to return to her husband and become pregnant shortly after this portrait was painted, only to die in childbirth the next year at age thirty-one.

Despite the tragic conclusion to Modersohn-Becker's actual pregnancy, the very fact that she painted herself as a nude pregnant woman and artist is an interesting challenge to the supposition that physical and spiritual pregnancy are necessarily entirely separate experiences. This is complicated somewhat by the fact that she presents her pregnant torso as more merged with the physical world around her than her head and upper torso. Does the state of physical pregnancy lead to such a merging? Or does the kind of spiritual pregnancy associated with artistic creativity achieve the same thing? Was this merging desirable or undesirable for an artist? We are left wondering.

Alice Neel is well known for her several portraits of pregnant nudes. She was herself pregnant several times, and returned many times throughout her long career to paintings of pregnant nude women. Sometimes, as in her portrait of her son Richard and his pregnant wife Nancy in 1971 and in her portrait of *Julie and Algis* (1967), the women appeared with their husbands. I concentrate on two of the works where the women appear both alone and hugely pregnant, *Pregnant Betty Homitsky* (1968) and *Margaret Evans Pregnant* (1978).

Neel painted both women with very close attention to the bodily changes reflective of pregnancy. Betty Homitsky, for instance, is a thin woman radically transformed by her enlarged torso. Her large breasts and stomach contrast strikingly with her twiglike arms and legs. Her slightly parted lips and flared nostrils suggest she has the difficulty in breathing that many women experience in late pregnancy as she seems to gasp slightly for air. She sits awkwardly but gazes directly at the audience, a named, unique pregnant individual, visually portrayed at one point in the transformation she undergoes while remaining Betty Homitsky.

Margaret Evans is also pregnant, naked, and sitting in a domestic interior. She is very pregnant, her enlarged nipples are clearly detailed, but her genitals are obscured by her pregnant belly. She faces her audience directly and appears vulnerable and proud, as well as somewhat happy, despite the awkwardness of her body language and the stiffness in her shoulders. Her body, moreover, both casts a shadow and is reflected in a mirror. In the mirror image we see the back of her chair and her face and body in profile, such that her body is partly obscured, so we are given simultaneously different views of Margaret Evans that emphasize and that downplay her pregnant torso. I find it striking that it is the view that emphasizes her pregnant body that also has her gazing directly and somewhat defiantly at the audience, as if she is saying: This, right now, is who I am, Margaret Evans pregnant.

Neel's pregnant nudes suggest to me the kind of experience of bodily transformation similar to that described by Carol Bigwood in the following passage, written when she was seven months' pregnant:

I try to adjust to active matter. All around, a thankless task. I have been infiltrated. My walk has changed, the way I sit, stand, eat, sleep, the way I breathe, the way

I make love. I can't sit up straight at my desk for long anymore. I have to lean back on the chair to write over my belly, legs apart, giving my belly as much room as possible. All of a sudden it seems my belly has become too big too fast for me to adjust to it as mine (1991, 66).

The ways in which Margaret Evans and Betty Homitsky sit, the tension in Evans's shoulders as she tightly grasps her chair base of her chair, as if she might otherwise fall, seem to reflect this sense of a sudden awkwardness in one's rapidly transforming and largely pregnant body. Both women, however, gaze directly at the audience. They are nude, they are pregnant, they are vulnerable, and they are dignified. They are uncomfortable, they are transformed, but they have not lost their sense of self. They appear neither to be lost in "the indolence of habit" nor to be experiencing the kind of delirious loss of self described by Kristeva as the only alternative responses to pregnant embodiment (Kristeva 1986). Instead, the women depicted in these images fit sociologist Lucy Bailey's observation of the thirty pregnant women she interviewed: "The dominant impression from these interviews, therefore, was not of a radical alternation within the women which was then radiated outwards, but a sense of their having entered, or being on the edge of, a 'whole new world' . . . which brought out different facets of their personalities" (Bailey 1999, 346).

The naked vulnerability and dignity of these women in their transforming bodies is interestingly echoed in Neel's *Nude Self Portrait* (1980), painted at the age of eighty. The artist is nude but not objectified. She holds a paintbrush and cloth and wears glasses, all emphasizing that she sees as well as is seen. Like Margaret Evans and Betty Homitsky she sits naked in a chair, and, like them, she has large somewhat droopy breasts and an enlarged abdomen. This self-portrait seems to me to emphasize the changes that occur in one's body, not only in pregnancy but as one ages, and suggests as well that one may take an aesthetic interest not only in the changes one's body experiences in pregnancy, but also in age.

The last artist I discuss is Elizabeth Mackenzie, a Canadian artist who works frequently with her own body and has made several works responding to aspects of pregnant embodiment, from *Identification of a Woman* (1986) to *Radiant Monster* (1996). In *Radiant Monster*, Mackenzie responds to the way the development of fetal ultrasound technology tends to diminish the importance of a woman's bodily knowledge during pregnancy and also to increase the sense of the fetus as an independent agent, which just happens to be temporarily contained within a pregnant woman's body (see Morgan 1996 and Mitchell and Georges 1997 for an account of this common dynamic).

*Radiant Monster* is a complex multimedia installation. A screen is mounted on the front of a large wooden box frame. The frame is draped in a soft light-colored fabric. On the screen, a hand reaches toward but cannot quite touch video images from an ultrasound of a fetus. Below the screen a number of phrases, including "radiant monster," "adorable demon," and "beloved, dreaded you," appear and disappear. Inside the frame, sound machinery plays a very loud version of the pumping of a pregnant woman's blood, a sound many visitors mistake for the fetal heartbeat (Ariss 1998, 43).

The work seeks, without in this case giving us a visual representation of a pregnant woman's body, to make that body nonetheless vividly present to its audience, while at the same time suggesting how fetal ultrasound can both serve as a means of connecting a pregnant woman to the unborn fetus within her and separating her from that fetus due to the way fetal ultrasound is performed and to the way in which images of fetuses have been appropriated in North American culture. The woman's hand reaches for but can never touch the video images, at the same time that her body is always already touching the fetus inside her. The constantly appearing and disappearing words capture the ambivalence of the pregnant woman's response to the life inside her and to the alternately dissolving and strict boundaries set up between herself and this new life. The work can therefore be seen as an exploration of the way that socio-cultural changes, such as the advent of new technologies, affect pregnant embodiment.

Although Mackenzie is responding to the way fetal ultrasound tends to obscure the presence of the pregnant woman, this tendency to view the fetus as an autonomous individual floating in its own self-contained atmosphere,[12] rather than a woman's body, preceded this technology, as is evidenced in a work by Marc Chagall painted long before the advent of fetal ultrasound. His *Pregnant Woman* (1913) shows a woman dressed as a Russian peasant with an oval section cut away from her skirt to reveal a standing and fully developed male child, presumably floating in uterine fluid but seemingly entirely unconnected to the mother's body. In this dreamlike vividly colored painting of a friend's pregnant wife, a cow floats in the sky and a young man chases an animal. The woman's body is cut away to reveal itself as a mere animal/physical container for the fully developed person within.

Chagall's work is one of the most dramatic instances of the representation of a pregnant woman as a mere house or physical container for the fetus within her, but it is clearly part of a long tradition of viewing pregnancy as a solely physical event, in which a woman's participation is limited to patiently waiting for (and not harming) the fetus within her.

In more recent popular and medical discourse about pregnancy, a woman's role is made more active. As she waits for the arrival of her child, she is to take vitamins, avoid toxins, exercise, and prepare for childbirth. However, in both, pregnancy is seen as a purely physical event, either one in which a woman passively waits for her body to do its work or one that she and/or medical personnel must actively manage. In both the understanding of pregnancy traced in Plato, Nietzsche, and Chagall and in the more contemporary version, pregnancy is important because it can lead to the birth of a child (whether this is desired or to be avoided) and requires control over women's bodies. In neither approach are women's experiences with pregnancy considered important.

The art works by Mackenzie, Modersohn-Becker, and Neel are a small sample of alternative ways to envision pregnant embodiment. They escape from a variety of potential traps, traps wherein pregnancy is seen (1) as purely physical and devoid of emotional or spiritual significance, (2) a threat to intellectual and artistic creativity, (3) valuable only for its product, or (4) an experience so threatening to identity that it can only be suppressed through the indolence of habit. They show pregnancy, instead, to be a much more complex phenomenon and one well worthy of further exploration, both philosophically and artistically.

Now that I have cleared away some false and distorting views of pregnancy found in art and philosophy and discussed some art works in order to focus attention on women's experiences of pregnancy, what emerges for our sustained theoretical attention? One possibility, already mentioned, is the set of issues concerning the borders of the self, as explored by Kristeva, which I discuss in the third chapter. Another possibility, which I take up in the next chapter, concerns a direction for further research initiated by feminist phenomenologists such as Bigwood and Young, and that is to focus on the role of change in pregnancy. I argue in that chapter for the importance of thinking about the enormous changes experienced by pregnant women, mainly in welcomed but also in unwanted pregnancies.[13] A third possibility, the one I take up in the last section of this chapter, is to search for those rare occasions when women's accounts of their own experiences of pregnancy make it into the public arena.

## 4. PREGNANT WOMEN'S STORIES

In examining these stories, we can be grateful that it has become more acceptable to acknowledge pregnancy socially, for instance, by representing pregnant women in advertising and other such public images. However, we not only need to have pregnancy acknowledged as occurring, and of significance, but need also to be sure that pregnancy is understood as more than a period when a woman waits for the arrival of a child and seeks to prepare her body for it. It is only when we start paying attention to women's complex experiences during pregnancy that we can begin to appreciate what these experiences may have to tell us both in terms of the richness of meaning these women attribute to pregnancy and in terms of the way their experiences are sometimes negatively affected by prevailing ideologies about the meanings of pregnancy and motherhood.

I begin by looking at a volume published in 2001 by author Cecilia Cancellaro, entitled *Pregnancy Stories: Real Women Share the Joys, Fears, Thrills, and Anxieties of Pregnancy from Conception to Birth. Pregnancy Stories* makes for a fascinating read. When she was pregnant, Cancellaro read voraciously on the topics of pregnancy and childbirth, but was unable to find many accounts of women's experiences of these events. Her book seeks to go some way toward making up for the dearth of women's accounts of pregnancy. It collects the stories of thirty-eight pregnant women, as well as a few of their partners, in an attempt to give its readers a sense of the diverse ways in which women experience pregnancy, birth, and the postpartum period.

The book is divided into ten chapters, with each chapter telling the stories of five to twelve women. The chapters are organized thematically and include, along with sections devoted to each trimester of pregnancy, birth, and the postpartum period, accounts of women's experiences with prenatal diagnostic testing, pregnancy loss, and pregnancy complications. The last chapter gives some perspectives of partners on pregnancy and childbirth. All the pregnant women live in the United States, and all are articulate and self-reflective, but they are otherwise diverse in age, social class, and whether or not they have been previously pregnant. Most are married, one is single, and one has a same-sex partner. All, despite some initial ambivalence, were experiencing wanted pregnancies.

The women are generous in sharing intimate details of their experiences, both regarding changes that happened to their bodies and their relationships and concerning their emotional reactions to these changes.

Many of their stories include accounts of physical and emotional discomforts, as well as some very serious complications and pregnancy losses. It provides a realistic sense of the amount of change that pregnant women experience and the mixed emotions, both negative and positive, that accompany this change. It also demonstrates that there are many different ways to be pregnant, that there is no one way to be a supportive partner of a pregnant woman, that the transition to motherhood is complicated albeit often replete with moments of joy, and that women somehow find ways to cope with stress, loss, and sorrow.

The volume is particularly important for how the women's narratives reveal how much their life changed in many dimensions because of their pregnancies, the extent to which their responses to their pregnancies involved work, thought, and often deliberate self-transformation, and the extent to which their pregnancies were for them times of great anxiety, both because of the changes in their lives and because of the extent to which they were made to feel that pregnancies involve a number of different kinds of measurable risks.

The narratives also give very clear examples of tensions between interpreting pregnancy as the beginning of the mother-child relation and interpreting it as tentative, which Barbara Katz Rothman has argued is associated with increased prenatal testing (Katz Rothman 1986). The women give accounts of themselves both bonding with their fetuses and trying not to bond, in case the pregnancy either ends spontaneously or they are asked to decide whether or not to terminate it, based on results from their prenatal testing. For instance, one woman writes: "It seems silly now, but I didn't want to tell everyone about my unexpected pregnancy only to go back and un-tell them should I lose the baby" (Cancellaro 2001, 19). Another is clear that this unwillingness to tell others is part of an attempt to avoid bonding with the fetus: "In my first trimester, I had dreamed of monsters, and guarded myself against bonding with the unknown fetus. Genetic testing resolves some fears, but others swooped in quickly to take their place" (Cancellaro 2001, 40).

The stories testify to the extent to which the women are simultaneously encouraged to think of their fetuses as their children and yet expected not to mourn the loss of those fetuses at least in the same way they would mourn the loss of an infant child. For instance, one woman, who mourned her miscarriage, writes: "My doctor told me that I might experience contractions before 'expelling' the 'product,' but the only pain I experienced that night was emotional" (Cancellaro 2001, 157). While the women in this volume who experienced pregnancy loss insist on the reality of their loss and feel anger at those who deny it, they do not tend to examine the tensions that exist between discourses around pregnancy and discourses around pregnancy loss.

The stories are also evidence of the extent to which the women accept risk and anxiety during pregnancy as natural and inevitable. Many of the narratives are full of accounts of anxiety. One woman writes: "Feelings of fear and anxiety consumed me, and I wasn't completely comfortable sharing them since they often seemed irrational. A life was growing inside me and I couldn't see it, feel it, or do anything to ensure its well-being. I never felt so out of control" (Cancellaro 2001, 27). Another woman is consumed with anxiety when told that tests reveal "about a 1 in 200 chance of Down's syndrome which is usual for a thirty-eight year old woman, but high for someone my age" (2001, 84). She decides to have a more in-depth ultrasound examination and finds out, as a result, "Our chances of having a Down's baby were now something like 1 in 350 and we were told to relax and enjoy the rest of the pregnancy" (2001, 86). Another woman similarly reports great relief at being told that, after undergoing testing, her risk of having a Down's syndrome baby is one in 360, instead of the one in 270 expected for a woman her age (2001, 89). None of the women in the volume blames her high anxiety on the testing routinely presented or speaks to the oddity of such small differences in risk assessment having a major impact on her level of calm or anxiety.

The lack of reflection on how risk is conveyed to them and why they respond as they do to risk assessments is one example of the limits of the usefulness of taking women's narratives of their experiences at face value. While it is incredibly important to bring women's subjective accounts of their own experiences of pregnancy into public discourse, we cannot assume that all of the factors influencing women's experiences of pregnancy will be transparent to them. Instead, as I argue in the next chapter, these narratives can be incredibly useful starting points for analysis of the factors affecting women's experiences of pregnancy. Thus, for instance, Deborah Lupton analyzed interviews with pregnant women in order to examine and interrogate their attitudes toward medical pronouncements about risks involved in pregnancy and in prenatal testing (Lupton 1999).

One other instance of where pregnant women's narratives require further reflection and analysis involves women's statements that they saw their pregnancies as useful preparation for childrearing. One woman, who was particularly ill during her pregnancy, with vomiting to the point of dehydration requiring intravenous fluids writes: "I know the experience taught me something. It prepared me for the reality of parenting. Some people say that the reason pregnancy takes nine months is so that you can slowly prepare for the disruptions having a child brings" (Cancellaro 2001, 25). Another woman writes: "It is my theory that pregnancy serves as a lead-in to child care. The increased attention to food intake prepares for nursing; the lack of sleep from frequent runs to the bathroom prepares for nighttime feedings; the discomfort of sitting in a movie theater prepares for the utter lack of films you will see as a new parent. I figure the way my body changed during pregnancy was meant to serve as a reminder that everything in my life would be upended by the coming of my daughter" (Cancellaro 2001, 214).

Feminist philosopher Louise Levesque-Lopman says something very similar, writing that she was grateful to the nine-month period of her pregnancy for allowing her to become ready for some of the changes that would occur once her child was born (1983, 256). Another feminist philosopher, Caroline Whitbeck, thinks that it is almost necessary to have given birth and experienced that vulnerability in order to be capable of responding appropriately to the vulnerability of children. She questions whether there are other experiences that both nonbirthgiving women and men can have that prepare them for recognition of their own and others' vulnerability. For Whitbeck, different experiences that women have as a result of their biology, experiences involved in pregnancy, labor, childbirth, nursing, and postpartum recovery, affect their childrearing (Whitbeck 1983b,186).

I believe these women are right to claim that the changes they experienced in pregnancy were helpful in preparing them for the kind of changes they experienced in becoming mothers. However, I find it interesting that the women tended to use gender-neutral language (parenting), while simultaneously claiming that bodily experiences available only to pregnant women prepared them for childrearing, since this kind of claim does not cause them to reflect on whether the connection they claim between childbearing and childrearing means that men and women who do not experience pregnancy will be inferior as childrearers to women who have been pregnant or whether there are other ways, besides pregnancy, to prepare for the responsibilities of childrearing. The tight association between childbearing and childrearing also tends to suggest that one person should be a child's primary caregiver, since only one person can have been pregnant with that child.

Earlier in this chapter, I cited Mackenzie's view that women will identify with culturally prevalent images even when these views might harm them. I believe that, in pregnancy, when women are experiencing dramatic changes and many of them are undergoing a transition to motherhood, they are peculiarly vulnerable to the impact of culturally prevalent images and ideologies about the role of pregnant women and mothers. They are therefore more likely to accept notions such as that pregnancy is the proper destiny of women. As a way of deferring worry about the responsibilities mothers often have in our society and in order to conform at this early stage to cultural tropes about what mothers should be like, they are also likely to agree that women who have experienced pregnancy are best suited to be the primary caregivers of infants and that they should care intensively, with others perhaps available to support them, as others supported them during pregnancy, but with no one able to replace them or share primary responsibility for care.

Sometimes women will have insight into the impact of culturally pervasive images and ideologies on their pregnancies. For instance, one woman writes that during pregnancy, "It felt as if I were fulfilling some evolutionary purpose, a biological design older than the ages, and carrying this baby was my destiny. I felt extremely feminine and proud of it. Every time the baby kicked, I was drawn into a private conversation to which no man would ever be invited" (Cancellaro 2001, 33). However, in reflecting back on her experience, she realizes, "The powerfulness of pregnancy masked my complete yet blissful ignorance of mothering an infant" (2001, 33). Sometimes this is not the case. In their study of African American women's personal experiences of pregnancy, Mann and her colleagues cite many women who viewed pregnancy as a passage to adulthood, womanhood, or wholeness. One woman writes: "[F]or me, it was so specifically about being an adult and being a woman" (Mann et al. 1999, 299). Another writes: "If I think about it, I used to hear my mother talking sometimes about women teachers in the school . . . who didn't have any children. She was scornful of them. What she would say is 'Neither chick nor child'" (1999, 299). Many of the women in Mann's study connect being a woman with being pregnant. Further, being pregnant is thought to make one a real woman (1999, 299–300). Just looking at women's narratives of their pregnancies, therefore, does not give us an explanation of the ways in which the cultural imaginary affects their pregnancies, for instance, the pronatalist attitudes that devalue the lives of women who do not give birth. (Meyers 2001 gives an excellent account of pronatalism and its impact on women's lives.)

Another limitation of collections of pregnancy narratives is that it is easy to miss what makes pregnancy distinctive for subgroups of women.

Academic articles that focus on the experiences of pregnancy for subgroups such as the one written by Mann et al., can overcome some of these limitations. Thus, for instance, Mann and her colleagues pay particular attention to African American women's experiences that their pregnancies are contributing to the survival of their minority community (1999, 300) and to the ways in which the largely impoverished women in their study differed from more privileged Caucasian women's pregnancies because of stresses around housing, monetary concerns, and the way the poorer African American women were treated in the health care system (1999, 298). Other studies of groups of women with some common features, such as Rudolfsdottir's (2000) study of the experiences of very young pregnant women, and Thomas's (1997) study of the pregnancy experiences of women with a variety of physical and mental impairments, can also help to correct a tendency to misinterpret pregnancy narratives as giving accounts of what it is like to be pregnant, rather than accounts of what it is like to be pregnant for women in particular kinds of situations. Thomas's study in particular points to the extent to which claims about pregnancy as the destiny for all women are not culturally applied to women with mental and physical impairments, as these women are often pressured not to have children.

Narratives and academic articles that seek to explore aspects of women's subjective experiences of pregnancy therefore need further analysis in order to make manifest how powerful ideologies around pregnancy and motherhood and about medical expertise have shaped women's experiences of pregnancy. Much work has already been done on the impact of what is termed the medicalization of pregnancy, and I do not focus extensively on this topic in this book. Instead, particularly in the third, fourth, and fifth chapters, I focus on what I term the ideology of motherhood, and how it shapes women's reproductive experiences.

I discuss the ideology of motherhood in more depth in those later chapters of this book, but say something briefly about it here. The ideology of motherhood involves claims about both what motherhood is like and what it should be like. Women who conform to it are culturally rewarded, if only by having a role that is central to their lives conform to social expectations. These expectations involve beliefs that pregnancy and motherhood are natural for women and that they are private activities that ought not to be carried on in the public sphere and do not need public analysis except when the mothering is done inadequately. Motherhood is supposed to involve endless self-sacrifice that is thought to come naturally to women, and furthermore this sacrifice is supposed to bring women happiness. Finally, mothers are expected to tend to all the needs of their children, on their own, with the exception of financial resources that are supposed to come from fathers. We can see how many of the women's narratives cited above reflect the impact of this ideology.

However, despite the limitations of narratives such as those in *Pregnancy Stories*, they are an important reminder that women's experiences of pregnancy are worth telling, that women need opportunities to reflect on their experiences, and that women experiencing or planning pregnancy will find other women's reflections an important resource. This is particularly important given that pregnant women are often expected to make important decisions about their pregnancies with very little time to reflect and with little access to stories about how others have handled similar critical decisions.

My remarks in the paragraph above stress how accounts of women's subjective experiences of pregnancy may be useful to other women experiencing pregnancy. The audience for the book *Pregnancy Stories* and pregnancy stories in general will probably chiefly consist of pregnant women, but such narratives and tales should be read or listened to by others as well. Those who have experienced pregnancy in the past might find that pregnancy narratives give them an opportunity to reflect on their own experiences, which are rarely made public. Those who are wondering whether or not to become pregnant and those who seek to support their partner through a pregnancy need to have realistic accounts of what women experience. It is also very important that those who will never be pregnant or support a partner through pregnancy begin to ask questions about pregnancy and social responses to it.

As I stress in the next chapter, women undergo enormous changes in many different dimensions of their lives during pregnancy. We are often fascinated by tales of the adventures people live even when we never expect to take on similar challenges. Why is it that the general public – those who are not planning a pregnancy or supporting a partner's pregnancy – do not show any interest in pregnancy narratives as stories people tell about their adventures? I suggest that the view of pregnancy we saw so clearly demonstrated in Plato and Nietzsche – of bodily pregnancy as a purely physical event, whether involving passive waiting or active bodily control, and of bodily pregnancy as significant only because it can lead to birth – is largely responsible for this lack of interest in an area of human life that involves remarkable and dramatic change. I would also agree with Gatens that embodied speech is less easily tolerated than speech that doesn't concern bodily processes, particularly when those bodies are women's.

However, I mean to suggest more than that we can or should turn to pregnancy stories out of vicarious interest in other people's adventures. There is also much that studying experiences of pregnancy can teach all of us, pregnant or not, capable of pregnancy or not, both in terms of what is unique to pregnancy and in terms of similarities between pregnancy and other kinds of experiences. These include those discussed in chapter 2 that involve making other sorts of plans that must adjust to phenomena outside one's control and experiences of some kinds of illness and impairment. Once we overcome the negative impact of the various misconceptions of pregnancy I have discussed in this chapter, we can be more open to seeing various reasons for making women's experiences of pregnancy part of public discourse.

# *Chapter 2*

# Reconceiving Pregnancy

## 1. INTRODUCTION

As I suggested in the first chapter, it can seem that we have great respect for pregnancy, at least those pregnancies that occur in the context of approved relationships and that involve the reproduction of people considered socially desirable. But while a pregnant woman may be held to be of more value and interest because of her pregnancy, this is because of society's interest in the child she may give birth to, rather than an interest in what she experiences between conception and delivery. Very little attention is paid to pregnancy as an experience.

Pregnancy as an experience is chiefly thought of as something uncomfortable and inconvenient that women must manage or endure. Nature is far more likely to be presented as an agent (as we speak of letting nature take its course) than pregnant woman are. The only way women appear to act reflectively with respect to their pregnancies is by choosing to continue with or to end those pregnancies (if they in fact have those options). In this chapter, I wish to challenge both misconceptions of pregnancy I outlined in the first chapter: the assumption that pregnancies are significant only because they can lead to the birth of a child and the assumption that pregnancy is chiefly a bodily event, either a passive period of expectation or a time in which a pregnant woman and/or medical professionals practice surveillance and control over her body, out of concern for her health and for fetal well being.

In feminist circles some writers have begun to claim that we should look past the medical model of pregnancy, in which pregnancies are valued only for their products, and examine the experience of pregnancy itself to see whether it has some value. In her discussion of midwives in the Netherlands, Barbara Katz Rothman writes that many of those midwives believe "that pregnancy itself has a meaning and a value in a woman's life, and that for women who want to become mothers, a good pregnancy and a good birth are good things to have" (Katz Rothman 2001, 185). But what might we mean by a good pregnancy, beyond or apart from a pregnancy that results in the birth of a desired child or a pregnancy that is less inconvenient than it might be?

To begin to investigate these questions, we need to ask what pregnancies are like for the women who are pregnant, a task I began at the end of the first chapter. Since I am interested in the embodied experience of pregnancy as a site of meaning, in my exploration of these questions I use the theoretical tools of phenomenology. I offer the following as a brief definition of phenomenology: the reflective description of human experience in an attempt to explore the meanings embodied in habit, feeling, and perception. In particular I draw on the framework generated by the work of Merleau-Ponty (1962) and his feminist appropriators and critics in order to look at the phenomenology of pregnancy.

To contest the assumption that pregnancy is of interest only because it can lead to the birth of a child, in this chapter I focus on aspects of pregnancy that go beyond questions about relations between pregnant women and the fetuses that grow inside them. Relationships between pregnant woman and the fetuses they carry are discussed in chapter 3, when I move on to discuss the ethical significance of pregnancy. I leave this to the next chapter because, if we think that this relationship is all that makes pregnancy worth taking seriously, we will still be caught up in the misconception that pregnancy is important only because it can lead to the birth of a child. Therefore, before discussing the ethical significance of pregnancy, I devote this chapter to analyzing aspects of pregnancy that are meaningful apart from the nature of the relationship between the pregnant woman and her fetus. I compare wanted pregnancies to other types of plans and projects and then compare them to the sudden onset of illness or impairment.

Moreover, a focus on the relationship between a pregnant woman and the fetus she carries can exaggerate the uniqueness of a woman's experience with pregnancy. Since it is only in pregnancy that the borders between the self and the other are first so fluid and then change so quickly, and it is only in pregnancy that one woman's choices with respect to her body have such an immediate impact on another being, a focus on the relationship between the woman and the fetus she carries may falsely suggest that pregnancy is an entirely unique experience, with no significant points of continuity with other experiences. I argue that this not only distorts pregnancy, but also suggests to those who have never been pregnant and will never be pregnant – including all men[1] and those women who know they are infertile – that pregnant women's experiences, while perhaps interesting as curiosities, could not possibly have any relevance for them, a view I argued against at the end of the first chapter. As I argue in the next chapter, even a focus on the ethical significance of pregnancy should not present pregnancy as entirely disconnected from other ethically significant relationships, but I hope that this chapter's analysis of the continuities and discontinuities between pregnant and nonpregnant experiences can prepare the way for that discussion.

Hilde Lindemann Nelson argues, as I do, against the "nearly universal belief that pregnancy in human beings is a purely biological process" (1994, 262). She reminds us that women transform "natural processes by valuing them or giving them meaning" (1994, 262) and suggests that there are four ways in which women do this to their pregnancies. First, women transform pregnancies into purposive activity when they become or remain pregnant for a reason or reasons. Second, by their emotional responses to their pregnancies and by their hopes and imaginings, pregnant women begin the "purposeful, creative activity of mothering long before birth" (1994, 263). Third, a pregnant "woman's acts of imagination, resistance, or welcome are not directed solely toward the future, in which there is a born child.... The pregnant woman is also actively doing something in the present moment for the fetus she carries" (1994, 264). Nelson stresses that women, unlike other animals, have the capacity to behave responsibly toward their fetuses. The fourth and final reason why we should recognize pregnancy as purposive involves the fact that all purposive activity, such as the purposive activity of an architect, involves accommodation to natural and social context, and so we should not think that the physical constraints of pregnancy make it remarkably different from other kinds of planned activity.

The first three reasons Nelson gives all revolve around the pregnant woman's relationship with her fetus or future child. In contrast, I concentrate in this chapter on those aspects of pregnancy that have been deemphasized, the ones that do not chiefly involve this relation. I also feel that the account Nelson has given of these three reasons perhaps overstresses the purposive, planned, or directed nature of pregnancies, rather than the intertwining of planning and accommodation that more accurately characterizes most women's experiences of pregnancy. I therefore concentrate on the fourth reason Nelson gives, which suggests that we may be overemphasizing the uniqueness of pregnancy in thinking of other types of projects as unconstrained in the ways that pregnancies are constrained, that is, by natural processes one cannot control and within a social context to which one can contribute but not control.

To draw our attention to commonalities as well as differences between experiences of pregnancy and other kinds of experiences involving planning and purposes, I compare pregnancies first to deliberately chosen projects, and second to types of physical illness and impairment that disrupt one's familiar bodily orientation to the world. I discuss pregnancy in relationship to women's projects and pregnancy in relation to illness and impairment in order to explore the extent to which pregnancy is an accommodation to features that are outside one's control and the extent to which it may involve conscious decision making and purposive meaning making. In particular, I hope to show that pregnancy is a particularly interesting phenomena and significant experience in the lives of many women precisely because of the mingling of accommodation and purposive activity or design throughout pregnancy.

In both comparisons, I emphasize the changes that pregnant women experience, although which changes they experience, and the meaning they give to these changes, will differ with women in different situations. Since most of the philosophical attention given to pregnancy has concentrated on ethical issues arising within unwanted pregnancies, I concentrate in this chapter on women's experiences with wanted pregnancies, and I conclude this chapter with a discussion of what my analysis reveals about the oppressive nature of unwanted pregnancies. The discussion of both wanted and unwanted pregnancy is intended to set the groundwork for the next chapter, because any adequate ethics of pregnancy must reflect awareness of the range of experiences women have during pregnancy. Before making comparisons between pregnancy and projects and pregnancy and impairment, however, I begin by giving an outline of the range of changes pregnant women often face.

## 2. PREGNANCY AND CHANGE

During pregnancy, women are faced with fast-paced and dramatic changes in their bodies, their emotions, and the social dimensions of their lives. Although I do not agree with her account of pregnancy as involving five distinct stages nor with her attempt to reinterpret the metaphor of woman as vessel in a more positive, gynecocentric light, I do agree with Kathryn Rabuzzi that "[p]regnancy, especially a first one, severely tests a woman's identity" and that "[i]t is a rare woman who does not experience some fundamental alteration of her core being during pregnancy" (Rabuzzi 1994, 54).

Most women experience pregnancy during that period of adulthood when they have already physically matured and are not yet experiencing dramatic signs of aging. They therefore experience pregnancy at a time when most changes to their bodies, if they are otherwise healthy, are slow, incremental, and more or less self-directed. Increases and decreases in fitness and increases and decreases in amount of food eaten lead to slow, small changes to their bodies, and such changes can be typically modified or reversed if a woman wholeheartedly chooses to do so.[2] Pregnancy, by contrast, is more akin to the sorts of bodily changes women experience either as girls going through puberty or as postmenopausal women. These are not changes that are generally self-directed (although women may delay the onset of menstruation by starving themselves or may postpone its end through hormonal therapy), and they make manifest what women can sometimes experience as their bodies' own agendas, separate from and uncontrolled by any projects they might undertake deliberately.

The power of the body to act, without needing direction from a woman's conscious plans, is made dramatically manifest during pregnancy. Moreover, it is not only a woman's size and shape that change during pregnancy; her body may also change in a number of other ways, including changes in visual acuity, the pigment of her skin, the onset of rashes, nausea, heartburn, raised blood pressure, increased congestion, difficulty catching her breath, and swollen hands and feet. It may well seem as if no part of her body has remained unchanged, as even her internal organs are dramatically rearranged. Many women speak of feeling out of control of their bodies during pregnancy, feeling, as Iris Marion Young (1984, 49), Lucy Bailey (1999, 340), and many other women put it, that they are no longer confident about what even counts as the borders of their bodies because of the presence of a fetus and also their bodies' changing sizes and shapes and because of a sense, as Robyn Longhurst puts it, that pregnant bodies are "leaky bodies" (2000, 15), leaking colostrum from breasts and fluids from the vagina, including shortly before birth.

Changes in a pregnant woman's social interactions are also often quite dramatic. In our society, mothers are expected to sacrifice a great deal for their children, and this is certainly expected as well of pregnant women, who may frequently be told that nothing they do could be more important than their job of bringing a child to life. Pregnant women often report being treated like public property. Robyn Longhurst observes that the bodily boundaries of pregnant women are frequently no longer respected, such as when strangers think it appropriate to pat their pregnant bellies (Longhurst 1998, 28). Joyce Davidson observes that pregnant women are subject to social surveillance, even by strangers, and are often lectured on what constitutes appropriate behavior, not only regarding smoking and drinking, but also regarding what is appropriate to wear (Davidson 2001, 289).

During late pregnancy, a woman's sex is immediately obvious even to strangers, and few of her interactions with strangers and casual acquaintances will be unaffected by social meanings given to sex and gender. Moreover, in the same way that a woman's sex influences her social interactions differently when she is a little girl, young woman, or older woman, attitudes toward what is appropriate for a woman also differ in many respects when she is pregnant. For one thing, wherever she goes in mid- to late pregnancy she is immediately tagged as someone's mother and supposed to look out for the well-being of her future child by limiting what she eats, drinks, and does.

There is a tension in our society between being a sexually desired and desiring woman and being a mother, and this tension affects how both men and women interact with a pregnant woman. Writing in 1984, Iris Marion Young observed that "our own culture sharply separates pregnancy from sexuality" (1984, 52). Lucy Bailey's study of thirty middle-class British pregnant women confirmed that many pregnant women have difficulty both experiencing themselves as sexual beings and being viewed as sexual by others. As Bailey puts it, because of a tension between sexuality and the mothering role, they experienced a "partial erasure of their sexuality" (Bailey 2001, 117) and "overwhelmingly regretted their difficulty in seeing themselves in sexual terms" during their pregnancies (2001, 117).

The women in Bailey's study spoke of a partial erasure – not an entire erasure – of their sexuality, and Rebecca Huntley (2000) suggests that the tension between maternity and sexuality does not prevent pregnant women from being eroticized. Relatively recently, they have begun to appear as sexual beings, both desired and desiring, in mainstream media such as the rather respectful depiction of the pregnant actress Lisa Rinna in the September 1998 issue of *Playboy* magazine. Pregnant women are also found, depicted in less respectful and maternal ways, in more hardcore pornography (web sites, films, and compilations of nude photographs sent in by readers of *Picture* magazine). Huntley examines mainstream and widely read pregnancy guides, such as Miriam Stoppard's book *Healthy Pregnancy*, which argues that sexual activity is safe, permissible, enjoyable, and possibly even good for the fetus in terms of both the role sexual activity can play in preparing the body for childbirth and its enhancement of the relationship of the pregnant woman and her partner (2000, 355–357). This suggests to Huntley that there are forms of sexual activity that are socially approved for pregnant women (and hence accepted in mainstream publications). Approved sex involves heterosexual couples and enhances the pregnant woman's relationship with the father of her child.

Pregnancy affects not only how a pregnant woman thinks of and experiences her own sexuality, but also her sense of herself as a woman or as feminine. In the previous chapter I cited several African American women who felt that their pregnancies confirmed not only their maturity, but also their womanhood. Many of the women in Bailey's study echoed these sentiments. Aby, who had previously felt as if she wasn't a proper girl or woman, found that her pregnancy reversed that (Bailey 2001, 117). Pregnancy can affect feelings about adequacy in meeting various gender ideals. Janey felt that she escaped from pressure to be thin because, in pregnancy, "You feel that your body's doing some function that it's meant to – that it's designed to. So it makes you feel your body – you know, positive about it" (Bailey 2001, 119). Bailey observes that many of the women in her study felt a "temporary release from the pressures of the slender imperative" (2001, 120). Rose Wiles similarly notes that some but not all overweight women "experience[d] their weight in a less negative way due to a greater social acceptability of fatness during pregnancy" (Wiles 1994, 33).

During pregnancy women re-evaluate what it means to be a woman and therefore may feel more or less confirmed in their gender identities. Some of the changes to a woman's gender identity during pregnancy are made particularly salient by examining the experiences of pregnant transitioning female to male transsexuals. In Sam Dylan More's study of nine female to male transsexuals who transitioned during or shortly after pregnancy, almost all of the pregnant men made it clear that pregnancy did not change their self-perceptions as masculine, and all of the people he studied were aware of their male self-identification before they became pregnant (More 1998, 322). However, many of them found it very difficult to reconcile their gender identity and pregnancy, not only because of the reactions of others, but also because of the many reminders pregnancy provided of their bodies as female.

Some chose to reconcile the tension by invoking a simple distinction between sex as biological and gender as social. For instance, Chris writes, "I'd come to terms with the incongruity of being pregnant and feeling non-female during my earlier pregnancies. I did that by realizing that pregnancy is a biological function indicative of genetic sex, not gender. I dealt with the 'general view of society' by ignoring it" (1998, 324). Matt and Del coped with the tension by seeing their bodies as those of female animals (both when pregnant and when breastfeeding) while they as social persons were fathers to be or fathers providing for their babies. While the tensions felt by these pregnant transitioning transsexuals are no doubt extreme, pregnancy clearly provides a reminder of the nature of the body and of changing social expectations that connect bodies and gender, especially pregnant bodies.

A pregnant woman is also, in western societies, very often a medical patient, and whether she plans a home birth with the support of a midwife or a hospital birth, she will face the prospect of her increased vulnerability during her pregnancy and during birth. The period of her first pregnancy will often be that in which she experiences the most significant relationship she has had with the medical establishment so far in her life; this is a point I expand on in the second section of this chapter.

Furthermore, when a pregnancy is welcomed, as well as sometimes when it is not, a woman frequently plans to raise the child herself once it is born, and this means that her pregnancy will alter her relations with her closest friends and members of her family. The child she carries not only is her child, but is her siblings' niece or nephew, her parents' or in-laws' grandchild, and her spouse or lover's child, whether biologically or by adoption. All members of a close-knit family will experience some change in their lives as a result of the imminent birth, and some members – her other children, her partner, her closest friends – will face dramatic change. While families and friends have the opportunity to prepare for the kind of change prompted by pregnancy, unlike those changes prompted by sudden deaths, for instance, these changes are unlike others in that people must prepare for the arrival of a person who will be very important to them and about whom they know almost nothing.

During wanted pregnancies most women face fears about the possibility of miscarriage and the possibility of having to make decisions about whether or not to continue a pregnancy when informed about significant health problems in a fetus. Beyond these kinds of fears and concerns about her own health and that of the fetus, every pregnant woman who plans to raise she child she carries also needs to come to terms with her welcoming of a creature who is already radically transforming her body, her social interactions, and her habits, who will always radically transform her life, and about whom she knows virtually nothing. Given the extent and pace of change, as well as the extreme difficulty a pregnant woman will most likely experience in attempting to ignore the changes she experiences, it seems remarkable that views of bodily pregnancy such as those found in Plato, Nietzsche, and Chagall have continued to be influential. Part of the explanation no doubt lies in the extent to which images of or discussion by pregnant or formerly pregnant women[3] that explore the changes they experience rarely make it into public discourse.

## 3. PREGNANCY, EXPERIENCE, AND PHENOMENOLOGY

In this part of the chapter I discuss how wanted pregnancies are similar to and different from other kinds of plans and projects, and, as mentioned, I draw on work in phenomenology to do so. This does not mean that I believe that all women will experience pregnancy in similar ways. Experience is affected both by social context and by a person's individual history and personality. Therefore, for instance, when one's pregnancy is socially acceptable, pregnancy will be experienced differently from when it is not, and differently when one has had a previous child or previous abortion. Moreover, as I discussed in the introduction to this book, in appealing to the significance of experience, I am not suggesting that we are either fully aware of what we experience or that our understanding of our experience is entirely veridical. For instance, I may feel that my decisions and experiences are not affected by social expectations, when others can see that they are, and I may be brought to see not only that they are but how they are. I elaborate on the first of these points in both this chapter and the next, as I suggest how a variety of factors may influence a woman's experience of pregnancy.

I discuss ways in which wanted pregnancies are similar to and different from more typical exemplars of deliberately chosen projects because I want to emphasize women's agency during pregnancy, rather than their passivity. Because women are sometimes presented as agents during pregnancy only in the ways they control their bodies, I explore ways in which women make use of their intellectual and creative capacities during pregnancy, as well as ways in which their agency may be thwarted. However, women's agency during pregnancy, even in the most hospitable environments, is complicated by, although not necessarily thwarted by, involuntary bodily changes. Therefore, after examining the ways in which women's experiences of pregnancy are like and unlike other activities they consciously undertake, I examine the extent to which pregnancy is similar to and different from some types of physical illness and impairment, in particular those which disrupt one's familiar bodily orientation to the world.

Vangie Bergum argues, "The goal of phenomenological research is to understand what a person's experience is from his or her point of view, as opposed to explaining actions, decisions, or patterns from an outside point of view or starting from a theoretical construct" (Bergum 1997, 5). In this chapter, I do not fully share that goal. I draw on the phenomenological method, but, because I am looking for patterns of commonality and difference in women's experiences of pregnancy, I am not primarily seeking to know how individual women think about their pregnancies. Instead, I look to women's experiences to discover what they see as meaningful about their embodied experiences but also look to features that structure and give meaning to those experiences in ways that may escape conscious awareness.

Merleau-Ponty's work is relevant because of his challenge to mind-body dualism and because of his concept of experience. As Elizabeth Grosz argues, for Merleau-Ponty experience is not a "neutral vantage point in establishing judgments – although clearly it must play some role in them. Experience is not outside social, political, historical and cultural forces" but neither is it entirely socially and ideologically fabricated (Grosz 1993, 40). Instead, experience is taken both as the starting point of his analysis and as a kind of "measure against which the vagaries of theory can be tested" (1993, 41).

Merleau-Ponty insists on the embodied nature of the mind and the significance of our bodily orientation to the world for all kinds of purposive activity. Unfortunately, as many feminist critics have pointed out, Merleau-Ponty paid scant attention to the way sex and gender affect bodily experience and also tended to take prototypically male experiences as exemplary (Grosz 1993, 1994; Butler 1989, 1997; Young 1984). For instance, in an observation particularly relevant to my project, Elizabeth Grosz has observed that Merleau-Ponty ignores all aspects of maternity (Grosz 1994, 104). Feminist authors have appropriated and critiqued his work, and some, such as Iris Marion Young (1984), Carol Bigwood (1991), and Louise Levesque-Lopman (1983), have begun to undertake a phenomenology of pregnancy. None of these authors, however, has focused on women's experiences of illness and impairment in pregnancy.

Levesque-Lopman writes that her phenomenology of pregnancy will involve "a reconstruction of the way I interpret my own experience of pregnancy and childbirth" (1983, 251) and claims that "the fact that it is now being reflected upon by one woman" does not "discount its meaningfulness for other women" (1983, 252). However, I am wary of claims that attempt to generalize about what one woman found meaningful about her pregnancy and indeed claims about "the phenomenology of pregnancy." I expand on the dangerous nature of such claims when I speak of the moral phenomenology of pregnancy in chapter 3.

In speaking of a phenomenology of pregnancy we must remember that meaningful embodied experience, which is what phenomenology seeks to describe, is shaped by culture, history, and social context, and we must as a result be careful not to either assume or give the impression that there is such a thing as a typical experience of pregnancy. Women's experiences of pregnancy will differ depending on many factors, including, but not limited to the following: (1) the extent to which they have been able to choose to become pregnant and the extent to which they desire, at various points, to continue to remain pregnant, (2) the physical changes they experience, some of which can be pronouncedly different from one woman to another, (3) women's attitudes toward their prepregnant lives and bodies, (4) the degree of social and economic support for their pregnancies and whether or not the women can expect continued support if they rear the children they bear, and (5) the response of their friends, lovers, and communities to their pregnancies.

In discussing the ways in which women's experiences of pregnancy are similar to and different from experiences with chosen projects and with illnesses that challenge them physically, I have attempted (in the section on pregnancy and change, above) or attempt to indicate below, at least briefly, how the first three factors listed above affect how women experience their pregnancies. In the next chapter, I discuss the remaining two. I do not in this chapter emphasize the impact of technological developments, such as ultrasounds and prenatal testing, on women's experiences of pregnancy for two reasons. First, a great deal of productive work has already been done on this point by Katz Rothman (1986), Martin (1987), Oakley (1987), Corea (1988), Franklin (1991), Davis-Floyd

(1994), and Squier (1994), for instance. Second, most of the impact of these technologies concerns how they affect the relationship between a pregnant woman and the fetus she carries and how the larger society views fetuses, and these are points I take up in the third chapter, which discusses the ethical significance of pregnancy.

## 4. PREGNANCY AS A PROJECT

There is not always a clear line between wanted and unwanted pregnancies. Decisions and attitudes can vary over the forty weeks or so of a pregnancy, and feelings of ambivalence are common throughout the period. Most typically, pregnancies are unwanted when a woman does not want to bear and rear a child at the time she becomes pregnant, but pregnancies may also be or become unwanted because of illness that a woman develops in her pregnancy or because features of the fetus, as suggested by diagnostic tests, make that particular fetus unwanted. They may also be unwanted because of the woman's resistance to the changes that occur during pregnancy, both changes to her body and changes in the way others relate to her. Because I am interested in the extent to which pregnancies can be experienced as both similar to and different from chosen projects, in this section I focus on pregnancies that are not entirely unwanted. When pregnancies are neither desired nor accepted, particularly when they are the result of coercion or are the unintended result of consensual heterosexual intercourse, they will have very little in common with chosen projects, and therefore it does not seem helpful to discuss them in this context.

However, I do think that a discussion of the phenomenology of wanted pregnancies can shed light on how invasive experiences of unwanted pregnancies can be, both because they may be experienced as deprivations of choice and purpose and because they will be experienced as significantly disruptive of the pregnant woman's bodily orientation to the world. I therefore, as mentioned above, conclude this chapter with a discussion of how attention to the phenomenology of pregnancy can help us understand why some pregnancies are unwanted.

In many ways, pregnancy seems very different from our typical understanding of a designed activity or consciously chosen project. Women often become pregnant without intending to do so, and at times they become pregnant despite specifically intending not to conceive. At other times they do not become pregnant despite desiring very much to conceive. Further, women sometimes stop being pregnant, or miscarry, despite desiring to continue with the pregnancy, and they sometimes continue to be pregnant despite desiring to end the pregnancy. Even in those instances where a pregnancy was intended and desired and its continuance was intended and desired, this does not mean that the women involved have a great deal of choice about either whether or how the pregnancy will proceed.

Pregnancy in particular involves many physical changes that by and large happen involuntarily. Some of those physical changes may be anticipated and desired, such as the stereotypical glowing complexion, but even they seem to happen without much design on the pregnant woman's part, and many changes that are not welcome occur nonetheless, such as itchy hands and feet, changes in vision, heartburn, or interrupted sleep. Even more seriously, there are illnesses and health problems that are either complicated by or caused by pregnancy, including gestational diabetes, pre-eclampsia, placenta previa, and hyperemesis, which not only happen involuntarily, but may also complicate a pregnant woman's other projects and in some cases threaten her life. These features of pregnancy all make it seem more like something a woman endures, willingly or unwillingly, than something she shapes and guides.

Iris Marion Young notes that the rapid changes one's body experiences during pregnancy bring one many moments of a sharp awareness of one's body. She therefore argues that pregnancy can be an important topic for phenomenologists to address, particularly as a corrective to the assumption, made by Merleau-Ponty, that clear awareness of one's body makes a person feel estranged and objectified, in that one cannot both attend to the physicality of one's body and use it as a means to the accomplishment of one's aims (Young 1984, 50). In those situations where women have either sought or welcomed pregnancy, they can do precisely this and experience the way in which the changes in their bodies connect to their aims and projects.

In the paragraphs above I noted that pregnancy has some features in common with both puberty and aging, in that aspects of the body change without one's conscious control in all three experiences. Pregnancies are unlike puberty and aging, however, in that they may be deliberately sought and sometimes deliberately timed, and they are also unlike puberty and aging in the speed with which the body changes. They are therefore a particularly striking example of the kind of phenomenon Young wants to assert against Merleau-Ponty's claim that clear awareness of the body is a sign of our experience of it as a roadblock to our conscious intentions. Wanted pregnancies lead to experiences where the body can be seen to function both independently of conscious direction and in accordance with a woman's deliberately undertaken projects and plans.

How well a woman can anticipate and direct the changes that will happen to her body and in many areas of her life will be a function of two things: first, her access to resources that allow her to be flexible in response to change and, second, how much knowledge she has about the changes she can expect, either from her own previous experiences of pregnancy or from her knowledge of other women's pregnancies. Since I argued in the previous chapter that women generally have very little knowledge about how their experiences will change (although they often have a great deal of information about how a fetus develops), we can see that this lack of access to women's accounts of their experiences of pregnancy can limit the amount of control pregnant women have over the changes they will experience. For instance, in their study of the experiences of pregnant women on home bed rest, Carrie Adler and Yosepha Zarchin found that access to an Internet discussion group involving other women who were or had experienced long periods of required bed rest during pregnancy helped many of the women feel more in control of their lives, even if only by letting them discuss such matters as when it was best to relinquish control of some plans and projects, and how to reclaim them (Adler and Zarchin 2002). Furthermore, since one woman's pregnancies can vary a great deal over time, even previously pregnant women need access to these kinds of accounts, as well, of course, as access to the kinds of resources – especially financial, emotional, medical, and material support – that can allow pregnant women to take some control over what happens to them during pregnancy.

To argue that pregnancy – the above features notwithstanding – is akin in many respects to a consciously undertaken plan or project, I compare pregnancy to two more typical exemplars of consciously undertaken projects: first, my plan to write this chapter on the phenomenology of pregnancy and, second, the project of improving one's soccer game. I choose these examples because the first is typically conceived of as intellectual labor, the other as primarily physical activity. The former may be thought to be a relatively solitary project, the latter, given that soccer is a team sport, a more collaborative project.

When pregnancies are deliberately sought and preserved, I argue that they share features with both types of project. However, I think that a realization that pregnancy can be a meaningful and purposive activity should also lead us to question our more typical understanding of projects as entirely within a person's control. Not only does this keep us from acknowledging the social nature of many supposedly individual projects, but it also makes an overly sharp distinction between aspects of the world we can actively control and aspects we can only passively accept. We then tend to dichotomize our experiences into those we must merely endure and those that we can control.

Levesque-Lopman compares pregnancy to a project very like my first example (of writing this chapter), in that she compares pregnancy to writing a novel. She writes that while a man writing a novel and a woman choosing to become pregnant both take projects on freely, "The man writing the novel, however, can also choose to set it aside and return to it another time, or abandon it completely. Moreover, the project is predominantly an intellectual endeavor: although the man's body is involved in it, its completion is not determined specifically by his body; it is neither dependent on another human being for its beginning or its completion, nor binding to his life in terms of commitment" (1983, 249). While I agree with her in some respects in the contrasts she draws, where abortion is available, women do have the option of abandoning their projects entirely, and when adoption is available, they also have the option of avoiding a life-long commitment to a child after the pregnancy ends. It is also important to recognize that the ability of the man to write the novel will depend on the state of his body and on other human beings and social institutions for its inception (all the other novels he has read, those who taught him to study literature) and for its completion (the paying job he has that foots the bills or an arts grant he has won, people who help to care for his children or elderly parents, his editor, etc.). We should therefore not overdraw the contrast between the intellectual labor involved in writing a novel or paper and the embodied labor of pregnancy, and should also avoid making either one appear an entirely private project.

Pregnancy might appear to differ from writing a novel or other such project chiefly in its necessary accommodation to natural phenomena. However, almost all of our projects involve some degree of accommodation to things we cannot control. Take, for instance, the example of planning a spring fair as a school fundraiser. This project will depend a great deal on the availability of volunteer labor from other parents, donations from local companies, and the vagaries of the weather. Pregnancy, in its combination of active planning and accommodation to what one cannot control, is therefore in many ways better modeled by projects such as this than the example of planning to write a book. This is because, in the way we typically understand the project of writing a book, the many contingencies that are beyond one's control, such as one's health, other demands on one's time, availability of adequate care for one's dependent children, and so forth, are de-emphasized or denied.

Once we recognize that wanted pregnancies are similar to some other consciously chosen projects, pregnancy may seem at first more akin to working on one's body, as in the soccer example, rather than working with and on the mind. However, we must remember that projects such as pregnancy, which involve working with one's body, also involve working with one's mind. Some of the intellectual work involved in pregnancy involves giving meaning to (and seeking to guide) the changes a woman experiences in her social interactions, self-image, and body, changes I discussed above. In Lucy Bailey's study of pregnant women, she notes, "Pregnancy was sometimes described as a 'full-time job.' As Linda stated: 'So almost everything I do is really about being pregnant in some way, whether I'm not doing it now, or whether I am doing it' (Bailey 1999, 343).

Bailey describes some of this work as involving practices of the self that are used both to negotiate the changes the women experienced and to "affirm continuities with the self whom they felt they had been before" (1999, 343). She also notes that many of the pregnant women she interviewed saw pregnancy as an impetus for change in many areas of their lives (1999, 339). Young notes something similar in terms of the extent to which pregnancy is a profoundly transformative experience but tends to emphasize the pregnant woman as a spectator to the physical changes she undergoes. She writes that "each day, each week, she looks at herself for signs of transformation" (1984, 54). I think it is important to note that pregnant women are not merely spectators to the physical changes they experience and seek not merely to change their self-understandings, as Bailey stresses, but also to change their situations, for instance, making changes at work and in relationships. As Bigwood describes a pregnant woman, "[s]he creatively takes up the changes of her body, constantly readjusting her body image and weaving subtle relations to a physical pulse that has emerged from elsewhere. Motivated by her new mothering body, she makes dramatic changes in her cultural, social and personal life" (1991, 68). I would argue that pregnant women are motivated by more than the physical changes that they undergo and that how they are motivated will differ with different factors of their experience, but I otherwise agree with

Bigwood as to the role pregnancy can play in motivating significant change.

Pregnancy is like other forms of intellectual labor that involve ordering experiences and events into meaningful patterns. However, in carrying on most kinds of intellectual work, we tend to pay attention to our bodies only when they thwart our plans: a headache or bout of nausea that makes concentration difficult, a sore wrist that inhibits writing or typing. As Merleau-Ponty emphasizes, a body that functions as we intend it to rarely commands our attention (Merleau-Ponty 1962, 82), and this is particularly true when we perform intellectual labour. There is a certain similarity to women's experiences of infertility or repeated miscarriages; the body and its fertility are focused on when they are experienced as unreliable or a barrier to our hopes and plans much more so than when the body functions as we want it to (Shanner 1996). This is in contrast to wanted pregnancies. In them, even when the body functions in accordance with our plans, it doesn't recede from attention. This is chiefly because it is a body that is undergoing rapid change, and because what we want to achieve depends on those changes. Both the changes themselves and the connection between those changes and our plans draw our attention toward the body.

The fact that a willingly pregnant woman aims at certain changes in her body, which she may not merely passively permit but actively encourage – as she changes her diet and those physical activities designed to keep her body fit for certain types of activity – has some similarities to the second kind of project I mentioned above, in which we aim at changes in the body, acquiring new habits, focusing our attention on our bodies, and monitoring our progress toward attaining a goal such as improving our soccer game. A pregnant woman may decide to eat more, to eat different foods, to exercise less, or to exercise differently, in the same way that an athlete switching from one sport to another may make these changes, and both women may monitor their bodily changes with interest in order to see the extent to which they have been able to modify their bodily contours and bodily habits in accordance with their plans.

However, there are also several discontinuities between the experience of the athlete and the pregnant woman. The most radical difference is in how directed the pregnant woman can be toward the changes in her body once they are well under way. The athlete, unless she is also pregnant, will not be experiencing major changes in the locations of major organs, she will not be experiencing a significant shift in her center of gravity, she will not be experiencing a large number of minor changes to her skin and possibly to her eyesight as a result of shifting hormone levels, although she may experience some hormonal changes if she lowers her percentage of body fat to the point that she ceases having menstrual periods. A pregnant woman, unlike an athlete who is not pregnant, can be purposive in relationship to her bodily changes that are the result of pregnancy largely in the way that she accommodates or resists those changes and in the way she gives meaning to them, welcoming or lamenting the changes in her contours, responding to or resisting her changes in appetite, resting in response to her increased fatigue or battling that fatigue. Much here will depend on the pregnant woman's prepregnant attitude toward her body and the way she and others around her view the combination of pregnancy and sexuality, and pregnancy and rigorous physical activity.

Pregnancy, like illness, not only involves changes to the body, but also presents challenges to our habitual routines as it, for instance, disrupts the way one moves through space, particularly when the bodily changes happen too quickly for one to incorporate them into one's self-image. Carol Bigwood, in her phenomenological analysis of pregnancy, describes her own pregnant body in the following: "I have to lean back on the chair to write over my belly, legs apart, giving my belly as much room as possible. All of a sudden it seems my belly has become too big too fast for me to adjust to it as mine" (1991, 66).

While it may seem as if the changes are happening to quickly for the pregnant woman to adjust to them, most of them do adjust and modify those adjustments, again and again. They make these adjustments to the way they sleep, perhaps changing their normal positions for sleep, perhaps taking naps and sleeping less at night. They make adjustments to what they eat, and how often, perhaps eating many small meals in order to minimize heartburn. They make adjustments in their sexual interactions, in their wardrobes, in their increased awareness of the proximity or lack thereof of washrooms. They change what they expect from acquaintances and strangers, adjusting perhaps to increased courtesy from strangers, increased resentment from colleagues, attempts at more invasive touching from strangers and acquaintances alike.

Three other differences between the woman who, not pregnant, sets out to improve her soccer game and a pregnant woman concern (1) how visible the two women's projects are to others, (2) how much these particular projects affect the women's attempts to carry out other plans, and (3) how obvious the social dimensions of each project are. Regarding the first difference, most though certainly not all pregnant women are clearly identified as pregnant by others in their last trimester, and most of those identified as pregnant find that others' interactions with them are significantly influenced by knowledge of their pregnancies. This is quite different from the case in which women undertake to improve a set of physical skills. Regarding the second difference, the decision to improve one's soccer game tends not to have a major impact on one's other projects; the only reason it would make it more difficult to pursue other projects, whether chiefly seen as physical or as intellectual labor, would be a limitation of time and energy. In pregnancies, by contrast, changes in one's energy level, changes in the way a woman moves through space, changes in her orientation toward time as the arrival of the child looms, and changes in her sensitivity toward perceived health risks may have a significant impact on her other chosen activities, as she withdraws from some activities, begins new ones, and alters the way she pursues others.

The third difference I mentioned above concerns how social or personal each project seems to be, and this difference is quite complicated. On the one hand, the pregnant woman's project of being pregnant may seem prototypically personal: Once conception has occurred, she doesn't seem to need anyone else to aid her in carrying the pregnancy to term, with the possible exception of medical personnel if she has any health problems. The woman improving her soccer game, by contrast, needs other soccer players to work with if she is to be able to undertake her project at all; although she may be able to work on her own at certain skills, she will not be sure that she is improving her game or working on the right skills unless she is able to play it. On the other hand, society often regards pregnant woman as vulnerable and requiring larger social support for their health and well being and possibly financial help as well if the pregnancy is physically debilitating.

I think here that a distinction between two ways in which we need social support for our projects may be helpful, and I make this distinction in reference to my earlier example of intellectual labor. In order for me to be able to undertake any project at all, including the project of writing this chapter, I need general social support for my being and my being able to undertake some projects rather than none at all, such as people who help to provide food, shelter, and care for my young children. I also need others to support this particular project – others who have written essays on related topics, for instance. We can easily see how this distinction maps onto the project of improving one's soccer game, but I think we cannot quite so easily make such a clear distinction when it comes to a woman's project of continuing a pregnancy from conception to delivery. Because the pregnancy requires the woman's overall well-being, physically and emotionally, there is not here as sharp a distinction between support for one's overall being and ability to carry on any projects whatsoever and support for one's pregnancy in particular, with the exception perhaps of some specific medical interventions such as hormone injections.

These three features, involving the high visibility of most pregnancies, the impact pregnancies have on many of pregnant women's other projects, and the blurring of the line between support for a pregnant woman's overall being and support for her pregnancy in particular, while different from most other consciously chosen or accepted projects, are features that pregnancies have in common with some varieties of physical illness and impairment.

I therefore turn now to the next aspect I wish to discuss about pregnancy, the ways in which it is and is not similar to physical illness or impairment. In setting out to discuss similarities and differences between women's experiences of some physical illnesses, impairments and their experiences of pregnancy, I want to make it clear that I do not draw this comparison because I concur with the medicalization of pregnancy. While some pregnancies, including mine, do require significant medical intervention and medical treatment, the majority do not. I find myself largely in sympathy with and impressed by the system of maternity care in the Netherlands in which midwives are the primary providers of maternity care, and there are criteria governing which women should be referred to physicians (Sandall et al. 2001, 129–133).

What is it to medicalize pregnancy? It involves interpreting pregnancy itself as a disruption of health that necessarily requires expert medical intervention, and thinking of pregnancy as primarily about health and illness. There are good reasons to resist the medicalization of pregnancy and birth. As Emily Martin suggests, regarding pregnancy and birth as medical problems tends to encourage health care practioners to see themselves as the agents involved and the pregnant or birthing woman as a patient to be worked on (Martin 1987, 147). It also encourages women to see their bodies as separate from their selves, thus contributing to a "fragmentation of the unity of the person" (1987, 19). However, we should not allow these reasons to keep us from acknowledging the many connections that do exist between pregnancy, illness, and impairment.

## 5. PREGNANCY, IMPAIRMENT, AND DISABILITY

As policy makers have sought to accommodate feminist demands to recognize women's distinctive role in reproduction, and the economic burdens women sometimes bear as a result, some attempts have been made to treat pregnancy per se as a disability or, more often, to consider particularly difficult pregnancies as temporary disabilities. For instance, in the United States, the Pregnancy Discrimination Act (PDA, 1978) requires employers to treat women with pregnancy-related illness or impairment in the same way in which they treat other employees with illness or impairment.

As mentioned above, feminists have largely been opposed to treating pregnancy itself as a disability, arguing that this contributes to the medicalization of what is a state of health and that it may encourage, rather than discourage, employers to discriminate against all female employees of childbearing years. However, some real gains have been made in requiring employers to treat employees with pregnancy-related illness or impairment as if they were disabled, particularly in the United States with the passage in 1990 of the Americans with Disabilities Act (ADA). As Jessica Wilson notes, when pregnant women are deemed to be disabled in accordance with the ADA, they can demand that reasonable accommodations be made for their pregnancy-related illness or impairment (Wilson 1999).[4] Mary Crossley notes that claiming that pregnancy is a disability in the terms of the ADA gives women more options than claiming that they have suffered discrimination due to their pregnancy, not only in terms of the demand for accommodation in the workplace, but also because the PDA applies only in the employment context, whereas the ADA applies also to public accommodations and to other public entities (Crossley 2000, 116). Moreover, increasing challenges, from disability activists and the social model of disability to the medicalization of disability, suggest that theorizing either some or all pregnancies as disabilities need not require us to medicalize pregnancy.

In this section of this chapter, I briefly review the current state of disability theory on the topics of how to understand and define disability, illness, and impairment and then argue that there are good reasons for feminists to look at pregnancy in relation to disability theory. In the same way that society is typically not structured to accommodate the public participation of people with illnesses or impairments, it is also not structured in ways that fully accommodate pregnant women. As disability theorists stress, people who are or are thought to be impaired may be healthy or ill, and significantly impaired or not significantly impaired, while still facing oppressive social attitudes and practices, or disablism (i.e., discrimination directed against people who have or are thought to have mental or physical impairments). Pregnant women may similarly be healthy or ill, slightly impaired or significantly impaired, and all may face barriers to their participation in public life. Some of the barriers faced by people with impairments are solely due to oppressive attitudes and practices, but some may involve illness or impairment, and this is also the case with pregnant women. Both people with impairments who are not pregnant and pregnant women who have not had other significant impairments may be in a position to have some insights into one another's situation. Finally, their experiences and reflections on those experiences can also be a valuable source of knowledge for people who have not been pregnant or impaired.

## 6. DISABILITY THEORY

Disability theory has been very much influenced by the social model of disability. To understand the social model of disability, we must first briefly review the model it is intended to replace. Disability theorists overwhelmingly reject the medical model of disability, according to which disability is a medical problem of individuals that should be prevented, cured, or managed by medical professionals. Those who view disability on the medical model chiefly see disability as a personal tragedy, which some rare individuals can overcome in order to be fully functioning members of society, while most people with disabilities will need assistance from medical professionals and economic support from the larger society in order to survive.

The social model of disability makes a sharp distinction between disability and impairment. Disabling attitudes and social practices such as discrimination and social exclusion are responsible for disability, and disablism is seen as on a par in many ways with sexism and racism: "Although the traditional individualistic medical model remains prevalent, many people across the world, including politicians and policy makers, now recognize that 'disability' is an equal opportunities/human rights issue on a par with sexism, heterosexism, racism, and other forms of social exclusion" (Barnes and Mercer 2001, 11).

The British Council of Disabled People defines impairment as follows:

> Impairment is a characteristic, feature or attribute within an individual which is long term and may or may not be the result of disease or injury and may 1. affect that individual's appearance in a way which is not acceptable to society, and/or 2. affect the functioning of that individual's mind or body, either because of, or regardless of society, and/or 3. cause pain, fatigue, affect communication and/or reduce consciousness. (cited in Morris 2001, 2)

Although various disability theorists differ on this point, generally the term "disabled people" refers to people disabled by disabling practices and attitudes, while the term "people with disabilities" is problematic because it uses the word "disabilities" to refer to impairments and draws attention away from oppression and discrimination directed against people who are or are thought to be impaired (Morris 2001, 3). Moreover, impairment is meant to be value-free, in that some impairments may be experienced by the people who have them as differences that are neutral or positive rather than necessarily negative.

In addition to making a sharp distinction between disability and impairment and drawing attention to disability as a human rights problem involving prejudice and discrimination, theorists of the social model typically also emphasize disability rather than impairment. For instance, influential theorists such as Vik Finkelstein, Colin Barnes, and Mike Oliver all argue in favor of minimizing talk of impairment (see Finkelstein 1996; Oliver 1996; Barnes 1998). They generally regard disability as an important political problem and see discussion of personal experiences of impairment as at best an improper use of energies and at worst divisive (because impairments differ radically from one another, whereas experiences of disability are shared) and dangerous (because focus on impairments may lend credence to the model of disability as a medical problem and personal tragedy, rather than a social and political problem). For similar reasons, and also because illness is generally associated with overall incapacity, they also seek to make a sharp distinction between illness and impairment.

Feminist disability theorists such as Liz Crow, Jenny Morris, Carol Thomas, and Susan Wendell praise the recognition of disability as a form of social exclusion but reject the taboo on exploring personal experiences of illness and impairment. This is partly because disabled women demand to speak about their lived reality, and feminists see the personal as political, and partly because they argue that the male social model theorists adopt a model of impairment and disability such that the typical disabled person is a healthy and fit young man who uses a wheelchair "and whose only needs concern a physically accessible environment" (Morris 2001, 9; see also Wendell 2001, 21). Feminist theorists argue that we need to recognize that impairments are not always stable or visible and often involve illness, including chronic illness.[5] Moreover, I argue that without attention to the particularities of impairments, we cannot be fully aware of how disabling attitudes and practices exclude people with impairments. Further, if disabled people are not to be socially excluded, we must examine not only the obviously social arenas of work, public transportation, and partisan politics, but also the social interactions that happen in people's homes with their friends and family and with other people they encounter in their daily living.

Finally, some feminist critics of the social model of disability, along with Bill Hughes and Kevin Paterson, are beginning to critique the sharp distinction between disability and impairment, with the former seen as social and the latter as a condition of the body (Hughes and Paterson 1997). As Bill Hughes puts it, we need to remember that disability is embodied and impairment has a social dimension (Hughes 2002, 66). After all, what is recognized as impairment, particularly impairment of a major life function as the ADA defines disability, depends on what are socially recognized as major life functions and the different manners in which people are able to carry out those functions in a particular social and physical environment. Although some, such as Morris, feel they need to make a sharp distinction between impairment and disability in order to be able to talk about impairment without giving up the importance of disability (Morris 2001, 9–10), others argue that attention to the personal experience of impairment can help to avoid the dangers of lending credence to the medical model of disability (Wendell 2001, 23).

I believe that attention to the phenomenology of impairment is not only a way to avoid the medicalization of impairment, but can also (1) serve to clarify the nature of relations among illness, impairment, and disability and (2) make us more aware, particularly but not only in the case of nonparadigmatic disabilities, of the fact that impairment is not simply a feature of minds and bodies, but reflects as well features of the physical and social environment.

In the remainder of this section of the chapter, I strive to look at pregnancy-related illness and impairment in light of the feminist version of the social model of disability. Pregnancy-related illness and impairment is more like the experiences of illness and impairment to which feminists such as Morris and Wendell wish to draw attention, and from which more women suffer, than the paradigmatic model of an otherwise healthy person with a stable impairment. However, there are also important differences between the experience of pregnancy-related illness and impairment and more chronic illness or long-term impairment, in terms of both the expected duration of the illness or impairment and how people respond to pregnancy versus nonpregnancy-related illness and impairment. Difference in response is partly due to the difference in duration – for it is easier to be sympathetic and accommodating to a person whose impairment has a definite endpoint – but also reflects the fact that pregnancy receives a far more positive social response. In the next few pages, I discuss first experiences of illness and impairment in pregnancy and then issues about forms of social exclusion and the need for accommodation that these experiences reveal.

## 7. PREGNANCY, ILLNESS, AND IMPAIRMENT

The definition of impairment I cited earlier in this chapter involves three parts. The first part refers to changes to one's appearance that are not acceptable to others. Most, though certainly not all, pregnant women are clearly identified as pregnant by others in their last trimester, and most of those identified as pregnant find that others' interactions with them are significantly influenced by knowledge of their pregnancies. However, unlike the case with most deviations from bodily norms, pregnancy in itself is generally not socially unacceptable, although appearing pregnant in public has been problematic at various points in history. What pregnancy-related physical changes have in common with more straightforward impairments is the extent to which they are not accommodated in public spaces; this is particularly clear in the case of seating in university desks, office spaces, theaters, trains and airplanes, auditoriums, and so on. These generally accommodate neither pregnant women nor others with nonstandard physiques, including people who are obese. Thus in even the healthiest of pregnancies, physical changes that happen in the last trimester may be experienced as impairments if they hamper or prevent pregnant women from carrying out tasks important to their daily living. Whether or not this will be the case depends on which tasks pregnant women have chosen to or been assigned to carry out before they became pregnant.

Mary Crossley argues that because pregnancy can impair women's daily functioning in particular contexts, even in the absence of illness, "perhaps we should be asking not whether a woman's pregnancy is characterized by some physiological disfunctioning or abnormality, but instead whether pregnant women, like people with disabilities, have been subject to social oppression because of their bodies' deviations from social norms" (Crossley 2000, 116). She adds, further, that if we want to know whether we should consider pregnancy per se or a particular woman's pregnancy as a disability, we need to think about whether and how the pregnancy in question affects a woman's ability to carry out her daily tasks.

As discussed in the first half of this chapter, the high visibility of most pregnancies and the impact pregnancies have on many of pregnant women's other projects are features that even the healthiest of pregnancies have in common with some varieties of physical illness and impairment, but there are other more intimate connections between pregnancy, illness, and impairment that correspond to the second and third parts of the definition of impairment, including affecting the functioning of one's mind or body and experiences of pain and fatigue.

First, like some illnesses, pregnancy increases a woman's risk of dying. Maternal mortality per 100,000 live births has decreased greatly since the beginning of the twentieth century. In 1918 there were 920 deaths per 100,000 live birth in the United States, whereas for the past twenty years, the rate has hovered between 8 and 9. In 1929 in Canada the rate was 564, but has dropped to between 3 and 5 since the 1980s. However, some groups remain more at risk than others, with black women experiencing a rate of approximately 20, and women over thirty experiencing a rate of approximately 34. Most of these deaths are attributable to embolisms, pregnancy-induced hypertension, and hemorrhage (Hoyert et al. 2000).

While maternal mortality remains relatively rare, pregnancy can greatly increase the rate of complications for women with ongoing illness and impairments, and pregnancies can make treatment of such illnesses, from diabetes to high blood pressure to cancer, more difficult. Moreover, women with ongoing illnesses and impairments who become pregnant often find that "most health care providers are unaware of how pregnancy affects physical disabilities" (Lipson and Rogers 2000, 17). Even specialists in high-risk pregnancies are often uninformed on this topic, since their focus tends to be on the fetus's well-being and on the pregnant woman's physical condition chiefly as it affects the fetus (ibid.). Women with pre-existing illness and impairment therefore often find their own health care needs unsupported during pregnancy, and many are encouraged both by friends and family and by health care practicioners to abort their fetuses (ibid.).

In addition to complicating the health, medical treatment, or both of women with pre-existing illnesses and impairments, pregnancy affects the well-being of women who have previously been without any significant chronic illness or impairment. These effects can be minor or major and often affect women's whole bodies. Pregnant women may experience changes in their eyesight. They are more likely to experience carpal tunnel syndrome, even to the point of requiring surgery on their hands and wrists, although symptoms typically abate after the pregnancy ends (Stahl et al. 1996). Extreme fatigue, of the sort that cannot be cured by a good night's sleep, is considered a normal feature of pregnancy, at least for the first trimester. It is routine for women to experience degrees of nausea and vomiting in the first four months of pregnancy that, in the absence of confirmation of pregnancy, would lead women and their health care providers to suspect a virus or food poisoning. Approximately 70 to 85 percent of women in the United States, for instance, experience significant nausea during pregnancy, and approximately one-half of all pregnant women experience vomiting. Vomiting two to three times a day for the first four months is considered perfectly normal.

Pregnancy complications that require medical intervention and treatment are, while not routine, far from rare. For instance, approximately 2 to 5 percent of all pregnant women in the United States have diabetes or develop gestational diabetes.[6] Approximately 5 percent of women pregnant for the first time develop pre-eclampsia,[7] which involves high blood pressure, fluid retention, and protein in the urine. This often requires bed rest and can lead to hospitalization. Between one and 20 in every 1,000 pregnant women develop hyperemesis gravidarum, losing more than 5 percent of their initial weight as a result of vomiting and typically requiring intravenous hydration and other forms of medical intervention. My own three full-term pregnancies involved hyperemesis, with vomiting eight to sixteen times a day for twenty weeks as the norm.

Slightly more than one-fifth of all women with a clinically recognized pregnancy experience bleeding, with 59 percent of those women going on to experience a miscarriage or spontanteous abortion (Krause and Graves 1999, 537). Overall, between 12 and 24 percent of all clinically recognized pregnancies end in miscarriage, with many women experiencing grief, and some of those women suffering from trauma (Lee and Slade 1996; see also Krause and Graves 1999). Finally, pregnancy-related impacts on a woman's health do not end when the pregnancy ends. For instance, 10 percent of adult mothers and 18 to 20 percent of adolescent mothers "experience a major depressive episode within the first postpartum year" with "up to 12.5% of psychiatric hospitalizations for women" occurring within the first postpartum year (Llewellyn et al. 1997, 28).

I am not in this chapter, interested in questions about the medical treatment of pregnancy; instead, I am interested in ways in which women's experiences of pregnancy do and do not resonate with their experiences of physical illnesses and physical disabilities. I am primarily interested in the ways both types of experiences involve disruptions of bodily habits. I therefore make no claims about similarities between experiences of pregnancy and experiences with impairments that are long-term and fairly stable, perhaps existing from birth, and that do not involve much change in bodily habits and bodily orientation.

In her discussion of the phenomenology of physical illness, S. Kay Toombs writes, "First and foremost illness represents dis-ability, the 'inability to' engage the world in habitual ways" (1988, 207). Physical illnesses challenge one's ability to engage with the world through one's body in familiar ways by changing one's lived spatiality, temporality, and gestural display and by making aspects of the body seem uncanny. A disruption of one's body is a disruption of one's being-in-the-world; it focuses attention on the limitations of the body, limitations that are always there regardless of one's level of health, but that are drawn forcefully to attention when the ordinary habitual ways of interacting with the physical environment are disrupted.

Toombs gives examples of a visually impaired person who walks into a table, a person who experiences a limp as a major change in bodily style, a multiple sclerosis patient who notices that on the occasions when she uses a wheelchair that strangers address her husband instead of her and refer to her in the third person. In these types of physical illness and impairment, "functional space suddenly assumes an unusually problematic nature" and particular "projects must be modified or perhaps set aside altogether" (211). Wishes, plans, and projects must incorporate not only changes in the way the person moves through space, but also changes in a person's orientation toward time, particularly when prognosis for the future involves progressive degeneration. It can take time for the person with the illness or disability to incorporate her new physical limits or new aids such as a cane or a walker into her bodily space in the way that a woman who routinely wears a hat with a feather intuitively incorporates that hat into her negotiation of habitual tasks. This process is complicated when the physical limits are constantly shifting.

Toombs also notes that in illness one often becomes aware of the body as "hidden presence" including events and processes over which we have no control and of which we are unaware (219). This can also make the body seem like an alien presence and appear uncanny in that something that seemed ultimately familiar suddenly reveals itself as other than what was expected (217). Illness makes it very difficult to experience the body entirely unreflectively.

Wanted pregnancies differ sharply from most physical illnesses and impairments, particularly progressively debilitating ones, in that they are desired and in that many of the most significant physical changes brought about by pregnancy are temporary. However, there are many similarities in the experiences of pregnancy and those illnesses and impairments that disrupt one's embodied existence. Pregnancy makes many women aware of bodily processes over which they have no control. It can render the body uncanny, although in welcome pregnancies, unlike most physical illnesses, the uncanny body may appear miraculous and powerful rather than threatening and unreliable.

Like physical illness, pregnancy draws attention to the body and bodily changes. Iris Marion Young argues that this gives us an opportunity to take an aesthetic interest in the body (1984, 51), and I think this is true, but it suggests that we are chiefly spectators in relationship to those changes, rather than active in response to them. By contrast, I argue that pregnant women, like people adjusting to illness and impairment, make many adjustments, some of them unconscious but many of them thought through in response to thwarted plans and changes in social expectations, to the changes they experience in their bodies. Like illness, pregnancy temporarily alters one's attitude toward horizons of time and changes – partly because of disruptions in bodily habits, partly because of one's altered orientation toward time, and partly because of changes in the attitudes of others – which of one's previously chosen projects one continues, which new projects one undertakes, and how projects both old and new are undertaken. With neither pregnancy nor illness or impairment does this mean the person who changes her plans is helpless or passive; instead, we can see that changes in one's bodily orientation toward space and time and increased awareness of one's body all provide opportunities for creative responses to the limitations and capacities of the body at the same time that they also increase both the limitations and the awareness of the limitations.

Pregnancy is also like some physical illnesses and disabilities in that it involves changes in one's gestural display or use of the body to convey meaning to others. Many aspects of the gestural display of illness and impairment, the lack of control over aspects of the body, and the use of aids to accomplish tasks, for instance, are taken by some who are not ill as a sign of a more general inability on the part of the ill person to communicate. Most people do not respond to pregnant women in a similar way. However, both in illnesses involving obvious physical impairments and in late pregnancy, the illness or the pregnancy are revealed whether one wishes to do so or not, and many people respond more to the pregnancy or the illness than they do to any specific intended communication. This social response to the physical condition of the speaker more so than to her conveyed meanings can definitely thwart the ability of either the person with an illness or the pregnant woman to carry out her projects, and both pregnant women and people with nonpregnancy-related illness and impairment are often treated as vulnerable and less capable than others to perform a wide range of tasks.

## 8. DISABLING BARRIERS AND ACCOMMODATION

Fatigue, high blood pressure, excessive water retention in one's hands and feet, nausea and vomiting, an inability to carry heavy objects, and other common symptoms of pregnancy do involve suffering and affect a pregnant woman's ability to carry out her daily tasks, whether in paid employment, domestic work, childcare, or interactions with friends and family, regardless of how accommodating her environment may be. Yet these aspects of illness and impairment will be experienced very differently depending on a number of factors, including whether or not she is obviously pregnant, how normal her pregnancy is considered to be, how flexible her workplace is, whether or not her illness and impairment can be cared for at home or in an institutional setting, and how many others volunteer or can be paid to assume some of the tasks that are ordinarily hers.

In terms of paid employment, many pregnant women wish that they could choose an alternative between working as usual and not working at all, even if generous disability leave with pay is available, yet this is usually the only choice. Particularly when a pregnancy is not yet obvious, pregnant women feel pressure to "pass" as entirely healthy and unaffected by any pregnancy-related illness or impairment, just as many men and women with less visible and more chronic impairments report feeling such pressure (see Wendell 2001).

When symptoms are considered to be those of a normal pregnancy, women are again supposed to cope, presumably on the understanding that they should have anticipated the impairments they experience, even if identical nonpregnancy-related symptoms would be thought to require rest. It is only when medical personnel identify a pregnant woman as unusual in her pregnancy-related illness or impairment that others accept her varying her routine, either in paid employment or in her private life and responsibilities.

How she needs to modify her routines and how much assistance she requires both in her daily care and in order to meet her other responsibilities will vary not only with the degrees of illness and impairment that she experiences, but also with the kinds of medical care that are available to her. Thus, my second and third pregnancies were quite different in that in the intervening three years in Ontario, Canada, home care had become increasingly routine, and portable intravenous fluid pumps were available. It made a great deal of difference being cared for at home, with access to my children, books and papers, and friends and neighbors, versus being attached to a six-foot-tall pole in a hospital room.

Because my own pregnancies were considered quite unusual, involving intravenous fluids and nasal tube feeding, I received a great deal of social support, as did those caring for me, particularly my partner, but it is far easier for friends and family to volunteer to take on extra tasks when there is a definite endpoint, whereas people with chronic illnesses would require more permanent and therefore more difficult accommodations from those in their social circle. If chronic illnesses were acknowledged more widely than they are, perhaps more people might be willing to make small modifications to their daily routines, including giving more time and notice of tasks and activities, rather than assuming that most of us are always able to do things quickly and immediately and that none of us need to cope with pain and ongoing illness. For instance, I was able to read graduate student work as long as I had a little more time than usual to do it, and I could call and speak to students as long as they understood that I was available for communication only for the period of time (from 1 to 4 P.M.) when I was least likely to vomit. What many people with illnesses and impairments need are alternatives to being either fully participatory on the same terms as everyone else or opting out of social life and accepting the position of being entirely dependent on others.

Susan Wendell writes that what people found most surprising in her book, *The Rejected Body*, was that she wrote that although she would accept a cure for her chronic illness if it became available, she does not need a cure and does not regret being ill (Wendell 2001, 30). My own experiences with pregnancy taught me many things, and although I am relieved that they are over, I am grateful for more than the three children that resulted. The changes I experienced in pregnancy, including those changes relating to illness and impairment, were opportunities for me to learn what it is like to live with a body that had become unreliable, that shifts and is uncanny, and that led me to experience vulnerability and dependence. Disability theory has helped me to further understand what I experienced, and I believe that feminists seeking to understand both pregnancy and nonpregnancy-related illness and impairment can only benefit from seeking to examine their similarities and differences.

I hope by now to have shown that wanted pregnancies have some similarities both to more typical exemplars of chosen projects, such as writing an academic essay or seeking to improve one's soccer game, and to illnesses and impairments, the onset of which disrupt one's bodily interactions with the environment. They are significant experiences precisely because of the ways in which women who are pregnant alternate between experiences of actively planning and accommodation, makeshift or otherwise, to changes outside one's control.

Levesque-Lopman writes that she was grateful to the nine-month period of her pregnancy for allowing her to become ready for some of the changes that would occur once her child was born (1983, 256). Pregnancy may give more than just time to prepare for the changes ahead as one rears a child; it may also give practice in walking the balancing act between directing and accommodating change that continues once a pregnancy ends and, for some, when childrearing begins, and this is something that I discuss in the third chapter.

However, women's experiences with pregnancy, precisely because of the extraordinary amount and degree of change they involve, and because of the abovementioned oscillation between directing and accommodating change, are experiences that should be of interest not only to those who are or might become pregnant or who do or might engage in childcare. They help to reveal to us the sometimes hidden role that the body plays in carrying out any project, and therefore also help us to understand what it is like for people with chronic illnesses and impairments when society refuses to accommodate their bodies and their experiences.

Although I have been at pains throughout this chapter to stress the degree to which pregnant women can direct and shape their experiences of pregnancy and have emphasized those aspects of pregnancy that involve women's agency and make it possible for them to learn and grow from their experiences, I wish now to conclude with some words about what this chapter can help to reveal about women's experiences with unwanted pregnancies.

## 9. EXPERIENCING UNWANTED PREGNANCIES

Many women are pressured to continue their pregnancies or are prevented from obtaining abortions, either because of legal or financial obstacles placed in their way or because of their own moral or religious attitudes. In an attempt either to persuade women to continue with unwanted pregnancies or, more often, to condemn women who sought or obtained abortions, pregnancy is sometimes spoken of as a minor inconvenience. According to this way of thinking, a woman should be willing to put up with a little inconvenience, for only nine months, with little more risk or pain than is involved in abortion, for the sake of the life of a child. Pregnancy is then viewed as a minor inconvenience, which ends in less than a year, albeit with some pain and with some small risk to the woman's life and health.

These views of pregnancy fail to acknowledge the enormous amount of change pregnant women experience and are expected to endure. At no other time will an otherwise healthy adult undergo such widespread, rapid, and undesired change in the shape and size of her body, in the way she moves, eats, and sleeps. In this chapter, I have given an account of how pregnant women's daily experience of living is transformed, sometimes by illness and impairment, but at other times simply because changes in what their bodies feel and do require them to make conscious adjustments to what were in many cases habitual ways of moving through the world. I have also argued that pregnant women experience changes in their understandings of their gender identity and sexuality and in most of their social interactions. Pregnancy can also cause or exacerbate many health problems, and in some cases, particularly when pregnant bodies are not accommodated in public spaces, it can lead a woman to give up some of her short-term or long-term projects, including work that provides her and any dependents she may have with their livelihood. She may find herself temporarily unable to work at her chosen occupation, and she will definitely find herself treated differently by even casual acquaintances and strangers, perhaps with increased consideration, perhaps with disdain if she is pregnant and very young, unwed, physically or mentally impaired, or poor.

Although I have not discussed this yet, since it is the focus of my next chapter, pregnancy also brings many moral demands with it, both from other people and often from the pregnant woman herself, since her body is growing another being inside it, one with the potential to become a person and a member of the social community. If guided by concern for the health of the fetus developing within her, she will also experience potentially dramatic changes in many of her habits, concerning what she eats and drinks, whether she smokes, what medicinal and recreational drugs she takes, how much she exercises, and what chemicals and other risks she exposes herself to. Most likely she will be frequently given intrusive advice and admonished to think of the life growing within her, as if she could forget something leading to such radical change in her body, her habits, and her social life.

The pace of change will be so fast, and the changes themselves so pervasive and inescapable, that she is likely to feel increasingly alienated from herself and to feel her body invaded, or itself invasive, powerful, changing, and active in ways contrary to anything she might will. Virginia Schmied and Deborah Lupton interviewed a number of pregnant women, most of them experiencing planned pregnancies, and found that many of them experienced a striking lack of control over their bodies. As one of their interviewees (who welcomed her pregnancy) described it: "Something is growing inside of me that I can't control at all. It's an invasion of my own body" (Schmied and Lupton 2001, 37). Schmied and Lupton note that many of their interviewees experienced pregnancy as "a distressing loss of control over their bodies and of the identity they had established before pregnancy" (2001, 38), and many of the pregnant women interviewed by Bergum reported similar feelings (1997, 145). It is important to remember that all of these were women experiencing wanted and in most cases also planned pregnancies.

In summary, pregnancy involves profound transformations in a woman's body, sense of self, and social relations. Even apart from any consideration of the long-lasting impact that some of these changes may have on a woman's body and sense of self, women's dramatic experiences of change during pregnancy should be taken into consideration by those who view pregnancy as a minor and temporary inconvenience. When these changes are the result of a pregnancy she has been unable to terminate or coerced into continuing, they are bound to be experienced as tremendous violations. An unwanted pregnancy threatens not only a pregnant woman's ability to direct her life and choose and carry out her projects, but also her sense of self, in almost every dimension, involving the shape, size, and abilities of her body, her gender, her sexuality, her understanding of her moral obligations, and her relationships with virtually everyone she knows.

Laura Purdy (1996) compares pregnancy to forced labor and argues that international conventions limit forced labor to labor that does not serve a private purpose, to work that involves no more than sixty days in any twelve-month period, work that does not exceed the normal work week without compensation at rates comparable to overtime, and so on. She argues that, because women have tended to be very reluctant to give their children up for adoption, they almost always end by rearing the children they bear and that childrearing, in its hours, lack of pay, and absence of any breaks, vastly exceeds the limits governing forced labor (1996, 151).

In her chapter on abortion and forced labor, she only briefly considers pregnancy in this context, noting: "Compulsory pregnancy would violate women's self-determination even if they had no qualms about adopting out their infants. But women are rarely willing to do that" (1996, 158–159.) In another chapter, entitled, "Are Pregnant Women Fetal Containers?" she notes that pregnancy itself involves what she terms sacrifices: "We should not forget that the sacrifices exacted by a well-run pregnancy may be considerable; they deserve recognition and perhaps even compensation; some may be too great to require at all. Forgoing small pleasures like an occasional drink is just the beginning. Imagine a bad cold, let alone more serious illness, without pain relief. Imagine, too, forgoing the therapy that will cure your disease, or being denied, as was Angela Carder, the only drugs that may prolong your life. What is it like to be a cocaine addict voluntarily – or involuntarily – going cold turkey? Imagine knowing that you need unavailable prenatal care or that its lack increases the probability that you will need dangerous treatment. Picture being required to undergo risky therapy for the sole benefit of another. Our anger rightly flares in response to those who take these situations for granted" (1996, 91). To my mind, a case can also be made about the tremendous burden that an unwanted pregnancy may involve, even without a focus on the sacrifices that the woman makes, voluntarily or against her will, for the fetus growing inside her. Even if a woman does not make decisions on the basis of what she feels pregnancy requires of her morally or what others feel it requires, almost every dimension of her life will be altered by the pregnancy, anyway.

Unwanted pregnancy, even without its added moral dimension, is therefore far more of a violation of a person's autonomy and sense of self than forced labor, and, like childrearing, there are no respites from its demands and its transformations of a woman's life. We must not let the fact that it is often desired or accepted, and can be regarded as intellectually or spiritually transformative, to obscure what some of these same changes may be like to someone who does not wish to continue with her pregnancy. There are many experiences, some of them also involving radical change – such as arduous and risky travel, mountaineering, and becoming involved as a social activist in places experiencing war, poverty, or civil strife – that people take on voluntarily. This is, of course, no argument for forcing people who have not sought out these experiences to climb mountains, parachute from airplanes, trek across deserts, or toil in dangerous situations. Carol Bigwood, in giving a phenomenological account of her own pregnancy, writes: "Going into my ninth month now; feeling heavy, out of breath, emptying my bladder every hour, bleeding hemorrhoids, sweating under my pendulous breasts.... Heavy like a stone. If this were a permanent female state...! To unwillingly bear a pregnancy like this in the center of one's being would be one of the worst forms of torture" (1991, 59).

Even though voluntary pregnancies are experiences far more common than the examples above, they also should be recognized as risky, occasionally to life, much more often to health, and always to one's plans, projects, and self-understanding. Moreover, there is evidence that even in terms of physical symptoms, unwanted pregnancies may well differ from wanted pregnancies. One of the largest studies (467 pregnant women) of the unpleasant symptoms of pregnancy documented that "psychological stress particularly contributed to the prevalence and frequency of concurrent symptoms and predicted symptoms up to 16 weeks later, independent of medical risk, smoking, and weight gain" (Rodriguez et al. 2001). We can expect the prevalence and frequency of unpleasant and threatening psychological symptoms to be even greater than that of physical symptoms for women undergoing the stressful experience of an unwanted pregnancy. An understanding of the range of difficult experiences women have even with wanted pregnancies will not give a full sense of what experiences with unwanted pregnancies may be like, but it should help to illumine the many ways in which unwanted pregnancies can be experienced as violations not only of women's bodies and autonomy but of their very identities.

# *Chapter 3*

# The Ethical Significance of Pregnancy

## 1. INTRODUCTION

By now I have given an account of some misconceptions of pregnancy found in lay and academic culture, in chapter 1, and provided a corrective account of women's embodied experiences of pregnancy in chapter 2. This second chapter stressed both the planning and purposes that can guide pregnant women, and the accommodations they must make to features outside their control. In neither chapter did I focus attention on the relationship between a pregnant woman and the fetus inside her. I turn now to this relationship, which must be considered in its social context, as I ask about the ethical significance of pregnancy. In speaking of ethical significance, I mean to indicate anything that is relevant to practices of moral evaluation and moral judgment.

While many aspects of pregnancy have been ignored by philosophers, ethical questions about it garner considerable attention. However, most of this attention has been focused on situations where women and fetuses are posited as adversaries: either where abortion is considered or chosen or when pregnant women engage in behavior that harms fetuses. Ethical questions about pregnancy tend to be presented as questions about whether women are morally justified when they make decisions without taking into consideration the welfare of their fetuses. As feminist philosophers Vangie Bergum, Eugenie Gatens-Robinson and Catriona Mackenzie, demonstrate, this is not how most women think about abortion. Of course, pregnant women might be misguided in their moral reasoning, and I do not argue that adequate moral reasoning must be in harmony with the actual moral experiences of pregnant women. Their moral experience does, however, give us prima facie reason to think that it may be wrong to theorize pregnant women and fetuses only or chiefly as potential adversaries. I return to the question of the relationship between reflection on the moral experience of pregnant women and moral reasoning about pregnancy later in this chapter.

I argue that pregnant women are right to think that the hard and interesting questions about pregnancy are not decided when we take a stand on whether or not fetuses should count for something in our moral deliberations. On my view, fetuses do matter, but a fetus is never the only factor in a pregnancy that has moral significance, and we are bound to err when we frame questions about pregnancy by thinking of pregnant women and fetuses as adversaries. However, this is not because a pregnant woman and her fetus are one entity; it is possible for their well-being to be at odds. It is instead because to think of them as adversaries is to suppose that fetal interests may be advanced only at some cost to pregnant women. This is both false as a matter of fact (for instance, better nutrition, shelter, and living conditions may advance the interests of both) and mistaken in its assumption that pregnant women are the only ones who can affect fetal well-being.

In reflection on their ethical significance, pregnancies tend to be divided into those that are wanted and welcome, in which case ethical issues are not thought to be salient, or else entirely unwanted, and then abortion is presented as the topic of ethical relevance. The ambivalent nature of many women's responses to pregnancy is ignored, as is the contribution women's partners and others in their communities make to whether or not a pregnancy is wanted. By contrast, recent work in epidemiology and anthropology suggests that "[a] partner's stability, status, feelings toward pregnancy, and level of dependability and support all had a significant influence on women's experiences of unwanted pregnancy," such that positive feelings and concrete social support from others "can have positive consequences for a mother's desire to carry out the pregnancy" (Kroelinger and Oths 2000, 112). The same study suggests that pregnancies can fluctuate between wanted and unwanted, or vary in the extent to which they were wanted, with such factors.

In addition, when pregnancies are wanted and welcome, profoundly significant ethical questions about them remain, including questions about how women are encouraged to make decisions that affect themselves and their fetuses and how they are often pressured to make personal sacrifices on the basis of inadequate information or discourses of risk that encourage anxiety and fear. Because the ethical significance of wanted pregnancies has been downplayed, I focus in this chapter more on wanted or welcomed pregnancies. In the last chapter I discussed how my work is relevant to the topic of unwanted pregnancies when I argued that philosophical reflection on abortion is bound to be wildly off the mark when it does not consider how profoundly transformative pregnancies can be, and how violating it can be to experience such changes when the pregnancies are not welcome.

Too often ethical theory concerns itself with pregnancy only in order to debate the legitimacy of abortion, rather than examining pregnancy as a kind of relationship that raises ethical issues, some of them unique to pregnancy and others that are similar to other kinds of relationships involving care and dependency. We need to address wanted pregnancies from an ethical perspective that respects both the unique nature of pregnancy and how thinking about it can be informed by and can inform our thinking about other kinds of ethically significant relationships. I therefore devote part of this chapter to comparing pregnancy to another female embodied experience, breastfeeding, which is another form of reproductive labor available only to women.

The discussion in this book is centered on recognition of pregnancy and childcare as forms of reproductive labor, as work. William Ruddick (1979) asked about the ethical consequences of the fact that pregnancy involves work in his essay "Parents and Life Prospects." He began by noting that sometimes parenting is seen as like gardening, and the analogy often sees the father, "planting his seed," as the gardener: "The analogy so sketched casts the father as gardener, the mother as nurturing, passive Mother Earth. But if the analogy is to be of use, the gardener must be female, even during pregnancy. A woman not only lends her body to the growth of the fetus, she must actively maintain her body, often in novel and onerous ways. . . . She is not 'with child' but 'making a baby.' She is not just 'in the family way'; she is already mothering. Pregnancy . . . is not a condition but an activity" (Ruddick 1979, 125). He asks what follows morally from recognition of woman's active role in pregnancy and notes that: "There is still a bar to her total control over her own product after birth – if perhaps not before – namely the peculiar character of the product itself," since the product of women's nurturing activity is potentially someone who can become a man or a woman (1979, 126). In what follows, I take up Ruddick's question about the moral or ethical significance of pregnancy.

In the first chapter, I discussed Kristeva's work on pregnancy. I found it very valuable for its critique of most systems of representation of maternity and benefited from her interpretation of pregnancy as replete with philosophical and ethical significance. However, I also disagreed with her claim that pregnancy involves near dissolution of a woman's identity as she comes close to merging with another. In "Stabat Mater," Kristeva writes that pregnancy teaches a woman that there are no rigid boundaries between persons. Certainly, I agree that there are no rigid boundaries between the body of a pregnant woman and that of her fetus. However, I think she is wrong not only to regard this as dissolving a woman's identity, as I stressed in chapter 2, but also to take the nonreciprocal relation between a pregnant woman and her fetus as a model for ethics more generally, as I discuss in this chapter.

According to Kristeva, pregnancy is ethically important because we can learn from pregnancy about how open we are to others: "what I call love is openness to the other" (Kristeva 1980, 144). For both Kristeva and Ewa Ziarek, the most important aspect of pregnancy is "the imprint of the other within the same" (Ziarek 1992, 102). Yet how are pregnant women to respond to the presence of otherness within their selves? Does an ethical approach require that they face a stark choice: Either end the pregnancy (when that option is in fact available) or be entirely open to that presence and all that it may demand, as suggested by Kristeva? This is certainly the choice that many feminist philosophers suggest a pregnant woman must make, including Vangie Bergum (1990), Rosalind Hursthouse (1991), Eugenie Gatens-Robinson (1992), Catriona Mackenzie (1992), and Elizabeth Harman (2000).

## 2. MATERNITY AND SELF-SACRIFICE

A choice between ending a pregnancy or deciding how to conduct it on the basis of fetal interests alone is also suggested by the dominant medical approach to questions of "Ethics in Fetal Medicine" as developed by Frank Chernevak and Lawrence McCullough (1999). They write: "The link... between a fetus and the child it can become, when the fetus is pre-viable, can be established only by the pregnant woman's decision to confer the status of being a patient on her pre-viable fetus" (1999, 493). Their principle of respecting pregnant women's bodily autonomy is valuable from a feminist perspective, as is their maintenance that a pregnant woman may "withhold, confer, or, having once conferred, withdraw the status of being a patient on or from her pre-viable fetus according to her own values and beliefs" (1999, 493). However, once a woman has conferred the fetus with the status of a patient, so long as she does not withdraw it, both then and after viability "aggressive management is the ethical standard of care," which involves "optimizing perinatal outcome by utilizing effective antepartum and intrapartum diagnostic and therapeutic modalities" (1999, 493). In other words, if a woman chooses to confer the status of "medical patient" on her fetus, then she should be willing to undergo whatever procedures the medical staff find necessary. As discussed by Cahill (1999) and Scott (2000), in some jurisdictions this has included caesarean section surgeries that a woman is required to undergo despite her objections.

Responding to this model, which has recently become dominant in North American medical practice, the feminist physician Lisa Harris notes a problem, in that "[f]etal needs exist only as a projection of a physician's or another party's determination of what is thought to be in the best interest of a fetus" (Harris 2000, 787). First, medical judgments are frequently mistaken (Harris observes that "data on court-ordered obstetric interventions suggest that in almost one third of the cases in which court authority was requested for a medical intervention, the medical judgment was wrong in retrospect" (2000, 787)). In addition, projection of fetal interests "carries with it an enormous risk of reproducing social and racial inequality" (2000, 787).

Harris concentrates on the way racism has been manifest in the treatment of pregnant women, but in this chapter I argue that gendered expectations regarding appropriate maternal behavior are particularly likely to require pregnant women to accede to whatever fetal interests are thought to require. It is interesting in this context that even midwives who pride themselves on their support for pregnant women "believe that women who refuse recommended treatment and risk their fetuses cannot be of sound mind" and that they therefore see such forced interventions as medically mandated caesarean sections as "wholly acceptable and justifiable" (Cahill 1999, 495). This is because of the commonly held belief that all reasonable mothers are willing to make whichever sacrifices are required to ensure the well-being of their fetuses or children.

French philosopher Emmanuel Levinas makes maternity his privileged exemplar of ethical being: "Maternity in the complete being 'for the other' which characterizes it, which is the very signifyingness of signification, is the ultimate sense of this vulnerability" (Levinas 1991, 108). As Astrid Thoné explains it, the pregnant woman is "open to the unknown" because, even when she chooses to be pregnant, she can never choose a particular child: "Thus the pregnant mother expects the unexpected and has literally offered herself to the other, and that is what Levinas calls ethics" (Thoné 1998, 119).

Maternity is presented, clearly by Levinas and implicitly by Kristeva, as the ultimate in willingness to give up one's own interests to another – just because of the other's needs, not because of any particular interest the subject has in this other. Thoné goes on to contest Levinas's depiction of pregnancy and motherhood as "detached from desire" and emphasizes the satisfactions women get from mothering. She writes: "Levinas eliminated every aspect of desire of the sensible relation between mother and child in order to make it possible to consider motherhood as an exclusively ethical relation" (1998, 122), and yet Thoné's examples of women's desires all involve interactions with infants who are born rather than women's desires during pregnancy. This suggests that pregnancy, at least, does conform to Levinas's model. She also fails to contest Levinas's vision of ethics as about complete self-sacrifice. Rather than merely maintaining the presence of mothers' desires, I think it is more important to question the appropriateness of this model of ethics and its application to pregnancy in a way that only reinforces the ideology of motherhood.

Iris Marion Young observes that the vitriol directed against pregnant substance abusers (as compared with ordinary addicts) is because "the mother is supposed to be the one who sacrifices herself. That's what mothering means" (1994, 36). Diana Meyers notes, "Mothers are culturally represented as self-sacrificial, unconditionally loving, and totally identified with their children" (Meyers 2003, 19). Janet Gallagher argues that "men's deviations from parenting ideals are largely ignored by officials and by the media, while pregnant women, in contrast, are confronted constantly with signs, pamphlets, and scolding strangers warning them not to drink alcoholic beverages or not to smoke" (1995, 359). This scolding of pregnant women – and the expectations that they should willingly make whichever sacrifices are required to ensure the well-being of their fetuses – depends on the vision of maternity emphasized by Levinas.

In contrast, Caroline Whitbeck argues against the demand that women's nurturing conform to ideals of self-sacrifice, writing that "the liberation of women's practice will mean that developing others will no longer be a matter of self-sacrifice on the part of those engaged in the practice, a self-sacrifice on the part of those engaged in the practice that ultimately contributes to the perpetuation of practices and relationships of domination and competition" (Whitbeck 1983a, 81).

However, in most nurturing activities, women's work could be shared with other women and with men, in order to avoid exploitation of women's labor. Solutions such as those of Diemut Bubeck (discussed in chapter 5) are possible; so that no particular person has to be "on call" twenty-four hours a day in order to meet the basic needs of people who are unable to meet their own needs (Bubeck 2002). Everyone can be educated to be a carer in a society where "the burden of care is socially recognized as an important task in society and distributed equally to all able members" (2002, 179); carers can be given systematic access to backup care (2002, 177); and every able person might be required to spend a certain portion of his or her time providing care (2002, 180). This is not the case with pregnancy, which suggests that pregnant women have only two ethical options: ending their pregnancies or giving themselves over to whatever those pregnancies demand. This, however, ignores the extent to which many of a pregnant woman's needs are created by her social context, and also that some of her needs, at least, can be met either by other persons who support her or by social and institutional responses.

Expectations of unstinting self-sacrifice are applied to pregnancy all the more strongly when it is assimilated to mothering, as is the case in many of the quotations above, or the nurturing of a child once it is born. As a result, many feminist philosophers try to use the more neutral language of embryos, fetuses, and pregnant women, rather than speaking of mothers and babies in their discussion of pregnancy. Robbie Davis-Floyd observes that the language we use has a deep impact on how women understand and interpret their own reproductive experiences[1] (2000, 288) and also notes that women experiencing wanted pregnancies often refer to their fetuses as babies, yet there are "baby-talk taboos" within much feminist discourse on pregnancy, because of the fear that speaking of babies will help society conceptualize the fetus "as a separate individual," and this language "can all too easily be co-opted into rendering the mother unimportant or invisible; she becomes the fetal environment and is treated accordingly" (2000, 284). Davis-Floyd also suggests that "feminist resistance to the idea of fetal consciousness comes from the possibility of its co-option by the patriarchy" (2000, 284). Of course, we would not have to worry that language assimilating pregnancy to mothering will be used to encourage self-sacrifice on the part of pregnant women if mothering were not so strongly associated with self-sacrifice and if all childcare were not so strongly associated with mothering, both assumptions I critique in chapter 5.

## 3. PREGNANCY, POLITICS, AND FETAL WELL-BEING

Just as Davis-Floyd fears that acknowledging how at least some women think of fetuses may be used against women's reproductive rights, Linda Layne notes that women experiencing miscarriages, stillbirths, and other forms of fetal loss have similarly been left out of most feminist discussions of women's reproductive rights because there is a fear that if fetal loss is taken seriously as a morally significant loss, such that we might blame someone who caused a woman to miscarry or criticize social conditions that contributed to the same, then this will be used to limit women's rights to decide to end their pregnancies (Layne 2003a, 2003b). In a similar vein, Cynthia Daniels writes that she has "been reluctant to talk about the nature of women's individual responsibility for fetal harm, particularly in cases involving drug and alcohol addiction," because the women involved have been abused by economic injustice, social workers, judges, lawyers, and often abusive partners, and also because this kind of talk may seem to legitimize calls for personal responsibility aimed at drowning out "any consideration of social responsibility" for fetal health, let alone the health of pregnant women (Daniels 1999, 83). In other words, attention to the particular moral issues that may be raised by questions of fetal well-being has seemed to be a threat both to the political position that women should have a right to govern their own pregnancies and to the position that it is society as a whole, particularly in its indifference to the health and welfare of pregnant women, not individual pregnant women, which is the greatest threat to fetal health.

Yet conservative attacks on pregnant women's bodily autonomy and similar attacks on pregnant women's failure to nurture their fetuses do not ignore these issues, and they therefore need response. Furthermore, we must pay attention to questions about fetal well-being if we are to acknowledge social responsibility (and the responsibility of some individual men) for harming or enhancing that well-being. Moreover, there is no inconsistency in maintaining both a commitment to women's political rights to conduct their pregnancies as they choose and a position that stresses that this conduct can nevertheless be morally significant and a suitable subject for moral evaluation. For instance, Davis-Floyd "interviewed twenty women who both fiercely defend women's right to choose and believe that babies are conscious. If they choose to carry their babies to term, they protect them from hurtful procedures. They are open to the possibility of a psychic connection with what they believe is a conscious being yet remain free to choose to abort" (2000, 284).

These women sought simultaneously to defend pregnant women's rights to make decisions about their bodies and their pregnancies without maintaining that those decisions were only about their bodies. Instead, the decisions involve a dependent being with whom they were in relation. In this chapter I stake out a position that defends the right of pregnant women to make their own decisions about their pregnancies, without claiming that practices and choices – of pregnant women, of other individuals, or society at large – that affect fetuses are morally innocuous and therefore not suitable material for moral reflection or moral judgment. In the process, I argue that we need to examine the phenomenology of pregnant women's experience (as discussed in chapter 2), in order to properly understand the moral significance of pregnancy. However, before developing how I think this phenomenology can be relevant to ethics, I need first to clarify the relation between my political position on pregnancy and my approach to the ethical significance of pregnancy.

I wholeheartedly agree with the position on pregnant women's political rights taken by Joan Callahan and James Knight. For political reasons, birth must be the point at which the fetus acquires a legal status. This is necessary, as they describe, in order to avoid incredible interferences with the decisions and daily lives of pregnant women (1993, 160–62), to ensure that pregnant women remain willing to seek out the health care they need (1993, 166), and to avoid criminalizing behaviors that are almost always influenced by social problems such as poverty and abuse (1993, 198). Similar reasons have been provided by Iris Marion Young, who objects to the punitive approach sometimes taken toward pregnant substance abusers (1994) and in studies of the most effective treatment programs for pregnant women with drug addictions (Howell et al. 1999, 195). Studies of such programs reveal that the best programs not only provide support services to pregnant women, but also address the social causes of pregnant women's substance abuse,[2] including poverty, the substance abuse of significant others, and family violence (1999, 195). To these reasons I add the observation that ensuring that women have the legal right to proceed with their pregnancies as they choose without facing criminal or civil sanctions for fetal harm is a way of avoiding the racist application of policies targeting lower income and black women on charges of causing fetal harm (Roberts 1997; Daniels 1999, 93; Mason 2000).

Cynthia Daniels notes that in contemporary North American societies, there is a tendency first to individualize responsibility for fetal harm and then to find only pregnant women to have this responsibility (Daniels 1999, 84–85). Callahan and Knight's analysis of case law in the United States also reveals this tendency to ignore the fact that "prenatal human beings are begotten by fathers, and fathers often encourage precisely the kinds of behaviors that may cause prenatal harm" (1993, 165). Daniels goes further in noting other ways that fathers' behaviors and situations affect fetal health and how social and environmental factors (from poverty through exposure to toxins) threaten fetal health and viability.

Daniels first cites and evaluates evidence that links fathers' occupational and environmental exposures to toxins to a variety of problems in their offspring. Such exposures (for instance, to pesticides or hydrocarbons or the fumes from steel welding) "are suspected of causing not only fertility problems but also miscarriage, low birth weight, congenital abnormalities, cancer, neurological problems, and other childhood health problems" (1999, 85). Life-style choices may damage sperm, and "studies of paternal smoking have also shown a link to lower birth weight for babies," while "paternal alcohol use has been correlated with low birth weight of babies and an increased risk of birth defects in children" (1999, 87). In addition to toxins (including ones in cocaine) affecting sperm, "men who are addicted to drugs or alcohol may not only produce damaged sperm; they may create a social context that harms maternal and fetal health" (1999, 89). Male partners may encourage or pressure pregnant women into joining them in drug or alcohol use, and they may physically abuse their partners.

While Daniels does not discuss this point, of course many individuals other than women's partners (male or female) may have an impact on pregnant women's experiences during pregnancy in a way that affects maternal and fetal health. Employers who accommodate a pregnant woman's changing needs (when her needs do in fact change) may positively affect her health, and employers who do not (or who require work that exposes the fetus to toxins or who fire women who refuse such work) also can bear individual responsibility for fetal harm. Friends or coworkers who smoke in her presence, who carelessly expose her to diseases that can affect her fetus, or who assist her in obtaining adequate nutrition can all have a significant impact on fetal health. However, maternal and fetal health are affected not only by individual decisions and practices, but also by collective ones, for instance, those that result in many pregnant women having insufficient nutrition (one of the leading causes of low birth weight and other problems in infants). Moreover, as Daniels points out, poverty exacerbates the negative effects of other exposures to toxins (Daniels 1999, 91). Environmental damage, as Layne observes, has been documented to produce significant effects on miscarriages and on fetal and infant health (Layne 2003b). It is therefore incredibly important, in our ethical evaluation of fetal harm, both to recognize that individuals other than pregnant women may contribute to this harm and to move beyond the illusion that individualizes responsibility for fetal well-being.

Callahan and Knight maintain that their arguments are meant to address not only the political and legal issues of whether or not sanctions against pregnant women's behavior make good law, but also whether "using legal sanctions to protect prenatal human beings from the potentially harmful actions of decisions of their mothers can be morally justified" (1993, 143). Now this is a question different from asking whether the potentially harmful actions or decisions themselves can be morally justified, but, as I suggested at the outset of this chapter, I think the latter question is also an important one to ask. This question needs to be asked, however, as noted above, in the context of a larger discussion of the moral dimension of individual women's and men's actions and decisions during pregnancy, as well as social practices that affect pregnancies, rather than with a focus only on what pregnant women do to harm their fetuses.

## 4. THE MORAL STATUS OF THE FETUS

Fetal well-being and fetal harm will have moral relevance only if we think that when people do things that affect fetal well-being, this matters morally. Often, attempts to answer this kind of question involve appeals to moral status. This is, indeed, the approach of Callahan and Knight, who argue that a fetus is a potential person and that one who will become a person is a future person. They argue that the point at which we decide a fetus (or an infant) has moral status is to some extent arbitrary and that, for the political reasons already discussed, we should decide that moral status is acquired at birth. However, we can separate political reasons to assign this status at birth from the question of whether or not we think fetuses, either because of their inherent qualities or because of some other properties they have, are beings with moral status. Moreover, we could also decide that what happens to fetuses matters morally because fetuses matter to others, people who themselves have moral status.

Elizabeth Harman (2000) makes a distinction between an early fetus, which is a "fetus before it has any intrinsic properties that themselves confer moral status" (Harman 2000, 310), and a late fetus, which is one that has moral status because of intrinsic properties (Harman leaves these unspecified, but they might include consciousness, the capacity to have sensations, or viability). She argues that some early fetuses may have moral status and others not, simply in virtue of whether or not they will actually live to the point that they acquire intrinsic moral status, which corresponds to the abovementioned distinction between a potential person and a future person. Therefore, the death of a fetus before the point at which it would have acquired moral status is morally innocuous, and the death of a fetus after that point is not.

This allows her to make sense of the claim that some abortions have no moral significance, while some fetal deaths (in late miscarriages) do, although it also requires her to say that other much mourned fetal deaths may involve a loss of hopes and dreams but do not involve the death of a being with any moral status. As a result, she writes that in the case of a pregnant woman facing a choice about abortion, "[i]f she chooses abortion, then it turns out that the fetus is morally insignificant. If she chooses to continue the pregnancy, then the fetus is the beginning of her child, and she owes it her love" (2000, 317). Once a woman chooses to continue a pregnancy, Harman also believes that "she is committed to a lifetime of responsibility to the child; even if she makes an adoption plan for the child, she has a unique responsibility and relation to that person" (2000, 323–324). The only sense in which a woman may reasonably regret an abortion is regretting "a lost possibility for her own life" (2000, 322).

Harman does consider one alternative to her view. She describes the Mother's Intention Principle, which "states that an early fetus has some moral status if and only if the woman pregnant with it is planning to carry it to term" (2000, 318) but considers this position absurd because the status of the fetus could fluctuate with the whims of the pregnant woman. She writes that "the intentions of the woman who carries a fetus are weak, relational properties of that fetus; they are not among the facts that can determine what kind of thing it is" (2000, 318). However, to my mind this is a caricature of the relational view of the fetus and also an overly voluntarized version of what having a relationship amounts to. All sorts of features of a pregnant woman's situation, beside her explicit intentions, affect whether or not she has a social relationship with her fetus. As already mentioned, language used to describe her experience will affect her. A pregnant woman's religious background, the responses of other people to her pregnancy, the proliferation of fetal images in our society, whether or not she sees the fetus in an ultrasound image, and how this experience is presented to her, and more can bring a woman into a relationship with her fetus or prevent her from having one.

While these features could also fluctuate and cause a pregnant woman to have different attitudes toward her fetus at different times, they would not depend on mere whims. Furthermore, Harman owes us an account as to why it is absurd to claim that the moral status of a fetus may fluctuate. If her position is that a fetus ought not to have its moral status entirely removed or added as a result of a woman's changing emotions, we can avoid that consequence of an intentional view of the moral status of a fetus by (1) recognizing that relationships are not founded or severed merely on whims and (2) recognizing that pregnant women are not the only ones who might have relationships with a fetus, although any other relationships would be necessarily mediated through the pregnant woman. Furthermore, we might offer a position that (3) combines, as with Harman's, the argument that at some point fetuses have intrinsic properties that grant them moral status with the argument that something else – in this case, social relations to a fetus, rather than whether or not it actually does develop to become a person – can also affect its moral status.

Feminist philosopher Susan Sherwin argues that "fetuses are morally significant, but their status is relational rather than absolute" (1991, 334). Rather than attempting to look at intrinsic properties of the fetus in order to determine their moral status, she suggests we look to the nature of the relationship between the fetus and the pregnant woman in whose body it develops (although such a view could also be modified to find the relationships other people have to the fetus to have relevance to determining its moral status). I believe we should modify Sherwin's view such that the moral status of a fetus may depend on both intrinsic and relational properties it has (with the relations to include and emphasize the relation between pregnant woman and fetus but not to be limited to it).

If, in asking whether a fetus has moral status, we mean, Does what happens to it have moral weight? then my own position is that the answer is yes, for several reasons. First, at some stage a fetus will have moral status because of intrinsic properties such as sentience and consciousness. Second, a fetus has some moral status at all stages of its development because of its potential to become a person, with more moral weight given when more of its potential has been realized. Third, what happens to a fetus will often matter morally because of social meanings given to fetuses and because of social relationships that others – especially but not only pregnant women – have with them.

One can have a social relationship only with another that has the capacity, if only in potential, to be in a social relationship with you. Therefore, a woman who thought she was pregnant but turned out not to be pregnant may mourn her lost hopes but has not had a relationship ended, although she attempted to start one. By contrast, a woman who was pregnant and had this pregnancy end, either because of her own decision or despite her desire to continue the pregnancy, will often have ended a relationship, albeit one that had only begun. Since social relationships have moral value (either positive or negative, depending on the nature of the relationship), when fetuses are helped or harmed, this matters morally not only because of the properties – potential or actualized – of the fetus, but also because of the moral significance of our social relationships.

Feminist anthropologist Lynn Morgan argues that "the fetus's capacity for relationality is not determined by its intrinsic characteristics, its personality or biological functions, but by meanings people give it in a social world" (Morgan 1996, 64). Whether or not the fetus is considered to be a social actor is not determined solely by the pregnant woman's attitudes toward it but by a larger social context (Morgan 1996, 53). I agree with Morgan that a fetus is a social actor not only as a result of a pregnant woman's attitude toward it, but also because of features of the larger social context. However, I disagree with her suggestion that a fetus's capacity for relationships and its moral status is solely a reflection of the meaning it is given.

To illustrate the distinction between her approach and my own, I suggest that we imagine a society in which most or many people believe in ghosts and in which individuals sometimes seek to harm and sometimes to help some of those ghosts, perhaps by writing letters to them, either loving or hateful. We could legitimately engage in moral evaluation of these people's characters, examining why they are willing to help or harm, and whether or not their intentions are appropriate moral responses to their situations. However, this would not (supposing we are in agreement that there are no ghosts or that they cannot be helped or harmed) mean that those individuals are right to believe that ghosts really do have moral status or that they are right to believe that they have social relations with ghosts. If someone were to stop them from their letter writing, they would interfere with their self-expression and cause them to regret lost hopes and plans, but they would not be ending a relationship.

It is not enough to feel oneself to be in a relationship in order for the other party to that relationship to exist and be in relation with you, even if there are social practices you share with others that support your belief that you are in a relationship with some other person or thing, such as the ghosts that played a role in the imaginary society of the previous paragraph. Therefore, I do not believe that the capacity of a fetus to enter into a social relationship is entirely determined by the meanings given to it within a social context. To have a capacity to relate, you must exist and you must have some intrinsic properties – even if they are only potentials for development – that legitimate other people's understandings that they are in a relationship with you.

If we sought to give a moral evaluation of people's intentions to help or harm ghosts, we would consider not only what they tried to accomplish, but also why they did what they did and whether they took care to explore the consequences of their actions. We would also ask questions about why they believed in ghosts and whether they were right to do so. Similarly, how we evaluate people – or institutions – who seek to harm or assist fetal well-being should involve not only what those people actually think about fetuses and how they might try to help or harm them, but also whether they take care to explore the consequences of their actions and decisions, and why they think what they do about fetuses. We should also explore why they don't think about them, if they don't, and what has influenced their attitudes and practices. We would furthermore need to consider the other factors that motivated their willingness to help or to harm. Most important, if they did seek to ensure fetal well-being or if they were willing to sacrifice fetal well-being, we would need to know about how their decisions and their actions were related to other goals they had.

When we were evaluating the decisions and actions of pregnant women, in particular, we would need to be sure that we did not expect those women to engage in unstinting self-sacrifice to prevent fetal harm. As with other decisions and actions that we evaluate morally, we would need to know whether the harm was avoidable and also whether avoiding fetal harm would lead to other kinds of harm that have moral relevance. Moreover, we would need to be sure that we did not apply standards to pregnant women, particularly ones that accord with the ideology of motherhood, different from those we applied to other actors (people or institutions) whose decisions and actions affect fetal well-being.

Unlike ghosts, we know that fetuses do exist, and we also know that many people (sometimes pregnant women and sometimes others who may know that woman) have strong feelings about fetuses and believe themselves to be in a social relationship with some particular fetus. We also know that a pregnant woman's relationship with her fetus is by no means solely a reflection of decisions she makes but will also reflect the social value placed either on fetuses in general or her fetus in particular. This may depend on broadly based social attitudes toward race and class or the fetus's possible illness or impairment, and it may reflect the actions of individuals in the pregnant woman's life, such as her partner or family, who may view the fetus as a threat to her health or as a welcome grandchild. As I discuss below in this chapter, the information that is presented to a pregnant woman and the technologies that are used in her pregnancy will also affect the nature of her relationship to her fetus. Other factors that can influence the nature of her relationship with her fetus include such things as whether she has been previously pregnant, had previously given birth to a living child, had previous experience caring for a dependent being, and how she became pregnant. I return to the implications of the relational view of the moral status of the fetus below in this chapter when I discuss how pregnant women's relations with their fetuses may differ depending on differences in their situations.

To return to Harman's view that a fetus has moral status either because it will become a person or because it has developed sufficiently to have morally valuable intrinsic properties, I agree with her strategy of thinking differently about fetuses at different stages, but her approach seems to me to miss both the moral significance of potentiality and the moral significance of the actual relationship a woman has – or lacks – with her fetus. It also seems odd to conclude that it is perfectly rational and reasonable for a woman whose early fetus will live to begin to love it, feel responsible for it, and recognize it as a being with moral status, whereas a woman whose early fetus ends up dying before the point at which it would have acquired intrinsic properties lost a being with no moral status. To return to my analogy about the society that believes in ghosts, for Harman, the latter woman would be in the category of someone whose letter writing to a ghost has been thwarted, while the former loves something that has moral significance. This is at odds with the experiences of mourning early fetal loss outlined by Layne, particularly in her chapter "'I Will Never Forget You': Trauma, Memory, and Moral Identity" (Layne 2003a), and with the dramatic rise and spread of pregnancy loss support groups. Moreover, Layne notes that women who face this experience (in the United States in 1992 there were an estimated 890,000 spontaneous fetal losses) often find their pain and grief increased by denial of the reality of their loss, a denial to which feminist silence has contributed (Layne 2003a, 239) and to which a position such as Harman's would unintentionally contribute.

Harman's position on the moral status of an early fetus is also at odds with the moral agonizing of women who make decisions selectively to terminate a fetus because of properties it may have or lack. Harman suggests that those decisions can be morally significant without the early fetus having any moral significance (2000, 323), because the decision to keep an early fetus is morally significant but the reactions and intuitions of women who selectively terminate their early fetuses, as well as the nurses who care for them, are radically at odds with this interpretation of their experience (Huntington 2002).

Of course, as I stressed earlier in this chapter, a philosophical position may be at odds with moral experience and yet be correct. Borrowing from Robert Audi (1996), Rosamund Scott labels "reflectionism" (Scott 2000, 434) the approach to ethical issues that starts with intuitions and seeks appropriate principles to explain the intuitions or potentially to correct them, in an ongoing oscillation between intuitions and general principles. This seems an accurate characterization of Harman's approach, and I generally endorse it, so long as in our oscillation between intuitions and principles we pay attention to questions about how ideological assumptions (such as those involved in the ideology of motherhood, which expects privatized responsibility for children's welfare and demands self-sacrifice as natural on the part of mothers) can shape those intuitions and principles.

Rosalind Hursthouse (1991) repudiates the position that we need to decide whether or not fetuses have moral status in order to decide whether harming or nurturing them is morally significant. She suggests, instead, that we investigate whether different ways of making decisions about or acting toward fetuses are virtuous or vicious. Yet it seems to me that she is thinking about the question of moral status in a narrow way, perhaps as the question of whether or at what point a fetus has a soul, as is suggested by her claim that the question as to whether a fetus has moral status is "not in the province of any moral theory; it is a metaphysical question, and an extremely difficult one at that" (1991, 235). She continues to argue that "to attach relevance to the status of the fetus . . . is to be gripped by the conviction that we must go beyond the familiar biological facts" (1991, 236). These are what she describes as the familiar biological facts: that pregnancy typically occurs as a result of sexual intercourse, that it lasts about nine months, during which the fetus grows and develops, that it generally ends in the birth of a living baby (1991, 236), that "childbearing is painful, dangerous, and emotionally charged," and that human parents "tend to care passionately about their offspring" (1991, 237).

Now it does seem to be a mistake to refer to these factors, some of which involve emotions and the nature of relationships, simply as biological facts. It also seems to me, since Hursthouse claims that ending a pregnancy deliberately is serious because it involves "cutting off of a new human life" (1991, 237), that Hursthouse has in fact decided that fetuses have moral status and that, moreover, this moral status increases over time both as a result of "gradual fetal development" (1991, 238) and because of the increased relationship one may have with a fetus over time. Hursthouse claims that the loss of an early fetus is not tragic (except in the sense of one's lost hopes), whereas the loss of a late fetus is tragic because "the mere fact that one has lived with it for longer, conscious of its existence, makes a difference. To shrug off an early abortion is understandable just because it is hard to be fully conscious of the fetus's existence in the early stages and hence hard to appreciate that an early abortion is the destruction of life" (1991, 239). I think Hursthouse is mistaken to think that the length of time a pregnant woman has been conscious of the existence of her fetus will always correlate with the closeness of her relationship with it (a mistake I discuss below in this chapter) and also wrong to think that, for many women, it is hard to recognize that an early abortion cuts off a potential human life.

## 5. PHENOMENOLOGY AND AN ETHICS OF CARE APPROACH TO PREGNANCY

Hursthouse's approach to asking whether the decisions and actions of pregnant women are virtuous and vicious is potentially a good one, but I do have some concerns about it which make me prefer an ethics of care approach, which seeks to find the most caring resolution to any given moral dilemma and which attends to the burdens and benefits involved in any caring relationship, over a virtue theory approach. First, while it would be possible to apply the arguments in Hursthouse's article to other people's actions and decisions toward fetuses, and she says that "with very little amendment, everything that has been said above applies to boys and men too" (1991, 243), she does not do so herself. Arguments of this sort tend to focus only on the decisions of pregnant women. This can also overemphasize the extent to which pregnant women's relationships with their fetuses are based on decisions. Also, by ignoring the social context of pregnancy (which Hursthouse mentions only in order to note that a social context can be so awful that it is not unreasonable or vicious of such pregnant women to place no value on fetal life), this can inappropriately place all the responsibility for fetal harm and health directly on a pregnant woman.

In contrast, an ethics of care approach that Young (1994) and Tong (1999) use in thinking about pregnant substance-abusing women clearly encourages us to think of the care owed not only to fetuses, but also to the pregnant women themselves. This kind of approach also lets us ask questions about how we can have caring institutions and how care can be provided in public contexts, while a virtue theory approach tends to focus, although it need not, on the actions of particular persons (whether only pregnant women or also the women and men in their lives). However, both approaches could be developed in ways that attend to the public dimension of responsibility for pregnant women and fetal well-being, and both may have areas of overlap. One significant advantage of an ethics of care approach is that it has been explored and extensively critiqued by feminists, who ask questions about how care is assigned in ways that illegitimately reflect racism and sexism. As a result, more so than a virtue theory approach, an ethics of care approach may also encourage us to think about the extent to which the virtues we expect of mothers and pregnant women may be inappropriately influenced by the ideology of motherhood and its naturalization of expectations of willing self-sacrifice on the part of mothers.

It is interesting in this regard to observe that conceptualizing the relationship between a pregnant woman and her fetus as the only significant factor involved in thinking about fetal health and harm can also cause us to forget about the role other women may play in supporting women as they proceed with or end their pregnancies, and the stress this support can involve. Annette Huntington reminds us that women experiencing mid-trimester pregnancy loss (either as a result of their own decisions, based on prenatal testing, or spontaneously) can experience great distress because of the "psychological and physical impact" of the event, but they are not the only ones emotionally affected; their nurses are, too. She writes: "Integrating feminist principles into practice can support both the woman experiencing the abortion and the nurse whose role in the event is sustained and intimate" (2002, 273). An ethics of care approach will not only focus on the pregnant woman-fetus dyad but will look at features of the social context of pregnancy, including how pregnant women are cared for or denied care in a variety of settings.

In addition to looking at social context, any attempt to apply an ethics of care perspective to pregnancy will necessarily attend to the details of women's experiences with pregnancy. In an article on moral phenomenology, Susan Dwyer (1998) writes that we cannot hope to understand the ethical significance of pregnancy unless we are familiar with its phenomenology. Attention to pregnant embodiment allows us to appreciate how it shapes pregnant women's moral identities and to understand what will be experienced as the drawbacks and benefits of alternative courses of action. Dwyer contrasts attention to pregnant embodiment with attempts to understand the moral significance of pregnancy by analogy. She argues that the latter approach inevitably distorts pregnancy by failing to appreciate its moral uniqueness. In no other experience do boundaries between self and other blur so greatly.

As was clear in chapter 2, feminist philosophers have begun to give us a phenomenology of pregnancy. Levesque-Lopman, Young, and Bigwood highlight its blurred boundaries between self and other, the enormous amount of change pregnant women experience, and the challenges to women's self-understandings that result from both (Levesque-Lopman 1983; Young 1984; Bigwood 1991). Moreover, feminist moral theorists such as Bergum (1990), Gatens-Robinson (1992), and Mackenzie (1992), in addition to Dwyer (1998), have engaged with phenomenological analysis of pregnancy in discussing women's choices about abortion.

This has prepared the groundwork for an adequate analysis of the ethical nature of pregnancy, but there are three important gaps in the work done so far. First, the phenomenological work has tended to claim as universal some features of women's experiences of pregnancy. The theorists acknowledge that there is no one experience of pregnancy and that pregnant embodiment will be shaped by both bodily changes and socio-cultural context (see, e.g., Mackenzie 1992, 148). However, they tend to attribute some features of the experience simply to the bodily changes and claim that these, at least, are universal. This is reminiscent of Hursthouse's (1991) description of mothers' emotional relationships to their babies as part of what she called familiar biological facts. Thus, for instance, Dwyer writes: "I do not assume identity between each woman's experiences of pregnancy; all I need for my case is that human fetuses grow inside women's bodies" (Dwyer 1998, 41). Mackenzie similarly claims that what happens to their bodies means that all pregnant women will experience a blurring of boundaries between the fetus and the self, all will feel increasing psychic differentiation from the fetus as it grows physically, and most will feel increasing emotional attachment based on that increasing psychic and physical differentiation and the expectation of future relationships with the beings that their fetuses will become (Mackenzie 1992, 148–149).

This tendency to identify universal features of experiences of pregnant women is understandable, because there is fear that otherwise the work will not have philosophical significance. However, we must recognize that while there may be some common features of many women's experiences of pregnancy, bodily changes, features of social context, and features of individual life histories will intertwine in shaping that experience. It is not the case that some features of their experience will reflect what is happening in their bodies, while others reflect factors that vary more widely. Moreover, as discussed in chapter 2, bodily changes in pregnancy vary substantially from one woman to another, and in the same women in different pregnancies.

Does this mean that phenomenological work will have no philosophical significance, since we will not be able to generalize about it? Instead, we can look to how widespread systematic patterns of differences in women's experiences of pregnancy have significance for them. Therefore, in order to engage in moral theory on pregnancy, we cannot simply proceed from philosophical reflection on our own pregnancies or those of other women we know well. Instead, we must draw on work in sociology and anthropology that attends to women's very different experiences of pregnancy. This is one place where we must be sure to address the concern raised by sociologist Linda Blum, as discussed in the introduction to this book. Blum observes that many feminist philosophers "pay little (or no) attention to the critical, qualitative sociology" that seeks to provide knowledge about particular communities (Blum 1999, 255).

For instance, Gatens-Robinson claims that we can divide pregnancy into four stages, depending on the development of the fetus and the embodied experience of the pregnant woman (claiming that quickening, when the fetus' movements are felt for the first time, always represents a transition from one stage to another in the relationship between a pregnant woman and her fetus; 1992, 62). However, sociological work on pregnancy by Margarete Sandelowski and Beth Perry Black reveals that pregnant women differ sharply from one another as to when or whether they regard their fetuses as real, babies, or their future children (Sandelowski and Black 1994, esp. 604).

Sandelowski and Black interviewed sixty-two (mainly white and middle-class) couples more than four times each as they experienced a transition to parenthood and observed that the couples "exhibited three overall patterns of managing the odd situation of the fetus' ontology: relating to the *in utero* being as a baby, relating to the *in utero* being as if it were a baby, and/or merging their dream, womb, and actual babies" (1994, 604). Moreover, they describe many of the men and women involved as wobbling back and forth between seeing the fetus as an embryo or a baby (604–605). Similarly, Schmied and Lupton argue against accounts of stages of relationship[3] between pregnant women and their fetuses, arguing that none of the pregnant women they studied "described her relationship with the foetus as a series of developmental stages, but rather saw it as fluctuating throughout pregnancy" (Schmied and Lupton 2001, 32).

Failure to reflect on the complexity of outstanding ethical issues that arise in wanted pregnancies is the second gap in the feminist philosophical work that takes pregnant embodiment seriously. These feminist theorists assume that once a pregnant woman has chosen not to abort her fetus, she has taken on parental responsibility for it that involves a commitment to provide the care needed for it to grow and flourish and become a child (see, e.g., Mackenzie 1992, 141). Like Harman and Hursthouse, these feminist theorists assume that once a pregnant woman has decided to continue with her pregnancy (assuming she has a choice), she now owes it both her unconditional love and her care. In one example, Vangie Bergum argues that morality in pregnancy involves "a woman's carefulness about entering, or continuing, a relationship that demands that she contribute the fertile, supportive ground from which to give life to the wanted and loved child" (Bergum 1990, 25). She clearly supports women's right to end their pregnancies and thinks that this can be the caring thing to do if they decide that they cannot commit to a responsible relationship to a fetus, but then she suggests that "[i]n response to the bab[ies] they carry, women are subject to self-denial. Is this responsiveness not really a transformed experience of responsibility for the Other, the child? Can we get a clue from the origin of the word 'responsibility'?

'Responsible' comes the Latin respondere, 'to promise in return.' As we respond to the presence of the child, then, we promise to look after that child, to be trusted by the child, to care for the child, to return always. No longer are we acting only for ourselves – we are 'one for the other'" (Bergum 1989, 84–85).

Mackenzie similarly distinguishes between decision responsibility – when the pregnant woman decides whether or not to continue her pregnancy, before which the fetus is, for Mackenzie, morally insignificant – and parental responsibility – the kind of responsibility she takes on whenever she decides to continue it. Once she has decided to carry the fetus to term, she owes the fetus her love and care and can expect to be required to engage in substantial self-sacrifice. This gives pregnant women precisely the same options as does Bergum (Mackenzie 1992, 152; see also Gatens-Robinson 1992, who stresses the self-sacrifice involved in pregnancy).

To some extent I agree (not that all willingly pregnant women owe their fetuses unconditional and unending love, but that they do owe them care in the absence of overriding concerns to the contrary), but I think it is important to acknowledge that providing care to a fetus is very unpredictable in terms of the amount of effort that may be required and the extent to which this will undermine or make impossible one's other commitments and concerns. Scott similarly observes (in the context of discussing a pregnant woman's right to refuse medical treatment thought to be needed by the fetus) that if we think that a willingly pregnant woman owes her fetus whatever it might possibly require, then "this, in effect, is to say that unless a woman is prepared to do anything for the fetus, notwithstanding, for instance, her religious faith, then she must either abort or decline to conceive" (Scott 2000, 432).

I have given examples of the extent to which some but not all pregnant women face significant illness and impairment during their pregnancies, and some but not all are forced to abandon other commitments in the preceding chapter. Therefore a host of ethical questions arise about how pregnant women are to balance a commitment to care for their fetuses with commitments to other people, including themselves. Are they to decide conflicts in the same way that they would decide conflicts with commitments to other children or other dependent beings? How can they resist social pressures that put responsibility for the care of the fetus solely on their own shoulders?

To suppose that the only way to give weight to fetal interests is by imposing obligations on pregnant women is to ignore the role that other people and social institutions can play in supporting both the well-being of pregnant women and fetal well-being and the role they can play in harming them as well. In the next chapter, I discuss feminist philosopher Eva Feder Kittay's (1997) ideal of "doulia" in which people who are the primary providers of care to other dependent people, a class of person she calls "dependency workers," receive support from others for their caring labor. The ideal of doulia is taken from examples of doulas who support and assist birthing and postpartum women in giving birth and then in caring for their children. In the next chapter I have some concerns about applying the doulia model to the work of caring for young children, but I find it much more applicable to supporting women in pregnancy (an application Kittay does not herself make). Giving public recognition to the work involved in pregnancy and the needs a pregnant woman may have – in terms of both her health and economic support and her other ongoing commitments and concerns – is one important way both to seek to avoid exploiting pregnant women with demands of total self-sacrifice and to recognize social responsibility for maternal and fetal well-being.

However, the doulia should not come merely in the form of increased assistance on the part of (paid and unpaid) individuals to others who are doing the work of care (such as a pregnant woman nurturing her fetus), but also in the form of accommodation on the part of individuals and institutions (including workplaces) to the increased that needs a woman may have as a result of the demands of her pregnancy. This is the only way we can make sure that the particular "dependency workers" who are pregnant women will not be exploited by demands that they seek to meet the needs (which at times can be overwhelming) required for fetal well-being.

My own pregnancies involved significant illness on my part and impaired my ability to care for myself and my other children, to work, and to carry on other activities that are important to me. Since I live in Ontario, Canada, my medical expenses and home care nursing were entirely publicly funded (weeks of hospital stay, twice-daily visits at home from nurses to insert, remove, and monitor my intravenous tubes or feeding tubes, as well as my general state of health to see whether I required hospitalization). My partner took up a much increased load of housework and childcare, and our family, friends, coworkers, and even acquaintances helped with the care of our children and with many other obligations one or the other of us had made. Moreover, my work was very flexible and I was able to continue to work to some extent, rather than being offered the choice many women have, of either not working at all (and being paid if one is extremely fortunate) or working exactly as before.

As I discussed in the second chapter, much of this assistance was available either because of public assistance or because of our fortunate situation in being blessed with many willing volunteers. The latter were aware of our needs because of the dramatic nature of my pregnancies (and part of some acquaintances' willingness to help was probably a reflection of the extent to which I was seen to be self-sacrificing, along the lines of the ideology of motherhood). By contrast, many pregnant women go unsupported because their pregnancies are considered "normal" – no matter how much they may need help not only in nurturing their growing fetuses, but also in caring for themselves and maintaining some sense of continuity with regard to other things they care deeply about. If I had lived someplace else, if my partner and I did not have the resources that we had, I would not have chosen to have my second and third children or been able to modify my life so much once I became ill in pregnancy. If other pregnant women are to get the assistance they need once they have decided to continue their pregnancies, then a model of the public provision of doulia will need to be established in a much more evenly distributed way.

## 6. PREGNANCY, ETHICS, AND THE ROLE OF ANALOGIES

The third gap in current feminist discourse around pregnancy and ethics involves the claim, made by others besides Dwyer (e.g., Whitbeck 1983b; Kristeva 1986, 1997; Bergum 1990; Hursthouse 1991; and Mackenzie 1992), that pregnancy is an entirely unique kind of experience. While I agree with these authors that some elements of pregnancy are unlike anything else women or men experience, there are also aspects that have continuity with other stages of reproductive labor. I discussed some of these parallels (for instance, with regard to illness, impairment, and disability) in the second chapter. In this chapter I draw some parallels between pregnancy and breastfeeding. Both are embodied ways of meeting the needs of a dependent being, and in both decisions about what to do with one's own body have a direct impact on that being. In both types of experience, women are subjected to intense pressure, reflecting what I call the ideology of motherhood.

The ideology of motherhood urges us to think that in all but the most unusual circumstances the best way to ensure children's development and happiness is to give them full access to their mothers. (DiQuinzio (1999) labels this as essential motherhood; Blum (1999) speaks of it as exclusive motherhood; and Fox and Worts (1999) describe it as privatized motherhood.) According to this ideology, for pregnant women, no sacrifice that could benefit their future children should be considered too great, and they are expected to engage in extremely rigorous practices of self-surveillance and self-control. For instance, one popular book of advice aimed at pregnant women, *What to Expect When You're Expecting*, urges women to ask of every mouthful of food that they swallow: "Is this the best bite I can give my baby?" (Eisenberg et al. 1997, 74).

Moreover, pregnant women are encouraged to take control not only of what, in some circumstances, they might possibly be able to control (such as their diet, in those circumstances when they are well resourced and have access to affordably good nutrition), but also of things over which it would be incredibly difficult for anyone to have control, such as their emotional responses to difficult and stressful events. Thus, recent studies published in obstetrical journals suggest that differing aspects of the moods of pregnant women, including depression, anxiety, and anger, can impact negatively on their fetuses and neonates. Field et al. conclude, "The infants of the high prenatal anger mothers had less optimal orientation, motor organization and depression scores" (Field et al. 2002, 263; see also Glover 2002). Although this is not mentioned by Lealle Ruhl in her article on the increasing rhetoric of self-control associated with what she calls the "willed pregnancy," it is entirely in keeping with it (Ruhl 2002). Ruhl suggests, moreover, that this emphasis on self-control, while it may have positive aspects in terms of advocating for pregnant women's autonomy, also has negative aspects in that it privatizes all responsibility for reproduction, both during pregnancy and childcare. If a woman's pregnancy does not turn out happily, then she is often implicitly or explicitly held to blame, something stressed as well by Layne in her analysis of women's responses to unhappy outcomes to their pregnancies (Ruhl 2002, 658; Layne 2003b).

These expectations of rigorous self-control, child-centeredness, and self-sacrifice on the part of pregnant women are applied equally to those who care for children rather than fetuses, and they are acutely applied to breastfeeding women. Moreover, breastfeeding mothers need to monitor their exposures to toxins and monitor their diet, their use of legal and illegal drugs, and alcohol and caffeine consumption lest they expose their infants to toxic substances in a way that is reminiscent of expectations for pregnant women. Interestingly, a Health Canada (Canadian government) publication stresses this connection, arguing that breastfeeding "continues the special relationship" begun in the womb and gives babies a continuing connection with their mothers' bodies (Wall 2001, 599).

Both pregnant women (who have decided to continue with their pregnancies) and infants' caregivers meet needs, provide care, enable growth, strive for preservation of life, and accept change, especially change directed toward increasing independence on the part of the infant or fetus cared for. Similarities are particularly acute when a lactating mother cares exclusively or near exclusively for an infant. Both breastfeeding and pregnancy are embodied ways of meeting another's needs, both involve intense physical contact, both keep the caregiver tied to another's needs, and in both decisions made by the caregiver about her own body have immediate and sometimes long-term repercussions for the recipient of her care.

However, there are also significant differences between the two sorts of experiences. Pregnant women and others with an interest in their fetuses have no possibility of immediate access to the fetus, since all access is mediated through the pregnant woman's body. As Sherwin notes, "[a] fetus is a unique sort of being in that it cannot form relationships freely with others, nor can others readily form relationships with it. A fetus has a primary and particularly intimate relationship with the woman in whose womb it develops; any other relationship it may have is indirect, and must be mediated through the pregnant woman" (Sherwin 1991, 335). Moreover, while the differences in terms of possibilities for independent existence are a matter of degree, in the case of an infant there is at least the possibility that others could care for that infant. While in both pregnancy and caring for a breastfed infant, there is a possibility for a network of persons to provide care, in the former case other persons can care for a fetus only by caring for the pregnant woman, while in the latter case (complicated as this can be by the ongoing breastfeeding), others can share in direct care for the infant. However, in both cases, the ideology of motherhood continues to shape expectations that one person, the pregnant woman or new mother, will continue to meet almost all of the needs for care on the part of the fetus or infant and that she will meet these needs with at best the private support of her partner and close friends or family. In both cases, moreover, the pregnant woman or new mother is expected to be willing to make almost any sacrifices necessary for the health and future happiness of the dependent being in her charge.

As Astrid Thoné points out, Levinas intended his observations about the ethical relationship between mothers and their children to capture both women's experiences of pregnancy and their experiences of breastfeeding (Thoné 1998, 119). Glenda Wall observes that "the focus on the baby in breastfeeding discourse also can be seen as an extension of the 'remoralization of pregnancy' that has accompanied recent technological advances in the monitoring and visualization of the fetus" (2001, 602). This suggests that, while there are aspects of pregnancy that are unique (as suggested above), there are also interesting ways in which it can be analogized to other experiences, particularly when we are looking to examine its ethical significance.

Moreover, just as the difficulties of pregnancy are minimized, Wall observes that medical and governmental literature advocating the benefits of breastfeeding tends to gloss over the real difficulties involved. Such difficulties include problems initiating breastfeeding, breast infections, added fatigue, and the enormous amount of time it can require, as well as "the isolation and confinement that result from having sole responsibility for nourishing a child while not feeling comfortable doing so publicly" (Wall 2001, 598).

Linda Blum, in a book discussing ideologies of breastfeeding and motherhood, stresses that breastfeeding is advocated almost exclusively in terms of the benefit to the baby (or to the woman's figure, which may be about pleasing her partner rather than herself). She writes: "Research and advice literature each pay less attention to maternal health and breastfeeding. Assumptions of maternal altruism run high and mothers particularly curious about the effects of breastfeeding on their bodies are likely to meet with frustration" (Blum 1999, 50–51; see also Wall 2001, 601). She notes that appeals to children's needs must be made with caution, since "they have so often invited demonization of mothers, making them shoulder the blame for larger social ills" (Blum 1999, 253). She remarks, in addition, that breastfeeding is often presented as a solution to third world infant feeding, without remarking on the problem of maternal malnourishment (1999, 52) and the contribution breastfeeding can make to such malnourishment (1999, 52). Moreover, the only solution typically advocated to combining breastfeeding with maternal paid employment is breast pumping, with no attention paid to the demands this can place on women, particularly in lower paid fields where working conditions are often less flexible and with fewer breaks than many higher paying jobs (1999, 58).

All of these phenomena point in their different ways to assumptions of maternal altruism (as well as to expectations of exclusive mothering rather than shared nurturing of children). As Jules Law points out, decisions about whether or not to breastfeed are presented entirely in terms of the best interests of the infant, but "what is missing from the debate is a sense of how the advantages and disadvantages of particular infant-feeding methods stack up relative to a host of complexly intertwined risks, family and work practices, child-care decisions, social goods, and labor arrangements" (Law 2000, 422). For instance, breastfeeding puts demands on women's bodies, time, and labor, while formula feeding puts demands on families (often men's) incomes (Law 2000, 438).

Although I do not pursue the claim at any length in this chapter, I think there are some interesting parallels (as well, of course, as many significant differences) between women's experiences of welcomed pregnancies and the experiences that many women and some men have in caring for very young children. These include pressures that reflect social expectations that those caring for children are engaged in private work, that they should put the needs of the children above their own needs in every instance, and that they should not demand social or economic support from the wider society for their work. I discuss the impact of this ideology of motherhood on the experiences of caregivers (women and men, paid and unpaid) in chapter 5.

## 7. HOW PREGNANCIES DIFFER IN ETHICALLY SIGNIFICANT WAYS

One of the most significant ways that pregnancies can differ from one another morally concerns whether or not the pregnancy is wanted. As I stressed earlier, because philosophers' attention to pregnancy has been dominated by unwanted pregnancies, I focus in this chapter on wanted pregnancies. While wanted pregnancies have been experienced by many women at many different historical periods, voluntary pregnancies have only recently become possible for some women, particularly those in industrialized countries with standards of living that support access to birth control and state policies that permit abortion. As I suggested above, when pregnancy is voluntary, and women as a result experience pregnancies that are wanted or not entirely unwanted, this does not mean that any ethical issues about pregnancy have been resolved.

Moreover, as argued above, what issues the women will see as ethically significant and what they will view as their possible courses of action will vary widely depending on features that make some experiences of pregnancy very different from others. Here I mention three such features. (1) The first involves how socially valued the pregnancies are. This will depend on both broad societal attitudes about the worth of children in general, the need for a new generation, and thoughts about the social value of reproductive labor, which will affect all women who are pregnant in a particular society and also reflect much more finely tuned attitudes about who is thought to be fit to reproduce and what kinds of children are valued. Therefore, pregnant women in the same culture are bound to experience pregnancy very differently. Pregnant women who are not wed or coupled to a male partner, those who are impoverished or very young, and those with physical or mental impairments receive messages about pregnancy very different from those who conform to social ideals for pregnancy.

For instance, Carol Thomas shows that women with physical and mental impairments are often urged to avoid pregnancy by means of sterilization or to end their pregnancies (Thomas 1997). Juliene Lipson and Judith Rogers similarly report, both on the basis of a U.S. survey of 1,200 parents with physical or mental impairments and on the basis of their own qualitative study of twelve recently pregnant women with mobility related impairments, that these women's pregnancies were not initially welcomed by their own families, the larger community, or the medical community to whom they turned for health care during pregnancy and birthing (Lipson and Rogers 2000, 15). Moreover, these negative attitudes had significant impacts on the nature and kind of resources these pregnant women could draw on. The women had to be unusually assertive in order to get their decisions respected and were often given no or false information and inadequate or no referrals to support services in occupational and physical therapy, even when these were available. By contrast, they were offered additional access to fetal testing and counseling that many of these women saw as encouraging them to get abortions.

The example of pregnant women with physical or mental impairments is meant to serve a general point about the extent to which some pregnancies are more socially valued than others, and some fetuses are thought to be either more innocent or more deserving than others, a point that can sometimes be lost when feminists oppose the emphasis on the welfare of fetuses rather than that of pregnant women. Carol Mason makes this point about the difference in social value given to different kinds of pregnancies and different kinds of fetuses very clear in her analysis of both the differential treatment of black as opposed to white mothers and the differential value placed on black versus white fetuses and babies. She points out (as does Dorothy Roberts 1997) that black mothers face greater suspicion of providing poor treatment than white mothers and also face a greater likelihood of prosecution for such things as delivering drugs to their fetuses in utero. She also observes that fetuses who are presented as innocents deserving protection are culturally coded as white (Mason 2000, 50). By contrast, "the so-called crack baby is the biologically and morally darker version of the image of fetuses used in 'partial birth' legislation" – "those 'normal,' 'healthy,' 'intact' fetuses who do not suffer 'genetic or other developmental abnormalities'" (2000, 50). This points to the way in which both racism and disabilism affect which pregnancies and which fetuses are thought to be of value and to require protection.

(2) The second feature that differentiates some pregnancies from others involves which kinds of information about pregnancy are available to women, whether they are given incomplete or skewed information, and what they are encouraged to do with this information. In North America, women are given increasing access to information about the development of their fetuses and about risk factors that affect the outcome of pregnancy, as well as general advice about how to cope with pregnancy-related changes and demands. However, they have very little access to information about experiences of pregnancy, particularly those that deviate from certain norms, and they are also expected to make significant life decisions on the basis of risk statistics of an order of magnitude that do not generally affect other life decisions.

Deborah Lupton observes: "Producing a 'perfect' infant is seen to be at least partly a result of the woman's ability to exert control over her body, to seek and subscribe to expert advice and engage in self-sacrifice for the sake of her foetus" (Lupton 1999, 82). This misrepresents the risks to a pregnant woman and her fetus as all due to her own decisions, contributing to and reflecting the ideology of motherhood. It also encourages pregnant women to make both small and large decisions about their pregnancies on the basis of very statistically small differences in levels of risk (as we saw in some of the women's narratives from *Pregnancy Stories* in chapter 1). It also encourages pregnant women to accept expert testimony about risk in the place of testimony about the subjective experience of outcomes that are deemed undesirable. For instance, information that the risk of having an infant with a certain condition is one in 287 suggests that it must be objectively bad or terrible to have that condition – otherwise, why would we be speaking about and calculating risks? This language of risk, as well as the availability of various prenatal diagnostic techniques, can therefore have a direct impact on the extent to which a pregnant woman bonds with her fetus or tries to keep herself from bonding. This effect was pronounced in Barbara Katz Rothman's important work *The Tentative Pregnancy* (1986), and it was also manifest in the narratives of pregnant women quoted in chapter 1. The impact on larger social attitudes toward people with the kinds of illnesses and impairments that prenatal diagnostics are intended to detect is increasingly explored in critical disability theory (Hubbard 1997; Shakespeare 1998; Sharp and Earle 2002).

Like prenatal diagnostic testing, much of the information given to pregnant women about their fetuses relies on technological innovations that allow them to hear their fetuses heartbeats or see their images (now available in three dimensions and color) through ultrasound technology. Ingrid Zechmeister, a sonographer and feminist social theorist, notes that in this new version of ultrasound technology, "additionally the fetus can be observed via real time when it kicks, excretes and yawns. This 'human behavior' reinforces its image of a person" (Zechmeister 2001, 393).

Feminists have intensively studied the uses and meaning of this technology, but what is of interest to me in this chapter is the way in which ultrasound is often used in an attempt to bring pregnant women into closer relationship with their fetuses. Although this is one of the reasons ultrasound is highly valued by many pregnant women experiencing wanted pregnancies, it is also used by medical personnel in an attempt to influence the behavior of pregnant women, in order to make their fetuses seem more real, and more like their babies, and hence worth making sacrifices for. Thus, for instance, Zechmeister observes that some obstetricians believe that seeing the fetus via ultrasound technology can trigger prenatal bonding and can help to influence the pregnant woman's "compliance and lifestyle" (Zechmeister 2001, 389). However, all of the information conveyed to pregnant women, not only the ultrasound technology, can affect how and whether they form relationships with their fetuses, as was clear from the way in which information about risk is presented.

(3) The third feature that differentiates pregnancies from one another and that can be ethically significant involves how disruptive – both of daily life and of women's long-term projects – the pregnancies are. How disruptive they are will depend on the nature of those projects, the nature

of the pregnancies, and the existence or lack of social support for both the pregnancies and the women's projects. As I stressed in the second chapter, some pregnancies will involve significant illness and impairment of daily functioning, all will involve radical changes in a woman's body and in her social relations, and many will involve changes in a woman's sense of her identity, particularly revolving around issues of gender identity.

## 8. CONCLUSION

The sheer amount and speed of change that women experience during their pregnancies increases their vulnerability to the ideologies of motherhood, in particular the demands that they be self-sacrificing and that they handle all of the demands of pregnancy by themselves without support from anyone beyond a private circle of family and friends. This will emerge as a theme in the brief chapter on birth that follows this one. Moreover, it is true that most of the ways in which a pregnant woman provides care to her developing fetus can be provided only by her, although often she will be able to provide this care only when she receives social support, both from the larger society and from her private resources.

We need to oppose stereotypes that pregnant women are particularly irrational and overly emotional and hence need others to help them to make decisions, without abandoning pregnant women entirely to their own private resources. Pregnant women need access to accurate information about the choices they are asked to make, both from medical experts and from people who have lived with the results of the kinds of choices pregnant women are asked to make. This will be reliably available only if discussion of the choices pregnant women make about ending their pregnancies or about how they proceed with them becomes part of public discourse. We also need as a society to recognize that pregnancy can seriously affect the health, energy, and opportunities of pregnant women and to ensure that social and economic support for pregnancy is available in ways that respect pregnant women's autonomy and dignity. Here, as I suggested in the second chapter, feminists may find an important ally in critical disability theory and the disability rights movement.

Feminists need to find ways to fight the demands that pregnant women engage in unstinting self-sacrifice, in part by interrogating discourses about risks to the developing fetus, without going to the opposite extreme of condemning women for providing care that cannot, in the nature of the relationship, be reciprocated. Complete self-sacrifice may be autonomy-negating,[4] but this should not mean that all relationships that cannot involve equity are wrong. This is a theme to which I return in the sixth chapter. Otherwise, all voluntary pregnancies, in which a woman takes on the responsibility of providing care to a developing being who cannot reciprocate by providing care to the woman, would be immoral. Instead, it seems clear that it would be ethically wrong to voluntarily become pregnant and continue with one's pregnancy if pregnant women were not prepared to provide some unreciprocated care. Yet providing unreciprocated care is not unique to pregnancy, and therefore our thinking about the ethical nature of this aspect of pregnancy can inform and be informed by reflection on other situations in which this happens.

In summary, while I agree with those feminists who urge us to take the phenomenology of pregnancy seriously in our moral theory, we must do this in a way that, first, pays attention to patterns of difference in women's experiences of pregnancy, seeking to identify which differences are ethically significant. Second, our approach must focus as much on welcome and wanted as unwelcome pregnancies and not make an overly sharp distinction between the two. Third and finally, our theorizing must attempt to appreciate both what is distinct about experiences of pregnancy and where there are areas of overlap between those experiences and other experiences of reproductive labor. Here we can analyze how ideologies of motherhood affect women who are pregnant or who breastfeed, as discussed above, as well as men and women who care for young children. The latter is the focus of the chapters that follow.

# Chapter 4

# What about Birth?

## 1. INTRODUCTION: THE OVEREMPHASIS ON BIRTH

As I mentioned in the introduction to this book, although I write about three important stages of reproductive labor – pregnancy, birth, and the provision of child care to young children – I do not devote a full-length chapter to birth, for several reasons. First, it is striking that only childbirth typically gets called "labor," while the other, more time-consuming aspects of reproductive labor, which require sustained effort and considerable skill and expertise, do not. A pregnant woman is described as "going into labor" when she begins to give birth to a child or having a labor that lasted nineteen hours, as if the previous months have not involved reproductive labor on her part and as if the labor will end when the child is born.

Next, probably because of the dramatic nature of birth, women's conscious experiences and accounts of pregnancy are already focused more on birth than on either the preceding nine months or the transition to becoming a parent. A study of 329 Finnish women reveals that women's fears relating to pregnancy and childbirth are mainly associated with childbirth (Melender 2002), especially concerning pain and distress during labor, their risk of caesarean section, their treatment by health care staff, and the health of their newborn babies. In addition to fear and anxiety, many women expect to feel great joy at birth, and so this emotionally loaded brief period can come to dominate their thoughts during pregnancy.

Moreover, the main form of education and group support that pregnant women in North America or Europe are likely to experience comes in the form of childbirth preparation classes. In my own case, my partner and I attended one two-hour "infant care" class before the birth of our first child and seven three-hour "childbirth preparation" classes, and this is the typical experience of most expectant parents who take part in such classes during pregnancy. Socially, it is also the case that birth is significant because it is the time when a child emerges, and the arrival of babies is of far greater interest to most people than the experiences of women during pregnancy. Since I have already argued that pregnant and birthing women are judged by an ideology of motherhood that represents these events in women's lives as only about the potential or newborn child, we should not be surprised that the time during pregnancy when the child first makes his or her appearance should be the period of pregnancy that gets most attention.

Anthropologist Linda Layne points to yet another reason why births – and conception – are often given more attention than the approximately nine-month period of pregnancy that may lie in between. She notes that "it is probably fair to say that most anthropological studies of reproduction have followed the medicine. As a result, most studies have focused on the two periods of pregnancy which are subject to the most medical intervention," and those are the beginning and the end (Layne 2003b, 1885). She continues to note that these are "what Katz Rothman has so aptly referred to as the two patriarchal moments: seeds goes in/baby comes out" (2003b, 1885).

## 2. FEMINIST WORK ON BIRTH

Moreover, feminist attention to reproductive labor has also focused more on birth than on the rest of pregnancy. As I discussed in the first chapter, Mary O'Brien's work was a relatively early and important feminist recognition that reproductive labor is indeed a form of labor, and an important human social activity, but her focus, particularly because of her use of Marx's analysis of productive labor, remains on the "product" of birth (O'Brien 1981, 199–200). She specifically notes that she is not interested in what she terms the psychology of pregnancy (1981, 50). Even those feminists I discuss in the next chapter, who concentrate on the elaboration of maternal thinking, as developed and exercised in caring for children, turn to discussions of birth, rather than pregnancy, when they wish to acknowledge the role played by biological mothers. Sara Ruddick writes an essay entitled "Thinking Mothers/Conceiving Birth" (1994), and Virginia Held devotes a chapter of her book *Feminist Morality* to claiming that we should recognize birth as a significantly human, social, and cultural event, in the same way that we recognize death as more than a natural event (the chapter is a reprint of Held 1989).

Ruddick fears that her own and other feminists' attention to the intellectual and moral work involved in childrearing tends to eclipse or direct attention away from the bodily work that women do in various stages of reproductive labor, including in pregnancy and birth. To counteract that tendency, she pays attention in her article (1994) to birth. Held, similarly, emphasizes birth, although in her case it is because she argues that as a society we recognize that death is not only biological but also social and that we have complicated social practices around death and social recognition of death, yet do not afford such social recognition to birth, at least insofar as it is an experience of women. Attention given to birth tends to be to the new person born, not to the person who has just given birth.

I share Held's determination to value women's experiences and activities (1989, 362), along with her more specific aims of understanding childbirth from the point of view of the birthing woman (366) and increasing our capacity for imaginative representation of birthing and mothering (369). I also share her criticism of other thinkers, such as Simone de Beauvoir (1953) and Hannah Arendt (1958), who interpret virtually all aspects of pregnancy and raising children as routine biological activity (375–376), rather than distinctively human social activities requiring a great deal of thought and care from those who undertake them.

However, despite the fact that I view Held's essay as groundbreaking, I also think that she underplays the importance of pregnancy in her emphasis on childbirth and childrearing. Although Held criticizes O'Brien for the latter's overemphasis on childbirth, Held thinks that O'Brien has paid too little attention to childrearing (383), rather than too little attention to pregnancy. Her emphasis on birth (when the child first appears) and childrearing (when the child is cared for) risks, in my judgment, exactly what she criticizes, and that is a forgetting of the importance of the pregnant woman's experience as an element worthy of attention in addition to any focus on the children produced or cared for.

Pregnancy is, moreover, as shown in the second chapter, a better example of reproductive labor as meaningful activity involving both choice and accommodation than birth typically is. The latter takes place over a shorter period of time and may physically overwhelm some women or even occur when they are anesthetized. Held attempts to counteract our impression of pregnancy, childbirth, and childrearing as purely natural biological activities by emphasizing a woman's capacity for conscious choice and control over her labor (if only in her decision to end her own life or that of the fetus inside her; 363), but this seems to me to overemphasize choice and control with potentially detrimental effects, which I discuss later in this chapter. Moreover, accommodation to the unexpected, undesired, and uncontrolled is as much an essentially human activity, with the potential for creative and meaningful experience, as is consciously purposive planning.

As with Held, when pregnancy is discussed by feminist theorists, it tends to be subsumed into a discussion of birth, as suggested by the titles and contents of such books and articles as Heather Cahill's "Male Appropriation and Medicalization of Childbirth" (2001) and Raymond DeVries et al.'s *Birth by Design: Pregnancy, Maternity Care, and Midwifery in North America and Europe* (2001). Both the article and the book make mention of pregnancy as well as childbirth, but concentrate to a very large extent on childbirth. Many feminists working in fields as diverse as anthropology (Davis-Floyd 1987, 1992; Martin 1992), medicine, midwifery, nursing, psychology, and sociology (Oakley 1980; Katz Rothman 1982), along with maternalists[1] in those fields, have offered important critiques of the biomedical model of childbirth and have taken an interest in women's experiences of birth, but a similar level of attention has not been directed to women's experiences with pregnancy before birth or to those wanted pregnancies that do not end in birth.

As a result, rather than devoting a full-length chapter to the topic of birth, I make some brief remarks in this short chapter that is the transition between the part of the book devoted to pregnancy and the part of the book devoted to childcare. In this interlude between the first three chapters about pregnancy and the next two chapters about childcare, I briefly summarize some of the important feminist work that has been done on women's experiences of birth. I concentrate on the critique of medicalized childbirth, recognizing its achievements, while also discussing the significance of many women's ongoing choice of hospitals as a birth setting and with awareness of the need for medical interventions in many births and pregnancies. I examine some of the important recent feminist work on childbirth that questions the stark dichotomy between medicalized childbirth and its feminist and maternalist rival and point to some commonalities between the two, particularly in their shared emphasis on control over childbirth (Fox and Worts 1999; Shaw 2002; Layne 2003b). Linda Layne, for instance, notes that both the medicalized and the alternative, more holistic approach emphasize control and the supposition that birth will end happily when control is properly applied (Layne 2003b, 1881).

## 3. THE MEDICALIZED MODEL OF BIRTH

What is the medical model of birth, according to its critics? As Cahill puts it, this model makes a fundamental assumption that "women's bodies are inherently defective" and in need of medical intervention during childbirth (2001, 334; see also Campbell and Porter 1997, 350). Sociologists Bonnie Fox and Diana Worts write that the medical model has been criticized because "medical professionals, acting on a definition of childbirth as hazardous, intervene in what is essentially a natural process. Their management of birth decreased the control of the birthing woman, fails to improve the physical and emotional outcome of the birth, and even alienates the woman from a potentially empowering experience" (Fox and Worts 1999, 327–328). Anthropologist Robbie Davis-Floyd argues that practices associated with midwifery and a more holistic model of birth are safer (2001) and enhance women's autonomy, instead of teaching them to defer to medical and technical expertise (1987, 1992).

Using Davis-Floyd's notion of birth as a rite of passage, Fox and Worts note that not only are birthing women socialized into a sense of the superiority of technology to nature, but also their experiences of birthing in a medical setting encourage them to think of mothering as essentially privatized. This is because they are given little or no support in caring for their newborn children while in the hospital (1999, 331). They write that "because medicalized childbirth offers only strictly delimited assistance, it communicates the message that the woman is alone (with perhaps the help of a partner) in her long-term responsibility for the care of the new child" (1999, 331). The privatization of birth is, of course, closely connected to the privatization of both pregnancy and childrearing, but this aspect of birth is rarely discussed. Medicalization, which is more closely tied to birth than to other aspects of reproductive labor, is more frequently the focus of feminist discourse.

Emily Martin observes that when birth is medicalized, for instance, with the use of ultrasound and fetal monitoring, "The doctor or technician literally turns his [sic] back to the woman to see the screen or printout describing what is happening inside her." She continues: "Mechanically, birth is seen as the control of laborers (women) and their machines (uteruses) by managers (doctors), often using other machines to help" (Martin 1992, 146). She also points out that during medical experiences of birth, women's experiences and feelings are effaced. For example, she describes one woman whose fetus was never in distress and notes that: "This woman's anger came from feeling that her own experience of the birth counted for nothing next to the welfare of her baby" (1992, 65).

These critics object to births necessarily taking place in a hospital, under the authority of medical expertise, and also to the medical and technological interventions women routinely experience there. Many of the critics of medicalized childbirth have been feminist, but as Kerreen Reiger points out, there have also been many maternalist critics of medicalized childbirth, who stress the importance of motherhood to women and the needs both to valorize motherhood and to make it more rewarding for women by paying attention to the needs of women and children to bond together in an atmosphere that does not intrude on their privacy and that respects women's wisdom about childrearing. This parallels Linda Blum's examination of the maternalist discourse around breastfeeding that has elements that are feminist and other elements that are not. For instance, Blum notes that the maternalist model puts greater trust in women and values their experiences but still sees exclusive, privatized motherhood as women's highest calling (Blum 1999, 37–38).

Maternalism and feminism in childbirth reform have had varying degrees of alliance in different countries (Reiger 1999, 586–587, 593). Sometimes the activism involved has led maternalist women who were originally hostile to or indifferent to feminism to take on a feminist identification, but this varies with the degree to which feminist movements in different countries have been dismissive of maternalism. Thus, Reiger suggests that in New Zealand and Canada in particular there have been close alliances between maternalist organizations and feminist ones, but in Australia, where "Australian feminist discourse on motherhood has focused mostly on its awful constraints," there has been little coming together of maternalist and feminist critiques of medicalized childbirth (1999, 588).

How much impact have these critiques had? Linda Blum remarks of U.S. women, "In 1900, less than 5 percent of women had hospital births. . . . By 1940, this was up to 55 percent . . . and by the 1970s, 99 percent of U.S. mothers had hospital births" (Blum 1999, 226). Pamela Klassen observes that this has changed little; as of 1994, the percentage of home-birthing North American women remained very low, at approximately 1 percent. (Klassen 2001b, 19). In the 1990s British women overwhelmingly (97 to 99%) gave birth in hospitals (Cahill 2001, 334), as did Canadian women (Bourgeault et al. 2001, 53), although the numbers of women giving birth outside a hospital remain higher at selected European countries, most notably 30 percent of all births in the Netherlands (Davis-Floyd 2001, vii).

However, this does not mean that the critique of medicalization has been ineffective. Not only are rates of home births slightly on the rise in many countries, but also substantial reforms have taken place within the hospital system. For instance, in Ontario in 1993, licensed midwives became legal, integrated into the health care system, and publicly funded (Bourgeault et al. 2001, 53). Many medical interventions that women found dehumanizing and unnecessary have been ceased, such as routine enemas and shaving, and concern over increasing caesarean section rates has led medical systems to examine the extent to which unnecessary caesareans have been performed. Layne observes that, largely due to the efforts of the alternative childbirth movement, "women are not as physically constrained during labor, many middle-class women now give birth in relatively cozy, lower-lit 'birthing-suites' in hospitals, babies are not swept away immediately from their mothers after birth, and breast feeding is encouraged" (Layne 2003a, 188).

These are all positive developments, but they also tend to conform to what Fox and Worts have revealed as the assumption of privatized motherhood. In other words, it is being made easier for mothers to immediately assume sole (or possibly, shared with a partner) responsibility for their children. It is therefore far from surprising that maternalist reformers would seek many of these kinds of changes to childbirth, since their conservative emphasis on women's destiny as mothers (despite their radical call for increasing the value given to this kind of work) is in complete harmony with an ideology of privatized and exclusive motherhood. Pamela Klassen observes that resistance to medicalization of birth is by no means entirely feminist and has often been rooted in valorization of women as domestic childrearers (2001b).

Fox and Worts (1999) point out that feminist critics often suggest that women who give birth in a hospital, at least when they make use of a variety of medical interventions, have surrendered their agency during birth. Fox and Worts argue that, while many women do report being alienated by their experiences of medical births, other women welcome medical interventions (1999, 328), and we should not assume that they are deluded in doing so, or overlook their agency. Robbie Davis-Floyd suggests that middle-class women are far more likely to be satisfied with medicalized childbirth, because their relatively powerful position in society gives them reason to identify with those norms that are privileged within it (Davis-Floyd 1994, 1137). She notes that "seventy of the one hundred women I interviewed for my first book . . . either actively sought or were generally comfortable with technobirth. Technological interventions tend to give women a sense of safety. . . . the feeling that all that can be done is being done" (Davis-Floyd 2000, 281–2).

However, this may be too quick a dismissal of women's reasons for being satisfied with medicalized birth. We must also examine the context of birthing women's choices. As Fox and Worts point out, given the assumption of individual mothers' privatized responsibility for their children, a hospital setting that provides pain control can at least make women feel more prepared to give this care. Women with strong social support (not only in the hospital but, more important, at home in terms of house care and infant care responsibilities) are the ones most likely to resist medical interventions to increase their comfort (Fox and Worts 1999, 337).

A number of recent feminist works have begun to contest the overly sharp dichotomy between the natural and the technological they see presumed in the critique of medicalized childbirth. Rhonda Shaw, for instance, argues that in New Zealand, she was offered only two choices – a medicalized childbirth or one that entirely rejected reliance on medicine and technology – and saw use of medicine as a desperate last resource in the case of dire emergencies (Shaw 2002). Ellen Annandale and Judith Clark suggest that the alternative childbirth movement has defined itself too sharply in contrast to the medical model of childbirth, and its critics are too quick to dismiss the value of technology (Annandale and Clark 1996). In contrast, they suggest that "cyborg imagery is . . . a way to deconstruct duality and challenge the theoretical positions which construct science/technology (including that around birth) as 'simply' male demonology" (1996, 38; see also Lim 1999 and Shaw 2002 for endorsement of the cyborg image of pregnant and birthing women; Davis-Floyd gives a nuanced account of four different ways in which this imagery can be used (2000, 287)).

Rona Campbell and Sam Porter respond to these criticisms by arguing that cyborg imagery is unlikely to deconstruct the "dualities of gender, in that those very dualities are intrinsic to the cyborg image, where the machine component signifies male impregnability, and the fragile flesh denotes the feminine," and they further suggest that this imagery is too "conducive to technologism" (1997, 355). Rudinow similarly points to the extent to which particular reproductive technologies are gendered and masculinity is constructed as "technophilic" (Rudinow 1996, 69). I am largely sympathetic to this response and think that "cyborg" imagery has little to offer women in making selective use of medical and technological approaches to birth, but I would be more persuaded by Campbell and Porter's response if they were to offer guidelines for assessing how to make such selective choices.

The assumption that pregnancy and childbirth are natural and normal activities that do not usually require medical intervention does too much to equate the natural, and even the normal, with the desirable. My own nearsightedness is both natural and relatively normal, and yet far from desirable, and many of the experiences women have as they birth can be ameliorated by medical interventions – just as my eyeglasses and contact lenses help me – without requiring the birthing women to accept a view of their bodies as defective or medical experts as those who should make all the decisions about their birthing experiences.

In the second chapter of this book, I discussed the extent to which illness and impairment occur in many pregnancies, including "normal ones," and it is important to recognize that birthing women will almost always need support for their birthing. Sometimes they will need medical solutions to the illness and impairment they experience (for instance, when their blood pressure skyrockets or they begin to bleed profusely). Sometimes impairment can best be met by social support (for instance, when they are unable to meet their own bodily needs or care for dependent children, others could do this work for them or help them to do it for themselves, depending on the birthing woman's degree of impairment and her preferences). Rather than offering overall positive (celebratory, technological) responses to medical and technological interventions or overall negative responses that see technology as patriarchal, ineffective, and alienating, birthing women should be given the opportunity to select those interventions that promise to be effective and/or necessary, without having to choose between two entirely opposed models of childbirth.

We need to be sure that we do not, in rejecting paternalistic and inappropriate uses of technology, celebrate birth as something that all women can experience naturally, if only we were not so civilized. Feminist religious studies scholar Pamela Klassen critiques the racist celebration of the so-called tribal woman who gives birth easily and naturally and stresses that women giving birth in conditions of poverty and deprivation are more, not less, likely to require medical assistance in pregnancy and childbirth. She writes: "When home-birthing women in North America claim the 'simplicity' of non-Western women as an inspiration, they not only romanticize the difficult realities of many women's lives but also perpetuate a mystifying form of racism for the empowerment of the 'civilized'" (Klassen 2001a, 139).

Despite the way that the medicalized critique of childbirth is sometimes described, this selective approach to the use of technological aids during birth is certainly consistent with the approach of many of the leading proponents of the alternative birthing movement. Davis-Floyd, for instance, notes, "To be sure, birth carries its own set of risks. In societies in which women are malnourished and overworked, rates of both maternal and infant mortality are high. But when women are healthy, well-nourished, and receive adequate social support, the percentage of complications in childbirth are low – well under ten percent" (2000, 292). Of course, 10 percent (what Davis-Floyd goes on to cite as the estimate of complications given by conservative obstetricians) is still far from rare, and women should certainly incorporate their awareness of the real possibility of complications into their plans for their birthing experiences, but need not rely on the medical model of childbirth in order to do so.

That this can well be the case is attested to by Christina, one of the home-birthing women studied by Klassen. Christina "considered her midwife to have medical knowledge on a par with that of a doctor, and thought her own medical training was an asset to having a home birth, since she had a 'knowledge of the basic physiology of the body.'" However, Christina was critical of the "meddling" of the medical system in the ways of birth, in that doctors made decisions for a woman "rather than allowing a woman's body to tell her what needs to be done" (2001b, 788). This home-birthing woman clearly distinguished between the medical knowledge and technological equipment associated with the medicalized model of childbirth and the minimization of interest in and respect for women's decisions and experiences that are also associated with that model.

Klassen notes, "Women giving birth at home who end up being transported to the hospital often experience chastisement by or disrespect from medical authorities as a result of their eschewing of a medicalized birth" (2001b, 780). She points out that "seeking a fulfilling experience is considered secondary to or even incompatible with the safety of a woman's baby in the eyes of some critics of home birth" (2001a, 38).

Many in the alternative childbirth movement not only maintain the safety of home birth, but also insist that women's choices in birthing should be respected because "childbirth is a life-shaping experience for the mother as well as for the baby," and "when women feel empowered in birth, they will also feel empowered in mothering, making for healthy babies and mothers in the long term" (2001a, 213). Klassen notes that we should be wary of a tendency to justify birthing women's exercises of agency by the benefits that flow as a result to children. Home-birthing women who make decisions about birthing based on "considerations of their own physical and emotional health, and the health of their babies," refuse "to accept a model of maternal sacrifice that eclipses the mother in touting the virtues of a mother's love" (Klassen 2001a, 214). This, even more than the extent to which they contest the need for many medical interventions during childbirth, may be one of their most potent challenges to contemporary management of birthing.

## 4. BIRTH, AGENCY, AND CONTROL

Most feminist accounts of childbirth stress women's agency and control, although, as Davis-Floyd (1994) and Fox and Worts (1999, 339–40) point out, control for birthing women can mean many differing things, from control over their bodies or over pain to the ability to remain conscious and aware, or the ability to shape the way in which the birth will take place. However, we may need at times to distinguish between what serves women's needs and respects their experiences and what increases their sense of being in control of birth, for different reasons articulated by Shaw, Layne, and Karin Martin.

Shaw argues that there may be ethical problems with one attempt to give women control over their birthing experiences, as exemplified in the contemporary "birth plan" in which a woman specifies in advance how she would like her birth to go, what kinds of interventions she welcomes, and so forth. Even when this plan includes the determination to be flexible (chiefly in response to medical emergencies), Shaw notes that this tends to equate control over birthing with the decisions of a "wholly head-oriented actor, a disembodied subject for whom the ethics of emotion, desire and affect as processes orienting the individual's ability to make choices and decisions about how to act are seen to be secondary or contingent considerations" (Shaw 2002, 137). By contrast, Shaw suggests that these birth plans ignore the "significantly vulnerable and dependent body event of giving birth" and tend to equate agency with the ability to control one's body and one's emotions and to decide what is wanted from other people before the birthing woman sees how they respond to her during labor (2002, 141).

Shaw also notes that the existence of the birth plan can also be used when anything goes wrong during birth to assign blame to the "patient/consumer for her failure to remain sufficiently reflexive enough to calculate potential risks to herself and the baby or to take steps to diminish these risks and remain adaptable to change" (2002, 141). Cahill similarly observes that birth plans "are being perceived increasingly as binding contracts," while instead "women must be able to change their mind[s] at any time" (Cahill 1999, 501). This is especially important since "it is precisely at the time of delivery that previously abstract images of childbirth become more real" (Cahill 1999, 500). Shaw suggests that we should understand birth to be profoundly transformative and not try to impose a plan devised in advance on the birthing body.

In a slightly different but interconnected vein, Klassen notes that many of the birthing women she studied did not equate agency with having control over the birthing process. Instead, many of the religious home-birthing women (from a wide variety of religious backgrounds) found "agency within surrender that for a time relinquishes control of their selves to multiple forces: nature, God, the energy of birth, their own bodies" (2001a, 215).

In yet another critique of the association between birthing women's agency and control, Layne observes that both practitioners of the medicalized model of birth and their alternative birthing critics tend to assume that control, if properly applied, can guarantee a happy outcome. This tends to privatize responsibility for good outcomes, ignoring the many things that are outside the control of women (and the medical personnel or midwifes who seek to assist them), including toxic environmental pollutants, accidents, and biological factors, all of which mean that "regardless of the quality of one's health care or the quantity of one's self-discipline and self-care during a pregnancy, there are countless things that can go wrong that neither would-be mothers or their care-givers can control" (Layne 2003b, 1885). The assumption that outcomes can be controlled can only, as Layne notes, exacerbate women's grief and sense of guilt when their birthing outcomes are not happy ones (2003b, 1881).

Furthermore, the reasons women may wish to exercise control over their birthing bodies may not always be benign. In her insightful article, "Giving Birth like a Girl," Karin Martin examines the extent to which birthing women, who are often depicted in the popular media as "screaming, yelling, self-centred, and demanding pain medication" (Martin 2003, 54), often instead constrain their behavior during birthing in order to "express selves that are relational, selfless, caring, polite, and subjected to the tyranny of nice and kind" (2003, 69). Martin argues that a gendered identity leads birthing women to "expend much energy on taking care of others and obeying gendered norms about politeness while they were in the middle of a profound physical experiences that takes considerable energy, agency, and willpower" (2003, 69). Women hesitated to make noise that would disturb their hospital neighbors, worried about their husbands, and attempted to reassure those who tried to assist them that they were being helpful even when the women were irritated by their presence or activities. These women sometimes asked for pain control so that they would be able to continue to be nice and kind model patients (Martin 2003).

I would suggest that not only did the women wish to conform to gender stereotypes, but also that birthing women are particularly susceptible to ideologies around maternal self-sacrifice when they are in the midst of a physically and emotionally overwhelming experience and are, furthermore, in many instances, about to begin their life as mothers. This is also suggested by sociologists Fox and Worts, who observed that during the process of birth, "many women did not distinguish between their own and their babies' interests," although "days later, women with healthy babies are more likely to distinguish their own needs from those of their babies" (1999, 334). This had been a prominent theme in the last chapter in my discussion of pregnancy and ethics and will continue to emerge as significant in the next chapter, as I go on to examine the influence of this kind of self-sacrificial ideology of motherhood on the experience of those who care for children once they are born.

# *Chapter 5*

# Mothers and Others

## Who Can Be "Maternal Thinkers"?

### 1. INTRODUCTION: FEMINIST PHILOSOPHY AND THE IDEOLOGY OF MOTHERHOOD

In the first four chapters of this book, I discuss two stages of reproductive labor, pregnancy and birth, which are available only to women. I turn now to a third stage, childrearing. This form of reproductive labor is still predominantly performed by women, both as unpaid and as paid caregivers. However, it is a kind of labor that can be performed by men, and one that not only can be but is undertaken by men, many as unpaid caregivers of their own children and a few as paid caregivers. In this chapter I examine the impact of the ideology of motherhood on the provision of childcare, an ideology that we have seen to have pernicious effects on women's experiences of pregnancy and birth. I approach childrearing from a perspective informed by the ethics of care, which also influenced my ethical analysis of pregnancy. As was the case in my study of pregnancy, an ethics of care perspective considers the needs and interests of caregivers and care receivers and considers questions about who gives care and how caregiving work is allocated. I begin my discussion in this chapter with an analysis of motherhood, but this leads to a much broader focus on childcare work in general, paid and unpaid.

Feminist philosophers have presented sharply contrasting analyses of motherhood. Shulamith Firestone in the *Dialectic of Sex* (1970) argued that women cannot be free until the biological family is entirely eliminated. Jeffner Allen famously called for the evacuation of motherhood, arguing that mere reform would be insufficient and that women should no longer deny themselves opportunities for creativity by unwisely giving of their time, energy, and bodies in order to rear the next generation.

She writes: "Motherhood always entails the death of a world in which women are free" (Allen 1983, 324). Proposals for different means of intercourse, pregnancy, and childraising "challenge, but need not break with, the ideology and institution of motherhood" (326). By contrast: "To not have children opens a time-space for the priority of claiming my life and world as my own and for the creative development of radically new alternatives" (326). More recently and in less sweeping terms, Claudia Card also writes in opposition to motherhood. She objects to the "involuntary uncompensated caretaking" involved in state enforcement of the child's access to its mother (Card 1996, 16–17) and worries about the vulnerability of children in such arrangements.

Other feminist philosophers are more sympathetic toward motherhood, seeing it as a source of women's strength, a practice making use of women's skills, and a potential new paradigm for ethical relations. These philosophers, including Annette Baier, Patricia Hill Collins, Virginia Held, Sara Ruddick, and Cynthia Willett, are careful to distinguish between the ideology of motherhood and motherhood as actually practiced by women. Furthermore, they distinguish between motherhood under patriarchy and more liberatory forms of motherhood.

To review my discussion in previous chapters, the ideology of motherhood, like all ideological constructions, makes claims both about what its subject is like and what it should be like, often blurring the line between the two. Patrice DiQuinzio labels the ideology of motherhood "essential motherhood" and writes: "Essential motherhood represents women's mothering as natural . . . inevitable, instinctive, and properly contained in its appropriate social realm, the private sphere" (DiQuinzio 1999, 10). The private sphere is conceived as a place where natural bodily needs are met, in contrast to the public sphere, where social matters are decided. Furthermore, essential motherhood requires "women's exclusive and selfless attention to and care of children" based on women's supposedly natural capacities for empathy and self-sacrifice (DiQuinzio 1999, xiii).

I would further characterize the ideology of motherhood[1] as committed to a view in which mothers meet all the emotional needs of their young children,[2] care for their bodies, and keep them safe, while fathers provide the material resources required for this mothering work. Neither mothers nor children are expected to have significant mental or physical impairments. Mothering work is meant to occur chiefly in private homes, and whenever children enter into more public domains, mothers are expected to continue not only to keep the children safe, but also to ensure that the children do not make significant demands on any other adults. Any mother who cannot meet these expectations is considered deviant or flawed. In broad strokes, according to the ideology of motherhood, with the exception of the necessary provision of material resources, mothers are thought to be necessary and sufficient for the happiness of their young children, and young children are thought to be necessary and sufficient for the happiness of their mothers.

In making claims about connections between the ideology of motherhood and conceptions of privacy, I do not here rehearse arguments about the existence and pervasiveness of the ideology of motherhood. Analysis of and evidence for it has come in many different forms, from sociological studies of parenthood (Uttal 2002), investigation of public policies around childcare (including the work of Tuominen 1997), studies of the experiences of paid childcare workers and their employers (Nelson 1990; Kousha 1995; Uttal 1996; Kyle 1997; Macdonald 1998; Murray 1998; Miedema 1999; Saggers and Grant 1999), and analysis of representations of mothers in literature and mass media (Ashe 1992; Bassin et al. 1994; Duquaine-Watson 2003; and many others).

However, I do not mean to imply that this ideal of motherhood is universally accepted, even in the middle-class North American, Australian, and Western European societies that I concentrate on here, which include the populations most likely to be able to live up to this ideal. First, there is evidence that black women are more likely to contest various aspects of this ideology, particularly in their assumptions of community responsibility for childcare (hooks 1984; Bailey 1994; Collins 2000) and in their construction of paid work as part of mothering (Reynolds 2001), rather than in tension with it. There are similar grounds for thinking that working-class women resist this ideology (Segura 1994), both because they can rarely live up to its demands and because their experiences can lead them to see paid work and mothering as complementary. Second, feminist ideas about the importance of male involvement in childrearing (at least paternal involvement) are encouraging men to take some responsibility for childcare, even though often not equitably. Finally, the increasing use of paid childcare may seem to be definitive evidence of the lessened hold of this ideal of motherhood. Certainly, paid work by mothers with young children is not only more likely to occur, but also less likely to be explicitly censured than in previous decades (Uttal 2002, 106). However, as I go on to discuss, the ideology of motherhood often retains some of its hold and affects both how that paid work is constructed and what maternal responsibility comes to mean. Moreover, childcare continues to be highly gendered, with, for instance, men constituting only 3 percent of the paid childcare work force in the United States (U.S. Department of Labor 1997).

This chapter focuses on how we can reconceive the work involved in caring for young children in ways that challenge the false and dangerous assumptions involved in the ideology of motherhood. I summarize one of the most important feminist philosophical challenges to essential motherhood. This challenge involves recognition that the provision of care to children is not natural and instinctive but is instead a social practice requiring specific skills and aiming at specific outcomes. Ruddick and Held speak, respectively, of this work as done by "maternal thinkers" or "mothering persons."

Next, I suggest that asking who counts as maternal thinkers or mothering persons is one useful way to organize our thinking about other important challenges to essential motherhood. Here we need not only to recognize the diverse persons who are actually doing the work, but also to think about how our recognition of this diversity requires us to change our understanding of what is involved in being a maternal thinker. In the process, it will become clear that there are problems in continuing to describe this work in terms that associate it with mothers.

Finally, recognition of the variety of different ways in which childcare may be provided needs to be supplemented by an evaluation of those differences. In this evaluation we must pay attention to several factors, some of which might push us in different directions in attempting to rank different forms of care. In keeping with the feminist ethics of care, we must focus attention on the needs and interests of both those who are receiving the care and those who are providing it.[3] Moreover, we must think about how the benefits and the burdens of childcare work are distributed differently to people of different sexes, social classes, and ethnicities and how the work itself is conceived differently when provided by people with those different characteristics.

## 2. MATERNAL THINKERS

Marxist feminists including Mary O'Brien (O'Brien 1981) have argued for decades that we should think of the activities involved in giving birth to and rearing young children as reproductive labor. In and of itself, this is an important challenge to the ideology of motherhood, which conceives of this activity as outside the world of work and indeed as a natural rather than a social activity. As I briefly indicated in the last chapter on birth, Ruddick and Held have expanded the challenge by encouraging us to recognize the provision of childcare not only as a form of labor and an essentially social activity, but also as a particular kind of practice requiring skills, talents, and aspirations both different from and related to those involved in other kinds of social practices.

Ruddick is emphatically opposed to idealizing motherhood and stresses that she is describing ideals inherent to certain practices. She draws analogies to ideals about scientific practice, which real scientists realize more or less but to which they are committed only insofar as they engage in scientific practice. She writes that "achievement, in maternal work, is defined by the aims of preserving, fostering, and shaping the growth of a child; insofar as one engages in maternal practice, one accepts these aims as one's own" (Ruddick 1983b, 234). In sharing this conception of achievement, "a mother engages in a discipline" (Ruddick 1983a, 214). When she engages well with it, she will develop certain intellectual capacities, need to make particular kinds of judgments, affirm some values, ask questions, make characteristic errors, and face characteristic temptations.

The three chief aims of maternal thinkers involve preserving children's lives, fostering their physical, intellectual, and emotional development, and ensuring their acceptability, both their overall social acceptability and their acceptability as children the mother can appreciate. Ruddick notes that these aims can sometimes conflict and also will lead to different kinds of practice depending on the different socio-economic situations of the mothers and children.

Baier, Held, Noddings, Ruddick, Willett, and others further claim that the work of mothering persons should be seen as a distinctively moral activity, and in fact all go on to argue that mothering work can serve as a central ethical paradigm. I discuss this argument in chapter 6. Here I note a danger that philosophers who focus on the moral aspects of the activity of care may be misinterpreted to accord with essential motherhood's understanding of care for young children as primarily requiring a certain emotional style. This danger is particularly acute when philosophers exaggerate the differences between caring activities and social exchanges where reason plays a more prominent role.

However, it is clear that both Ruddick and Joan Tronto do not see the moral element of caregiving to involve our emotions in a way that excludes our capacities to reason. For instance, Tronto speaks of attentiveness as one of the most important characteristics of caring for others[4] (Tronto 1995). To be attentive to others' needs, we need knowledge about them – and this requires us to be, as Alison Jaggar notes, "properly critical of the moral validity of felt, perceived, or expressed needs," to "avoid permitting or even legitimating morally inadequate responses to them" (Jaggar 1995, 189). Tronto argues that this requires not only close observation and other forms of gathering knowledge about others, but also substantial self-knowledge to prevent caregivers from projecting their own needs onto those of the care receivers.

Sara Ruddick is similar to Tronto in arguing that a moral orientation should never be thought to reduce to an emotional style. While she does speak of the characteristic maternal virtues of clear-sighted cheeriness and attentive love, along with the vices of cheery denial and self-denial (Ruddick 1983b, 237), she does not mean this to be an exhaustive account of maternal thinking. For her, care is a moral orientation, and moral orientations involve "distinctive cognitive capacities, appeal to distinctive ideals of rationality, elicit distinctive moral emotions, presume distinctive conceptions of identity and relationships, recognize distinctive virtues, and make distinctive demands on institutions" (Ruddick 1995, 204). The distinction between feelings of care and adequate caring work is most clear when Ruddick speaks of the possibility of emotionally caring but nonetheless assaultive mothers who "may believe that assault is a useful or even necessary instrument of training" (213). Therefore, there is a sharp distinction between emotional feelings of care and caring work that meets its aims.

Mistaking the focus on morality to imply that caring work is primarily a matter of an emotional orientation is one specific form of a more general tendency to recognize that particular capacities and talents are involved in mothering work but to interpret them as natural. Held, Ruddick, and Tronto, among others, encourage us to see caring work as involving skills that some men and women may possess more than others and that are developed and perfected with experience and training. Held observes that in nonfeminist moral theory, mothering is almost totally absent: "Until Sara Ruddick wrote her paper 'Maternal Thinking,' there had been virtually no philosophical recognition that mothers think, that there are characteristic standards for reasoning in this activity, and that one can discern moral values being striven for and expressed in this practice" (Held 1993, 88).

Failure to appreciate the extent to which skills are required to do a good job caring for children not only can lead to failure to meet the real needs of children, but also can devalue what caregivers have to offer. Understanding the work involved in childcare as unskilled childminding is then used to justify either no or very poor rates of pay for those who do this work. Baukje Miedema writes, for instance, that when the Canadian government advertises for foster mothers, the advertisements claim that no particular skills are required, just a loving heart (Miedema 1999). Certainly, the low rates of compensation for foster parents in Canada suggests that the rate of pay is in keeping with the view of this work as both unskilled and something that should be performed as a labor of love, rather than for money.

Many who provide care for children interpret their work as being natural, and they associate this naturalness with motherhood. Those who provide paid care who interpret themselves as "motherlike" in accordance with the ideology of motherhood are likely both to see themselves as unskilled and to set themselves up for exploitation by governments or other employers, since good mothers love children naturally and care for those children whether or not they are recompensed for their work.

By contrast, arguing, as Ruddick does, that persons who care for children are engaged in maternal thinking, involving their intellectual and emotional capacities and requiring skills in order to do the work well, is a significant challenge to many aspects of essential motherhood. Some of the intellectual demands Ruddick speaks of include welcoming change, "the most exigent intellectual demand on those who foster growth" (Ruddick 1989, 89); "concrete thinking," which involves disciplined attention to children and their circumstances (98); developing the ability to relish complexity, tolerate ambiguity, and multiply options; and learning how to tell stories that help both the mother and the child to understand the child as attempting to construct a coherent self (93).

We do not want, on the other hand, to underemphasize the embodied aspects of care or to reject continuities between other animal species and human caregiving. Cynthia Willett argues that if society valued socialization itself, the pleasures and praxis of the caregiver may be discovered to occur in other animal species "without that labor being reduced to the work of Cartesian machines" (Willett 1995, 40). However, she seems to overemphasize the physical and emotional aspects of the caregiver-child relation and to devalue the mental work and attention involved. Her account of caring for children focuses almost exclusively on such activities as cradling, touching, tickling, and nursing. While physical contact is an important part of caring for young children, and thinking can be embodied in such activities as pattern making and music making with those children, we need to recognize that maternal thinkers, in meeting the needs of children, do work that is simultaneously physical, intellectual, and emotional.

## 3. WHO CAN BE MATERNAL THINKERS?

### *(a) Maternal Thinking and Biological Motherhood*

Recognizing the work involved in caring for young children as a distinctive practice involving characteristic skills, virtues, and aims is one important step in challenging the ideology of motherhood. But we are still left wondering whether all forms of caring for children involve maternal thinking and who is capable of engaging in this practice. One of the most obvious questions raised by calling this maternal thinking or work done by mothering persons is the question of whether men can be maternal thinkers. Both Held and Ruddick are with some qualifications happy to recognize men as maternal thinkers. Ruddick explicitly acknowledges that "although maternal thinking arises out of actual child-caring practices, biological parenting is neither necessary nor sufficient. Many women and some men express maternal thinking in various kinds of working and caring with others" (Ruddick 1983a, 225). Held similarly notes that she intends the phrase "mothering person" to be gender-neutral (Held 1993, 198): "A child is mothered by whoever protects, nurtures, and trains her" (35). If men feel uncomfortable having their work described that way, she notes, perhaps this echoes women's discomfort at being described as "economic men." She continues: "To a large extent the activity of mothering is as open to men as to women. Possibly fathers could come to be as emotionally close, or as close through caretaking, to children as mothers are" (80).

However, both Held and Ruddick agree with Susan Rae Peterson (Peterson 1983) that for now, at least, the work should be given a name associated with mothers, rather than the more universal term parenting, so as both to not give a false picture of gender neutrality regarding who currently does the work and to honor the greater amount of work women have done. Both also have some reservations about making a sharp separation between the kind of mothering work done by women who are pregnant and give birth, which of course is available only to women (and not all women at that) and the kind of mothering work that is in principle open to anyone who cares for a child once born.

Whitbeck is more extreme than Ruddick and Held in that she thinks that it is almost[5] necessary to have given birth, and experienced that vulnerability, in order to be capable of responding appropriately to the vulnerability of children. She downplays the extent to which there are other experiences that both nonbirthgiving women and men can have that prepare them for a recognition of their own and others' vulnerability. For Whitbeck, it is not just socialization that causes men and women to care differently for their children, but different experiences women have as a result of their biology, experiences involved in pregnancy, labor, childbirth, nursing, and postpartum recovery (Whitbeck 1983b, 186).

Ruddick and Held do not make as strong a connection as Whitbeck does between biological reproductive experiences and activities involved in caring for young children, but both have some degree of discomfort with entirely divorcing pregnancy and birthgiving from the work involved in caring for children once they are born. As discussed in the previous chapter on birth, in her 1994 essay, "Thinking Mothers/ Conceiving Birth," Ruddick expresses concern that in separating "mothering" from birthgiving, she demoted birthing women to breeders and promoted the mental over the physical. Perhaps the problem here is the assumption that if we find it easy to recognize that men and those women who have never been pregnant can be mothers, then we should think of pregnancy and birth as essentially different in kind from the work carried out by maternal thinkers, and therefore as merely biological events. However, as my arguments in the preceding chapters have shown, we can make a clear distinction between the work involved in carrying and giving birth to a child from the work involved in caring for the child once he or she is born without being in any way required to see pregnancy and birthgiving as purely natural activities.

Instead, we can recognize pregnancy and birthgiving as social activities, as forms of caregiving, and as involving both choices and periods of intellectual activity, without as a result thinking of the work done by men and others who do not give birth to the children they care for as anything less legitimate than the mothering work done by birthgivers. I suspect that the only reason we might think there is a problem here is because we assume that there is always one person who is the real mother, such that if we accept that stepmothers and fathers and adoptive parents can be the real maternal thinkers, we seem to have denied the role of mothers and maternal thinkers to birthgivers, particularly those who do not continue to be engaged with the children they birth. If we disabuse ourselves of the notion that one and only one person must be recognized as a child's mother, then we can recognize that there are no legitimate reasons to argue that only biological mothers can be maternal thinkers.[6]

### *(b) Maternal Thinking and Gender*

While actively involved fathers and other male caregivers, adoptive parents, lesbian co-parents, and others who did not give birth to a child are all challenges to that aspect of the ideology of motherhood that suggests that motherhood is essentially a natural biological relation, they represent different levels of challenges to other aspects of that ideology. The ideology of motherhood assumes not only that mothers are biological mothers, but also that they are heterosexual women married to and financially dependent on husbands. Heterosexual women who remain outside the paid work force to raise a child they have adopted with a man to whom they are married and on whom they are financially dependent are much less of a challenge – if they also maintain traditional gender divisions in their labor – to the ideology of motherhood than are two gay men or two lesbians who co-parent a child biologically related to one or neither of them.

The gay couple or the lesbian couple may also act in ways that mirror traditional gender roles, with one person being designated the stay-at-home primary caregiving "mother" and the other designated the less involved, income-providing "father." To this extent, their family arrangements may be more in keeping with some aspects of essential motherhood than those of heterosexual couples who are both biologically related to the child they care for in some more collaborative manner. Single parents, including biological mothers, biological fathers, and adoptive parents, similarly challenge the assumption that care is and should be provided by one parent who is with the children all the time while another parent is the breadwinner.

As Diana Meyers observes, "after a quarter of a century of feminist critique and activism, little progress has been made in uncoupling care giving from gender" (Meyers 2003, 19). As a result, women who perform caregiving work, whether or not they are birthgivers, heterosexual, married, or employed outside the home, do not represent threats to gendered associations between femininity and care in the same way as men do. This is true not only when children are cared for by fathers, but also when children are cared for by paid male childcare providers.

Susan Murray observes that childcare is a gendered occupation in at least three different senses. Childcare workers are expected to be female;

female childcare workers are socially (although not economically) rewarded for their work; and childcare is seen to be in continuity with the feminine role accorded women within a gendered division of labor within the family (Murray 1996, 371). Male childcare workers are hired, but they make up only 3 to 6 percent of the childcare work force, and they tend to be singled out by employers, other daycare workers, and parents as "being something other than a child care worker" because of their sex (373). They tend to be differentially rewarded for being male childcare workers and assigned a higher status and sometimes pay as a result, but also are regarded with suspicion. For instance, they are often either explicitly or tacitly prevented from performing some types of childcare activities (such as cuddling with and soothing an upset child) that are considered to be legitimate only when women undertake them.

Men who perform a significant amount of primary care for young children, whether as paid caregivers, actively involved fathers, or in other roles, certainly represent a challenge to the role laid out for them in the ideology of motherhood. Cynthia Willett suggests that while there are no legitimate reasons to argue that only biological mothers can be maternal thinkers, men can be maternal thinkers only if they are open to redefining masculinity. Nurturers become nurturers in interaction with a child: "This social interaction with the parent not only transforms the infant; it also transforms the subjectivity of the one who takes care of the child. For men, this transformation can occur only if manhood is redefined to include not only fathering but also parenting the child" (Willett 1995, 56).

We need, first, to challenge the implicit view here that fathers are the only men to act as caregivers for young children. Willett has a tendency to speak interchangeably of the mother-child relation, the parent-child relation, and the caregiver-child relation (Willet 1995, 40). This may sound progressive, in that she recognizes that fathers and other caregivers can act as primary nurturers to young children. However, her claim that men can become nurturers only if they redefine the meaning of fatherhood suggests that only men who are fathers will act in this capacity.

Moreover, we also need to ask whether the redefinition of manhood that Willett rightly suggests means that men can become maternal thinkers only when they come up with ways of distinguishing between masculine and feminine forms of childcare. It is clear that some male caregivers do this. For instance, Murray notes that some male paid childcare providers think of themselves as delivering what women cannot – fatherlike care – and certainly many of those who come into contact with these male daycare providers see themselves as bringing masculinity to their daycare work (Murray 1996, 374). But do we have any reason to think that men engaged in actively caring for young children will necessarily see themselves as doing something other than what women do? Might not they instead redefine the work of childcare in order to highlight aspects of this work that are congruent with more hegemonic masculinity?

Male daycare workers tend to emphasize the academic and intellectual nature of the work they do (Murray 1996, 374). While this differentiates them from their colleagues who emphasize the emotional nature of the work they do, this emphasis is also shared by many of their female colleagues, especially those who argue that daycare should be seen as a profession. The most innovative work in theorizing childcare argues that this work should be seen both as a profession requiring skills, education, and training and as a form of highly emotionally charged work (Kyle 1997). But whichever approach one may take to defining paid childcare, none of these approaches has any reason to endorse the view that men and women should do the work of caring for children differently, although men and women may differentially highlight aspects of the work that are more congruent with their masculine or feminine gender identities. Is this different when the care is provided not by paid workers but within the family? If paid male daycare workers can do "mothering work," can unpaid fathers also be "maternal thinkers"?

In Ruddick's earlier work, her reflections on the feminist psychoanalytic work of Nancy Chodorow led her to suggest that maternal thinking is different for women and men, because women are daughters, and women's role in mothering tends to produce an identification between mother and daughter (Ruddick 1983a, 236). Yet this does not provide us with reason to believe that maternal thinking, as a practice guided by specific aims, would or should differ for men and women. If anything, it instead suggests that men may find it difficult to overcome the extent to which they are encouraged to separate from their mothers and motherly activities, but it does not tell us anything about how they might behave when they reject the expectation that they should not be active caregivers and begin to engage in caregiving activities.

Since hegemonic masculinity is associated in contemporary western societies with income-generating work, it is in tension with performing unpaid work as a father, particularly when the father is a primary caregiver and leaves the paid work force. Men who choose to perform this role emphasize their willingness to depart both from the assumption that their value is determined in the paid work force and from the role of fathers assigned by the ideology of motherhood. In Brandth and Kvande's study of Norwegian men who took year-long paid parental leave, the authors found that the men in many ways borrowed aspects of ideal motherhood, particularly its emphasis on closeness, frequent contact, and everyday acts of caregiving, in their construction of their fathering work.

However, these men also differed from women in their vision of the work involved in caring for young children in three ways: They sharply differentiated housework from childcare (a distinction largely made possible by their wives' labor); they integrated their children into their ongoing interests and work lives; and they saw themselves as teaching their children, even very young infants, to be independent (Brandth and Kvande 1998). In this way, and also by stressing the skills involved in their childcare work and their sense of accomplishment, they were able to incorporate their childcare work into their understandings of themselves as masculine. Brandth and Kvande argue that the childcare work they did should be entitled "masculine care" (310), and yet in their account the men differ little from women in their daily interactions with their children. Where they differ is in their attitudes toward this work, its continuity with their other projects, and in their sharp separation of housework and childcare work.

Why are some feminist researchers nonetheless committed to theorizing the existence of a masculine form of care, seen as meeting children's needs, but nonetheless in a manner distinct from maternal care? Radhika Chopra objects to any ideal of fathering that assimilates it to mothering because, she claims, "An irresolution lies at the heart of this apparently seamless move by these new fathers into nurturing practice . . . an irresolution that centres around masculinity itself. Does identification with a nurturing, care giving, overtly 'mothering' role entail a consequent repudiation of masculinity?" (Chopra 2001, 447). Because Chopra holds that it does, and fears that men's forays into active care for their children will be unstable so long as this requires them to repudiate their masculinity, she searches nonwestern societies for evidence of distinct but active fathering and turns as well to films in search of models of nurturant masculinity.

However, it is dangerous to celebrate a different form of fathering work without asking to what extent it meets the needs met by mothers who do this work. Why should we suppose that children would have different needs when being cared for by mothers or fathers? Does this form of masculine care exist not as an alternative to maternal care but as a supplement to it, since the fathers in this study could assume that whatever they left undone would be done by the mothers? Sara Ruddick warns that given the persistence of patriarchal ideologies, attempts to endorse an idea of "distinctive fatherhood" are likely to end up in support of male superiority (Ruddick 1996). Since men would already have to depart from traditional models of fathering and hegemonic versions of masculinity in order to become actively involved fathers – and many do express unhappiness with the model of fathering supported by the ideology of motherhood – it seems more promising to draw on male tendencies to highlight different aspects of childcare work in order to come up with a description of this work that shows ways in which this work is congruent with activities seen as traditionally feminine as well as those seen as traditionally masculine.

Fathers' accounts of the ideals governing their caring for young children might also be instructive in developing a fuller account of the virtues involved in this work, particularly if we contrast the virtues with characteristic temptations and vices with which fathers must struggle. Rather than celebrate the Norwegian fathers for their ability to feel that they were doing a good enough job with the children in their care and blame the Norwegian mothers for their higher standards and concomitant guilt, we might instead see that ideal practice veers away both from the fathers' intentions to disrupt their lives as little as possible in order to accommodate their infants and the mothers' extreme willingness to do so.

### *(c) How Many People Can Be Maternal Thinkers in Relation to One Child?*

When we ask whether a man can be a maternal thinker, we may be asking whether a man can serve as a primary caregiver, or we may be asking whether we can see men as participating equally with women in mothering a child. When we ask about the connections between biological mothering and maternal thinking, we may be asking whether others can substitute for the work of biological mothers, or we may be asking whether they may supplement it such that, for instance, stepmothers should be recognized as maternal thinkers when children continue to have relationships with their biological mothers as well (Downe 2001).

Some of these questions require us to ask about how many persons can function as maternal thinkers in relation to one child.

Lorraine Code argues that Ruddick's account of maternal thinking is chiefly applicable only to middle-class, two-parent, relatively affluent families (Code 1991, 94). In other words, maternal thinking conforms too closely to many aspects of the ideology of motherhood. This criticism may seem unfair in that nothing in my characterization of maternal thinking so far suggests that maternal thinking, with its focus on the preservation of children's lives and the enhancement of their growth and social acceptability, would take place only in the circumstances Code describes. However, some of the details of Ruddick's approach, particularly when she speaks of the difficulty mothers have in separating from their children as those children increase in their capacities for independence, does suggest a model of one woman working alone, tending to all the needs of and emotionally very attached to her children.

Black feminist theorists, including bell hooks and Patricia Collins, point to some of the limitations of the models of mothering work as carried out by one or perhaps two people in a family. In contrast, they acknowledge the important role "othermothers" play in the caretaking of children. "Othermothers" may be kin to a child – aunts, grandmothers, or grandfathers – or they may be friends of the child's parents or members of a close-knit community. The model of one or two parents as solely responsible for raising their children does not adequately capture the reality of the circumstances in which many African American and African Canadian families raise their children (hooks 1984; Collins 1992, 1994; Hunter and Ensminger 1992; Bailey 1994). Patricia Hill Colllins's work played a major role in leading to the recognition that children may be mothered by more than one person. The involvement of extended kin and what Collins calls "fictive kin" in providing care for young children represents a significant challenge to the assumption that children are and should be raised by a small number of people living in one home.

Collins writes that there is an African American tradition of serving as othermothers to children whose mothers are unwilling or unable to provide for them. Some aspects of this tradition, particularly the notion of a communal responsibility for children, are radical breaks with the ideology of motherhood, but many of the examples Collins gives involve one woman, whether grandmother, aunt, or kind neighbor, taking over a role usually assigned to a generally absent biological mother, whom she calls a "bloodmother" (Collins 2000, 178–188).

Her suggestion that extended kin and fictive kin could supplement the involvement of biological mothers, rather than replacing them, is more of a challenge to essential motherhood, as is her observation that othermothers can serve to mediate the emotional intensity of relationships between bloodmothers and their daughters. Here it is a manner not simply of one person (in all of Collins's examples, a woman),[7] replacing another in the role of primary caregiver but of several persons sharing the work and the responsibility for children's care.

Perhaps in response to these criticisms, in Ruddick's more recent work she notes that some mothers "may work so closely with others that it is impossible to identify one 'mother'; others may share their work with many mothering persons, and some work primarily in couples" (Ruddick 1994, 35). Virginia Held similarly observes that "various persons may participate in mothering a child" (Held 1993, 206). However, Alison Bailey argues that Ruddick's formal acknowledgment of diversity is not reflected in her actual analysis of mothering work (Bailey 1994, 192). Held also sees the work involved in caring for young children as generally involving one person who is in a permanent and irreplaceable relation to a child (Held 1993, 206). We need to think more about how mothering work could be shared.

Another aspect of the ideology of motherhood's assumption that one mother can meet all the needs of her children is reflected in the assumption that mothers and the children they care for have no significant mental or physical impairments. This assumption is rarely challenged in feminist philosophical accounts of mothering. When parents with mental or physical impairments and parents of children with impairments write about their experiences, however, they make important challenges to the view of mothering work as something carried out by an isolated individual. I first discuss the claims made by mothers who have written about what mothering work means to them when they use other people, particularly personal care assistants (PCAs), to provide some hands-on care to their children. I then discuss the claims made by parents of children with mental or physical impairments, who have found it necessary to work with others to meet their children's needs

Mothers with mental or physical impairments dispute legal guidelines and government policies that will pay for PCAs who enable them to work outside the home but that refuse to pay for PCAs who would enable them to be productive by caring for young children (Reinelt and Fried 1992). Their accounts of the ways they share their mothering work with spouses and paid caregivers open up new opportunities to recognize mothering work as distributed across several persons.

However, in some of this discourse there is a problematic tendency to devalue the work of paid assistants, by seeing this work as not itself a form of mothering work, and also to make an overly sharp distinction between the "real" mothering involved in supervising and being aware of what needs to be done and the mere manual labor of those who are in physical contact with the child (Reinelt and Fried 1992). While I am sympathetic to the attempt by mothers with physical or mental impairments to get recognition for their care for their children as mothering, I think that we would not need to devalue the work of their paid assistants if we did not think that mothering work must be assignable to only one individual. This devaluing of the hands-on labor also suggests one danger associated with the term "maternal thinking" such that we could come to think of the real work involved in caring for children as the planning involved in seeking to preserve their lives, encourage their growth, and ensure their social acceptability. This would then devalue physical, hands-on care.

In other words, we might overemphasize the cognitive element involved in maternal thinking, overlook the extent to which much of this thinking must be embodied, and end up with a picture of supervisory maternal thinkers working with assistants who do not need to think but instead merely carry out their orders and use their bodily capacities to meet the bodily needs of the children. In relation to Berenice Fisher and Joan Tronto's distinction between taking care of and caregiving, this understanding of maternal thinking would be linked more to the former than to the latter. "Taking care of" involves assuming responsibility for what one cares about but may, as Fisher and Tronto observe, involve delegating the tasks involved in caregiving to another (Fisher and Tronto 1990). In "caregiving," by contrast, "the caregiver must be ready to revise her care giving strategy according to moment-by-moment or day-by-day conditions. To make such revision requires experience, skill, and ultimately, judgment" (1990, 43).

As Barbara Katz Rothman points out, there is already a literature addressed to employed mothers encouraging them to think of their relationship to paid caregivers in a way that downplays the skills involved in hands-on caregiving. Katz Rothman finds that reading such books and listening to such conversations is deeply troubling in part because she observes that she is "listening to women talking about the mothering work of other women in a way that sounds to me like Victorian fathers must have talked about their wives" (Katz Rothman 1994, 202). This will often have implications for how children learn about social classes. Katz Rothman notes that if a child begins with a strong attachment to his or her caregiver and then switches it to his or her mother, a person with more social power, this is like the switch in allegiance from mother to father, but instead of gender, it involves class (205).

While mothers with mental or physical impairments challenge some aspects of ideologies of motherhood, mothers of children with significant impairments have also spoken of the problems created for them by the assumption that one mother should be able to address on her own all the needs of her children. As Barbara Hillyer observes, professionals have often criticized mothers of children with impairments, "frequently assuming that the child's 'treatment' should be the sole or central focus on the mother's life, though the mother should not, of course, be overprotective" (Hillyer 1993, 88). Mother blaming, as a result, is pervasive. These mothers highlight the need for a more collective approach to the work done by mothering persons. Hillyer writes of how enormously difficult it was for her personally to surrender some of her many roles of interpreter, teacher, trainer, and therapist and to recognize that she was simply not strong enough to simultaneously fulfill the many roles needed to meet her daughter's needs (1993, 247).

In calling for a recognition of the need for a collective approach to mothering work, Hillyer and Kittay, both mothers of daughters with physical and mental impairments, also warn of the dangers of devaluing hands-on care and overvaluing the expertise and specific roles of clinical experts. Hillyer, for instance, writes that after her daughter was institutionalized, "the representatives of the 'direct-care staff' who attended her primary planning meeting were never those who knew her best; their status was too low to qualify them to attend staffings. On those rare occasions when such people did attend, they were invariably silenced by their lower status; they contributed their extremely valuable information only if I was able to consult them outside the meeting" (182). Hillyer provides an important warning about how the understanding of those who provide hands-on care as inferior to professionals sets up "barriers to mutuality . . . or even communication between members of the care giving network" (182). Kittay similarly speaks of a "rift between professionals and mothering person," a rift created by the different virtues guiding the two kinds of care and aggravated by the professionals' tendency to focus on only one aspect of the child (Kittay 1999, 22).

In her account of mothering her profoundly impaired daughter, Sesha, Kittay speaks of confronting the falsity of her initial belief that "with shared parenting one should be able to care for a child and still pursue an additional life's work" (11). She learns that mother and father are not enough; even the addition of a paid caregiver, Peggy, is not enough, and Kittay writes of reluctantly being forced by Sesha's overwhelming needs to move to a model of "distributed mothering" (13). Kittay clearly has some uneasiness with the model. She writes that she "never wanted to hire help to care for my child" (11) and also acknowledges that her conception of herself, her husband, Peggy, and others working as a team is sometimes less accurate than her unhappy recognition that her relationship with Peggy is sometimes "like the patriarchal relation of husband to wife vis-a-vis their children" (15). Moreover, Kittay does not suggest that the model of distributed mothering may be appropriate to describe what happens when children without profound mental or physical impairments are cared for by multiple caregivers. In this way, her departure from the model of mothering work as privatized is not seen as a potentially fruitful way for others to challenge this aspect of the ideology of motherhood. It is seen as something necessitated in some cases by the needs of a child, but also lamented.

### *(d) How Privatized Is the Work of Maternal Thinkers?*

As we have seen, the understanding of mothering work as private can and does involve several separate assumptions, and there are, accordingly, many different ways of challenging the claim that this is private work. Childcare is seen as a private activity because it tends to bodies and emotions in contrast to the less intimate, less insistently physical, and less emotional realm of civil society. Privacy is associated with the forms of physical and emotional intimacy thought to be appropriate to relations among friends, families, and lovers. Mother work is also considered to be private when it is associated with parental autonomy, with the freedom of parents to raise their children in ways they see fit (except when abuse is suspected). Responsibility for childcare is privatized when children are seen as private goods and therefore neither a public resource nor a public responsibility. Finally, mother work is seen as private in that the motivations for undertaking it are seen to be ideally ones of love and care rather than economic gain.

Feminist criticisms of the public-private distinction have been explored extensively for at least the past two decades (Elshtain 1981;

Pateman 1988; and Boyd 1997 are but a few of the thinkers). In summary, presenting the distinction between the private and the public as natural and unchanging can obscure the workings of power in the private realm. It can hide the way problematic organizations of private life along sexist lines shape public life, and it may cause us simultaneously to romanticize and denigrate aspects of life considered private.

One aspect of privacy is the understanding that a mother is working alone. Even if she shares her work with others, this work may still be seen as private if each person works one at a time. This is often accompanied by the assumption that whoever cares for young children will do so in a private home, rather than in a setting where many individuals work together and have frequent contact with one another and other members of the public. A third and related aspect of conceiving of childcare work as private is the assumption that this work happens in the family. Even when it takes place outside the family, parents and caregivers may see the work as being family-like. Each of these elements – working alone, working in a home, and working within the family – could be separately contested, without necessarily contesting the other assumptions.

A fourth aspect of understanding of mothering work as private is the assumption that the work involved in caring for young children is a private or familial responsibility as opposed to a larger social responsibility. Children may be cared for in ways that challenge the assumption of privacy in several ways: They may be cared for outside the family, in a relatively public setting such as a daycare center, and by several people working as a team. However, if the parents are seen as solely responsible for choosing and paying for that child's care, then elements of the understanding of mothering work as private have been retained.

We need to make sure that we do not essentially privatize our conception of maternal thinking. While feminists such as Jean Bethke Elshtain recognize that the work involved in caring for young children contributes essentially to the public good and argue that we should see the work as therefore a public activity, she and others still think of mothering work as taking place chiefly or solely within private homes and to be the chief responsibility of private families. DiQuinzio points out that Elshtain tends to suggest that the only alternative to raising children in private homes is to raise children in a coldhearted institutional setting, in which they are not allowed to form emotional bonds with their caregivers, or in an anti-authoritarian commune, in which they are inadequately supervised and left pretty much to their own devices (DiQuinzio 1999, 82).

In her discussion of "Family and Polis," Held argues, much like Elshtain, that we can rethink family relations not only in terms of the reproduction of persons, but also regarding their rearing, and suggests that as a result we can question the association of women with the domestic and men with the political and public. As discussed in the previous chapter on birth, I am in full agreement with her insistence that we see "giving birth and mothering as central human activities rather than as merely natural, biological events" (Held 1993, 134) and her claim that family relations have political significance. However, I think we also need to rethink our expectation that childrearing either occurs within the family home or must model family relations. Instead, we must acknowledge how much childrearing occurs outside the family home and how much childrearing is done by paid providers, whether inside or outside the family home.

In yet another kind of challenge to the idea that mothering work belongs to the private realm, Amy Rossiter's analysis of difficulties that new mothers experience in being expected to do their mothering work in isolation in private homes led her to argue that mothers must be made more comfortable when they venture out of private homes with their children. It is important for women to feel that they can take their young children into public places without censure, whether to nurse their babies in public, to socialize with others, or to carry out tasks they need to accomplish. However, they or their surrogates are still thought to be moving through the public world in a manner consistent with their chief or sole responsibility for the children in their care (Rossiter 1988).

Calls for social support for mothering work, for instance, by Australian social policy researcher Marty Grace and U.S. philosopher Eva Feder Kittay, represent another kind of challenge to the ideology of motherhood's privatization of motherhood. Marty Grace calls for governmental financial support for mothering. She argues against the view that "having children is some sort of private indulgence that brings individual benefits to parents, and is of no public value" (Grace 1998, 410) and argues that when we see that raising children is of public value, we should stop exploiting mothers in particular by holding them responsible for raising their children. Grace proposes that the way to remedy this is to ensure that public resources are attached to the mother role. These resources could then be used either to provide adequate material resources for mothering work done by the mothers themselves or to "purchase services to reduce their amount of work related to that role" or to pay for childcare that the women could use to "participate in sports and recreation, education and training, and professional development activities as well as to undertake paid employment" (411).

There are many aspects of Grace's proposals, including her call for studies of the activities involved in the work of caring for children of different ages "to establish work value and some benchmarks of the time required to provide a reasonable level of care" (412), that represent significant advances in the understanding of the work involved in caring for young children. Her reminder that even children who attend long hours of daycare still require a great deal of work from their parents, usually mothers, in their hours at home, her calls for adequate financial support for mothering work, her criticism of the categorigation of the work of caring for young children as nonwork and unskilled, and her focus on the "continuing exploitation of the labor of the women who carry out the vast bulk of the unpaid work of caring for young children" (410) are all important, as is her insistence that we should not think that "any remuneration would taint the purity of maternal devotion" (410).

However, I do have some concerns about the way in which mothers appear to get the social recognition and financial remuneration for caring for their children, possibly at the expense of the people, mainly women, who are hired while their mothers are in paid employment, leisure activities, and professional development. Grace insists that in order to resist dichotomizing mothers into working and nonworking, she defines mothers' responsibilities for the care of their children to mean "personally caring for, or responsible for arranging alternative care for young children" (402). If, as she writes, resources are attached to the mother role, and some of these resources are to be used to purchase services that reduce the workload associated with that role, this seems to give both lower status and less money to the women from whom they would purchase these services. While her proposals are progressive in recognizing that both mothers doing paid work outside the home and mothers providing hands-on care are still engaged in forms of mothering work, it sets up potential exploitation of those others, typically women, who will be doing the paid work. It also suggests, despite her insistence on the value of the actual work involved, that the "true mothering person" is the one who pays for and supervises, rather than the one who performs, the daily work. Since I agree that taking care of young children is work, and this work requires adequate material resources to support it, it appears to me that the public funds should be used to remunerate those who actually do the work, as well as to provide them with adequate resources, food, toys, and space in order to care for the children in a way that encourages their growth, meets their bodily needs, and keeps them safe.

Eva Feder Kittay offers a doulia model of social caring that, like Grace's proposal, is in some ways a significant challenge to the privatization of care, but this still suggests that childcare responsibilities would be met by one person, usually the mother, who would then receive support from another caregiver not in meeting the needs of her child but in meeting her own needs. Kittay's insistence that people meeting the needs of dependent persons, who form a class she calls dependency workers, need and deserve social support for their work is an important challenge to an understanding of dependency as solely the responsibility of private families. She writes: "Let us use the term 'doulia' to refer to an arrangement by which service is passed on so that those who become needy by virtue of tending to those in need can be cared for as well" (Kittay 1997, 233).

Moreover, as mentioned earlier, elsewhere Kittay, in her philosophical reflections on her care for her daughter, does explicitly discuss the need for several persons to share the work of meeting her daughter's needs, but I remain concerned that her model of doulia, when applied to the work of mothering persons, as she does herself, in itself suggests that the needs of the child are best met by one person, who then herself needs support. The example of a doula assisting a postpartum mother suggests that the work involved in caring for young children is exhausting, but the emphasis on the mother's need for bodily recovery from childbirth can make it seem as if once the mother was physically recovered, she would not need assistance in meeting her child's needs. Moreover, I worry that if the doula was thought to be a kind of personal assistant to the mothering person and was paid to help her, a hierarchical relationship would be set up in which the mothering work would be conceived of as most important, and the work of the doula would be secondary to allowing the mother to meet the needs of her child. This is similar to the worry expressed by Diemut Bubeck. She writes that even if "a carer has systematic access to care provided by others – 'third parties' . . . such access cannot be provided privately, either unpaid or via the market, without raising further problems about the uneven provision of such access and the exploitation of badly paid caregivers" (Bubeck 2002, 177). As a result, she concludes that "private provision of care does not solve the problem" (177).

In the works of Elshtain, Held, Ruddick, and Willett, and even in that of Grace, Kittay, and Rossiter, the provision of child care is still linked to privatized motherhood. Moreover, the work involved in caring for young children is still primarily characterized by many feminists and their targets alike as in sharp contrast to work performed in public and in exchange for pay. Feminist philosophers seem not to have let their knowledge that much of the care that children receive is performed by workers who are paid for their labor (albeit insufficiently) and who make decisions about whether or not to take on and continue this work partly out of economic motives sufficiently affect their conceptualizations of mothering work. Instead, Held, for instance, describes mothering work as involving a permanent relation to a child in which the work is undertaken for reasons that are entirely different from the reasons we have to enter into contracts with one another. She writes: "The relation between mothering person and child is not voluntary and therefore not contractual. The ties that bind mothering person and child are affectional and solicitous on the one hand, and emotional and dependent on the other. . . . The relation should be voluntary for the mothering person, but it cannot possibly be so for the young child" (Held 1993, 204). She also speaks of the relation between mothering person and child as normally being a permanent and irreplaceable relation (206) that is generally not the case for paid caregivers.

While Held is right that parents and others rarely choose to care for children for economic reasons alone, many people who provide childcare do this work for pay, and parents and others who provide it also sometimes make decisions about whether or not they will be the ones doing the childcare work for partly economic reasons. Moreover, while some people do provide childcare for pay, Held is right to observe that the contract would be not between the caregiver and child, but instead between the caregiver and whoever pays her, whether a parent or a public agency. However, we need to be careful not to make too sharp a contrast between mothering work and paid work, or we will end up with a picture of child care that legitimates low salaries and a lack of clear limits on workload because of ambivalence about the very existence of childcare for pay.

### *(e) Can We Pay People to Be Maternal Thinkers?*

Must those who care for young children be volunteers in order to count as maternal thinkers or mothering persons? One prominent feature of Patricia Hill Collins's analysis is that the othermothers she writes about all volunteer and work for free. Collins suggests that "purchasing services appears to be the hallmark of American middle-class existence. In this context, stopping to help others to whom one is not related and doing it for free can be seen as rejecting the values of the capitalist market economy" (Collins 2000, 182). This may be a challenge to capitalism, but it also leaves people, mostly women, taking on additional work without compensation, and this may leave them without resources needed to meet their own needs, as well as those of the children for whom they care.

Why might we think that those who care for young children compromise their ability to do their work when they are paid for it? Joan Tronto speaks of a tension in one primary virtue required of care providers: "In order to be attentive to the needs of others one must relinquish the absolute primacy of the needs of the self. In this regard, attentive care is incompatible with the paradigmatic relationship of modern society, exchange" (Tronto 1995, 107). The paradigm of market relations "involves the assertion that one knows one's own interests best"; it "involves putting one's own interests first"; and "it involves reducing complex relationships into terms that can be made equivalent" (1995, 107).

While this may be an accurate description of the paradigmatic relationship of modern markets, it is not, as Tronto would clearly acknowledge, an accurate description of the working lives of many paid caregivers. Feminist economist Julie Nelson argues that we fear that "if an activity were, in some sense, fully paid for, then it would come to obey the laws of anonymous, objectified, self-interested exchange" (Nelson 1999, 44). This view leads us to make sharp dichotomies between the market economy and caring labor. Nancy Folbre, for instance, defines caring labor as work "undertaken out of affection or a sense of responsibility of others, and with no expectation of immediate pecuniary reward" (Folbre 1995, 75).

Nelson notes that the need to make an overly sharp distinction between caring labor and the paid economy, such that we actually worry about whether or not it is appropriate to pay people to care, is because we have a tendency to confuse "the market" as a "complex metaphor which we can use as one lens for examining social interactions" with concrete reality (Nelson 1999, 45). Actual markets may differ quite dramatically from the idealized market, and childcare markets, in particular, "tend to be examples of 'rich' markets in which the movement of money is only one dimension in a complex relationship of child, caregivers, and parents including elements of (when it is going well) trust, affection, and appreciation. A market relation between people who don't know each other, who are each acting in their 'own interests' in a transaction of pure commodity exchange, is only one of many possibilities" (1999, 46).

Even solutions such as that presented by Virginia Held, which argue that we can come to accept the legitimacy of paid childcare if we see it as in the market in the sense that it is paid and yet not in the market in the sense that it is not governed by market norms (Held 2002), suggest that there is a tension between providing good care and acting from self-interest. This logic suggests that whether or not family day care or nanny care would be problematic would depend on the motive of the caregiver, with the appropriate motive presumably being the intention of providing excellent care, rather than the intention of obtaining things the worker herself needs. This oversimplifies the complex motivations women have for performing paid childcare, which often include beliefs about the value of the work, their suitability for it, the importance of providing unpaid care to their own children, the need for income, and their disinclination or inability to obtain other kinds of employment.

In giving an adequate account of caring labor, such as that undertaken by those who provide childcare for pay, we need to be careful to avoid making overly sharp distinctions between care as a feature of relationships and care as a kind of labor. In her more recent work, Ruddick begins to make such a distinction, arguing that she now intends to "distinguish more clearly two aspects of practice – work and relationships in excess of work" (Ruddick 1998, 22). She recognizes that there is significant emotional work involved in caring for children, whether this is paid or unpaid, writing that caring labor requires "an ability to interpret, control, and encourage emotions" (1998, 24). This is in keeping with the most innovative work in theorizing child care, which argues that this work should be seen both as a profession requiring skills, education, and training and as a form of highly emotionally charged work (Kyle 1997). However, I have some discomfort with the contrast Ruddick draws between emotionally involved mothers and fathers, as opposed to caring and controlled daycare workers "trained to respond appropriately to emotions" (Ruddick 1998, 12).

Borrowing the concept of intensive mothering from Sharon Hays (1996), Ruddick contrasts the intensive caring of those who are emotionally and intellectually engrossed in the well-being of those they care for with the care provided by paid helpers. These intensive carers then "engage personally and thoughtfully in the selection of helpers – day care centers, child tenders in their homes, health aides, who participate less intensively in caring work" (Ruddick 1998, 17). Ruddick seems to me to make too sharp a distinction between the caring relationship involved in the parent-child relationship and the less intensive caring provided by the paid "helper." This can seem uncomfortably close to the model in which mothers (and fathers) hire paid caregivers to provide purely custodial care, chosen and closely supervised by them, and ended whenever it suits them.

I am confident that Ruddick would not intend this distinction to legitimate parental control over paid caregivers, to the point where the paid caregivers would not be licensed to use their own judgment in responding to the needs of the children in their care, for this would be in tension with her work that recognizes maternal thinking as growing out of the practice of caring for children. I do not, moreover, have clear suggestions as to how to balance the competing values, needs, and priorities of parents and paid caregivers who both have a stake in shaping the care that is provided. What I wish to do instead is to make a modest suggestion: that we recognize that both do have a stake and begin to make explicit decisions about how to resolve such conflicts and bring such debates into public discourse.

Paid caregivers consistently speak of themselves as engaged not only in meeting a child's needs for physical comfort, safety, and opportunities for growth, but also in performing a kind of emotional labor.[8] Whether caregivers are paid or unpaid, they need to moderate the display of their emotions around the children they care for, and they are bound to feel a wide variety of emotions, such as anger at a child who persists in injuring others or attacking the caregiver, pride in the accomplishments of the children and in their own work and its impact, delight in the spontaneous affection and joy of the children, and worry when the children are not doing well or experience threats to their well-being. What paid caregivers often find most difficult to manage are discontinuities between their powerful feelings for the children in their care and the expectation that they will moderate the display of these emotions, particularly around parents (Kousha 1995; Macdonald 1998; Murray 1998). Macdonald, in particular, observes that, in service of the ideology of motherhood, mothers and nannies often perform extra work devoted to downplaying the work and emotional involvement of the nanny in order to create an image of the self-sufficient nuclear family (Macdonald 1998, 49).

They need to do this extra emotional work precisely because of the way parents, especially mothers, often feel threatened by the bonds formed between caregivers and the children in their care. Feminist sociologist Lynet Uttal has studied the "microideologies" that employed mothers develop about paid child care. Microideologies manage tensions between ideologies and aspects of lived experience. As she notes, microideologies differ in the extent to which they adhere to or challenge dominant ideologies, in this case the ideology of motherhood. She observes that there are three primary strategies used by employed mothers to explain the meaning they give to having other persons regularly care for their children, in light of the dominant expectations that mothers are best suited to meeting all the needs of their children. Some mothers set sharp limits on what the child care providers were supposed to do and make sharp distinctions between mothering care and custodial care. Paid providers are thought to deliver custodial care, "providing adult supervision and meeting immediate physical and emotional needs (such as feeding, physical safety, diaper changes, and attention to minor hurts)" (Uttal 1996, 298). Moreover, the mothers see themselves as supervising and controlling this type of care, even in their absence. As Uttal notes, this does challenge the ideology of motherhood's requirement that the mothers always be physically present; no other aspects of the ideology are challenged.

In particular I am concerned that this approach to paid care encourages us to think of the work involved in caring for young children in terms analyzed by Rosanna Hertz, who speaks of parents who take a market approach to hiring other people to care for their children. While I think Hertz is wrong to think that this market approach necessarily brings with it a de-skilling of motherhood, breaking apart a set of practices once thought to belong together as a whole, she is right to criticize parents who break the mother role into separate components, especially those who sharply separate the emotional and intensively physical care thought to be appropriate for young infants, and often associated with nonwhite women, from the more educated professionally skilled care thought to be provided by white western European caregivers.

It is not the turn to the market economy that is the problem. Instead, the problem is the fragmentation of labor involved in parceling out different aspects of the job of mothering as if they could be carried out by separate and easily replaceable individuals. In their discussion of the dangers of fragmentation of labor, Uttal and Tuominen warn that childcare is not a type of work that, when done well, can be easily divided into discrete and clearly defined components. When the work is fragmented, moreover, the authors observe that the lowest status element of this work – the physical care – is frequently delegated to women at the lower end of racial and class hierarchies.

We have seen the dangers involved in the strategy adopted by mothers who fragmented the labor involved in caring for young children. In Uttal's study of employed mothers' interpretations of the work of the paid providers they hired, a second group of employed mothers saw the paid providers as surrogate mothers and sought out paid providers who would act as mothers to the children they were paid to care for. These mothers challenged the assumption that mothering can be accomplished only by a child's mother but continued to see mothering in alignment with the ideology of motherhood.

Moreover, while Uttal focuses only on the meaning that employed mothers give to their childcare arrangements, it is also important to think about the consequences of having the paid providers adopt this model of care. Ample sociological evidence suggests that many paid providers see themselves as surrogate mothers, or the "true mothering person," because of the time they spend with a child, meeting the child's needs and encouraging his or her development. This is demonstrated in Margaret Nelson's study of family daycare providers. Family daycare, a form of childcare provided in a private home other than the child's own, is the most common form of out-of-the-home care for very young children in North America. Nelson observes that most "family day care providers align themselves with mothering (rather than with a more professional stance) as a model for the care they give" (Nelson 1990, 211).

In some cases this conception leads the paid providers to be hostile toward the mothers, who are seen to voluntarily or too easily leave their children with another "mother." In other cases, for instance, in Baukje Miedema's study of foster mothers, this microideology encourages foster mothers to think of the biological mothers they replace as bad mothers who cannot be redeemed and should not be worked with, rather than as mothers who could benefit from their expertise or who need to enhance their skills.

Moreover, when paid providers think of themselves as surrogate mothers, they sometimes have difficulty insisting that they be paid for their work. For instance, Margaret Nelson observed many instances in which family daycare providers were exploited, especially when parents threatened to seek out alternative childcare arrangements if the providers were not willing to provide additional hours of unpaid work. The family daycare providers are reluctant to surrender children whom they have "mothered" to the socially recognized mothers who have the power to make decisions about who will look after their children.

In addition to microideological interpretations of childcare as custodial care and surrogate care, in Uttal's study a third group of employed mothers saw the paid providers as working in concert with them to provide coordinated care. This approach is the most significant challenge to the ideology of motherhood in that it "reconstructs mothering as not only a transferable activity but also one that can be jointly accomplished by several caregivers" (Uttal 1996, 309). The mothers and the paid providers work together, learn from one another, and see themselves as socializing children as well as seeing to their emotional and physical safety. Uttal sees this as the most promising approach in terms of the best interests of women and children and also sees it as a redefinition of childrearing from a privatized activity to a social one. While I agree that it has important advantages over models of custodial care or surrogate care, I am concerned that interpreting paid providers as "comothering" and "like parents" (303) may not be enough to recognize this work as public rather than private. It may also encourage parents and paid providers to think about paid care in terms that, like surrogate care, set up a tension between caring and working for pay.

Finally, it may, very much like the concept of "maternal thinking" itself, obscure differences between the role of a parent and that of a child's caregiver. The intellectual, bodily, and emotional work involved in seeking to meet a child's needs may be called "maternal thinking" by Ruddick and "mothering work" by Held, but this work is quite separable, both practically and conceptually, from other aspects of being a child's mother or parent. Parents are held to have financial and legal responsibility for the actions of their children. They have power to make decisions about that child's religious upbringing and education; they decide where the child will live and who he or she will socialize with. They also have reason to expect that their relationship with their children will be long-term and that the parent and child will belong to a network of ties to other family members and family friends. All of the above color a parent's emotional relationship with a child, but so, too, does the daily work of provision of care color one's emotional relationship with a child. Parents may or may not be actively involved in the daily work of meeting a child's needs, but this is by no means all there is to their relationships with their children.

If maternal thinking is what emerges from the work involved in caring for young children and is in itself a characteristic kind of practice, we must be careful not to conflate maternal thinking with all that a parent might think and feel because of the additional elements of his or her relationship with a child, and I think we must also be careful to distinguish the thoughts and practices that occur when one is involved in daily care giving from the activities that shape one's relationship with a child when one is not. To my mind, the debate over whether "mothering work" or "maternal thinking" should be redescribed as parental thinking or parental work in many way misses the boat overlooks this point, because daily caregiving is a particular kind of practice regardless of who does it, whether they are paid or not. I think that we also miss out on some of the important features of this kind of practice when we forget that sharing the work with other caregivers and attempting to balance the competing needs of many other children are important parts of the thinking and feeling involved in this kind of work.

## 4. HOW SHOULD CHILDCARE BE STRUCTURED?

Once we have enlarged our understanding of the kinds of situations in which people provide childcare for young children, and therefore modified our understanding of maternal thinking or mothering work to include the possibility of multiple caregivers with differing types of relationships with children, we can move on the third task of this chapter, and begin to think about the proper basis for ranking different childcare arrangements. Any actual ranking would require a great deal of empirical study, but what I can do here is recommend a three-pronged approach to evaluating modes of delivering childcare, guided by the feminist ethics of care, in which we focus on the needs of the care receivers and the needs of the care providers, while keeping in mind overall concerns about equality among people of different genders, races, and social classes. In this book I focus mainly on the needs of the care providers, because the needs of the children have typically been all that are considered in evaluating different forms of childcare.

If we use a three-pronged approach, we would not think that one factor alone, such as the needs of the children being cared for, is definitive. Thus, for instance, even if we were to agree with strong (and to my mind implausible) versions of attachment theory and believe that children need to have a strong attachment to a primary caregiver who meets all of their needs, we could argue that our concern with caregivers' needs requires social support for the caregiver. This could come in many forms, including financial support and Kittay's model of doulia, where other people would take on the work of supporting the care provider and helping to meet his or her needs. If we took the needs of caregivers as seriously as we did the need of care receivers, we would not think that theories about children's interests are all that we need in order to answer questions about the delivery of care. We would remember that we might need to be innovative in attempting to harmonize the needs of care receivers and care providers.

We also need to be careful to avoid assuming that it is a simple matter to assess what children need and to avoid assuming that all children have similar needs. Not only do we need to remember that some children, including those with significant mental or physical impairments, will have needs that may go beyond the norm, but we also must remember that our judgments about what children need are affected by our vision of their future prospects. These latter judgments, in turn, depend not only on a child's access to resources, but also on our vision of the culture in which we expect them to function.

As discussed earlier, Claudia Card is very critical of motherhood. Her evaluative approach is similar to mine in that it has three foci: She critiques traditional mothering for its impact on the mother, its impact on the child, and its larger social consequence: "My concerns . . . are as much for the children as for the women that some of these children become and for the goal of avoiding the reproduction of patriarchy" (Card 1996, 4). Regarding the first concern, she welcomes "revolutionary parenting" (hooks 1984, 133–146) because it "dilutes the power of individual parents" (Card 1996, 17). She does not spend much time on the second concern, the potentially oppressive effect of mothering on women. The issue she discusses the most is the unfairness of legally establishing the "mother's answerability for her child's waywardness" (ibid.).

Her lack of attention to the specifics involved in mothering work also means that she does little to envision alternative arrangements of childrearing with any concreteness. She seems to recommend (although she may just be describing what she sees as historical reality) a situation in which children are "raised by a variety of paid caretakers with limited responsibilities" (Card 1996, 19). Furthermore, she suggests that if public safety were sufficiently improved, "there might be no need for motherhood – which is not to say that children would not need to bond with and be supervised by adults" (18). If emotional connection and supervision are eliminated from mothering work, what would remain on Ruddick's account would be concern with children's social acceptability and enhancement of their capacities for growth. Since it is unclear how either of these goals would be met by increasing public safety, Card's suggestion above shows that she is operating with a limited picture of mothering work in which mothers are responsible for keeping their children safe and out of the way of other adults.

Card writes that she is most interested in the standpoint of the child. Any alternative to privatized mothering would have to meet the needs of children, which she describes as follows: "Children . . . need stable emotional bonds with adults" as well as "supervision, education, healthcare, and a variety of relationships with people with a variety of ages" (1996, 16–17). However, as mentioned above, Card does little to tell us how these various needs could better be met. Moreover, when we consider alternatives to privatized mothering, we need to ask not only how children's needs could be met, but also whether those who would end up doing the work of meeting those needs would be paid and by whom. We need also to ask how fragmented the work of childcare could be and still remain rewarding for those men and women of various social classes who would do it, as well as how well it could meet the needs of children for stable, intimate bonds.

These concerns complicate, I think, any possible application to childcare of the model suggested by Bubeck, who argues for the advantages of requiring every able person to contribute his or her fair share to a "universal caring service" as a means of providing backup care to primary carers (Bubeck 2002, 180). When the care involved is for children, few would be willing to have their backup care provided by persons randomly recruited from this universal caring service, and it would be extremely difficult for members of this service to do anything more than provide brief respite care in emergency situations. Furthermore, any such solution would, for the most part, keep mothers caring for children in a privatized context, albeit with a publicly provided safety net in place. By contrast, I agree with Meyers that "only degendering and redistributing default dependency work – that is, granting women a full range of allocation options – can contravene women's 'natural' responsibilities and ensure their full autonomy" (Meyers 2003, 31). However, degendering caring labor (and ensuring that it is not thought necessarily to happen best in private households) will not be enough. We must also strive to avoid making certain kinds of childcare associated with people whose race, ethnicity, or social class make them more vulnerable to exploitation than others. Childcare is a form of work that is gendered, such that DiQuinzio argues that we cannot disentangle ideological beliefs about women from those about mothers (DiQuinzio 1999, xiii), but it is not only gendered. Joan Tronto argues that in general, care is not only feminized but associated with race and social class (Tronto 1993, esp. 110–115).

We need to achieve greater recognition of the worth and nature of paid and unpaid childcare. Macdonald and Merrill (2002) advocate job shadowing, in which parents spend a day observing the work of caregivers in childcare centers. This is a good first step, but it is equally important for people who do not have children to learn about the demands of this kind of work, which is essential for the public good (Grace 1998). We also need to find ways to recognize the bond that forms between paid caregiver and child, in a way that does not inappropriately assimilate paid caregivers to mothers or presuppose that there are problems about being paid for caring for children.

There are many advantages to sharing the work involved in caring for children. Caregivers who do not provide full-time care are given the opportunity to participate in a wider range of types of activity, drawing on different skills they possess and offering different kinds of rewards. Caregivers working in concert can learn from one another and challenge one another to question unreflective assumptions about children's needs and how to meet them. Children have access to people with different skills, knowledge, values, and personal styles, and they also have more than one person they can turn to in times of trouble or if one of their caregivers fails in his or her work, whether due to abuse, neglect, lack of skill, or misunderstanding of the demands of the work.

However, in keeping with Tronto's warning, we must be sure that it is shared in a way that doesn't falsely separate different aspects of the work and assign them to people of different social classes, genders, or ethnicities. Regarding childcare in particular, there are powerful associations between different aspects of that work and ideas about social class. Middle-class and upper-class mothers, for instance, sometimes complain that they did not expect when they engaged in childcare to find themselves performing so much manual labor, as opposed to the intellectual labor for which they received compensation in the paid work force.

Sociologists have repeatedly found that different meanings are assigned to childcare when men and women of different ethnicities and social classes perform the work. Race, ethnicity, and class are likely to play significant roles in shaping the microideologies used to account for the way childcare is shared. It is therefore vital that we consider the needs of all interested parties, children, their parents, and the children's assorted caregivers in evaluating different proposals for providing care to young children. Finally, we need to make sure that our understanding of the work involved in caring for young children and the kind of thinking it requires and inspires accurately reflect the actual practice of the many differently situated men and women who engage in this work.

# Chapter 6

# Caring for Children, Caring for Friends, Caring by Children

## 1. INTRODUCTION

In the previous chapter, I argued that, rather than thinking about caring for children on a model of mothering, we should recognize and theorize about the different ways in which children receive care. In this chapter I ask what thinking about children and their caregivers in this broader context can reveal to us about other kinds of caring relations. This is in keeping with one of the overarching aims of this book, which has been to recognize the relevance of experiences with reproductive labor to other kinds of experiences.

In this chapter, rather than making a very general claim about connections between caring for children and all other kinds of caring relationships, I choose to compare relations between children and their caregivers with friendships between mature and morally competent adults. My discussion in this chapter is positioned with respect to a debate within feminist theory over the relevance of the mothering relation for thinking about the ethical nature of other human relationships. I distinguish my position both from those who claim that the caregiver-child relation should have a privileged role in theorizing ethical relationships and from those who argue that this relation serves best as a point of contrast to caring relations between adults, rather than a paradigm for them. The concluding section of the chapter examines the way in which "young carers" – school-aged children who provide care to their parents – have been made into a social problem. Both aspects of the chapter are intended to argue against what I interpret as the paradigmatic caregiver-child relationship.

My own view is that a comparison between the caregiver-child relationship and caring relationships between adults reveals both interesting points of continuity and significant differences and that we need to avoid making too sharp a contrast between these different types of caring relations if we are not to distort our understanding of both. An overly sharp distinction distorts both the possibilities for mutuality and some forms of reciprocity in relations between caregivers and young children. It also prevents us from acknowledging the existence of inequality and dependence in relationships such as friendships between morally competent adults. It becomes difficult for us to understand how children can make the transition from one type of relationship to the other as they mature and can obscure the extent to which kinds of inequality, degrees of dependence, and even occasionally paternalism may exist appropriately within some friendships.

Maturity and moral competence can seem falsely to be an all-or-nothing matter, rather than accomplishments slowly achieved or intermittently left behind. This can cause us both to exaggerate the difference in moral status between children and adults and to think, inappropriately, of adults with varying degrees of dependency on others as child-like. We need, instead, to interpret children and adults as existing along a continuum, with both, at different times and sometimes for different reasons, dependent on a variety of supports given by others.

A final reason to compare relations between young children and their caregivers with friendships between morally competent adults is because, unlike other relationships between adults involving elements of care and dependence, such as the doctor-patient or teacher-student relationships, both friendship and caregiving for young children tend to involve all four of the phases of care distinguished by Joan Tronto: caring about, which involves recognition of a need and commitment to the view that the need should be met; taking care of, which involves assuming some responsibility for meeting the need; caregiving, which involves direct meeting of needs for care; and care receiving, which involves the response of the one cared for (Tronto 1993, 105–108). It may also be fruitful to compare caring for children and friendships with these more formal relationships involving varieties of care, but this is not what I seek to do in this chapter. This is because I am as concerned to correct misunderstandings of the nature of the relationships between children and their caregivers as I am to illuminate the concept of friendship. I turn now to the next section of this chapter, in which I give an account of debates within feminist theory over whether or not mothering should serve as a model for other caring relations.

## 2. MOTHERING AS ETHICAL PARADIGM: THE FEMINIST DEBATE

Can relationships between caregivers and young children serve as an ethical model for other personal relationships? Are there important similarities between those caring relationships and friendships between mature adults? Or are the differences far more salient than the similarities? Feminist theorists disagree. Jean Elshtain, Virginia Held, Paul Lauritzen, Nel Noddings, Sara Ruddick, Caroline Whitbeck, and Cynthia Willett either state or imply that the mother-child relation can serve as a valuable model for other sorts of ethical relationships, including friendship.[1]

Before going any further, it is important to note that there is a lack of clarity involved in speaking of the mother-child relation. Mothers continue to care for and think about their children when those children reach adulthood and beyond. As noted in the previous chapter, I find it implausible to claim that maternal thinking about and maternal care for a one-year-old infant and a forty-five-year-old bank teller would have much in common. Those who speak of the mother-child relation clearly use the term to describe relations between mothers and their young dependent children. They speak of children being dependent on their mothers for their preservation, growth, and social acceptability, and they do not describe these children as being greatly influenced by others, such as teachers. This indicates that the children they have in mind are young, generally younger than school age. Another potential confusion involves the fact that many of these theorists, for instance, Held and Ruddick, believe that both men and women may "mother" a child, although more women than men currently mother. As I observed in the previous chapter, these and other theorists who intend the term "mothering" to be gender-neutral retain the association with mothers in order to reflect the fact that throughout history and still today it is women who have performed the bulk of this kind of work.

Having cleared up some potential confusion regarding the meaning of the phrase "mother-child relation," I turn now to claims made for the paradigmatic status of this relation. Virginia Held writes that if we are to understand human relationships in all their complexity, we must replace "the paradigm of economic man with the paradigm of mother and child" (Held 1993, 195). Cynthia Willett writes that the relationship between mothers and young children is of central importance for developing ethical theories because "[f]rom the standpoint of the mother-child relation, we can address the major concern of contemporary ethics, namely the possibilities of a prosocial desire" (Willett 1995, 53). Paul Lauritzen claims that, so long as we make the practice of rearing, rather than bearing, children central to our understanding of mothering, then the intellectual and emotional skills required for mothering can serve as a model for a feminist ethic of care and compassion (Lauritzen 1989, 39–42.) Nel Noddings uses the relation between a mother and her child both as an example of natural caring and as a model for a feminist ethic of caring (Noddings 1984). Sometimes the paradigmatic status of this relation is implied rather than explicit. Lorraine Code observes of mothering practices that "[n]either Whitbeck nor Ruddick claims explicitly that these practices have paradigmatic status. But the generalizability claims that they make carry paradigmatic implications" (Code 1991, 90).

While these theorists suggest that the mother-child relationship carries paradigmatic implications, they tend not to explore issues of the continuities between the mother-child relation and other ethically significant personal relationships in detail. For instance, in Held's contrast between the mother-child relation and contractual relationships, she does not consider where we might place friendships. Friendships clearly line up alongside the mother-child relationship in comparison to contractual relations in that the former are paradigmatically both caring and noncontractual. However, to the extent that friendships involve reciprocity of exchange of goods and services, as many argue that they do, this would align them in some respects with contractual relations. Friendships would be decidedly less formal, and they are relationships in which we typically do not intend to use legal frameworks to enforce the reciprocity but hope it will be voluntary. The emphasis on reciprocity of exchange, however, would suggest that friendships have something in common with both types of relationships that Held contrasts so sharply.

In opposition to the feminists who defend the paradigmatic status of the mother-child relation, Linda Bell, Claudia Card, Lorraine Code, Mary Dietz, Marilyn Friedman, Jean Grimshaw, Sarah Lucia Hoagland, and Barbara Houston argue that mothering should not have a central place in theorizing other sorts of ethical relations. Alisa Carse and Hilde Nelson observe: "It is precisely the asymmetries of power, authority, and vulnerability in parent-child relationships that lead many to deem them ill-suited as moral paradigms, for they permit (even require) forms of domination that are morally inappropriate in relations among equal adults" (Carse and Nelson 1999, 24–25). Hoagland writes: "I do not think that mothering can be used as a model for an ethics of caring" (Hoagland 1991, 249; see also Houston 1987, 253). Friedman argues more specifically that mothering is a poor model for friendships among mature adults (Friedman 1993, 151). Other theorists of friendship see the contrast between friendships and the parent-child relation as so great that they have generated a debate over whether or not parents can become friends with even their adult children (see Thomas 1987 and Kupfer 1990). This debate about the nature of relationships between adult children and their parents is conceptually separable from the question of whether or not friendships have much in common with the relationship between young children and their caregivers. However, the debate is clearly generated by the view that the contrast between paradigmatic friendships and relations between caregivers and children is far greater than any similarities.

Focusing on questions about the similarities between the caregiver-child relation and other personal relationships may give the impression that the former are worthy of philosophical discussion only if they can serve as a model for other relationships. This is clearly not the view of philosophers such as Ruddick, who have written extensively of their significance, and it does not seem to be the intent of the latter group. For instance, Code recognizes that mothers are an important influence on children's moral development, and the relationships between caregivers and children are ethically significant at least for that reason (1991).

In their relationships with their caregivers, children learn how to trust, receive, give, and care. Even if there are no significant points of contact between relationships shared by children and their caregivers and other types of ethically significant relationships, the former will be ethically important not only because of their role in shaping children's moral development, but also because they draw on moral capacities from both caregivers and children.

This part of the chapter seeks to compare relationships between caregivers and children with friendships between morally competent adults. With reference to the debate over the paradigmatic status of the mother-child relation, I agree in important respects with those who argue that significant differences in the two sorts of relationship militate against using the mother-child relationship as a model for ethical relationships more generally. For brevity, I call these the "nay-sayers."

## 3. DISAGREEMENTS WITH THE NAY-SAYERS

I disagree with the nay-sayers in three respects. (1) My first disagreement is not only with the nay-sayers, but also with those who claim that relationships between caregivers and young children can serve as a model for other relationships. The range of relationships between caregivers and the children in their care is reduced to the dyadic, familial relationship between a mother and her child. Despite definitions of mothering, by Ruddick, for instance, that equate mothering with gender-neutral provision of childcare,[2] mothering relationships as analyzed by Held, Noddings, Ruddick, and Willett conform in most respects to practices stereotypically expected of middle-class mothers with relatively noninvolved but income-providing partners. Jean Grimshaw argues that this causes Ruddick to "conceive of mothering as a task whose demands arise simply within the mother-child nexus and to adopt an ahistorical view of the ways in which these demands are understood" (1986, 248).

These theorists understand mothers to be solely or chiefly responsible for the care of children. Each is expected to do her caring work alone in a private home and to have long-term responsibilities toward her child, a great deal of power to make decisions on behalf of the child, and authority over the child. However, as discussed in the previous chapter, many children in contemporary Canada, the United States, and Europe, as well as most children in other historical periods and in developing countries, have not been cared for in this way. In contemporary Canada and the United States, many children are cared for by a group of caregivers working together in a childcare center. Often, children's caregivers are paid, the relationships are not expected to last long, and caregivers' responsibilities and power are limited. As discussed at length in the previous chapter, Patricia Hill Collins, bell hooks, and Alison Bailey have all pointed to ways in which Ruddick's account ignores the role of "othermothers" within African American communities who each voluntarily take on the role of a child's mother. Some of these othermothers simply replace a child's "biomother"; others share the work of raising a child (see hooks 1984; Bailey 1994; Collins 1994). To appreciate the ethical significance of relationships between children and their caregivers, we need to acknowledge and theorize about the range of relationships between young children and their caregivers, not simply the relationships between children and some types of mothers.

This criticism chiefly applies to the work of Elshtain, Held, Noddings, Ruddick, Whitbeck, and Willett. However, for the most part, despite their critics' recognition of the limitation of this model of caring for children,[3] the nay-sayers themselves do not seek to provide a richer understanding of the range of relationships between children and their caregivers, but instead criticize the mother-child relation as if it were a good model for all relations between caregivers and dependent children.[4] Some of the similarities between relationships involving mature adults and relationships of children and their caregivers may be harder to observe when we conceive the work of caring for young children in accordance with the ideology of motherhood, something I have discussed at length in the previous chapter.[5]

As I argued in several of the previous chapters, the ideology of motherhood not only idealizes and proscribes maternal care for young children, but also makes care provision a private responsibility. Like many other feminists, I think the ideology of motherhood is false as a description of the wide variety of situations in which children are cared for and is deeply flawed as an ideal. As a result, I rework the question about whether relations between mothers and children can serve as a model for other ethically significant relations. In this chapter I begin a project of studying a range of relationships between caregivers and children in order to contrast them to and compare them with relationships between morally competent adults. The caregivers can be male or female, paid or unpaid, or have long-term or short-term relationships with a child but they will not be considered caregivers for the purpose of this chapter unless they are on intimate terms with the child and strive to meet his or her needs for preservation, growth, and development.

(2) To return to the terms of the debate between those who do and those who do not encourage us to use the relationship between caregivers and children as a model for other relationships, I have a second point of disagreement with the nay-sayers. Those who argue that we should not use the relationship between caregivers and children as an ethical paradigm do not adequately distinguish among various features of the relationships between caregivers and the young children in their care. (a) The fact that children are dependent on their caregivers, (b) the fact that children and their caregivers have different abilities and different social power, and (c) the fact that young children, unlike most of their caregivers, are often legitimately believed not to be the best arbiters of their own interests are all conflated. Dependency, inequality, and paternalism[6] are seen as necessarily connected. My objection is not to the depiction of relationships between young children and their caregivers as ones in which the caregivers may legitimately make decisions

for children, seeking to promote their interests. I agree that this is the case. However, I think the nay-sayers are too quick to suppose that all relationships involving dependency and inequality will promote paternalism. This leads to my third point of disagreement with the nay-sayers.

(3) Nay-sayers make an overly sharp contrast of relationships involving caregivers and dependent children with relationships between adults who are equals in every respect. They also suggest that the former relationships necessarily lack mutuality. For instance, Friedman writes, "Relationships vary considerably. We can relate to others in ways which approach equality and mutuality, or we can relate to others in ways which involve forms of dependency or hierarchies of power and authority" (Friedman 1989, 3). The dependency, inequality, and paternalism that characterize relations between very young children and their caregivers are then contrasted with features presented as appropriate to friendship. The latter is described as a relationship between equals, in which neither is dependent on the other and neither makes decisions for the other. As we see below, it can come to seem as if any failures of reciprocity, such as prolonged dependency of one person on the other, and any significant inequalities in power and ability between the two parties inevitably leads to paternalism. Moreover, just as the caregiver-child relationship is presented as dyadic, friendship is also presented primarily as a relationship between two individuals, instead of a social network.

Code makes a similarly sharp contrast between friendship and the caregiver-child relation in "What Can She Know?" She also claims, "Friendship can occupy the space claimed for the best forms of maternal thinking" (96). Yet the best relations between caregivers and young children involve dependency and severe inequality in both power and abilities, and this is not how Code conceives of friendship, which is presented as a relationship between equals.

## 4. FRIENDSHIP AND RECIPROCITY

Of the nay-sayers, Friedman gives the most extensive account of friendship, and it is to her analysis of friendship and its contrast with the caregiver-child relation that I turn. In her "What Are Friends For?" Friedman argues that reciprocity in care is a moral requirement in relationships between "morally competent adults." In some sense this is uncontroversial. Adults should not seek to exploit one another and should be willing to give as well as receive. Sandra Bartky (1990) and

Claudia Card (1990) examine failures of this kind of reciprocity. For instance, Bartky argues that in relationships between women and men who are their social superiors, women's caring attention to their male friends and attempts to boost their self-esteem and validate the men on the latter's terms, when not reciprocated, can lead women to compromise their values and minimize their own self-esteem.

These theorists are right to argue that a friendship in which only one party seeks to provide emotionally significant care can be damaging to the psychological health of the giver and moral status of the receiver. Card warns that "lack of reciprocity is probably a major cause of the breakup of friendships among peers" (Card 1990, 205). In particular, she worries that in our primary relationships, when only one person in a relationship values the other apart from his or her utility, this lack of reciprocity of valuing harms the self-esteem of the person who is not independently valued (205). However, questions remain about what is required for reciprocity. In the literature there seems to be a variety of types of reciprocity, often not clearly distinguished, including reciprocity of valuing, reciprocity of caring, and reciprocity of the exchange of goods and services. Furthermore, since the differences between the types of reciprocity are generally not acknowledged, there are no clear arguments that the different types are linked.

Some strands have little to do with others. Moreover, honoring some strands requires us to forego insistence on others. First, reciprocity of caring should not lead to reciprocity in the exchange of goods and services should the needs and resources of the parties involved differ sharply. If two people care for one another and strive to meet one another's needs when they can, yet one friend has more resources than the other – perhaps financial resources, perhaps availability of leisure time – reciprocity of caring would discourage demands that the friend with lesser resources seek always to provide gifts of equal value to the more well-off friend or to refuse to accept gifts whose overall value he could not reciprocate. While we might insist that the friend should be given other kinds of goods and services of "equal value" (thoughtful phone calls, emotional support during difficult times), it seems perverse to me either to insist on the equality of value or to attempt to provide some common measure, whether in terms of money or utility, that would make it possible for us to assess whether or not he has reciprocated equally. Moreover, it seems equally perverse, should one friend have more serious needs than the other, for him to refuse to accept help at the point where he predicts that he is unlikely to be able to reciprocate and perverse as well for his friend to stop giving so as to preserve the reciprocity of the exchange of goods and services.

However, despite my claims that it is morally problematic to always require reciprocity of exchange of goods and services within a friendship, the experiences of people who have suddenly acquired serious illnesses and impairments makes it clear that they frequently experience a withdrawal of friendship when their needs are greater than they were before. Carol Thomas describes this withdrawal as one of the psycho-social effects of disability, where disability is defined as social oppression and exclusion directed at people who have physical or mental impairments.[7] In her chapter "Disability and the Social Self," she quotes long excerpts from the testimony of several people who were neglected or abandoned by friends after they became impaired. Interestingly, several of the women found that it was longstanding friends who found it most difficult to abandon entrenched expectations about the equality involved in the friendship, whereas friends who were more recently acquired were often more flexible about changing the nature of the friendship to include seeking to meet the now much greater needs of their friends (Thomas 1999, 46–61). It was also clear that friends were more accepting of short-term illnesses and impairments than anything long-term or permanent.

One of the reasons that demands for reciprocity of exchange of goods and services within friendship seem perverse and that abandonment of friends with increased needs can be a violation of friendship is because an unwillingness to tolerate anything less than reciprocity of exchange of goods and services conflicts with another type of reciprocity, one that is more essential to an intimate friendship, and that is reciprocity of valuing. Since reciprocity of valuing, as defined by Card, is contravened whenever a person is not valued apart from his or her utility within the relationship, it cannot be said to exist in relationships that cannot tolerate failures in the reciprocity of exchange. If friendships lose some or all of their stability and value[8] when friends are not equally useful to one another, giving and taking in approximately equal amounts, then those friendships do not actually involve reciprocity of valuing.

Theorists of friendship generally insist on both equality overall and the equality of giving and taking in particular within a friendship. For instance, Joseph Kupfer argues that the reason to think parents and their grown children might be friends is because "young children become adults able to contribute to their parents' lives in ways comparable to what their parents have done for them" (Kupfer 1990, 15). By contrast, the reason he decides parents cannot really be friends with their adult children is because the history of the inequality between them prevents them from interacting as equals forever afterward (16). Even Nicholas Dixon, who argues that friendships might be possible between people who are not obviously equal in needs and abilities, such as a person who physically assists her physically impaired friend, suggests that this is because "the alleged inequality in such relationships may be only superficial, since the able-bodied person may gain just as much in terms of emotional satisfaction and intellectual stimulation as she gives in physical assistance" (Dixon 1995, 81). While I certainly would not dispute the possibility, it troubles me that friendships are presented either as no longer possible or as morally flawed whenever the "give and take" involved are not roughly equal. Are inequalities of resources and needs always a threat to the moral value of a relationship between adults? To suppose so conflates willingness to give and ability to give.

I find it implausible to think that the kinds of support we provide for our friends, whether providing meals for someone temporarily bedridden, shopping for someone who is permanently physically impaired and unable to access stores, assisting in caring for the children of a recently bereaved friend, or supporting a friend who challenges social mores, would or should always be reciprocated equally. I find it more plausible to demand that the various parties to a friendship be prepared to meet the needs of their friends, depending on their resources and abilities, but not that they should seek to provide goods and services of equal value to what has been received. To the extent that a friend refuses to accept help because she does not expect to be able to repay it, I think most of us would see this as a weakness in the friendship. Similarly, we do not expect caregivers to refuse to provide, or children to refuse to receive, that which they do not expect to be reciprocated.

Audrey Thompson points out that "the distinctive character of responsibility in friendship, which we might call co-responsibility, calls for shared rather than distributive attention to the conditions of the friendship" (Thompson 1989, 72). In her example, if one friend has significant obligations to spouse and daughter as well as to work and to an aged parent, and the other friend has obligations to work and to a spouse but not to dependents, it would be inappropriate for the friends to impose equivalent demands on one another. Her suggested solution is for one friend to assume some of the burdens of caring for the other's dependents, not in order to receive quid pro quo extra attention from the more burdened friend, but instead as "the boundaries of the friendship are widened to include caring for what the friend cares for" (72).

However, Thompson then goes on to make an absolute contrast of friendship to relationships between parents and children. She states that the latter relationships preclude mutuality, since "caretaking imposes necessarily differential responsibilities, whereas caring between equals allows for co-responsibility" (73). Here I think it is significant that her solution to the situation where friends do not have equal time and resources to devote to a relationship is that one friend care for the other's dependent daughter. For her, caretaking that meets dependency needs is something that an adult may provide to a child, but not something that one adult friend may provide for the other. It emerges that, despite her call for co-responsibility that does not require reciprocity in the sense of equivalence in the exchange of goods and services, whenever differential care is provided, it must be to one's friends' dependents, and not to one's friend, for this would be caretaking of the sort appropriate for parents to provide to children, not for equal friends to provide at times one for the other. Caring for equals is contrasted with the caring that an adult may provide to a child, and dependency is considered appropriate only for the child, a point to which I return at length in the last section of this chapter.

Marilyn Friedman, in a move similar to Audrey Thompson's, appears to allow for a notion of reciprocity broader than that of equivalent exchange but holds back from making sense of dependency in friendship. Friedman argues that she does not require a "*quid pro quo* accounting of services in personal relationships." However, while she may not require an accounting of services, she does seem to require that the goods and services exchanged be equivalent in value. She writes: "Something is amiss . . . if a close personal relationship between morally competent adults lacks an overall approximate reciprocity in the diverse ways of caring. This mutuality seems, on the face of it, to be a moral requirement for those morally competent persons who genuinely care for each other" (Friedman 1993, 159–160).

In a footnote to this paragraph, Friedman observes, "My generalization is intended to allow for exceptional cases; sometimes one partner is infirm or otherwise deeply needful of care and unable to reciprocate this care for a prolonged period of time" (160). However, she does not tell us what justifies the exceptional cases or whether she believes the relationship is sustainable (either practically or as a moral relationship) if the inability of one partner to reciprocate on an equal basis is sustained or can be expected to continue indefinitely, as in the situations of people who acquire permanent impairments. Moreover, if we consider the percentage of the population who experience illness and impairment, whether because of how a person is born, accidents, environmental toxins, disease, or aging, it seems odd to consider these to be exceptional circumstances in the course of long-term friendships.

In the same footnote, Friedman goes on to distinguish between mutuality and reciprocity but makes it clear that reciprocity is a necessary though not sufficient component of mutuality: "'Reciprocity' suggests that specific actions are met with corresponding actions as repayments; 'mutuality' suggests, in addition, the sharing of interests or concerns. 'Mutuality' identifies a richer relationship than that of mere repayment for good turns rendered. Nevertheless, reciprocity is not irrelevant to personal relationships; it would seem to be a part, even though only a part, of what mutuality involves" (160).

I believe that Friedman is mistaken to claim that mutuality always requires reciprocity in the broad sense of repayment for care received. As I argue below, we can see mutuality in relations between children and their caregivers even before reciprocity is aimed at and certainly before it is achieved. However, I believe that this is true of relations not only between children and caregivers. Close personal relationships between morally competent adults do not require this kind of reciprocity to involve mutuality and to be morally valuable relationships.

Friedman's concern, echoing Bartky and Card, is that women, particularly in their relationships with men, will care for more than they will be cared for, either because they are actively abused or because they are exploited by having their caring activities taken for granted and not reciprocated. There are real grounds for this concern. We often encounter relationships where one member has sufficient emotional and financial resources, as well as time and talent, to provide for the other member's needs, but chooses not to do so or to do so in a very limited way, while continuing to draw on the other person's resources.

However, there are also relationships where failures of reciprocity are due not to one person's unwillingness to do her or his fair share or lack of commitment to the relationship but to the person's lesser resources or greater needs. Sometimes, as Friedman indicates, this period of greater need may be prolonged – in fact, it may be permanent. For example, one friend, due to aging manifested during the relationship, may come to have physical impairments, which make it more difficult for her to provide goods and services to her friend, even while she continues to care for and about the friend, to value the relationship, and to have mutual interests with her friend. The physical limitations, such as difficulty walking, chronic fatigue, or problems with fine motor control, may also limit her opportunities for employment, reduce her income, and lower her social status as compared with her friend. Reciprocity, independence, and equality of status may therefore all be threatened.[9]

Except for the one sentence in a footnote discussed above, Friedman ignores friendships that face these kinds of issues. This failure on her part is linked to her sharp distinction between "caring by mature persons for those dependent on them and the caring that can and should go on among morally competent adults" (Friedman 1993, 155; see also 188–189). Because she considers only these two alternatives, she risks making all persons who are dependent on others for care, whether or not they are mature, appear morally incompetent. While this stark contrast is particularly clear in Friedman, it operates as well in other theorists of friendship. For instance, Laurence Thomas privileges reciprocity of self-disclosure as the criterion of friendship. He considers the objection that this obscures other features of friendship, such as providing material help to one's friend, and notes that he has "assumed that by and large companion friends are self-sufficient or, in any case, that the material help each provides the other is quite ancillary to the friendship" (Thomas 1987, 227). Not only does this ignore the many times in which friends are not self-sufficient and have real dependency needs, but he also makes an overly sharp distinction between the affective component of a friendship (which involves the exchange of confidences) and material help. Those who care for young children are well aware of the emotional intimacy involved in acts of bodily care, and the provision of material help to adults, including such actions as helping one's friend to recover from surgery or illness, can be similarly deeply emotional.

## 5. CARING FOR YOUNG CHILDREN

Friedman also rejects the possibility that work focusing on the philosophical significance of care for dependent children may be relevant for thinking about relationships between adults. Ruddick argues that maternal thinking is characterized by concern for a child's preservation, growth, and social acceptability. This involves seeking to ensure that a child thrives physically and grows and develops emotionally, intellectually, and morally. As a result, the characteristic virtues aimed at in maternal thinking involve being responsive to growth, accepting of change, and attentive to particularity, context, and individual differences. If we view friendship between two people as static, these aims and virtues do not apply, but if we see friendship as characteristically long-term and capable of accommodating and encouraging change, then they do seem relevant. Friedman argues, "Morally competent adults, in relationships with each other, do not usually have mother like responsibilities for each other's preservation, growth, or social acceptability" (151).[10] If we think of mother-like responsibilities according to the ideology of motherhood, in which one person is assigned moral and legal responsibility for achieving these outcomes for her child, then friendship is indeed dissimilar. However, if we reject this ideology and refuse to limit responsibility for children's development to one or two persons, who may well have inadequate resources and talents to achieve their aims, then the contrast to friendship is not as great.

Nonetheless, in some respects, Friedman is surely right; there are significant differences between caring for children and caring for adults. One important difference involves the extent to which young children in particular may lack insight into their long-term interests and needs and may lack the ability to delay gratification in order to meet those needs. While children at different ages have different levels of insight into their needs and interests, and caregivers should never ignore children's expressions of those interests, caregivers also have responsibilities to look out for children's long-term interests as well as the capacity to help shape what those interests may turn out to be. This makes the work of the caregiver morally difficult, but we must be careful not to make moral judgments about this relationship that would be appropriate only if the relationship were one of morally competent adults.

Linda Bell, following Sartre, makes just this mistake and finds all relationships between caregivers and children to involve violence: "To keep the child from consequences she or he does not intend, the adult limits the child's freedom. Though done with the best of intentions for the child's welfare and though perhaps truly necessary to keep the child from harm or to provide for her or his future freedom, the limitation is nonetheless violence" (Bell 1993, 201). She therefore argues: "Vulnerability of the child and the power imbalance between the child and adult(s) render this relationship inherently violent and thus a poor model for caring and moral adult relationships" (200). While Bell is right to argue that the paternalism of the child-caregiver relation "simply cannot be taken as a model for relationships between individuals who are both responsible adults" (201), she is wrong to consider vulnerability of one person in a relationship and a power imbalance between the parties always to threaten the moral status of that relationship. Relationships between mature adults should not characteristically involve profound paternalism, but they may well involve unequal vulnerability and dependency. Of course, vulnerability may be abused, and one person may illegitimately take another's dependency as a sign that he or she lacks the capacity to make decisions for his- or herself. However, since friends are paradigmatically vulnerable to one another in many ways, it is odd to think that we need to worry about only the kinds of vulnerability produced by dependency.

While Friedman is right that caring for adults differs significantly from caring for children, she is like Bell in closely relating inequality, dependence, and paternalism. Friedman rejects the caregiver-child relation as a model for ethics and replaces it with friendship, characterized in opposition to the former. Instead, we should look to paradigmatic features of various types of caring relationships to investigate whether or not one type, such as friendship, may sometimes have features associated more often with relationships of another type, such as the relation between caregivers and children. This is in keeping with philosopher Annette Baier's observation that there is something wrong with most moral theory's focus on relations between equals and her insistence that we examine the moral experience of "those whose daily dealings are with the less powerful or the more powerful" (Baier 1994, 116). Unlike Baier's point, it is also to insist that we should not make an overly sharp distinction between those relations that involve people with unequal power and those that do not, and those that involve children and those that are between adults. While there are important differences between these types of relationships, there can also be interesting points of similarity, particularly when one adult is dependent, temporarily or permanently, partially or totally, on another or others for preservation or spiritual, intellectual, or emotional growth. This dependence may be much easier for both the dependent person and that person's supporter to bear when a network of persons shares the task of providing support, as Aronson argues (1998). But this response to dependence is obscured by Friedman's emphasis on friendship as dyadic.

One of the reasons Friedman downplays areas of overlap between relations between caregivers and the children in their care and relations between friends has to do with her uneasiness about relations of dependence between mature persons. Another reason may be because

Friedman reduces the former to familial relationships. This is because she ignores the relationships between children and those of their caregivers who are not bound to them by familial ties, and also because she downplays the extent to which men and women who care for children may challenge the roles socially ascribed to family members, particularly those challenging the ideology of motherhood.

What are some of Friedman's worries about family ties? She considers them to involve "great differences in status and power between family members" often due to age differences or gender inequality (214). This is often true; however, she also claims that kinship relations are marked by a "crusty rigidity" (219). She describes family ties as nonvoluntary; they are socially ascribed relations (209). When we recognize that caregivers are not always family members, some of these worries about the caregiver-child relationship may be diminished, and certainly the contrast Friedman draws between friendships and the caregiver-child relationship need not be so sharp. Differences in status and power due to age and ability remain, but there is no reason to think that all relationships between children and their caregivers will be characterized by crusty rigidity or governed by expectations about relations between kin. Moreover, even when caregivers have some abilities that the children in their care lack, the children may have some abilities that the caregivers lack. For instance, some quite young children serve as translators for their immigrant parents, and others care for an ill parent or assist a parent by providing information he or she lacks, for instance, due to blindness. However, while some caregivers may voluntarily choose to work with children, the children in their care generally cannot opt out of the relationship. This may seem like a sharp distinction between friendships and the role children play in their relationships with their caregivers, but just because a friendship may be voluntarily started, this does not mean a friend can easily opt out of his or her ties to those on whom he or she depends.

Just as some of Friedman's concerns about the caregiver-child relation are better represented as criticisms of traditional mother-child relations, so, too, are some of Hoagland's. For instance, in her "Some Thoughts about 'Caring,'" Hoagland worries about the inequalities involved in relations between mothers and children – both in that mothers are expected to care for their children (perhaps unconditionally) without being cared for in return and in that mothers have authority to make decisions for their dependent children. Here it is unclear whether Hoagland finds the inequality itself problematic, as she objects to Noddings's focus on "the unequal relationship between mother and child" (250), or whether she worries only that the authority of the parent may lead to domination of the child.

She suggests that "group mothering may be the key" to avoiding one mother's singular authority over her children (253; see also Card 1996, 16–17). In group mothering, inequalities of power and ability between adults and children would remain, as would children's dependence on the adults. Presumably, paternalism would also be involved, at least in relations with very young children, but there would not be as many opportunities for abuse of power, and the entire burden of a child's needs would not be placed on any one person. This would suggest that inequality and dependence, and potentially also paternalism, are not in themselves problematic features of relations between adults and children, although they may become so when one person has sole responsibility for and authority over a child.

Paternalism is rarely appropriate in relations between morally competent adults, but I am reluctant to say that it is never appropriate in friendship. If limited to specific periods of time and specific areas of decision making, in times when moral competence and autonomy in general may be compromised due to significant stress, such as bereavement, temporary drug or alcohol abuse, an area where our friend is massively self-deceived, and similar threats to the friend's insight into his or her interests and situation, then paternalism between friends may be a legitimately caring act. Friends may act to prevent their friend from making irretrievable decisions in times of grief or when judgment is clouded by alcohol or emotion. One friend may try to keep another friend, who just had a sexual relationship end badly, from engaging in a sexual encounter he or she suspects his friend would deeply regret. Another may temporarily remove a large supply of sleeping pills from the medicine cabinet of a just widowed friend. These decisions may be mistaken, and the mistakes could have very bad consequences, but I do not feel that occasionally paternalistic acts of this sort would nullify a friendship. In fact, we may feel that failures to intervene in these ways, when no one else is as well acquainted with the shaky or vulnerable nature of our friend's ability to think about his or her long-term interests, would be a failure of friendship. We can sometimes make too sharp of a distinction between moral competence and incompetence. We need to recognize not only that may we make poor decisions about alcohol or suffer stressful events that temporarily render us incompetent, but also that friends are sometimes aware of others' areas of weakness and vulnerability and can seek to shield one another from the effects of bad decision making.

Nonetheless, I would agree that there is a significant difference of degree in the amount of paternalism appropriate in caring for young children and caring for our friends, albeit one that shifts slowly as the child ages and develops his or her abilities. What about those other prominent features of caring for young children, inequality and dependence? Hoagland suggests: "The very purpose of parenting, teaching, and providing therapy is to wean the cared-for of dependency" (251). I agree that in most cases, although not all, these practices do and should aim to end dependency in the one cared for. In other relationships, however, enabling the cared-for person to mature or develop skills may not end dependency. Sometimes all that can realistically be aimed at, even in relations between morally competent adults, is diminished dependency. For instance, a frail senior may depend on his partner for some kinds of care; a woman may depend on her network of friends for support in her terminal illness.

Do these kinds of relationships necessarily lack mutuality and reciprocity? For Friedman, it appears that they do. By contrast, Noddings, thinking about relations between infants and adults, offers a minimalist notion of reciprocity in which mere acknowledgment of care received is a kind of reciprocity. Hoagland worries that in this model, "there is no need for the child to turn and exhibit concern for the mother's projects" (254). She writes that "[n]onreciprocity-beyond-acknowledgment" does not show respect for the other and undermines the ability of the cared-for to learn to become caring. However, is this a problem with the caregiver-child relationship per se, or is it a problem with Noddings's characterization of that relationship, particularly when the child is still an infant?

## 6. CHILDREN, THEIR CAREGIVERS, MUTUALITY, AND RECIPROCITY

Here I would like to advance three claims, which I can only sketchily defend. First, relationships between children and their caregivers can involve mutuality in the absence of various sorts of reciprocity. Second, we should tolerate the lack of reciprocity only when the child lacks the abilities required for that kind of reciprocity. Third, children at various ages are capable of various sorts of reciprocity, and even young children are capable of the kinds of reciprocity that involve intent rather than equivalence in exchange, for instance, reciprocity of valuing and reciprocity in seeking to give one another joy.

Children are capable of much more than mere acknowledgment of care received, and the mutuality of a relation between caregivers and children can come in the form of shared activities and shared joys, rather than in the child's contribution to those of the caregiver's projects that existed before the relationship with the child.[11] Children and their caregivers, including those caregivers who are with a child only for a few months or years, share stories and share experiences. Both sides may engage in self-revelation (with the adult keeping to age-appropriate topics, of course). Young children and their caregivers may mutually maintain the living space they use to eat, sleep, and play. This is not to say that the contributions of the children and the adult caregivers will be equal as they tidy up, fix meals, or play together, but it is to insist that children are capable of contributing to the tasks involved in their care. In good relationships, children and their caregivers have mutual trust, are physically affectionate with one another, and share at least some aspects of a sense of humor. Such good relationships are rewarding for the caregivers as well as the children and are one explanation for the interest some women and men have in paid caregiving as a career, despite the poor financial compensation.

Many caregivers seek to teach children physical, emotional, and moral skills by means of play. Some of this play, particularly when a caregiver is not expected to be the sole adult participant and available for the entirety of a child's waking hours, can be fun for the caregiver as well. While many of these forms of mutuality require a child to seek to reciprocate the care he or she receives, they certainly do not require him or her to be equal in contributing to what he or she shares with the caregiver. Moreover, some of what children give to their caregivers does not involve any specific intention to give. For instance, some of it comes in the form of a transformation of the caregiver's world. Christine Gudorf talks about some of what her physically impaired children have given her: "new communities, new loyalties, new insight – new identities" (Gudorf 1985, 179).

Reciprocity requires both parties to seek, explicitly or implicitly, to provide something to the other. The reciprocity may be in the exchange of goods and services, and it may aim at equivalency, or it may be reciprocity in valuing or reciprocity in seeking to bring one another joy. Mutuality is broader. Mutuality is a matter of what the relationship to which each contributes achieves for the other, such as moments of fun, opportunities for growth and learning, and the making of new connections to others outside the immediate relationship. This should not be taken to excuse those who have the ability to contribute more directly to the other person and choose not to because the other is seen as unworthy of care. However, it does provide us with models of reciprocity and mutuality that permit the participants, whether children or adults, to be unequal in status, abilities, and resources, while still having an ethically valuable relationship.

If friendships between mature adults may involve varieties of inequality and dependency and absence of reciprocity of some kinds, does this mean that relations between caregivers and young children can or should be friendships? We often hear of parents mistakenly trying to be friends with their young children. The mistake here is not the pursuit of mutuality. Possibilities for mutuality and reciprocity should not make us forget that relations between caregivers and young children continue to involve not only more inequality and dependency than is typical in friendship, but also some significant paternalism on the part of the caregivers. Caregivers have responsibilities to strive to preserve children's lives, health, and opportunities. These responsibilities may require them to override children's wants and decisions, albeit reluctantly, when those children do not manifest the capacity to make reasonable and informed judgment about what is required to meet their needs or what are likely to be the consequences of their choices.

The responsibility that the caregivers have may suggest that the caregivers have duties to give, with no corresponding requirements on the children. However, abandoning reciprocity as a goal to be worked toward within the relationship would have many negative consequences. Failure to work toward reciprocity within that relationship threatens the moral development of the children, who learn to subordinate others' needs to their own. It threatens the happiness and mental health of the caregivers. It weakens the relationship between the child and his or her caregivers, and it deprives both caregivers and children of real joys, including but not limited to the opportunity to learn about those who differ from one's self.

When we make an overly sharp contrast between friendship, seen as a relationship involving mutuality and reciprocity, and relations between caregivers and children in their care, we make it difficult to see how children could make the move from one type of relationship to the other. We impede working toward mutuality and reciprocity as goals in caregiving, and we also discourage people from engaging in caregiving, leaving the work instead to those who are most culturally devalued, because of their gender, class, race, or ethnicity. However, my encouragement of the pursuit of mutuality and reciprocity in relations between children and their caregivers is not meant to burden caregivers and children with the expectation that they will share all of one another's interests, any more than I would endorse the ideology of motherhood's expectation that one person can and should meet all of the needs of a child.

Instead, this should give us further reason to strive toward caregivers working in groups or networks. The networks should be small enough to coordinate the work of caregiving and to let the children and caregivers form intimate bonds, yet large enough to minimize the potential for abuse of authority and the stress of people seeking to meet needs they are not suited or don't have the resources to meet. One reason the networks must be reasonably small is that caregiving requires intimacy of at least some types. Caregivers require intimate knowledge of the bodies, moods, and character traits of those they care for, if they are to meet their needs. This intimate knowledge, however, makes those who are cared for particularly vulnerable to abuse by their caregivers. While groups of caregivers are as capable of abusing the vulnerability as individuals are, and so the potential for abuse can never be reduced to zero, it does seem plausible that members of a caregiving network would be more nervous about abusing those they are supposed to care for when they know that evidence of this abuse would be available to others in the network. They might also be less likely to abuse the children in their care if they were not overwhelmed by the demands of those children, as well as social expectations about their abilities to meet those demands.

Another potential advantage of providing care for young children in networks concerns the paternalism involved in this work. As Grimshaw observes, Ruddick can make it seem as if discovering what a child really needs is solely a matter of attentive love (Grimshaw 1986, 248). Yet what someone is taken to need depends also on ideologies imposed on this caregiving work, social expectations of the child, and possibly the unconscious expectations and needs of the caregiver him- or herself. If caregiving for young children were provided by groups working together, the caregivers would first need to become self-consciously aware of their conception of the long-term interests and short-term needs of the child, and then possibly to defend or alter that conception when faced with the alternative conceptions of the other caregivers. Even if the power dynamics of the caregiving network were such that one or two persons' conceptions of the best interests of the child were more likely to dominate, the process involved in articulating that conception (if only so the other caregivers can be expected to share it or act on it), could at least help to expose that conception to the scrutiny of other adults and would require articulation and therefore conscious reflection. This could be a safeguard against some of the abuses potentially involved in paternalism. However, whenever the caregiving network is relatively homogeneous, this would not prevent the conception of the best interests of the child from being parochial and possibly sexist, racist, or classist.

Speaking of caregiving networks in the context of childcare may seem like a radical proposal, given our common conceptualization of this work as being done by lone individuals (typically mothers) or pairs (typically parents). However, as argued in the previous chapter, this common view fails to acknowledge the many ways in which the ideology of motherhood is already undermined. It ignores practices such as othermothering and the involvement of an extended community in rearing a child that Bailey, Collins, and hooks see occurring in many African American communities. It ignores the roles played by many people in caring for a child, including medical professionals, neighbors, and extended families. It also ignores the fact that childcare is often shared by parents and paid caregivers. In part, what I am proposing is that we begin to think of this work as shared by a network, rather than of one caregiver as a surrogate for another. Sociologist Lynet Uttal argues that parents sometimes think of paid caregivers who care for their children as temporary surrogates or replacements for the parents. She notes that a few parents instead think of themselves as working in coordination with their caregivers.

As I argued in the previous chapter, I find the latter approach preferable for a variety of reasons and believe that it is not only parents who need to think of paid caregivers in this way, but also the paid caregivers and the wider society (see Uttal 1996). This approach would facilitate recognition that all of those who provide significant care for a child have insight into the needs and abilities of that child, and all have a legitimate interest in securing the child's well-being. It is also important to remember that, just as children may grow to accept unjust relations between the sexes when they observe significant disparities in the role of men and women in their care, so, too, they may grow to accept unjust relations between social classes or races when they observe how hierarchically their caregivers interact with one another. Thinking of the caregiving that is already shared as part of a network of providing care makes some of these caregivers more visible to those with more power and may provide an opportunity to reflect more self-consciously about the power dynamics involved in the network. Finally, when thinking about who is part of the network of caregivers, we should also remember the historical and international role that children have played as caregivers of younger children. The role of children as companions for and teachers of younger and similarly aged children should be encouraged and celebrated, so long as we see them as sharing in the work of caregiving with others, including adults, who have skills and capacities that they themselves lack.

The dependency of a child makes some forms of caregiving more ideal than others, especially those that limit opportunities for abuse of authority and encourage the sharing of the work and decision making involved in caregiving. This may also be applied to relationships between mature adults, particularly when one or some of those adults have needs that make them obviously dependent on others. We might be prompted to move toward a model of friendship in which people participate in social networks, rather than solely dyadic relationships.

Appreciating both the differences and the commonalities between the caregiver-child relation and friendship between mature adults can help to shape our ideals about both sorts of relationship. By contrast, when we are given only two models of relationship – friends who are equal in status and who contribute equally to the relationship and caregivers who provide care to dependents, particularly parents to children – all failures of reciprocity threaten to reduce a dependent person to the status of a child. However, there are important differences between dependency in relationships between morally competent adults and relationships between a child and a caregiver. Although I have argued that paternalism may occasionally be appropriate in friendships, in most friendships between morally competent adults, including those involving substantial dependency, we should not take the person who is dependent to have less insight into his or her interests than the other person. While morally competent adults can sometimes misconstrue their own interests, and friends may occasionally have more insight into one another's needs than into their own, there is no reason to think that dependency alone makes one incapable of understanding and seeking to realize one's goals. In fact, experiences of dependency can help to clarify what really matters most to one.

We need not interpret all relationships in which one party has more ability or more resources than the other as morally compromised because we need not see all such relations as equivalent to the caregiver-child relation, which involves inequality, dependency, and extensive paternalism. Hoagland argues that differences in ability need not compromise our seeing our intimates as equal: "When interacting with those we consider our peers, we do not treat each other as though our abilities were the same, and we do not treat each other as lesser or unequal because of it.... So when we interact with someone in a way that is premised on a difference of power, it is not simply because we perceive them as not having abilities we have. Often it is because we perceive them as incompetent or less competent than we are in being able to make decisions in general" (Hoagland 1991, 251).

Hoagland is right to try to make space for relations between peers that do not involve equivalence in abilities, but there also needs to be space to recognize that sometimes these differences in abilities – and differences in needs – will make one person dependent on another or others, and this should not make us see the dependent person as incompetent. Similarly, we should not think of children beyond the age of infancy as generally incompetent. Instead, we should recognize that both children and adults are on a continuum in which they possess a variety of kinds and degrees of competency, which in turn lead them to need a variety of supports in they are to flourish.

When friendship is presented in sharp contrast to the caregiver-child relation, we may well be tempted to see the person with lesser abilities or more needs as like a child and incompetent to make decisions for his- or herself. This distorts the nature of relations both between friends and between children and their caregivers. As long as we distinguish between the degrees of paternalism, inequality, and dependency involved in relations between caregivers and young children and those that may be permissible or required in relations between friends, we should avoid this temptation and may begin to operate with broader conceptions of reciprocity and mutuality than those involving equivalent exchanges of goods and services. This should, in turn, allow us to develop richer conceptions of friendship and the caregiver-child relationship alike.

## 7. YOUNG CARERS: THE NEGATIVE EFFECTS OF THE PREDOMINANT MODEL OF MEETING CHILDREN'S NEEDS FOR CARE

In the bulk of this chapter, I have been considering relationships between adult caregivers and what I termed "very young children." In this concluding section of the chapter, I consider relationships between slighter older, school-aged children and their caregivers. When we consider relationships between caregivers and children, we typically think of the caregivers as surpassing those children in every respect and without dependency needs of their own. The adult, with fully developed cognitive, emotional, and physical skills and capacities, cares for a child whose skills are latent or just beginning to develop. When the adult caregiver lacks some of the skills or capacities that the child does possess, and when, moreover, the child successfully responds to some of the adult caregiver's needs, the temptation is very strong to say that roles have been reversed, such that the child is now the caregiver, and the adult is the dependent. This is precisely how the situation is described, both in the popular media and in some academic literature on the topic, when children help to meet some of the needs of their parents, particularly when those parents have physical or cognitive impairments (Keith and Morris 1996, 92).

When children care for their parents, especially when they care for a single parent with physical or cognitive impairments, they are described as "young carers." As Tony Newman points out, in the 1990s in Great Britain, young carers became "well and truly on the map of child welfare services" (Newman 2002, 614). They were recognized in parliamentary legislation, and services specifically dedicated to them in the United Kingdom ballooned from two in 1992 to 110 in 1998. The recognition of the capacity of children to provide care and the fact that many of them make use of that capacity are important and help to deconstruct the understanding of the relationship between children and their caregivers that I have been at pains in this chapter to critique. This recognition could, therefore, help to move us toward a fuller picture of the kinds of mutuality and reciprocity that are possible between children and their adult caregivers.

Unfortunately, this is not how the existence of young carers has been perceived. Young carers are thought to be evidence of a social problem, and because the understanding of the caregiver-child relationship remains resolutely one in which there is no significant mutuality or reciprocity, they are said to have inappropriately reversed roles, and to be "parenting their parents" who are, in turn, infantilized and put in the place of a child. How are young carers defined? Sometimes they are defined as young people who are "carrying out significant caring tasks and assuming a level of responsibility for another person which would normally be undertaken by an adult" (Walker 1996, 3). However, as

Newman points out (Newman 2002, 616), sometimes they are defined much more broadly as people whose lives are in some way restricted by the need to care for someone who is ill, elderly, or impaired; as people who care for or about people with an illness or impairment and who, as a result, find their lives significantly restricted, or, most broadly, as "[a]ny child or young adult whose life is or may be affected because they are involved with someone who is restricted by illness, disability, mental distress, or substance misuse" (Seddon et al. 2001, 29).

On these, progressively broader definitions, young carers become virtually any children whose family members are ill or impaired, even if their lives are restricted simply because of the restrictions their parents face (including those due to disabling attitudes and barriers, rather than those that reflect impairment alone). Whenever the parents (or, occasionally siblings or grandparents) have needs that are greater than those who are not ill or disabled, the parents are thought to be dependent, and therefore the children are described as carrying out the roles of parents in caring for their own parents – whether or not the children actually provide care to them.

Feminist disability theorists and activists, such as Lois Keith, Jenny Morris, Tony Newman, and Michele Wates, have pointed in recent work to the many ways in which oppressive attitudes toward people with impairments have helped to shape the debate about young carers. Newman observes that the supposedly toxic effects of being a young carer are assumed rather than shown, and evidence of positive effects on children of their caring for family members is ignored (Newman 2002, 614–615). Like Newman, Keith, Morris, and Wates, point out that society is more interested in supporting what are portrayed as heroic and exploited young children than in providing adequate services, accessible housing, and other social supports that would enable the parents with impairments to avoid inappropriate reliance on the assistance of their children.

There has also been some attention by disability activists and theorists to questions about exactly what kinds of care provided by school-aged children to their parents are inappropriate. As Keith and Morris observe, it is relatively easy to note that such children should not be expected to do work that exceeds what their bodies can withstand without damage and that they therefore should not be expected to do heavy lifting, for instance, or other tasks that "adversely affect their emotional, social, and educational development" (Keith and Morris 1996, 108). However, outrage at the work carried on by young carers is often directed at the claim that they are doing what their parents should be doing for them. It is therefore often claimed that whenever children do what adults normally do (whether grocery shopping or laundry), they are taking on too great a burden and are acting as parents rather than children. This is especially the case when they provide intimate care for their family members, helping them with dressing, for instance, or picking up things dropped from a wheelchair. While it may be the case that having a child help with certain intimate tasks, such as toileting, may be emotionally distressing for parent and child, it seems to me that when certain tasks are associated with parents or other caregivers caring for children, we are too quick to assume that someone who cannot take care of him- or herself in that manner is immature, dependent, and helpless and therefore not fit to parent someone else. Rather than recognizing that we all need help of various kinds to meet our needs, people with certain needs, in particular, physical or mental impairments, are defined as dependent and are therefore identified as childlike, since it is only in children that we accept obvious dependence.

Feminist disability theorist Susan Wendell makes a similar observation when she points out that "[w]hile most non-disabled people in industrialized societies believe that being able to perform the so-called 'activities of daily living' . . . such as washing, dressing, cooking, shopping, cleaning, and writing, by and for oneself is a necessary condition of independence, and therefore regard people with disabilities as dependent if they cannot perform them, they do not recognized their own dependence on services, such as the provision of water that comes out of the tap, as obstacles to their own independence" (Wendell 1996, 145).

She argues that technology can be developed that would render many people with impairments independent, and indeed many disability activists define independence as having choice and control over the assistance they receive (Shakespeare 2000, 72). However, there is a profound difference between relying on water coming out of a tap or relying on the availability of social services more broadly and relying on a particular individual to help with one's care – not in that the former does not involve dependence, but in that the latter makes a person very vulnerable (see Morris 2001, 13) to another person, including vulnerability to abuse, but also reliance on another person's goodwill, receptivity, and understanding. Another difference, which Wendell does not remark on, is that some kinds of dependence are associated with being a child: needing someone to help you wash, dress, get food to eat, and so forth, whereas other forms of dependence are not noticed as such, I argue, precisely because they are shared by all or most in a given society. It is when adults need the kind of help we ordinarily associate with children that they are inappropriately infantilized and made to seem dependent on some particular parent-like caregiver, and this is why anyone who meets their needs is put in the role of a parent. While it is beyond the scope of this chapter to discuss, I believe that something similar happens when elderly parents need and receive care from their adult children: They are often described as having reversed roles, with the parents described as childlike.

As Grue and Laerum point out, "disabled people on the whole are primarily still looked upon as being dependent on other people's help and care. In short, they are looked upon by professionals and lay people as receivers, and not as carers" (2002, 671). Lloyd notes, "Disabled women have to grapple with the dilemma that, because they need, to a greater or lesser extent, care or assistance themselves, they are not deemed capable of providing care. In the context of motherhood this subjects them to a degree of scrutiny by health professionals which would not routinely be applied to non-disabled women, and makes them vulnerable to the charge of inadequate and also damaging parenting" (Lloyd 2001, 720).

Morris further observes that it is not only social service professionals and laypersons who stigmatize people with impairments in this way, but also some feminists who do research on carers. She points out, "This research divided women into 'carers and their dependents' and made invisible the experiences of women who need" support with daily living tasks (2001, 6). She further observes that dichotomizing people into two groups – carers and their dependents – "has particularly undermined disabled mothers" (7). Examining how the parenting of people with impairments is often misconceived makes it clear that it is not only disabling prejudices against these people that cause their parenting to be suspect, but also the pervasive influence of a model of meeting needs in the private context, such that people who need bodily care and assistance with what was described above as the tasks of daily living are equated with dependent children, and children who provide care for adults, whenever they carry out tasks that are normally associated with adults, are thought to be parenting their parents. In other words, those who have needs we normally associate with children are thought to be dependent and immature, whatever their other skills and capacities might be, and those children who meet needs normally met by adults are thought to be acting in a parental role, despite the other ways in which their own needs for care may be met by the adults in their lives.

In Thomas's study of British mothers with a variety of physical impairments (and in one case, a mental health problem) and Grue and Laerum's study of Norwegian mothers with physical impairments, the researchers made remarkably similar observations. The mothers felt enormous pressure to prove they were good enough, faced fear that their children would be taken away from them if they could not demonstrate their capacity to care for them entirely unaided, and therefore found it very difficult to either ask for or receive appropriate assistance in caring for their children (Thomas 1997; Grue and Laerum 2002). Even when they were able to receive assistance, the assistance often took the form of having someone else care for their children, rather than being helped to care for them. Thomas, for instance, quotes one woman who thought there should be "more emphasis on helping, not doing it – helping mum not doing it for the baby" (637). Grue and Laerum found that "mothers who asked for practical help found that this was sometimes used as proof that they were inadequate as mothers" (678).

Although Norway does not officially recognize young carers as a social problem, the Norwegian mothers studied in many instances restrained themselves from asking their children for any help – not only care the mothers needed for themselves, but also household help, which is often expected of children, because of "other people's concern that their children were made into assistants who were exploited by their disabled mothers" (679). The authors point out that when the mothers are impaired, the children's helping out is seen "within a discourse of disability and not within a discourse of socialization" (679). Interestingly, when these children started attending school, their kindergarten teachers complained that they were very lazy and not used to doing anything for themselves; this, too, was blamed on the mothers, who then had to balance fears that they would be seen as exploiting their children with fears they would be seen as not teaching their children to be independent and to care for themselves. However, some of the mothers in the Norwegian study resisted the social messages they received about the negative impact of their own needs on their children and were proud that they had raised children who "were able to see when other people needed a helping hand, and they interpreted this as an important value acquired by a child growing up with a disabled mother" (680). It is precisely this kind of resistance to dominant messages about what care that is given to children is supposed to be like that can help us to reconceptualize that care to include aspects of mutuality and reciprocity.

The experiences of the mothers in the Norwegian study point to contradictions inherent in the model of the all-giving adult care provider and the entirely dependent child who receives that care. Children are, after all, expected to acquire the ability to meet and to identify many of their own needs and those of others and an interest in or motivation toward meeting those needs. If they are given no opportunities to recognize others' needs and little opportunity to seek to meet their own needs or those of others in their lives, it is difficult to see how they can become responsible and caring adults; at the least, they will surely do better at acquiring responsibility and caring attitudes when provided opportunities to develop these skills and attitudes, rather than being suddenly expected to possess them when separated from their caregivers.

If, instead, we were to reconceive caregiving relationships between children and adults as appropriately involving varieties of mutuality and reciprocity, young carers, insofar as they are seen as a social problem, would be defined much more narrowly, after we had determined that in certain instances, children's acts of providing care were harmful to them. This would help to remove the stigma from parents with impairments of failing to be adequate parents whenever they cannot meet all of their children's needs on their own, while also recognizing that sometimes a child may appropriately care for a parent and receive care from that parent. As Thomas, Keith and Morris, and Grue and Laerum point out, a parent is still parenting and providing care for a child when others help in providing this care, and parents are entitled to assistance in providing care, rather than being forced to choose between providing all of a child's care on their own or having the child taken away from the home (Keith and Morris 1996, 113; Thomas 1997, 637; Grue and Laerum 2002, 678).

## 8. CONCLUSION

The above recalls the conclusions of the preceding chapter, in that we need to recognize that there are many situations, applying not only to parents with illnesses or impairments, but also to parents in poverty and parents with significant other demands on their time, such as paid employment, and so forth, in which networks of care are required to meet the needs of a child. Moreover, there are many other circumstances in which networks may not be absolutely needed, if a parent is amply supplied with time and resources, but in which children may nevertheless be well served by having their needs for care met by several persons rather than one alone.

We must refuse to think of the paradigmatic child's caregiver as someone who has no significant care needs of his or her own and refuse also to think only of the caregiver who gives and never receives care from the children in his or her care. If we can do so, we will be moved closer to the recognition that relationships do not come only in two types, ones in which we meet each other entirely as equals without significantly differing needs and ones in which we are either the dependent care receiver or the all-powerful care provider. The existence of "young carers" and the way they have been perceived solely as a social problem is a powerful reminder of the pervasive influence of the negative influence of operating with overly simplistic and dichotomous paradigms of personal caring relationships. Taken together with my arguments in the first section of this chapter, in which I compared friendships with relations between young children and their caregivers, these considerations suggest that caring relationships between children and their caregivers not only are an important subject for philosophical study in themselves, but also that a proper consideration of them can help to illuminate many other caring relationships. Once again, as throughout this book, we observe that philosophical investigations of experiences in reproductive labor have lessons to teach us about other parts of life, as significant errors and omissions occur when we think that relationships between children and their caregivers are the only ones that appropriately involve dependency.

# Conclusion

Throughout this book I have argued for increased recognition of pregnancy, birthing, and childrearing as social activities that involve simultaneously physical, intellectual, emotional, and moral work from those who undertake them. This work calls for a number of skills and also requires broad social support if it is to be done well by pregnant women, birthing women, and male and female providers of childcare in a number of different kinds of social circumstance.

The first three chapters of this book were devoted to philosophical analysis of pregnancy. I argued that pregnancy is a subject that has been overlooked or distorted by an emphasis only on ethical issues that arise in unwanted pregnancies. This discussion was followed by a brief chapter on birth in which I argued that focus on the medicalization of birth needs to be supplemented by increased awareness of how privatized women's experiences of birth are encouraged to be and how we should not think of birth as involving minds controlling bodies to the greatest extent possible. The following two chapters were devoted to the next stage of reproductive labor, caring for children once they are born. In chapter 5 I argued that our understanding of caring for children needs to be extended to include the many different situations in which children are and can be cared for and that we need to consider the needs of both care providers and care receivers in evaluating these different situations. In the chapter that followed, I suggested that we can learn a great deal from comparing, rather than simply contrasting, friendship and the caregiver-child relation.

I have suggested that in analyzing these forms of reproductive labor it is important to approach them from the perspective of the pregnant and birthing women and male and female caregivers, paid and unpaid, who perform them. It is a mistake to focus only on the needs of fetuses or children. This is for two reasons. First, for ethical reasons, we should consider the needs and interests of all the parties involved. Second, children will not be well served if they have access to only one or two caregivers who do not themselves receive support for their own needs. As a result, any attempt to focus only on the needs of children will be self-defeating. We must therefore think broadly about how to support caregiving and how to allocate more fairly the provision and receiving of care, particularly in ways that do not illegitimately reflect prejudices about impairment, race, sex, class, or ethnicity.

Another broad theme running throughout the book has been the importance of considering a range of experiences of people engaged in reproductive labor, rather than taking as paradigmatic the worker envisioned by the ideology of motherhood, a woman working alone, financially supported by a male partner, with no significant needs of her own, and totally absorbed in her work. We need to recognize that reproductive labor is undertaken by paid as well as unpaid caregivers, by men as well as women, and by men and women with physical and mental impairments.

When we theorize about the many different men and women in varying circumstances who provide reproductive labor, we enrich our understanding of the work and can begin the kinds of nuanced ethical and political debates the subject requires. Gendering reproductive labor has excluded men from its rewards as well as sheltering them from its demands, and it has kept both men and women from developing skills and acquiring knowledge that are required by and emerge out of the different types of undertaking from which they have been excluded. I have argued against developing separate ideals of male and female childcare, while arguing for recognition of the role played by traits deemed both masculine and feminine in various aspects of reproductive labor.

Respecting the value of paid reproductive labor encourages us to contest sharp distinctions between self-interest and care and between work and emotional involvement. Recognizing the extent to which a number of different caregivers often share care for a child allows us to develop models of collective or cooperative caregiving that respect the value of paid care while also attending to the difference between being a child's caregiver and being his or her parent.

A focus on the impact of physical and mental impairments (and disabling practices and prejudices) – whether these affect the workers or the children cared for – has many lessons to teach us. It leads us to rethink associations between care receiving and childhood or dependency. It challenges the assumption that any one person can meet all the needs of any child. It also leads us to contest any sharp contrast between friendship and the caregiver-child relationship. Last, it demands that we think about how both caregiving in general and caregiving by people with impairments in particular is made more difficult by social failure to acknowledge and accommodate the demands of the work.

In clarifying the nature and demands of reproductive labor, whether in pregnancy, birthing, or caring for children, I have opened up space to challenge assumptions that self-sacrifice should be the norm without going to the opposite extreme of concluding that acts of unreciprocated care are unhealthy. I have approached an ethical analysis of caregiving relations from a point of view that neither assumes that these relations pit caregivers and fetuses or children against one another nor optimistically concludes that their interests will always coincide. Moreover, I have argued throughout the book about the need to recognize that reproductive labor places ethical demands on the larger social context in which this work is located. This may come in the form of social support of various kinds for pregnant and birthing women and less privatized conceptions of these kinds of reproductive labor or in the form of more collective responsibility for caring for children once they are born.

Finally, I have argued throughout the book that experiences of reproductive labor have relations to and relevance for other kinds of experiences. For instance, in chapter 2 I argued that women's experiences with pregnancy can lead us to rethink our division of life into the mental and the bodily, the passive and the purposive, as we can instead recognize that our projects always depend on both our minds and bodies. Moreover, goals and purposes require us not only to plan in advance, but also to respond flexibly to what we cannot predict or control. I also argued that theorizing about pregnancy and theorizing about some forms of impairment can be mutually illuminating. In chapter 6 I argued that reflecting on relations between caregivers and children can lead us to rethink our models of ethical relations more generally, to avoid holding such relations to require either self-sacrifice or complete reciprocity.

Failure to acknowledge and reflect on experiences of reproductive labor therefore not only keeps us from understanding the requirements of the work, the demands it makes on people who undertake it, and its ethical import, but also deprives us of insights into other kinds of experiences. These insights are available only when we compare these different types of experience with one another, and therefore the former must be acknowledged and theorized about not only for their own sake.

This book has aimed to initiate or to continue both sorts of reflection, presenting experiences with pregnancy and childcare as both worthy of study for themselves and with important connections to other kinds of experience, whether of impairment, transformation and growth, or other types of caring relationship. If it also contributes to increasing the dialogue among philosophers and other scholars and laypersons with an interest in these topics, it will have succeeded in one of its main goals.

# Notes

## INTRODUCTION

1. Virginia Held has some reservations about the use of the phrase "reproductive labor," arguing that while it represents a significant advance to recognize the work involved, "it may be almost as inappropriate to think of childbirth and rearing as forms of 'production' as it is to think of them as forms of mere 'reproduction'" (Held 1989, 382). Instead, she argues that they may be closer to forms of artistic expression than to the production of material objects. I agree that we should not think of reproductive labor as akin to producing material objects (although children are, of course, material subjects) and use the term to indicate that productive and socially necessary work is involved in being pregnant, giving birth, and raising children.

## CHAPTER 1: PREGNANCY MISCONCEIVED

1. See Matthews and Wexler 2000 for an excellent account of shifts in the images of pregnant women throughout the twentieth century. See Duden 1993 for an analysis of how the development of fetal ultrasound technology has diminished the significance of fetal quickening as an important transition in women's experiences of pregnancy.
2. See Parkes 1994 for a careful examination of the ways this metaphor is elaborated in each case.
3. Alison Ainley quotes this passage in full and argues that Nietzsche offers us an alternative to feminist readings of maternity as oppressive as well as an enriched understanding of the self as other than self-contained (Ainley 1988, 124–125). However, she virtually ignores the many places where Nietzsche manifests his disdain for merely physical pregnancy and also fails to note the fact that while Nietzsche seems to recognize the presence of otherness within the self, in his talk of the spiritual child as unknown to the parent, he ultimately claims that he is giving birth to himself.
4. This and all further references to Plato's dialogues are taken from Plato 1961. References within the text will be given to the name of the dialogue and the section number.

5. Socrates, in addition to being a historical figure who significantly influenced Plato, also appears as a character, often the most dominant character, in most of Plato's dialogues. He is generally taken, at least in the early and middle dialogues, as something very close to a mouthpiece for Plato's own views.
6. In a letter written to Peter Gast on December 22, 1888 (in one of his last moments of sanity), Nietzsche writes that he was in the past unable to appreciate the impact of his works and says, "It is the case of the mother with her child – she may perhaps love it but she is stupidly ignorant of what the child is" (Nietzsche 1921, 258). In an earlier letter to Hans Von Bulow in December 1882, Nietzsche writes, "It seems to me that the state of pregnancy is the only one that binds us ever anew to life" (276).
7. Lucy Lippard offers a concise definition of "body art" as art that "focuses upon the body or body parts usually the artist's own body, but at times, especially in men's work, other bodies, envisioned as extensions of the artist him/herself" (Lippard 1995, 99). Writing in 1976, she notes as a curious fact that "no women dealing with their own bodies and biographies have introduced pregnancy or childbirth as a major image" (112).
8. To the extent that they succeed in negotiating between these extremes, I read them as consonant with the excellent work done by Iris Marion Young and Carol Bigwood, which I discuss in the next chapter. Each of these feminist philosophers interprets pregnancy as a process of change (rather than simply an event) that involves constant readjustment of one's habits and self-understanding. See Young 1984 and Bigwood 1991.
9. See Mulvey 1975 and Kelly 1987. Both writers are complex theorists and artists, and I do not pretend to do more than engage with one way in which their work has been taken up, as issuing in a prohibition against the objectification of women's bodies.
10. One of the important philosophical issues raised by experiences of bodily pregnancy, which involve one woman's body shaping and containing that of another living being, concerns the question of where we locate the boundary of a person. Thus Kristeva, for instance, locates the maternal body as one of the primary sites of the abject. Rich, similarly, writes of the experience of pregnancy as revealing "something inside and of me, yet becoming hourly and daily more separate" (Rich 1986, 63). Since the fetus inside the woman's body is experienced "neither as me [nor] as not me," this challenges a woman's understanding of the borders of personal identity.
11. Sjoo's belief in a great Goddess who is a cosmic mother to us all puts her in an essentialist camp, and in her writings she often speaks of a universal feminine essence.
12. Rosalind Pollack Petchesky has importantly observed how this tendency has been used in anti-abortion campaigns (Petchesky 1987).
13. While the border between wanted and unwanted pregnancies might not always be clear or fixed, and a woman may change her mind many times about whether or not her pregnancy is welcome, this distinction does nonetheless capture a difference that is very important to women's experiences of their pregnancies.

## CHAPTER 2: RECONCEIVING PREGNANCY

1. This assertion that all pregnant persons are women is complicated somewhat by the existence of pregnant people who are transitioning transsexuals (see More 1998). However, all of the transitioning transsexuals in this study had some discomfort with the idea and the reality of their pregnancies because they experienced pregnancy as very female, both in terms of others' expectations of them and in terms of feeling like female animals during pregnancy. None of them saw herself as having completed the transition from females to males until after the pregnancy.
2. This is not to deny that women, as well as men, often have very complicated and ambivalent attitudes toward dieting, exercise, and their bodies, which may well make it extremely difficult for women to be wholehearted about these kinds of undertakings.
3. When I wrote the first draft of what would become this chapter, I was nine months' pregnant and the mother of two children. I now have three young children.
4. Wilson notes that the courts have been inconsistent in sometimes deeming pregnancy-related illness and impairment to count as a disability and sometimes not.
5. I use the definition of chronic illness offered by Susan Wendell. Chronic illnesses are those that do not go away by themselves within six months, cannot reliably be cured, and will not kill the patient any time soon. Wendell 2001, 20.
6. "Understanding Gestational Diabetes," http://www.nichd.nih.gov/publications/pubs/gesttoc.htm. Accessed December 15, 2002.
7. "Pre-eclampsia," http://www.nichd.nih.gov/new/releases/PREEC998.htm. Accessed December 15, 2002.

## CHAPTER 3: THE ETHICAL SIGNIFICANCE OF PREGNANCY

1. See Martin 1998 for an interesting discussion of a number of different metaphors that have been used in medical texts to describe the relation between a pregnant woman and a fetus, including fetus as intruder, as tumor, and as conqueror.
2. What is the extent of the problem? A 1995 U.S. National Household Survey on Drug Abuse suggests that "nationally 7.2% of women ages 15 to 44 who were not pregnant used an illicit drug at least once during the past month, compared to 2.3% of pregnant women . . . suggesting women reduce substantially their use of drugs during pregnancy" (Howell et al. 1999, 197). A National Pregnancy and Health Survey (conducted in hospitals after delivery) undertaken in 1992 showed that 5.5 percent of pregnant women used an illicit drug at some point during the pregnancy (mostly marijuana), while 18.8 percent used alcohol and 20.4 percent smoked cigarettes (Howell et al. 1999, 197).
3. Vangie Bergum has engaged in extensive and important empirical study of women's experiences with pregnancy but tends to report those experiences

in ways that exaggerate somewhat the presence of distinct stages in the relationship between pregnant woman and fetus; also, the women she studied had relatively similar social contexts. See Bergum 1989.

4. Sarah Lucia Hoagland argues that self-sacrifice undermines autonomy and that it is particularly dangerous in unidirectional mothering, which is supposed to involve unconditional love and unreciprocated care. (1990, 288)

## CHAPTER 4: WHAT ABOUT BIRTH?

1. As Linda Blum points out, historians have labeled "maternalists" those (largely female) reformers who "used the rhetoric of gender difference, invoking women's motherly virtues, to gain a distinct voice as the defenders of children" (Blum 1999, 23).

## CHAPTER 5: MOTHERS AND OTHERS: WHO CAN BE "MATERNAL THINKERS"?

1. This ideology is sometimes called "privatized motherhood" (Fox and Worts 1999), intensive motherhood (Hays 1996), or exclusive motherhood (Blum 1999).
2. Mothers continue to care for and think about their children when those children reach adulthood and beyond. I find it implausible to claim that maternal thinking and maternal care of a one-year-old infant and a fully grown son or daughter would have much in common. Furthermore, the ideology of motherhood is really targeted only at mothers with fairly young children. Mothers are not thought to be both necessary and sufficient for the happiness of their teenaged children. By "very young children" I mean children who are not yet expected to be away from their caregivers for substantial periods of time to attend school.
3. Feminist sociologist Lynet Uttal makes a similar observation when she asks, "How can child care support mothering, and how do mothers and child care providers coordinate their care giving in the best interests of children?" (Uttal 1996, 309). While this makes sense in the context of her focus on the meanings mothers give to their childcare arrangements, it leaves out questions about which forms of caregiving and which conceptions of caregiving are in the best interests of the paid care providers.
4. Tronto is well aware that this kind of virtue may be developed by people because they are oppressed. She writes: "insofar as caring is a kind of attentiveness, it may be a reflection of a survival mechanism for women or others who are dealing with oppressive conditions, rather than a quality of intrinsic value on its own." It might be "otherwise understood as the necessity to anticipate the wishes of one's superior" (Tronto 1995, 112).
5. Whitbeck grants that different socialization and different temperaments may make up for the sex differences she has discussed (Whitbeck 1983b, 271).
6. Assisted reproductive technologies and practices such as surrogate motherhood have similarly led at times to debates about who is a child's real mother,

versus acknowledgment that several different women may serve in different aspects of this role.

7. Collins claims that this is not because African American men do not share the commitment to shared childrearing but that this is because of differences in male and female labor force participation (Collins 2000, 180). Given the high unemployment among African American males, I find this an implausible explanation.
8. Arlie Hochschild introduced the concept of emotional labor in Hochschild 1983.

### CHAPTER 6: CARING FOR CHILDREN, CARING FOR FRIENDS, CARING BY CHILDREN

1. Some of these theorists, such as Elshtain (1981) and Ruddick (1989) also make claims about the significance of the mothering relationship to political thought. Their claim is engaged by Patricia Bowling (1991) and critiqued by Mary Dietz (1985). I do not discuss the relevance of the caregiver-child relationship to political thought, but I do find some interesting parallels between the debate over its significance for ethical thought and the debate over its significance for political thought. In particular, those who dispute the significance tend to conceive of politics as a place where equals meet and deny the significance of meeting dependency needs for politics. See, for instance, Dietz 1985, 34.
2. "To be a 'mother' is to take upon oneself the responsibility of child care, making its work a regular and substantial part of one's working life" (Ruddick 1989, 17).
3. See, for instance, Code 1991, 94.
4. Hoagland (1991) does briefly explore possibilities of group mothering, as does Card (1996), as discussed at the end of the previous chapter.
5. For instance, the mother-child or parent-child relationship is typically contrasted with friendship with the former described as formal and highly structured and the latter as minimally structured. See, for instance, Thomas 1987, 218–219. I believe the contrast would not be as sharp if we considered a range of caregiver-child relationships.
6. I am using "paternalism" here in a gender-neutral way to describe any relation in which one person makes decisions for the other on the basis of what the decision maker believes to be the best interests of the one decided for.
7. As in other chapters of this book, I follow many disability activists and theorists in distinguishing between physical or cognitive impairments, with impairment briefly defined as "lacking all or part of a limb, or having a defective limb, organism or mechanism of the body" (Crow 1996, 212) and disability. Disability (not impairment) is a form of social oppression, including prejudice and bigotry, but also a failure to accommodate the needs of people with impairments. However, the terminology is still quite unsettled in this area, and some of the authors quoted in the last section of this chapter refer to, for instance, "disabled mothers," by whom they mean mothers with impairments, and conflate disability and impairment. For a fuller discussion of

the distinction between impairment and disability, and for a more nuanced definition of impairment, see Morris 2001, 2.

8. A loss of moral value is suggested by those, like Friedman, who argue that ethically ideal friendships require reciprocity of exchange.
9. Friedman (1993) also thinks that mutuality is reinforced by "an approximate overall equivalence of status and authority of the friends, and by an approximate equivalence in their mutual confidences and disclosure of vulnerabilities" (210).
10. Despite her explicit denial, Friedman herself argues that friends can be an invaluable resource for enabling moral growth, including the growth possible when we "learn to grasp our experiences in a new light or in radically different terms" (Friedman 1993, 196). She also argues that we depend on others for our social acceptability, even when we are adults and even when we are morally competent adults (1993, 207). Concerning both growth and support for one's social acceptability, Friedman's analysis of friendship suggests there are similarities between friendship and maternal thinking as Ruddick (1989) describes it.
11. Another way to think about reciprocity between parents and children is to think that, in the long term, children will have opportunities to repay their parents, perhaps when the parents become dependent. Few parents endorse this ideal. Moreover, this type of reciprocity is available only when the caregiving relationship is itself long-term, such as the relationship between mother and child is expected to be.

# References


Adler, Carrie L., and Yosepha Rose Zarchin. 2002. "The 'Virtual Focus Group': Using the Internet to Reach Pregnant Women on Home Bed Rest." *JOGNN Clinical Studies* 31, no. 4: 418–427.

Ainley, Alison. 1988. "'Ideal Selfishness': Nietzsche's Metaphor of Maternity." In *Exceedingly Nietzsche*, ed. David Farrell Krell and David Wood. London: Routledge.

Allen, Jeffner. 1983. "Motherhood: The Annihilation of Women." In *Mothering: Essays in Feminist Theory*, ed. Joyce Trebilcot. Totowa, N.J.: Rowman and Allanheld.

Ambert, Anne-Marie. 1994. "An International Perspective on Parenting: Social Change and Social Constructs." *Journal of Marriage and the Family* 56, no. 3 (August): 529–548.

Annandale, Ellen, and Judith Clark. 1996. "What Is Gender? Feminist Theory and the Sociology of Human Reproduction." *Sociology of Health & Illness* 18, no. 1: 17–44.

Arendt, Hannah. 1958. *The Human Condition*. Chicago: University of Chicago Press.

Ariss, Rachel. 1998. "Mackenzie, Elizabeth: The Radiant Monster." *Herizons* 12, no. 2: 43–44.

Aronson, Jane. 1998. "Lesbians Giving and Receiving Care: Stretching Conceptualizations of Caring and Community." *Women's Studies International Forum* 21, no. 5: 505–519.

Ashe, Marie. 1992. "The 'Bad' Mother in Law and Literature." *Hastings Law Journal* 43: 1017–1037.

Audi, Robert. 1996. "Intuitionism, Pluralism, and the Foundations of Ethics." In *Moral Knowledge: New Readings in Moral Epistemology*, ed. Walter Sinnot-Armstrong and Mark Timmons. New York: Oxford University Press.

Baier, Annette. 1994. *Moral Prejudices: Essays on Ethics*. Cambridge, Mass.: Harvard University Press.

Bailey, Alison. 1994. "Mothering, Diversity, and Peace Politics." *Hypatia* 9, no. 2: 188–198.

Bailey, Lucy. 1999. "Refracted Selves? A Study of Changes in Self-Identity in the Transition to Motherhood." *Sociology* 33, no. 2: 335–352.

Bailey, Lucy. 2001. "Gender Shows: First-Time Mothers and Embodied Selves." *Gender and Society* 15, no. 1: 110–129.

Barnes, Colin. 1998. "Review of the Rejected Body by Susan Wendell." In *Disability and Society* 13, no. 1: 145–146.

Barnes, Colin, and Geoff Mercer. 2001. "The Politics of Disability and the Struggle for Change." In *Disability, Politics, and the Struggle for Change*, ed. Len Barton. London: David Fulton.

Bartky, Sandra. 1990. "Feeding Egos and Tending Wounds: Deference and Disaffection in Women's Emotional Labour." In *Femininity and Domination: Studies in the Phenomenology of Oppression*. New York: Routledge, 99–119.

Bassin, Donna, Margaret Honey, and Meryle Mahrer Kaplan, eds. 1994. *Representations of Motherhood*. New Haven: Yale University Press.

Bell, Linda A. 1993. *Rethinking Ethics in the Midst of Violence: A Feminist Approach to Freedom*. Lanham, Md.: Rowman & Littlefield.

Bergum, Vangie. 1989. *Woman to Mother: A Transformation*. Granby, Mass.: Bergin & Garvey.

Bergum, Vangie. 1990. "Abortion Revisited: Toward an Understanding of the Nature of the Woman-Fetus Relationship." *Phenomenology and Pedagogy* 8: 17–26.

Bergum, Vangie. 1997. *A Child on Her Mind: The Experience of Becoming a Mother*. Westport, Conn.: Berge & Garvey.

Betterton, Rosemary. 1996. A*n Intimate Distance: Women, Artists and the Body*. New York: Routledge.

Betterton, Rosemary. 2002. "Prima gravida: Reconfiguring the Maternal Body in Visual Representation." *Feminist Theory* 3, no. 3: 255–270.

Bigwood, Carol. 1991. "Renaturalizing the Body (with the Help of Merleau-Ponty)." *Hypatia* 6, no. 3: 54–73.

Blum, Linda. 1999. *At the Breast: Ideologies of Breastfeeding and Motherhood in the Contemporary United States*. Boston: Beacon.

Bourgeault, Ivy, Eugene Declercq, and Jane Sandall. 2001. "Changing Birth." In *Birth by Design: Pregnancy, Maternity Care, and Midwifery in North America and Europe*, ed. Raymond Devries, Cecilia Benoit, Edwin R. Van Teilingen, and Sirpa Wrede. New York: Routledge.

Bowden, Peta. 1997. *Caring: Gender-Sensitive Ethics*. New York: Routledge.

Bowling, Patricia. 1991. "The Democratic Potential of Mothering." *Political Theory* 19, no. 4: 606–625.

Boyd, Susan B. 1997. "Challenging the Public/Private Divide: An Overview." In *Challenging the Public/Private Divide: Feminism, Law and Public Policy*. Toronto: University of Toronto Press.

Brandth, Berin, and Elin Kvande. 1998. "Masculinity and Child Care: The Reconstruction of Fathering." *Sociological Review* 46, no. 2: 293–313.

Brennan, Samantha, and Robert Noggle. 1997. "The Moral Status of Children: Children's Rights, Parents' Rights, and Family Justice." *Social Theory and Practice* 23, no. 1: 1–26.

Bubeck, Diemut. 2002. "Justice and the Labor of Care." In *The Subject of Care: Feminist Perspectives on Dependency*, ed. Eva Feder Kittay and Ellen K. Feder. New York: Rowman & Littlefield.

Butler, Judith. 1989. "Sexual Ideology and Phenomenological Description: A Feminist Critique of Merleau-Ponty's Phenomenology of Perception." In *The Thinking Muse: Feminism and Modern French Philosophy*, ed. Jeffner Allen and Iris Marion Young. Bloomington: Indiana University Press, 85–100.

Butler, Judith. 1997. "Performative Acts and Gender Constitution: An Essay in Phenomenology and Feminist Theory." In *Writing on the Body: Female Embodiment and Feminist Theory*, ed. Katie Conboy, Nadia Medina, and Sarah Stanbury. New York: Columbia University Press.

Cahill, Heather. 1999. "An Orwellian Scenario: Court Ordered Caesarean Section and Women's Autonomy." *Nursing Ethics* 6, no. 6: 494–505.

Cahill, Heather A. 2001. "Male Appropriation and Medicalization of Childbirth: An Historical Analysis. *Journal of Advanced Nursing* 33, no. 3: 334–342.

Callahan, Joan C., and James W. Knight. 1993. "On Treating Prenatal Harm as Child Abuse." In *Kindred Matters: Rethinking the Philosophy of the Family*, ed. Diana Tietjens Meyers, Kenneth Kipnis, and Cornelius F. Murphy, Jr. Ithaca, N.Y.: Cornell University Press.

Campbell, Rona, and Sam Porter. 1997. "Feminist Theory and the Sociology of Childbirth: A Response to Ellen Annandale and Judith Clark." *Sociology of Health & Illness* 19: no. 3: 348–358.

Cancellaro, Cecilia A. 2001. *Pregnancy Stories: Real Women Share the Joys, Fears, Thrills, and Anxieties of Pregnancy from Conception to Birth*. Oakland, Calif.: New Harbinger.

Card, Claudia. 1990. "Gender and Moral Luck." In *Identity, Character and Morality: Essays in Moral Psychology*, ed. Owen Flanagan and Amelie O. Rorty. Cambridge, Mass.: MIT Press, 197–216.

Card, Claudia. 1996. "Against Marriage and Motherhood." *Hypatia* 11, no. 3: 1–23.

Carr, Karen L. 1995. "Optical Allusions: Hysterical Memories and the Screening of Pregnant Sites." *Postmodern Culture* 5: 2.

Carse, Alisa L., and Hilde Lindemann Nelson. 1999. "Rehabilitating Care." In *Embodying Bioethics: Recent Feminist Advances*, ed. Anne Donchin and Laura M. Purdy. New York: Rowman & Littlefield.

Chervenak, Frank A., and Laurence B. McCullough. 1999. "Ethics in Fetal Medicine." *Baillière's Clinical Obstetrics and Gynaecology* 13, no. 4: 491–502.

Chodorow, Nancy. 1999. *The Reproduction of Mothering: Psychoanalysis and the Sociology of Gender*, 2nd ed. Berkeley: University of California Press.

Chopra, Radhika. 2001. "Retrieving the Father: Gender Studies, 'Father Love' and the Discourse of Mothering." *Women's Studies International Forum* 24, no. 3/4: 445–455.

Code, Lorraine. 1991. *What Can She Know? Feminist Theory and the Construction of Knowledge*. Ithaca, N.Y.: Cornell University Press.

Collins, Patricia Hill. 1992. "Black Women and Motherhood." In *Rethinking the Family*, ed. B. Thorne and M. Yalom. Boston: Northeastern University Press.

Collins, Patricia Hill. 1994. "Shifting the Center: Race, Class, and Feminist Theorizing about Motherhood." In *Representations of Motherhood*, ed. Donna Bassin, Margaret Honey, and Meryle Mahrer Kaplan. New Haven: Yale University Press.

Collins, Patricia Hill. 2000. *Black Feminist Thought*, 2nd ed. New York: Routledge.

Corea, G. 1988. *The Mother-Machine: Reproductive Technologies from Artifical Insemination to Artificial Wombs*. Boston: Beacon.

Crossley, Mary. 2000. "Impairment and Embodiment." In *Americans with Disabilities: Exploring Implications of the Law for Individuals and Institutions*, ed. Leslie Pickering Francis and Anita Silvers. New York: Routledge.

Crow, Liz. 1996. "Including All of Our Lives: Renewing the Social Model of Disability." In *Encounters with Strangers: Feminism and Disability*, ed. Jenny Morris. London: Women's Press.

Daniels, Cynthia. 1999. "Fathers, Mothers, and Fetal Harm: Rethinking Gender Difference and Reproductive Responsibility." In *Fetal Subjects, Feminist Positions*, ed. Lynn R. Morgan and Meredith W. Michaels. Philadelphia: University of Pennsylvania Press.

Davidson, Joyce. 2001. "Pregnant Pauses: Agoraphobic Embodiment and the Limits of (Im)pregnability." *Gender, Place and Culture* 8, no. 3: 283–297.

Davis-Floyd, R. E. 1987. "The Technological Model of Birth." *Journal of American Folklore* 100: 479–495.

Davis-Floyd, Robbie. 1992. *Birth as an American Rite of Passage*. Berkeley: University of California Press.

Davis-Floyd, Robbie. 1994. "The Technocratic Body: American Childbirth as Cultural Expression." *Social Science and Medicine* 38: 1125–1140.

Davis-Floyd, Robbie. 2000. "Afterword: Technologies of the Exterior, Technologies of the Interior – Can We Expand the Discourse of Reproductive Studies?" In *Body Talk: Rhetoric, Technology, Reproduction*, ed. Mary M. Lay. Laura J. Gurak, Clare Gravon, and Cynthia Myntti. Madison: University of Wisconsin Press.

Davis-Floyd, Robbie. 2001. "Foreword." In *Birth by Design: Pregnancy, Maternity Care, and Midwifery in North America and Europe*, ed. Raymond Devries, Cecilia Benoit, Edwin R. Van Teilingen, and Sirpa Wrede. New York: Routledge.

De Beauvoir, Simone. 1953. *The Second Sex*, trans. H. Parshley. New York: Bantam.

De Lauretis, Teresa. 1988. "Aesthetic and Feminist Theory: Rethinking Women's Cinema." In *Feminist art Criticism*, ed. Arlene Raven, Cassandra Langer, and Joanne Frueh. New York: HarperCollins.

De Vries, Raymond, Cecilia Benoit, Edwin R. Van Teilingen, and Sirpa Wrede, eds. 2001. *Birth by Design: Pregnancy, Maternity Care, and Midwifery in North America and Europe*. New York: Routledge.

Diethe, Carol. 1989. "Nietzsche and the Woman Question." *History of European Ideas* 11: 865–875.

Dietz, Mary. 1985. "Citizenship with a Feminist Face: The Problems with Maternal Thinking." *Political Theory* 13: 19–37.

DiQuinzio, Patrice. 1999. *The Impossibility of Motherhood: Feminism, Individualism, and the Problem of Mothering*. New York: Routledge.

Dixon, Nicholas. 1995. "The Friendship Model of Filial Obligations." *Journal of Applied Philosophy* 12, no. 1: 77–87.

Donath, Susan. 2000. "The Other Economy: A Suggestion for a Distinctively Feminist Economy." *Feminist Economics* 6, no. 1: 115–123.

Downe, Pamela J. 2001. "Stepping on Maternal Ground: Reflections of Becoming an 'Other-Mother.'" *Journal of the Association for Research on Mothering* 3, no. 1: 27–40.

Duden, Barbara. 1993. *Disembodying Women: Perspectives on Pregnancy and the Unborn*, trans. Lee Honicki. Cambridge: Harvard University Press.

Duquaine-Watson, Jillian. 2003. "All You Need Is Love: Representations of Maternal Emotion in Working Mother Magazine, 1995–1999." *Journal of the Association for Research in Mothering* 5, no. 1: 91–103.

Dwyer, Susan. 1998. "Learning from Experience: Moral Phenomenology and Politics." In *Daring to be Good: Essays in Feminist Ethics*, ed. Bat-Ami Bar On and Ann Ferguson. New York: Routledge, 28–44.

Eisenberg, A., H. Murkoff, and S. Hathaway. 1997. *What to Expect When You're Expecting*, 2nd ed. New York: Harper Collins.

Elshtain, Jean Bethke. 1981. *Public Man, Private Woman*. Princeton: Princeton University Press.

Field, Tiffany, M. Diego, Maria Hernandez-Reif, F. Salman, S. Schanberg, Cynthia Kuhn, Regina Yando, and Debra Bendell. 2002. "Prenatal Anger Effects on the Fetus and Neonate." *Journal of Obstetrics and Gynaecology* 22, no. 3: 260–266.

Finkelstein, V. 1996. "Outside, Inside Out." *Coalition* (April): 30–36.

Firestone, Shulamith. 1970. *The Dialectic of Sex*. New York: Bantam.

Fisher, Berenice, and Joan Tronto. 1990. "Toward a Feminist Theory of Caring." In *Circles of Care: Work and Identity in Women's Lives*, ed. Emily K. Abel and Margaret K. Nelson. Albany: SUNY Press.

Folbre, Nancy. 1995. "Holding Hands at Midnight? The Paradox of Caring Labor." *Feminist Economics* 1, no. 1: 73–92.

Fox, Bonnie, and Diana Worts. 1999. "Revisiting the Critique of Medicalized Childbirth: A Contribution to the Sociology of Birth." *Gender & Society* 13, no. 3: 326–346.

Franklin, Sarah. 1991. "Fetal Fascinations: New Dimensions to the Medical-Scientific Construction of Fetal Personhood." In *Off-Centre – Feminism and Cultural Studies*. New York: Harper Collins.

Friedman, Marilyn. 1989. "Friendship and Moral Growth." *Journal of Value Inquiry* 23: 3–13.

Friedman, Marilyn. 1993. *What Are Friends For? Feminist Perspectives on Personal Relationships and Moral Theory*. Ithaca, N.Y.: Cornell University Press.

Gallagher, Janet. 1995. "Collective Bad Faith and 'Protecting' the Fetus." In *Reproduction, Ethics, and the Law: Feminist Perspectives*, ed. Joan C. Callahan. Bloomington: Indiana University Press, 343–379.

Gatens, Moira. 1992. "Power, Bodies and Difference." In *Destablishing Theory*, ed. M. Barrett and A. Phillips. Cambridge: Polity.

Gatens, Moira. 1996. *Imaginary Bodies: Ethics, Power and Corporeality*. New York: Routledge.

Gatens-Robinson, Eugenie. 1992. "A Defense of Women's Choice: Abortion and the Ethics of Care." *Southern Journal of Philosophy* 30, no. 3: 39–66.

Glover, Vivette. 2002. "Effects of Antenatal Stress and Anxiety." *British Journal of Psychiatry* 180: 389–391.

Grace, Marty. 1998. "The Work of Caring for Young Children: Priceless or Worthless?" *Women's Studies International Forum* 21, no. 4: 401–413.

Grimshaw, Jean. 1986. *Philosophy and Feminist Thinking*. Minneapolis: University of Minnesota Press.

Grosz, Elizabeth. 1993. "Merleau-Ponty and Irigaray in the Flesh." *Thesis Eleven*, no. 36: 37–59.

Grosz, Elizabeth. 1994. *Volatile Bodies*. Bloomington: Indiana University Press.

Grue, Lars, and Kristin Tafjord Laerum. 2002. "'Doing Motherhood': Some Experiences of Mothers with Physical Disabilities." *Disability and Society* 17, no. 6: 671–683.

Gudorf, Christine. 1985. "Parenting, Mutual Love and Sacrifice." In *Women's Conscience: A Reader in Feminist Ethics*, ed. C. Gudorf and M. Pellauer. Minneapolis: Minnesota Winston.

Harman, Elizabeth. 2000. "Creation Ethics: The Moral Status of Early Fetuses and the Ethics of Abortion." *Philosophy & Public Affairs* 28, no. 4: 310–324.

Harris, Lisa H. 2000. "Rethinking Maternal-Fetal Conflict: Gender and Equality in Perinatal Ethics." *Obstetrics and Gynecology* 96, no. 5: 786–791.

Hays, Sharon. 1996. *The Cultural Contradictions of Motherhood*. New Haven: Yale University Press.

Held, Virginia. 1989. "Birth and Death." *Ethics* 99: 362–388.

Held, Virginia. 1993. *Feminist Morality*. Chicago: University of Chicago Press.

Held, Virginia. 2002. "Care and the Extension of Markets." *Hypatia* 17, no. 2: 19–33.

Hertz, Rosanna. 1997. "A Typology of Approaches to Child Care." *Journal of Family Issues* 18, no. 4: 355–385.

Hillyer, Barbara. 1993. *Feminism and Disability*. Oklahoma City: University of Oklahoma Press.

Hoagland, Sarah Lucia. 1990. "Lesbian Ethics and Female Agency." In *Lesbian Philosophies and Cultures*, ed. Jeffner Allen. Albany: SUNY Press.

Hoagland, Sarah Lucia. 1991. "Some Thoughts about 'Caring.'" In *Feminist Ethics*, ed. Claudia Card. Lawrence: University Press of Kansas.

Hochschild, Arlie. 1983. *The Managed Heart: Commercialization of Human Feeling*. Berkeley: University of California Press.

hooks, bell. 1984. *Feminist Theory from Margin to Center*. Boston: South End.

Houston, Barbara. 1987. "Rescuing Womanly Virtues: Some Dangers of Moral Reclamation." In *Science, Morality and Feminist Theory*, ed. Marsha Hanen and Kai Nielsen. *Canadian Journal of Philosophy* suppl. vol. 13: 237–262.

Howell, Embry M., Nancy Heiser, and Mary Harrington. 1999. "A Review of Recent Findings on Substance Abuse Treatment for Pregnant Women." *Journal of Substance Abuse Treatment* 16, no. 3: 195–219.

Hoyert, Donna L., Isabella Danel, and Patricia Tully. 2000. "Maternal Mortality, United States and Canada 1982–1997." *Birth* 27, no. 1: 4–11.

Hubbard, Ruth. 1997. "Abortion and Disability: Who Should and Should Not Inhabit the World." In *The Disability Studies Reader*, ed. L. J. Davis. London: Routledge.

Hughes, B. 2002. "Disability and the Body." In *Disability Studies Today*, ed. C. Barnes, M. Olive, and L. Barton. Cambridge: Polity.

Hughes, B., and K. Paterson. 1997. "The Social Model of Disability and the Disappearing Body: Towards a Sociology of Impairment." *Disability and Society* 12, no. 3: 325–340.

Hunter, Andrea G., and Margaret E. Ensminger. 1992. "Diversity and Fluidity in Children's Living Arrangements: Family Transitions in an Urban Afro-American Community." *Journal of Marriage and the Family* 54, no. 2(May): 418–426.

Huntington, Annette D. 2002. "Working with Women Experiencing Midtrimester Termination of Pregnancy: The Integration of Nursing and Feminist Knowledge in the Gynaecological Setting." *Journal of Clinical Nursing* 11: 273–279.

Huntley, Rebecca. 2000. "Sexing the Belly: An Exploration of Sex and the Pregnant Body." *Sexualities* 3, no. 3: 347–362.

Hursthouse, Rosalind. 1991. "Virtue Theory and Abortion." *Philosophy and Public Affairs* 20, no. 3: 223–246.

Jaggar, Alison M. 1995. "Caring as a Feminist Practice of Moral Reason." In *Justice and Care: Essential Readings in Feminist Ethics*, ed. Virginia Held. Boulder, Colo.: Westview.

Katz Rothman, Barbara. 1982. *In Labor: Women and Power in the Birthplace*. New York: Norton.

Katz Rothman, Barbara. 1986. *The Tentative Pregnancy: Prenatal Diagnosis and the Future of Motherhood*. New York: Viking.

Katz Rothman, Barbara. 1994. "Beyond Mothers and Fathers: Ideology in a Patriarchal Society." In *Mothering: Ideology, Experience, Agency*, ed. Evelyn Nakano Glenn, Grace Chang, and Linda Rennie Forcey. New York: Routledge.

Katz Rothman, Barbara. 2001. "Spoiling the Pregnancy: Prenatal Diagnosis in the Netherlands." In *Birth by Design: Pregnancy, Maternity Care, and Midwifery in North America and Europe*, ed. Raymond DeVries, Cecilia Benoit, Edwin R. Van Teilingen, and Sirpa Wrede. New York: Routledge.

Keith, Lois, and Jenny Morris. 1996. "Easy Targets: A Disability Rights Perspective on the 'Children as Carers' Debate." In *Encounters with Strangers: Feminism and Disability*, ed. Jenny Morris. London: Women's Press.

Kelly, Mary. 1987. "Interview with Mary Kelly." In *Visibly Female: Feminism and Art: An Anthology*, ed. Hilary Robinson. London: Camden.

Kittay, Eva Feder. 1997. "Human Dependency and Rawlsian Equality." In *Feminists Rethink the Self*, ed. Diana Tietjens Meyers. Boulder, Colo.: Westview, 219–266.

Kittay, Eva Feder. 1999. "'Not *My* Way, Sesha, *Your* Way, Slowly': 'Maternal Thinking' in the Raising of a Child with Profound Intellectual Disabilities." In *Mother Troubles: Rethinking Contemporary Maternal Dilemmas*, ed. Julia E. Hanigsberg and Sara Ruddick. Boston: Beacon.

Kitzinger, Sheila. 1984. *Giving Birth: Alternatives in Childbirth.* New York: Penguin.

Klassen, Pamela. 2001a. *Blessed Events: Religion and Home Birth in America.* Princeton: Princeton University Press.

Klassen, Pamela. 2001b. "Sacred Maternities and Postbiomedical Bodies: Religion and Nature in Contemporary Home Birth." *Signs* 26, no. 3: 775–809.

Kousha, Mahnaz. 1995. "African American Private Household Workers, White Employers and Their Children." *International Journal of Sociology of the Family* 25, no. 2: 67–89.

Krause, Susan A., and Barbara W. Graves. 1999. "Midwifery Triage of First Trimester Bleeding." *Journal of Nurse-Midwifery* 44, no. 6: 537–548.

Kristeva, Julia. 1980. *Desire in language*, ed. Leon Roudiez, trans. Thomas Gora, Alice Jardine, and Leon Roudiez. New York: Columbia University Press.

Kristeva, Julia. 1986. "Stabat Mater." In *The Kristeva Reader*, ed. Toril Moi. New York: Columbia University Press.

Kristeva, Julia. 1997. "Motherhood According to Giovanni Bellini." In *The Portable Kristeva*, ed. Kelly Oliver. New York: Columbia University Press.

Kroelinger, Charlan D., and Kathryn S. Oths. 2000. "Partner Support and Pregnancy Wantedness." *Birth* 27, no. 2: 112–119.

Kupfer, Joseph. 1990. "Can Parents and Children Be Friends?" *American Philosophical Quarterly* 27, no. 1: 15–26.

Kyle, I. 1997. "Private and Public Discourses: The Social Context of Child Care." *Canadian Journal of Research in Early Childhood Education* 6, no. 3: 203–222.

Lauritzen, Paul. 1989. "A Feminist Ethic and the New Romanticism: Mothering as a Model of Moral Relations." *Hypatia* 4: 29–44.

Law, Jules. 2000. "The Politics of Breastfeeding: Assessing Risk, Dividing Labor." *Journal of Women in Culture and Society* 25, no. 2: 407–450.

Layne, Linda L. 2003a. *Motherhood Lost: A Feminist Account of Pregnancy Loss in America.* New York: Routledge.

Layne, Linda L. 2003b. "Unhappy Endings: A Feminist Reappraisal of the Women's Health Movement from the Vantage of Pregnancy Loss." *Social Science and Medicine* 56: 1881–1991.

Lee, C., and P. Slade. 1996. "Miscarriage as a Traumatic Event." *Journal of Psychosomatic Research* 40, no. 3: 235–244.

Levesque-Lopman, Louise. 1983. "Decision and Experience: A Phenomenological Analysis of Pregnancy and Childbirth." *Human Studies* 6: 247–277.

Levinas, Emmanuel. 1991. *Otherwise Than Being*, trans. Alphonse Lingis. Boston: Kluwer.

Lewin, Ellen. 1994. "Negotiating Lesbian Motherhood: The Dialectics of Resistance and Accommodation." In *Mothering: Ideology, Experience and Agency*, ed. Evelyn Nakano Glenn, Grace Chang, and Linda Rennie Forcey. New York: Routledge.

Lim, Hilary. 1999. "Caesareans and Cyborgs." *Feminist Legal Studies* 7: 133–173.

Lippard, Lucy. 1995. "The Pains and Pleasures of Rebirth: European and American Women's Body Art." In Lippard, *The Pink Glass Swan*. New York: New Press.

Lipson, Juliene G., and Judith G. Rogers. 2000. "Pregnancy, Birth, and Disability: Women's Health Care Experiences." *Health Care for Women International* 21: 11–26.

Liss, Andrea. 1994. "The Body in Question: Rethinking Motherhood, Alterity and Desire." In *New Feminist Criticism*, ed. Joanna Frueh, Cassandra L. Langer, and Arlene Raven. New York: HarperCollins.

Llewellyn, A. M., Z. N. Stowe, and C. B. Nemeroff. 1997. "Depression during Pregnancy and the Puerperium." *Journal of Clinical Psychology* 58, suppl. 15: 26–32.

Lloyd, Margaret. 2001. "The Politics of Disability and Feminism: Discord or Synthesis?" *Sociology* 35, no. 3: 715–728.

Longhurst, Robyn. 1998. "(Re)presenting Shopping Centres and Bodies: Questions of Pregnancy." In *New Frontiers of Space, Bodies, Gender*, ed. Rosa Ainley. London: Routledge.

Longhurst, Robyn. 2000. "Corporeographies of Pregnancy: 'Bikini Babes.'" *Environment and Planning D: Society and Space* 18: 453–472.

Lupton, Deborah. 1999. "Risk and the Ontology of Pregnant Embodiment." In *Risk and Sociocultural Theory: New Directions and Perspectives*, ed. Deborah Lupton. Cambridge: Cambridge University Press, 59–85.

Macdonald, Cameron L. 1998. "Manufacturing Motherhood: The Shadow Work of Nannies and Au Pairs." *Qualitative Sociology* 21, no. 1: 25–53.

Macdonald, Cameron Lynne, and David A. Merrill. 2002. "It Shouldn't Have to Be a Trade: Recognition and Redistribution in Care Work Advocacy." *Hypatia* 17, no. 2: 67–83.

Mackenzie, Catriona. 1992. "Abortion and Embodiment." *Australian Journal of Philosophy* 70, no. 2: 136–155.

Mackenzie, Catriona. 2000. "Imagining Oneself Otherwise." In *Relational Autonomy: Feminist Perspectives on Autonomy, Agency, and the Social Self*, ed. Catriona Mackenzie and Natalie Stoljar. Oxford: Oxford University Press.

Martin, Emily. 1987. *The Woman in the Body: A Cultural Analysis of Reproduction*. Boston: Beacon.

Martin, Emily. 1992. *The Woman in the Body*. Boston: Beacon.

Martin, Emily. 1998. "The Fetus as Intruder: Mother's Bodies and Medical Metaphors." In *Cyborg Babies: From Techno-Sex to Techno-Tots*, ed. Robbie Davis-Floyd and Joseph Dumit. New York: Routledge.

Martin, Karin A. 2003. "Giving Birth like a Girl." *Gender & Society* 17, no. 1: 54–72.

Mann, Rosemary, Priscilla Abercrombie, Jeanne DeJoseph, Jane S. Norbeck, and Renee Smith. 1999. "The Personal Experience of Pregnancy for African-American Women." *Journal of Transcultural Nursing* 10, no. 4: 297–305.

Mason, Carol. 2000. "Cracked Babies and the Partial Birth of a Nation: Millenialism and Fetal Citizenship." *Cultural Studies* 14, no. 1: 35–60.

Matthews, Sandra, and Laura Wexler. 2000. *Pregnant Pictures*. London: Routledge.

Melender, Hanna-Leena. 2002. "Experiences of Fears Associated with Pregnancy and Childbirth: A Study of 329 Pregnant Women." *Birth* 29, no. 2: 101–111.

Merleau-Ponty, Maurice. 1962. *The Phenomenology of Perception*, trans. Colin Smith. New Jersey: Routledge and Kegan Paul.

Meyers, Diana T. 1998. "Tropes of Social Relations and the Problems of Tropisms in Figurative Discourse." In *Norms and Values: Essays on the Work of Virginia Held*, ed. Joram G. Haber and Mark S. Halfon. New York: Rowman & Littlefield.

Meyers, Diana Tietjen. 2001. "The Rush to Motherhood – Pronatalist Discourse and Women's Autonomy." *Signs* 26, no. 3: 735–773.

Meyers, Diana. 2003. "Gendered Work and Individual Autonomy." In *Recognition, Responsibility and Rights: Feminist Ethics and Social Theory*, ed. Robin N. Fiore and Hilde Lindemann Nelson. New York: Rowman & Littlefield.

Miedema, Baukje. 1999. *Mothering for the State: The Paradox of Fostering*. Halifax, Nova Scotia: Fernwood.

Mitchell, Lisa M., and Eugenia Georges. 1997. "Cross-cultural Cyborgs: Greek and Canadian Women's Discourses on Fetal Ultrasound." *Feminist Studies* 23, no. 2: 373–401.

More, Sam Dylan. 1998. "The Pregnant Man – An Oxymoron?" *Journal of Gender Studies* 7, no. 3: 319–328.

Morgan, Lynn M. 1996. "Fetal Relationality in Feminist Philosophy: An Anthropological Critique." *Hypatia* 11, no. 3: 47–70.

Morris, Jenny. 2001. "Impairment and Disability: Constructing an Ethics of Care That Promotes Human Rights." *Hypatia* 16, no. 4: 1–16.

Mulvey, Laura. 1975. "Visual Pleasure and Narrrative Cinema." *Screen* 16, no. 3: 6–18.

Munro, Vanessa. 2001. "Surrogacy and the Construction of the Maternal-Foetal Relationship: The Feminist Dilemma Examined." *Res Publica* 7: 13–37.

Murray, Susan B. 1996. "We All Love Charles: Men in Childcare and the Social Construction of Gender." *Gender and Society* 10, no. 4: 368–385.

Murray, Susan B. 1998. "Child Care Work: Intimacy in the Shadows of Family Life." *Qualitative Sociology* 21, no. 2: 149–168.

Nelson, Hilde Lindemann. 1994. "The Architect and the Bee: Some Reflections on Postmortem Pregnancy." *Bioethics* 8, no. 3: 247–267.

Nelson, Julie A. 1999. "Of Markets and Martyrs: Is It Okay to Pay Well for Care?" *Feminist Economics* 5, no. 3: 43–59.

Nelson, Margaret K. 1990. "Mothering Others' Children: The Experiences of Family Day Care Providers." In *Circles of Care: Work and Identity in Women's Lives*, ed. Emily K. Abel and Margaret K. Nelson. Albany: SUNY Press.

Newman, Tony. 2002. "'Young Carers' and Disabled Parents: Time for a Change of Direction?" *Disability and Society* 17, no. 6: 613–625.

Nietzsche, Friedrich. 1921. *Selected Letters of Friedrich Nietzsche*, ed. Oscar Levy, trans. Anthony Ludovici. Toronto: Doubleday.

Nietzsche, Friedrich. 1967. *Ecce Homo*, trans. Walter Kaufmann. New York: Vintage.

Nietzsche, Friedrich. 1969. *Thus Spoke Zarathustra*, trans. R. J. Hollingdale. London: Penguin.

Nietzsche, Friedrich. 1990. *Beyond Good and Evil*, trans. R. J. Hollingdale. London: Penguin.

Nietzsche, Friedrich. 1997. *Daybreak*, ed. Maudemarie Clark and Brian Leiter, trans. R. J. Hollingdale. Cambridge: Cambridge University Press.

Noddings, Nel. 1984. *Caring: A Feminine Approach to Ethics and Moral Education*. Berkeley: University of California Press.

Noddings, Nel. 1990. "A Response to Claudia Card, Sarah Hoagland, and Barbara Houston on Nel Noddings' Caring." *Hypatia* 5, no. 1: 120–126.

Oakley, A. 1980. *Woman Confined: Towards a Sociology of Childbirth*. Oxford: Martin Robertson.

Oakley, Ann. 1987. "From Walking Wombs to Test Tube Babies." In *Reproductive Technologies*, ed. Michelle Stanworth. London: Polity, 36–56.

O'Brien, Mary. 1981. *The Politics of Reproduction*. Boston: Routlege and Kegan Paul.

Oliver, Mike. 1996. "Defining Disability and Impairment: Issues at Stake." In *Exploring the Divide: Illness and Disability*, ed. C. Barnes and G. Mercer. Leeds: Disability Press.

Overall, Christine. 1996. "Reflections of a Sceptical Bioethicist." In *Philosophical Perspectives on Bioethics*, ed. L. W. Sumner and Joseph Boyle. Toronto: University of Toronto Press.

Parkes, Graham. 1994. *Composing the Soul*. Chicago: University of Chicago Press.

Partington, Angela. 1987. "Feminist Art and Avant-Gardism." In *Visibly Female: Feminism and Art: An Anthology*, ed. Hilary Robinson. London: Camden.

Pateman, Carole. 1988. *The Sexual Contract*. Cambridge: Polity.

Petchesky, Rosalind Pollack. 1987. "Foetal Images: The Power of Visual Culture in the Politics of Reproduction." In *Reproductive Technologies: Gender, Motherhood and Medicine*, ed. Michelle Stanworth. Minneapolis: University of Minnesota Press.

Peterson, Susan Rae. 1983. "Against Parenting." In *Mothering: Essays in Feminist Theory*, ed. Joyce Trebilcot. Totowa, N.J.: Rowman and Allanheld.

Plato. 1961. *Collected Dialogues*, ed. Edith Hamilton and Huntington Cairns. Princeton: Princeton University Press.

Purdy, Laura M. 1996. *Reproducing Persons: Issues in Feminist Bioethics*. Ithaca: Cornell University Press.

Rabuzzi, Kathryn Allen. 1994. *Mother with Child: Transformations through Childbirth*. Bloomington: Indiana University Press.

Rawlinson, Mary C. 2001. "The Concept of a Feminist Bioethics." *Journal of Medicine and Philosophy* 26, no. 4: 405–416.

Reiger, Kerreen. 1999. "'Sort of Part of the Women's Movement. But Different': Mothers' Organizations and Australian Feminism." *Women's Studies International* 22, no. 6: 585–595.

Reinelt, Claire, and Mindy Fried. 1992. "'I am this child's mother': A Feminist Perspective on Mothering with a Disability." In *Perspectives on Disability*, 2nd ed. Palo Alto: Health Market Research.

Reynolds, Tracey. 2001. "Black Mothering, Paid Work and Identity." *Ethnic and Racial Studies* 24, no. 6: 1046–1064.

Rich, Adrienne. 1986. *Of Woman Born*. New York: Norton.

Rich, Ruby B. 1978. "Women and Film: A Discussion of Feminist Aesthetics." *New German Critique* 13: 82–107.

Roberts, Dorothy. 1997. *Killing the Black Body: Race, Representation, and the Meaning of Liberty*. New York: Pantheon.

Rodriguez, Alina, Gunilla Bohlin, and Gunilla Lindmark. 2001. "Symptoms across Pregnancy in Relation to Psychosocial and Biomedical Factors." *Acta Obstetrica et Gynecologica Scandinavica* 80: 213–223.

Rossiter, Amy. 1988. *From Private to Public: A Feminist Exploration of Early Mothering*. Toronto: Women's Press.

Ruddick, Sara. 1983a. "Maternal Thinking." In *Mothering: Essays in Feminist Theory*, ed. Joyce Trebilcot. Totowa, N.J.: Rowman and Allanheld.

Ruddick, Sara. 1983b. "Preservative Love and Military Destruction: Some Reflections on Mothering and Peace." In *Mothering: Essays in Feminist Theory*, ed. Joyce Trebilcot. Totowa, N.J.: Rowman and Allanheld.

Ruddick, Sara. 1989. *Maternal Thinking: Toward a Politics of Peace*. New York: Ballantine.

Ruddick, Sara. 1990. "Thinking about Fathers." In *Conflicts in Feminism*, ed. Marianne Hirsch and Evelyn Fox Keller. New York: Routledge.

Ruddick, Sara. 1994. "Thinking Mothers/Conceiving Birth." In *Representations of Motherhood*, ed. Donna Bassin, Margaret Honey, and Meryle Mahrer Kaplan. New Haven: Yale University Press.

Ruddick, Sara. 1995. "Injustice in Families: Assault and Domination." In *Justice and Care: Essential Readings in Feminist Ethics*, ed. Virginia Held. Boulder, Colo. Westview.

Ruddick, Sara. 1996. "The Idea of Fatherhood." In *Feminisms and Families*, ed. Hilde Lindemann Nelson. New York: Routledge.

Ruddick, Sara. 1998. "Care as Labor and Relationship." In *Essays on the Work of Virginia Held*, ed. Joram G. Haber and Mark S. Halfon. New York: Rowman and Littlefield.

Ruddick, William. 1979. "Parents and Life Prospects." In *Having Children: Philosophical and Legal Reflections on Parenthood*, ed. Onora O'Neill and William Ruddick. New York: Oxford University Press.

Rudinow, S. A. 1996. "Ultrasound Discourse: Contested Meanings of Gender and Technology in the Norwegian Ultrasound Screening Debate." *European Journal of Women's Studies* 3: 55–75.

Rudolfsdottir, Annadis Greta. 2000. "'I Am Not a Patient, and I Am Not a Child': The Institutionalization and Experience of Pregnancy." *Feminism and Psychology* 10, no. 3: 337–350.

Ruhl, Lealle. 2002. "Dilemmas of the Will: Uncertainty, Reproduction, and the Rhetoric of Control." *Signs* 27, no. 3: 641–663.

Saggers, Sherry, and Jan Grant. 1999. "I Love Children, and Four-Pence a Week Is Four-Pence! Contradictions of Caring in Family Day Care." *Journal of Family Studies* 5, no. 1: 69–83.

Sandall, Jane, Ivy Lynn Bourgeault, Wouter J. Meijer, and Beate A. Schuecking. 2001. "Deciding Who Cares: Winners and Losers in the Late Twentieth Century." In *Birth by Design: Pregnancy, Maternity Care, and Midwifery in North*

*America and Europe*, ed. Raymond DeVries, Cecilia Benoit, Edwin R. Van Teilingen, and Sirpa Wrede. New York: Routledge.
Sandelowski, Margarete, and Beth Perry Black. 1994. "The Epistemology of Expectant Parenthood." *Western Journal of Nursing Research* 16, no. 6: 601–622.
Schmied, Virginia, and Deborah Lupton. 2001. "The Externality of the Inside: Body Images of Pregnancy." *Nursing Inquiry* 8: 32–40.
Scott, Rosamund. 2000. "The Pregnant Woman and the Good Samaritan: Can a Woman Have a Duty to Undergo a Caesarean Section?" *Oxford Journal of Legal Studies* 20, no. 3: 407–436.
Seddon, D., K. Jones, J. Hill, and C. Robinson. 2001. *A Study of Young Carers in Wales*. Bangor: Report to the Wales Office of Research and Development.
Segura, D. 1994. "Working at Motherhood: Chicana and Mexicana Immigrant Mothers and Employment." In *Mothering: Ideology, Experience and Agency*, ed. Evelyn Nakano Glenn, Grace Chang, and Linda Rennie Forcey. New York: Routledge.
Shakespeare, Tom. 1998. "Choices and Rights Eugenics, Genetics and Disability Equality." *Disability and Society* 13, no. 5: 665–681.
Shakespeare, Tom. 2000. *Help*. Birmingham: Venture.
Shanner, Laura. 1996. "Bioethics through the Back Door: Phenomenology, Narratives, and Insights into Infertility." In *Philosophical Perspectives on Bioethics*, ed. L. W. Sumner and Joseph Boyle. Toronto: University of Toronto Press.
Sharp, Keith, and Sarah Earle. 2002. "Feminism, Abortion and Disability: Irreconcilable Differences?" *Disability and Society* 17, no. 2: 137–145.
Shaw, Rhonda. 2002. "The Ethics of the Birth Plan in Childbirth Management." *Feminist Theory* 3, no. 2: 131–149.
Sherwin, Susan. 1991. "Abortion through a Feminist Ethics Lens." *Dialogue* 30: 327–342.
Sjoo, Monica. 1987. "Interview with Monica Sjoo." In *Visibly Female: Feminism and Art: An Anthology*, ed. Hilary Robinson. London: Camden.
Squier, S. 1994. *Babies in Bottles: Twentieth-Century Visions of Reproductive Technologies*. New Brunswick, N.J.: Rutgers University Press.
Stahl, Shalom, Zeev Blumenfeld, and David Yarnitsky. 1996. "Carpal Tunnel Syndrome in Pregnancy: Indications for Early Surgery." *Journal of the Neurological Sciences* 136, nos. 1–2: 182–184.
Thomas, Carol. 1997. "The Baby and the Bathwater: Disabled Women and Motherhood in Social Context." *Sociology of Health and Illness* 19, no. 5: 622–643.
Thomas, Carol. 1999. *Female Forms: Experiencing and Understanding Disability*. Buckingham: Open University Press.
Thomas, Carol. 2001. "Feminism and Disability: The Theoretical and Political Significance of the Personal and Experiential." In *Disability, Politics, and the Struggle for Change*, ed. Len Barton. London: David Fulton.
Thomas, Laurence. 1987. "Friendship." *Synthese* 72: 217–236.
Thompson, Audrey. 1989. "Friendship and Moral Character." *Philosophy of Education* 45: 61–75.

Thoné, Astrid. 1998. "A Radical Gift: Ethics and Motherhood in Emmanuel Levinas' *Otherwise than Being*." *Journal of the British Society for Phenomenology* 29, no. 2: 116–131.

Tong, Rosemarie. 1999. "Just Caring about Maternal-Fetal Relations: The Case of Cocaine-Using Pregnant Women." In *Embodying Bioethics: Recent Feminist Advances*, ed. Anne Donchin and Laura M. Purdy. New York: Rowman & Littlefield.

Toombs, S. Kay. 1988. "Illness and the Paradigm of the Lived Body." *Theoretical Medicine* 9: 201–226.

Tronto, Joan C. 1993. *Moral Boundaries: A Political Argument for the Ethic of Care*. New York: Routledge.

Tronto, Joan C. 1995. "Women and Caring: What Can Feminists Learn about Morality from Caring?" In *Justice and Care: Essential Readings in Feminist Ethics*, ed. Virginia Held. Boulder, Colo.: Westview.

Tronto, Joan C. 1996. "Care as a Political Concept." In *Revisioning the Political: Feminist Reconstructions of Traditional Concepts in Western Political Theory*, ed. Nancy J. Hirschmann and Christine Di Stefano. Boulder, Colo.: Westview.

Tuominen, Mary. 1997. "Exploitation or Opportunity? The Contradictions of Child-Care Policy in the Contemporary United States." *Women & Politics* 18, no. 1: 53–80.

U.S. Department of Labor. 1997. *Facts of Working Women*. No. 98–1. Washington, D.C.: Government Printing Office.

Uttal, Lynet. 1996. "Custodial Care, Surrogate Care, and Coordinated Care: Employed Mothers and the Meaning of Child Care." *Gender and Society* 10, no. 3: 291–311.

Uttal, Lynet. 2002. *Making Care Work: Employed Mothers in the New Childcare Market*. London: Rutgers University Press.

Uttal, Lynet, and Mary Tuominen 1999. "Tenuous Relationships: Exploitation, Emotion, and Racial Ethnic Significance in Paid Child Care Work." *Gender and Society* 13, no. 6: 758–780.

Walker, A. 1996. *Young Carers and Their Families*. London: Stationery Office.

Wall, Glenda. 2001. "Moral Constructions of Motherhood in Breastfeeding Discourse." *Gender & Society* 15, no. 4: 592–610.

Wates, Michele. 2001. "'Young Carers': Disabled Parents' Perspective," http://www.disabledparentsnetwork.org.uk/young_carers.html. Accessed November 1, 2002.

Wendell, Susan. 1996. *The Rejected Body: Feminist Philosophical Reflections on Disability*. New York: Routledge.

Wendell, Susan. 2001. "Unhealthy Disabled: Treating Chronic Illness as Disabilities." *Hypatia* 16, no. 4: 17–33.

Whitbeck, Caroline. 1983a. "A Different Reality: Feminist Ontology." In *Beyond Domination*, ed. Carol Gould. Totowa, N.J.: Rowman & Allanheld.

Whitbeck, Caroline. 1983b. "Maternal Instinct." In *Mothering: Essays in Feminist Theory*, ed. Joyce Trebilcot. Totowa, N.J.: Rowman and Allanheld, 265–273.

Wiles, Rose. 1994. "'I'm not fat I'm pregnant': The Impact of Pregnancy on Fat Women's Body Image." In *Women and Health: Feminist Perspectives*, ed. Sue Wilkinson and Celia Kitzinger. London: Taylor and Francis.

Willett, Cynthia. 1995. *Maternal Ethics and Other Slave Moralities*. New York: Routledge.

Wilson, Jessica Lynne. 1999. "Technology as a Panacea: Why Pregnancy-Related Problems Should Be Defined without Regard to Mitigating Measures under the ADA." *Vanderbilt Law Review* 52, issue 3 (April 1999): 831–868.

Young, Iris Marion. 1984. "Pregnant Embodiment: Subjectivity and Alienation." *Journal of Medicine and Philosophy* 9: 45–62.

Young, Iris Marion. 1994. "Punishment, Treatment, Empowerment: Three Approaches to Policy for Pregnant Addicts." Feminist Studies 20, no. 1: 33–57.

Zechmeister, Ingrid. 2001. "Foetal Images: The Power of Visual Technology in Antenatal Care and the Implications for Women's Reproductive Freedom." *Health Care Analysis* 9: 387–400.

Ziarek, Ewa. 1992. "At the Limits of Discourse: Heterogeneity, Alterity, and the Maternal Body in Kristeva's Thought." *Hypatia* 7, no. 2: 91–108.

# Index